THE POLITICS OF CHANGE

The Transformation of
the Former Soviet Union

THE POLITICS OF CHANGE

The Transformation of
the Former Soviet Union

CAROL BARNER-BARRY
CYNTHIA A. HODY

The University of Maryland

St. Martin's Press
New York

To
Amelia, Brian, Colleen, Dan, and Joey, our future;
Wellspring, our present;
and in memory of Jeanne Pernet, our past.

Executive editor: Don Reisman
Managing editor: Patricia Mansfield Phelan
Project editor: Alda D. Trabucchi
Production supervisor: Alan Fischer
Art director: Sheree Goodman
Cover design: Heidi Haeuser
Cover art: Brodsky & Utkin, *Amphitheater,* 1989–90, etching, 42″ × 31″, Courtesy
Ronald Feldman Fine Arts, New York

Library of Congress Catalog Card Number: 94-65222

Manufactured in the United States of America.

9 8 7 6 5
f e d c b a

For information, write:
St. Martin's Press, Inc.
175 Fifth Avenue
New York, NY 10010

ISBN: 0-312-09079-X (paperback)
    0-312-12264-0 (cloth)

CONTENTS

PREFACE

The collapse of the Soviet Union threw the entire field of Soviet Studies into disarray. Soviet scholars made jokes about having been transformed into historians virtually overnight. Underneath the levity, however, was a deeper sense of disorientation and challenge. During the Gorbachev era, the Soviet political system had constantly been subject to rapid change. Just keeping up was a full-time job. It was exhilarating and fascinating, but unless one had nothing else to do, it was difficult to analyze the changes—let alone discern any reasonably stable overall picture. The failed coup of August 1991 was the grand finale of this period. It left analysts out of breath and thinking about how to approach their transformed area of study.

For us, the former Soviet Union affords a fascinating laboratory for the study of political change. What has happened and is happening there is unprecedented in history and raises many interesting questions that we think are best considered within the framework of fundamental political concepts such as power and authority. Most of the concepts used in the analysis will not be new to readers, but many have had to be modified or more narrowly delineated in order to be useful in the analysis. Thus, this book has become both a vehicle for the analysis of change in the former Soviet Union and an exercise in the reconsideration and modification of some of the most basic concepts used in the study of politics. This has been an exciting and challenging task for us. We hope that it will form the basis for further conceptual refinement and many more detailed analyses of the continuing changes taking place in the newly fledged countries that once made up the Soviet Union, as well as the Eurasian regional and international systems.

For young scholars this unprecedented situation presents many valuable research and analytical opportunities. There is a new cohort of researchers preparing to become experts on the countries that were once the non-Russian Soviet republics. Some have graciously shared their current findings with us while we were preparing *The Politics of Change*. They are, however, only the first wave. In working on this book, it became apparent to us that there is almost unlimited opportunity for those who wish to expand our knowledge of the fascinating part of the world that was the Soviet Union. In doing so, they have the opportunity both to add to our knowledge of that part of the world and to test (and, possibly, refine) key social science concepts in order to make them more useful for the study of major societal transformations.

The Politics of Change, however, is not just for scholars. It is for anyone who is looking for help in understanding the implications of the rapid changes taking place in the post–Cold War world. It is designed to be a guide to the forces that blew apart the Soviet Union and that still play a major role in the destinies of the newly independent countries. The transition from a Soviet-dominated Eurasia to a post-Soviet Eurasia is far from over. While some patterns seem to be emerging, none has achieved much stability. Thus, for the general reader this book presents a set of concepts and a background survey that can be used as aids in understanding the unfolding situation in the former Soviet Union.

We think that it is not yet possible to study any part of the former Soviet Union without reference to the whole and to the shared past of the newly independent countries. They once made up a giant superpower, and they are still tied together in a multitude of ways that are constantly changing. Consequently, this book focuses on trasitions, attempting to bridge the gap between what has been and what is to come. In trying to do so we have had to make difficult choices about what to include and what to leave out. These choices have been guided largely by our conceptual framework and by our interest in keeping the book to a manageable length. In the final decision making, we listened to reviewer suggestions, considered them carefully, and incorporated those which we thought feasible given the central focus of the book.

Transliteration is a constant problem in works of this sort. Russian terms and Russian language sources have been transliterated using a modified form of the Library of Congress system. This was intended to facilitate recovery of the original Cyrillic for students of the Russian language. Names and places, however, are often daunting to the English-speaker who is not familiar with Russian. Thus, in these cases we tried to use the most recognizable versions. For most names we used the Latin alphabet spelling commonly found in popular sources such as the *Washington Post* and the *New York Times*. For most places we used the Latin alphabet spelling on the National Geographic Society map (published March 1993).

Many people have graciously given their time and energy to help us with this project. First and foremost, we would like to thank our self-designated "library troll," Sylvia Moritz, who has been an enthusiastic research assistant from the beginning. Also enormously helpful were the comments of the students in a special seminar in which we used the manuscript: Richard M. Call, Jeff Goldsmith, Maureen (Mo) Johnson, Harold L. Katz, Michael Landers, Susan E. McAvoy, Sally M. Otto, Kenneth R. Rainey II, George D. Tullos Jr., and Stephen Ward. The reviews commissioned by St. Martin's Press were an important source of guidance thanks to the time and effort expended by the following readers: Steven Burg, Brandeis University; Mark A. Cichock, University of Texas at Arlington; Patrick Dale, St. Olaf College; Zvi Gitelman, University of Michigan; Philip G. Roeder, University of California, San Diego; Gordon B. Smith, University of South Carolina; Laurence Thorsen, Eastern Illinois University; and John P. Willerton, University of Arizona.

Others who helped in a multitude of ways, both large and small, include Michael Bradley, Bhavna Dave', Nancy Miller, Arthur O. Pittenger, Meredith Peruzzi, Michael Schlitzer, Cynthia Snavely, and Adam Yarmolinsky. We would also like to acknowledge the staff of the Albin O. Kuhn Library for their hard work and patience. Finally, Don Reisman, Mary Hugh Lester, and Alda Trabucchi at St. Martin's Press have been unfailingly encouraging and helpful. On a more personal level, we would like to acknowledge the patience and forbearance of our families and friends, particularly John Munro.

As is the custom, we would like to absolve all of those mentioned above from responsibility for what appears in this volume. All final decisions were made by us and, thus, we take sole responsibility for the content of this book. Finally, we would like to emphasize that the best thing about collaboration is how much you learn from each other. So, the most important person each of us would like to acknowledge is the other. Neither of us could have done it alone.

Carol Barner-Barry
Cynthia Hody

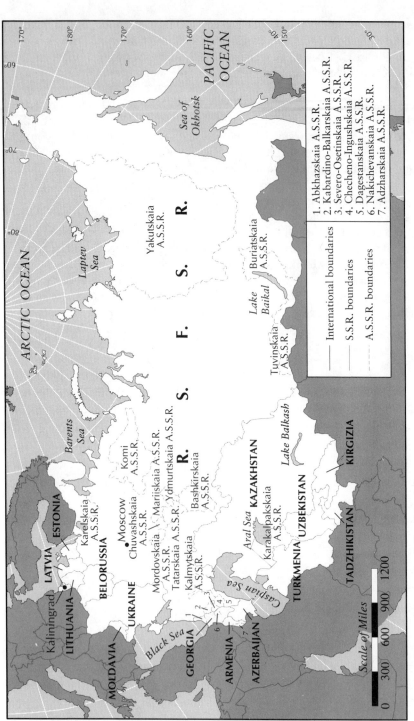

MAP 1 The Union of Soviet Socialist Republics

S.S.R. = Soviet Socialist Republic *A.S.S.R.* = Autonomous Soviet Socialist Republic

Source: U.S. Information Agency (1974). *Problems of Communism*, 23 (3), 3.

· Introduction ·

WHEN COUNTRIES DIE AND ARE REBORN

Imagine taking a trip into space. You expect to spend a few months circling the earth on a space station. Instead, you are stranded there for ten months. You leave as flight engineer in the space exploration program of one of the two most militarily powerful countries on earth. You return to the place you left, but it is now a foreign country. The superpower you worked for has split into fifteen smaller countries, and you have returned not to your native Russia but to Kazakhstan. The insignia on your clothing and equipment is obsolete, the insignia of a country that no longer exists. To rejoin your wife, you must cross an international border. Your hometown is no longer Leningrad but St. Petersburg. Science fiction? No, it happened to Cosmonaut 3rd Class Sergei Krikalev.

Anyone who took the time to look closely at the Soviet political-economic system knew that it had problems—serious ones. The history of the Soviet Union (and the Russian Empire before it) was one of survival despite overwhelming odds in the face of natural disasters or man-made ones like the German invasion during World War II. Somehow, the Soviet Union had always managed to muddle through. Thus, although scholars and other commentators kept pointing out the intractable problems that the Soviet leadership faced, no one anticipated that the country itself would rapidly collapse and disappear anytime soon. No one seemed to realize just how vulnerable it was.

When we began the research for this book, the central question seemed to be: Why did the Soviet Union collapse so quickly and completely? This was a country that the United States had perceived as so great a threat that it had generated an enormous debt in its efforts to ward off the so-called Red menace. We decided that we needed to rethink the entire Soviet experience before it would be possible for us to analyze the new political and economic order emerging on the territory that had once been the Soviet Union. To do this rethinking, it was necessary to get a new perspective. For this, we turned to theory.

Soviet studies have historically been focused primarily on facts and events. There have been some notable efforts to apply theory to these facts and events, but the emphasis was on an inductive approach. Few writers started with basic

1

political science, economic, and psychological concepts and tried to use them to shed light on the nature of the Soviet political-economic system. Much was simply assumed away. To take one example, many scholars referred to the Union of Soviet Socialist Republics as "the Soviet Empire" but left the term *empire* undefined. Without a clear definition of empire, there was no way to determine whether the Soviet Union was, in fact, an empire. Those who used the term tended to treat their assertion as self-evident.

We decided to start by trying to ascertain exactly what kind of a political animal an empire is—no easy task, we found. This investigation led us into a literature that explored the vulnerability of empires and the reasons for that vulnerability. When we viewed the Soviet experience through the prism of this theoretical perspective, it was clear that the Soviet political order was indeed an empire. Further, it was clear that the Soviet Union, like all empires, carried within its basic political structure the seeds of its own downfall. George Kennan was right in 1947 when he observed that the Soviet Union had the capacity to change "overnight from one of the strongest to one of the weakest and most pitiable of national societies." (Kennan, 1947, p. 580) A major reason for this was the fact that its basic political structure was an anachronistic and unstable one (empire), rather than a modern and relatively stable one (nation-state).

This led us to a more basic conceptual level. To make sense of the disintegration of the Soviet political-economic system we had to define and delineate some of the most fundamental concepts of political science, economics, and psychology: namely, power, authority, persuasion, and exchange. But identifying them was one thing, defining them quite another. For example, in much political science writing, *power* and *authority* are used as synonyms. Alternatively, one (usually power) is used to describe what we view as two different types of behavior with basically different effects.

By distinguishing *power* (based on coercion and compliance) from *authority* (based on legitimacy and internalization), we were able to explore the implications of the fact that the Soviet Empire, like all other empires, was based on power and that this power was the root source of its instability. In fact, it could be said that the fatal flaw of the Soviet Union was its overreliance on power in both its political and its economic systems. A Soviet Union based on authority would have been much more stable and less likely to collapse. Civil societies are built on legitimacy, and in them coercion is used only as a last resort. Differentiating *power* from *authority* allowed us to explore the efforts of the Soviet leadership to achieve legitimacy and the reasons why they were not successful enough to prevent disintegration. Differentiating *power* from *authority* also facilitated our analysis of the efforts (or lack of same) by the successor countries to build institutions based on authority rather than on power.

In short, we devote much more time to the exploration of concepts than is usual in Soviet or post-Soviet studies. As a result, we have reached some conclusions that—to a greater or lesser degree—are different from what we initially considered to be received wisdom. Also, we have conceptualized parts of the Soviet experience in nontraditional ways. For example, we treat Marxism-Leninism as primarily a mythology rather than an ideology. Of course it was both, depending on how it was used, but we think that the mythological aspect is more important than the ideological to understanding the collapse of the Soviet Union. Marxism-Leninism was intended to be the basis for the creation of a Soviet nation that transcended the diverse ethnic makeup of the USSR. Such a transformation was a necessary step in converting the Soviet Union from an unstable empire to a more stable nation-state. To accomplish this, however, Marxism-Leninism had to be made accessible to everyone. Accessibility could be more easily accomplished by a mythological presentation that tapped people's emotions (and did not even require basic literacy) than by an ideological presentation that depended on a certain degree of intellectual sophistication.

The Soviet Union not only was politically vulnerable to collapse but also had an economic system that could not function effectively without breaking its own rules. When the Soviet command economy is viewed in light of contemporary, mainstream theory in political economy, it is clear that it was capable of only short-term gains. In the long run, it was both unworkable and ultimately unreformable. In fact, a basic mistake made by Soviet leaders from Nikita S. Khrushchev to Mikhail S. Gorbachev was the belief that a bit of tinkering would get the economy running smoothly and effectively. In the face of all evidence to the contrary, they held on to the belief that they had a superior economic system. What they actually had was a system that no amount of tinkering could fix. In addition, when the Soviet political and economic systems are considered together, it is clear that the Soviet Union could not have kept up with the technological revolution that was sweeping the world—except, perhaps, in the military sector, which was run differently in some important ways from the rest of the economy.

In short, internal problems were much more a threat to the existence of the Soviet Union than was any external enemy. It had a political system that would ultimately self-destruct and an economic system that was fundamentally unworkable. Paradoxically, *external* threats—both real and perceived—may have prolonged the existence of the Soviet Union by giving it a much-needed focus for internal cohesion. Thus, we moved from asking why the Soviet Union collapsed so rapidly and completely to asking why the Soviet Union lasted as long as it did.

Chapter 1 focuses on the definition of a basic set of theoretical concepts that we use throughout the book. Our discussion of political-economic systems and mechanisms of social control (power, authority, persuasion, and exchange) is based primarily on ideas drawn from political science, economics, and psychology. We also use the same sources to explore the nature of social structures and the relationship between rule systems and conflict. The concrete examples that we use are drawn from the Soviet experience. We also compare and contrast domestic and international politics.

The Soviet Union was once a large domestic political system. What remains is an international system composed of fifteen separate successor countries. Thus, although the territory to be studied has not changed, much of what used to be domestic politics is now international politics. In short, our aim in the first chapter is to introduce concepts and information about the fall of the Soviet Union—the pivotal event around which the book revolves.

Chapter 2 surveys the historical and cultural basis of the Soviet Union. Our definition of the term *political culture* is followed by a discussion of the Russian political culture that strongly influenced the leadership of the Soviet Union. Also important to an understanding of the Soviet Union is its revolutionary heritage. We turned to social psychology for a definition of *revolution* that is not tied to any particular revolutionary experience and that permits a distinction to be made between *revolutionary conflict* and *revolutionary change*. This distinction lets us compare and contrast three major revolutionary periods: (1) the 1917 revolutions and their immediate aftermath; (2) Stalin's "revolution from above," which laid the basic foundations of the Soviet political-economic system; and (3) Gorbachev's "reform," which resulted in a revolutionary change, the disintegration of the Soviet Union. In all three periods there was an attempt to significantly modify the underlying political culture.

Chapter 3 begins with a discussion of the history of the Russian Empire and goes on to examine the characteristics and control mechanisms of the Soviet Empire. We then explore why empires are highly vulnerable to decay and collapse and how this applies to the Soviet experience. The decay that took place during the last decades of the Soviet Union contributed to its eventual breakup. Finally, Chapter 3 closes with a discussion of the problems to be overcome if an empire is to be transformed into a nation-state.

Relevant to that transformation is the creation of a common national identity among the peoples of the empire. In the case of the Soviet Union, this involved combining well over 100 different ethnic groups into a common "Soviet" people. The major device used in this process was a state-imposed system of socializing the people to believe in a common mythology based on Marxism-Leninism. On the surface, the system seemed to work—as long as political heresy could mean punishment or even death. When glasnost loosened the grip of coercion, however, interethnic problems erupted. Soviet policymakers, who did not seem able to grasp the extent to which their system of education, agitation, and propaganda had failed, did not understand or deal effectively with the problems stemming from nationalism. Those factors, discussed in Chapters 4 and 5, eventually tore the Soviet Union apart and remain a source of problems in most of the successor countries.

As in the political system, force was the hallmark of the economic system. The Soviet people could own no property except their personal possessions. In theory, everything else was the property of the entire Soviet people. As a practical matter, it belonged to the state. All important economic decision-making took place within the state apparatus (primarily the Communist Party) and was implemented by the government. It was a command economy in which everyone—from a lowly store clerk to the head of a giant enterprise—had to follow and fulfill their plans. Plans were nothing more than directives from the state. This sytem was crafted during the Stalin period and, despite several attempts to reform it, remained in place until the end—gradually becoming more and more dysfunctional.

Chapters 6 and 7 outline the basic characteristics and history of the Soviet command economy and set forth the reasons why it was doomed to fail in spite of attempts by Gorbachev and others to make it work. This command system created major economic problems for the fifteen successor countries. In fact, the survival of many of them, as well as their ability to create democratic institutions, may hinge on their leaders' ability to get them out of the economic mess created by the Soviet command system. The needed measures inevitably will inflict considerable pain on the people—who are also voters in those newly independent countries currently experimenting with democracy.

At the time of the disintegration of the Soviet Union, all of the former Soviet republics claimed to want to become democratic. Chapter 8 begins with a discussion of the Gorbachev regime's efforts to accommodate the demands for sovereignty and independence that glasnost had unleashed. The failed coup of August 1991, however, changed everything because it made all of the former union republics independent countries whether they wanted independence or not. In order to assess the democratic potential of each newly independent country, we identify some of the preconditions which must exist for stable democracy. This is followed by examples, drawn from the experience of the successor countries, that indicate good or poor potentials for creating these preconditions. The discussion continues in Chapter 9, where we cluster the countries into their traditional geographical groups and analyze the major problems challenging each group.

These regional groupings indicate something about the age-old relationships among the peoples of the former Soviet Union. Chapter 10 explores the international relations of the countries that used to be republics of the Soviet Union. Currently, the principal organization tying the region together is the Commonwealth of Independent States (CIS). With the exception of the Baltic countries, all of the former Soviet republics are members of the CIS or have significant ties with it. We explore the nature of international governmental organizations and examine the history of several that may be pertinent to the CIS. We then attempt to evaluate the potential of the CIS for creating a viable system of regional cooperation.

Because Russia still represents a huge and dominant presence in the region, we pay particular attention to Russia's role and the relationships it is establishing with the rest of the successor countries—called the "near abroad" by the Russians. Russia also presents an unusual problem because it is similar to the Soviet Union in size and diversity. This similarity raises the issue of whether Russia itself can resist pressures to disintegrate into smaller ethnically defined countries, whether it will succeed in becoming a viable democratic federation, or whether it will return to empire. The path it follows will have a profound effect on the other newly independent countries, as well as on the rest of the world.

Chapter 11 explores the implications of the ending of the Cold War and the ways in which it has transformed global international relations. Again the topic of power becomes important, because economic and military power are the currency of international relations. Thus, Russia plays the most central role of all the successor countries because of its size and potential. At this point in history, the fact that Russia has profound political and economic problems creates a challenge for the rest of the world, particularly the developed nations and international organizations. Although what happens in Russia will affect the new world order of the twenty-first century, it is difficult for the United States, the European Union, Japan, and China to decide what is the best course of action and what the consequences of their action (or inaction) might be. The other newly independent countries will also have a role to play in the international system. The Muslim republics, for example, have a choice to make. Will they follow the lead of countries like Iran and embrace Islamic fundamentalism? Or will they become more secular states like Turkey? Whichever way this decision goes, its effects will be felt both in the region and around the world.

The Soviet Union is dead. Although its demise eliminated one set of problems, it created another. These years will be remembered as a time of major transformation. No longer can we lump together most of Eurasia and look to Moscow to understand it. Rather, the part of Eurasia that was once the USSR is now a host of countries, each with its own characteristics and problems. Each will find its own way into the twenty-first century. We hope that this book will make a small contribution to the understanding of what the fall of the Soviet Union means and what the rest of the world might expect from the newly independent countries of Eurasia.

REFERENCES

Kennan, G. ("X"). (1947). The sources of Soviet conduct. *Foreign Affairs, 25,* 566–582.

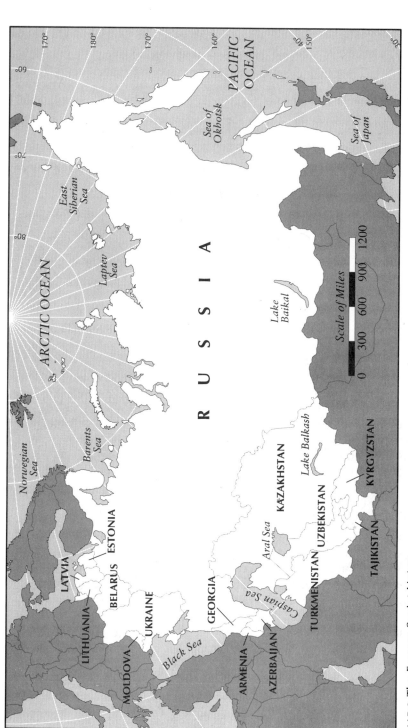

MAP 2 The Former Soviet Union

Source: Modified from Goldman, M. (Ed.). (1992). The Commonwealth of Independent States—Central/Eastern Europe. Guilford, CT: Dushkin.

· 1 ·

THE SOVIET POLITICAL-ECONOMIC SYSTEM AND THE NATURE OF POLITICS

Conflict is a given datum in life. Wherever there is life, there is conflict. Where there is no conflict, there is death.
EDUARD C. LINDEMANN (Seaburg, 1968, p. 69)

Politics is about conflict. Conflict exists in any situation where there is not enough for everyone—when people think they may get less than they want or perhaps nothing at all. (Brickman, 1974) Because humans live in a world of limited resources, they have had to devise ways of deciding who will get what, when, and how. (Lasswell, 1958) The outcome of some of these conflicts affects only the participants. Many, however, also have an impact on society. In such cases, it is important for society to have some say in the way the conflict reaches resolution, as well as the type of solution that emerges.

The political arena is the place where decisions are made about the values and goals that limit and channel societal conflict. Frequently, these decisions are recognized as explicit or implicit rules of the political game. The most important explicit rules are constitutional provisions and laws (for domestic politics) and treaties and other formal international agreements (for international politics). Implicit rules are usually more difficult to pin down, because they take the form of traditions or unwritten norms of behavior, sometimes referred to as political culture. Both types of rules structure conflict in order to minimize the use of violence. To the extent that violence is avoided, humans escape an existence where, as the political philosopher Thomas Hobbes wrote in 1651, life is "nasty, brutish, and short." (Hobbes, 1962, p. 100) Rules communicate to the players what behavior is acceptable and what behavior is not. The outcome of the political game is supposed to be decisions that benefit society.

But who should decide what rules will govern the political game? Politics is not just about the rules. It is also about the creation, maintenance, reform, decay, destruction, and re-creation of the political relationships that determine how the rules of conflict will be made and who will make them. The Russian

8

revolutions of 1917 destroyed the set of political relationships that made up the tsarist political system and began the creation of a new set of relationships— the Soviet political system. For the better part of the twentieth century, this sytem maintained a set of political relationships that answered the *how, when,* and *who* questions surrounding the rules of social conflict in the Soviet Union. In addition, the Union of Soviet Socialist Republics (USSR) was a central actor in international politics, where relationships among sovereign states create a different kind of political system. In the international political arena, "Might makes right." States enter into treaties and agreements designed to minimize violent conflict, but no authority exists to enforce such treaties and agreements. Thus, Soviet leaders gave tremendous emphasis to the creation and mainte- nance of the political and economic factors that built up their military might.

The reforms of Mikhail Gorbachev began the formal dismantling of the political and economic relationships that had characterized the Soviet system since 1917. The failed coup attempt of August 1991 shattered most of what remained, although much survives—to a greater or lesser extent—in the Soviet successor countries. The breakup of the Soviet Union produced fifteen emerg- ing political-economic systems. Moreover, in the international domain, one superpower became fifteen legally independent but economically interdepen- dent actors. Some are joined by loose political ties; all are affected by the legacy of empire—Russian and Soviet.

The magnitude of the changes that have occurred and will occur can scarcely be overestimated. These changes span the two major domains of politics—the domestic and the international. They also bridge the major fields in the social sciences, most obviously political science and economics. An appreciation of the complexities and dynamics of the multiple processes of transformation that continue within and among the former Soviet republics demands a firm theoreti- cal basis. Thus, our first step is to look closely at the traditional view that the political system and the economic system are separate. After that, it will be possible for us to introduce the basic mechanisms of social control in a way that highlights their usefulness in analyzing the Soviet Union and the dynamics of the current transition.

POLITICAL-ECONOMIC SYSTEMS

In the United States, people are accustomed to thinking of the political and economic spheres as separate. After all, there is a public sector and a private sector. For most of this century, politics and economics have been studied as if they were independent centers of social activity that only occasionally interact. In economics, scholars and students studied markets and exchange relation- ships; in political science, they studied governments as well as social power and authority relationships.

In recent years, there has been a growing recognition of the interdependence of politics and economics and a greater appreciation of the importance of political economy to both economics and political science. This development is particularly important to any analysis of the Soviet system. There was no division between the public and private sectors in the Soviet Union. At least in theory, the government ran it all—mostly by means of legally binding directives based on policy decisions made by the political leadership and issued from such organizations as Gosplan (the State Planning Committee). In fact, much of what Westerners regard as desirable private sector activity was illegal. An example would be the crime of "speculation" (*spekuliatsiia*), which is defined in Article 154 of the Russian Republic Criminal Code as "the buying up and resale of commodities or other articles with the goal of profit."[1] (*Ugolovnyi kodeks RSFSR,* 1990, p. 94)

Thus, it is impossible to analyze the Soviet political and economic systems separately without seriously distorting Soviet reality. In fact, it is also necessary to go beyond political science and economics. To approximate an adequate understanding of the Soviet political-economic system, concepts from the fields of "sociology, social psychology, political and moral philosophy, and history" should be included. (Kornai, 1992, p. 12) Our analysis therefore draws on research from those disciplines on an as-needed basis. By using this approach, we tacitly acknowledge that the divisions among the social sciences are essentially artificial and that the strands of any social fabric are intricately intertwined.

In 1977 an American scholar, Charles Lindblom, compared the ways in which various political-economic systems operate. In *Politics and Markets* he emphasized three mechanisms of social control: authority, persuasion, and exchange. These, he asserted, are the building blocks for all political-economic systems. The identification and examination of these basic building blocks is necessary because each of the fifteen Soviet successor countries is in the process of dismantling one system and trying to replace it with another. To explore this process (or, more accurately, these processes), it is necessary to return to the fundamentals.

Our discussion of the methods of social control, however, differs from Lindblom's in one important way. In his discussion of domestic politics, Lindblom treats power (coercion) as an aspect of authority. For purposes of analyzing the Soviet Union and its successor countries, it is much more useful to examine these concepts separately. Power and authority have different bases; therefore, each has a different psychological motivation for behavior.

The contrast between power and authority is most evident when we compare international relations and domestic governments. Power dominates in international political systems, but authority is paramount in domestic political systems with stable governments. Because one of our aims is to analyze the transformation of one country into fifteen, domestic politics and international politics are equally important. To treat power and authority as the same phenomenon would invite misunderstanding of two fundamentally different kinds of social behavior. In addition, the way in which the Soviet Union was gov-

---

1. Unless otherwise noted, all translations from the Russian are by Carol Barner-Barry.

erned makes it important to distinguish between situations in which coercion played a decisive role and situations in which it did not.

MECHANISMS OF SOCIAL CONTROL

Controlling human behavior is the key to managing or resolving social conflict in political-economic systems. Dallin and Breslauer (1970, p. 2) define such control as "the shaping and channeling of . . . behavior either to secure compliance with particular directives or to mold attitudes so as to assure . . . stability through the voluntary acceptance of a given authority structure, its norms of social conduct, and its directives." Mechanisms of social control are the building blocks for social structures and institutions. These, in turn, allow people to deal with the conflicts that unavoidably arise in a world of limited resources. There are four basic methods by which human behavior can be controlled: power, authority, persuasion, and exchange.

Power and authority are typically identified as the unifying concepts of political science. Politics, however, also involves persuasion and exchange. Persuasion operates in the dissemination of political information and beliefs; it is also the vehicle for political socialization. Exchange is at the heart of most day-to-day relationships between political leaders and followers. (Burns, 1978) It is also a major characteristic of the relationships between and among politicians, government officials, public and partisan organizations, and states. "You scratch my back and I'll scratch yours" is the essence of practical politics.

Power

Power is the ability to compel someone to do something he or she would not otherwise have done or to refrain from doing something he or she otherwise would have done. The practical basis of power is the ability to coerce. Coercion can range from the infliction of physical harm to the withholding of a reward. In other words, the exercise of power can involve both sticks and carrots. In either case, the response to coercion is simple compliance. Whether the person being coerced thinks that what is being demanded is right or wrong is irrelevant. The motivation is to avoid the physical or psychological pain that can result from either loss or the failure to gain. (Kelman, 1958; Kelman & Hamilton, 1989, pp. 104–116)

The link between pain and the negative exercise of power (the stick) is obvious. A person complies in order to avoid future harm. The presence of pain is less apparent but no less real when positive power (the carrot) is exercised. A promise of reward is made contingent on behavior that is desired by the person controlling the rewards. If the party being coerced refuses, there will be no reward. In the Soviet Union, people who complied were often rewarded with things that were difficult to obtain. For example, the person casting the deciding vote to expel the Nobel Prize–winning writer Alexander Solzhenitsyn from the

Writers Union (and thus take away his ability to publish his work in the Soviet Union) was rewarded with a new apartment. (Burg & Feifer, 1973, pp. 341–342) Because of the extreme scarcity of desirable housing, this reward was very tempting. But the cost of complying and getting a reward is the loss of the ability to act freely and voluntarily. Frequently, the people who compromised their principles to obtain the rewards the Soviet leadership offered regretted their choices. The person who cast the deciding vote against Solzhenitsyn in return for better housing later got very drunk and wandered around cursing himself.

Distinguishing between sticks and carrots is not always easy. Whether an instrument of coercion is viewed as a reward or a punishment depends on how those involved perceive the situation. (Doob, 1983, pp. 126–127) For example, to a hard-working employee expecting a Christmas bonus of $100, a bonus of $50 will not be seen as a reward. The employee is likely to feel deprived, even though the well-meaning employer believes "a bonus is a bonus." In this example, one person's carrot is another's stick.

A similar scenario unfolded with regard to economic aid to the new Russian Federation. Shortly after the Soviet Union fell, the International Monetary Fund (IMF) and the Group of Seven (G-7)[2] promised Russia an aid package of $24 billion—*if* Russia made rapid and disciplined progress toward a market economy. Clearly, the IMF and the leaders of the G-7 thought they were offering a reward for desirable behavior (a carrot). But there were those in Russia (both inside and outside the government) who saw the potential for pain in this so-called reward. They thought that meeting the requirements of the IMF and the G-7 could cause social chaos in the form of mass unemployment and thousands of bankruptcies. (*Washington Post*, August 27, 1992, p. A22)

The bottom line is that Russia *was* being coerced. The advanced industrial states were wielding money as an instrument of power to get the behavior they wanted. Their goal was the rapid transformation of the Soviet command economy into a fully privatized market economy, and they wanted it done their way. The exercise of power, however, seldom flows in one direction—even when it seems that one of the parties possesses virtually all of the power. The example of aid to Russia is no exception. Russia was targeting the industrialized countries with some coercion of its own. The implied threat was that the global community would face dire consequences if the economic aid was denied and Russia degenerated into economic collapse and social upheaval.[3]

Authority

Like power, authority confers on those possessing it the ability to cause someone either to do something she or he would not have done or to refrain from

---

2. The Group of Seven is composed of the seven capitalist countries with the largest gross domestic products: Canada, France, Germany, Great Britain, Italy, Japan, and the United States.
3. Other equally undesirable possibilities included the reversion to a militaristic, absolutist state that would threaten a return to Cold War conditions.

doing something she or he would otherwise have done.[4] The basis for authority, however, is different from the basis for power. Those who possess authority have been given it by those who will be affected by their decisions and actions. Thus, authorities possess the virtual certainty that their commands will be carried out, because their right to issue such commands will be respected. (Kreml, 1985, p. 119) In other words, their acts are legitimate.

Legitimacy is the belief that something is right and proper and is in conformity with significant values. Legitimacy leads people to act in accordance with the decisions of authoritative leaders because they think they should. Thus, "from a psychological viewpoint, the government of a nation-state is legitimate insofar as the population perceives it is (a) reflecting its ethnic and cultural identity and (b) meeting its needs and interests." (Kelman & Hamilton, 1989, p. 116) Saying this implies a value judgment. A person who is making a decision about acting in response to an order matches the source of the order against his or her "salient norms" (Eckstein & Gurr, 1975, pp. 204–221) and decides what to do.

What sorts of norms are involved? In general, authority in political-economic systems flows from three possible sources. (Eckstein & Gurr, 1975) The first is personal. A person may have authority because he or she occupies a certain position in the political-economic system or has relevant expertise. Thus, for most of the history of the Soviet Union, the top leader was the General Secretary of the Communist Party of the Soviet Union (CPSU). Even though this was not a government office, the leaders of other countries understood that possession of this title implied the ability to make decisions on behalf of the USSR. Authority based on skill or expertise was relatively less important. One of the core problems of the Soviet Union during most of its history was the tendency of its leaders to subordinate too much of the work of scientists and technical experts to the demands of ideology. By refusing to recognize the authority of experts, the USSR suffered serious losses in almost all areas, including the important areas of industrial growth and military strength. (McCauley, 1981, p. 148) As the democratic countries of the developed world experienced the technological revolution of the second half of the twentieth century, the Soviet economy fell further and further behind.

The second normative basis of legitimacy is substantive. What is the content of the order? The decision to carry out an order depends on an evaluation of its content. The values applied may range from the practical (What's in it for me?) to the abstract (Is this for the good of my country?). At the time of the 1991 Soviet coup attempt, Russian President Boris Yeltsin called on the Soviet people to resist. Those who gathered to defend the Soviet parliament building (the center for opposition to the coup) did so for a variety of reasons. Some budding businessmen joined the defenders because they thought that a successful coup would destroy their new lives and careers—"their right to wheel and deal."

4. There is a rich literature on authority. For a good summary of historical and contemporary conceptions of authority, see Kelman & Hamilton (1989, pp. 53–76).

(*Washington Post,* September 26, 1991, p. 1) Others saw the same action in a more philosophical (though equally personal) light. For example, a professor who was among the defenders later made the observation: "[T]he main feeling [among the defenders], in the end, was one of liberation from the constraints of political dogmas and stereotypes—the realization of one-self [*sic*] as a human being whose point of view can be changed by the power of persuasion, but not the persuasion of power." (*Woodrow Wilson Center Report,* November 1991, p. 2) Finally, when Yeltsin climbed on top of a tank to address the crowd outside the parliament building, the crowd chanted: "You are right, Boris Nikolaevich[5] [Yeltsin]. We will defend democracy." (*Washington Post,* August 20, 1991, p. A17)

The third normative basis for legitimacy is process. How was the command generated? The basic source of legitimacy in the American political system is democratic procedure. Was there a vote, and were all eligible persons given the chance to participate? In the United States, a law is usually regarded as authoritative because it was passed by a majority of legislators who were freely elected by the citizens. A major factor in the minds of those choosing to respond to Yeltsin's call for resistance was the fact that he was the first popularly elected president in the history of Russia. An American who was in Moscow at the time of the coup went to Manezh Square outside the Kremlin where an anticoup rally was being held. He described a speaker who told the crowd that a resistance movement was being organized and that its leader was Yeltsin. The speaker kept repeating: "Elected! Yeltsin we have elected!" (*New York Times Magazine,* September 29, 1991, p. 33)

This example also points out that legitimacy is seldom based on only one factor. Rather, it is based on a combination of factors that hold value for the persons who decide that the authority should be obeyed. At the time of the coup, Yeltsin possessed all three bases of legitimacy. He held the position of President of the Russian Republic (RSFSR), which gave him a personal basis for legitimacy. His order to the Soviet people was to help defeat the coup, and many who decided to respond saw the defeat of the coup as being good both for their country and for themselves. This perception gave his order a substantive basis for legitimacy. Finally, Yeltsin, the official who had issued the call to resist, was President by virtue of the first truly free popular presidential election ever held in Russia. The people who led the coup were asserting their right to take command by force. Yeltsin clearly had a procedural basis for legitimacy that the coup leaders lacked.

Thus, a legitimate order is in line with the value system of the people expected to carry out the order. Acting out cherished values is usually psychologically satisfying. *Internalization* is the word social psychologists use to characterize

---

5. It is a custom in Russia for persons in certain situations or positions of authority to be addressed by their name and patronymic (a middle name based on the first name of their father). For example, Russian schoolchildren traditionally address their teachers this way. In this case, it is clear that Yeltsin's father's first name was Nikolai.

such behavior. A classic example of internalization is the act of voting. Citizens vote because they believe in the merits of what they are doing. They view voting as the civic duty of a citizen of a democratic country, even though they understand that the vote of any one individual seldom changes the outcome of an election. Voting is a satisfying act because it symbolizes internalized norms about the importance and superiority of democracy. Many of those who openly resisted the attempted coup did so for reasons which indicate that they were acting on the basis of deeply internalized norms. One woman who had helped defend the Russian parliament building, potentially risking her life, told a reporter: "We are not heroes, but we are patriots." A young man asserted: "We will never again bend our spines beneath their pistols, the way our fathers did." (*Washington Post*, August 22, 1991, pp. A1, A27)

Correspondingly, one of the reasons the coup failed was that the military was divided. Faced with the possibility of having to fire on their own people, many officers and enlisted men experienced deep ambivalence based on two clashing but internalized norms. Military organizations are very hierarchical— you obey your superior's orders, period. Soldiers, however, are not supposed to be shooting at the very people they are sworn to protect and defend. Thus, the soldiers sent to Moscow to support the coup had to contend with experiences like having a gray-haired woman scream: "Tanks against whom? Boys! Boys! You are our children! What are you doing! What do you want?" (*Washington Post*, August 20, 1991, p. A17)

It is not surprising that many of the troops defected and helped the defenders of the parliament building. Others showed the people around them that their weapons were not loaded. Finally, when it was over, a young tank commander expressed his relief: "It's over! We got our orders! Thank God, we're heading home." (*Washington Post*, August 22, 1991, p. A25) He was clearly relieved that he had not had to choose which internalized value to uphold and which to violate.

Internalized norms can change. People can reconsider the basis of their behavior; they can reevaluate the merits of their actions. The experience of the coup led many Soviet citizens to question and reject their formal behavioral norms. To a people long known for passivity, defiance of the coup meant empowerment. A Soviet woman told her story while the events of the coup were still unfolding and the outcome was uncertain:

> I am ready to die here, right on this spot. I will not move. I am 55 years old and for years nothing but obedience and inertia was pounded into my brain. The Young Pioneers, the Young Communist League, the unions, the Communist Party, all of them taught me not to answer back. To be a good Soviet, a bolt in the machine.
>
> But Monday morning my friend called and said, "Turn on the radio." I didn't need to. I heard a rumbling and went out on my balcony and saw the tanks. . . . These monsters! They have always thought they could do anything to us! They have thrown out Gorbachev and now they are threatening a government I helped elect. I will ignore the curfew. I'll let a tank roll over me if I have to. I'll die right here if I have to. (*Washington Post*, August 21, 1991, p. A1)

Legitimate social institutions are characterized as much by their authority relationships as by the goals they claim to further. Very small groups may rotate decision-making authority among members according to an agreed-upon schedule. Larger organizations establish authority relationships that are more formal and hierarchical. Corporations, labor unions, professional and trade associations, political parties, and interest groups all have authority structures designed to complement their objectives. The same is true of governments.

Governments, however, are different from all other types of social organizations. Only governments can legitimately use physical violence (power) to enforce their decisions. (Max Weber in Gerth & Mills, 1958) Under ordinary circumstances, citizens accept the government's right to use force appropriately to threaten or punish those who do not obey the law. Government use of coercion that the people consider excessive, unnecessary, or lawless, however, can erode the foundation of authority so critical to successful governance. Whatever authority the Soviet state possessed was largely based on an acceptance of the assumptions and predictions of Marxist-Leninist ideology, which was tied to an elaborate mythology about the nature and destiny of the Soviet Union. According to Lev Timofeyev, a journalist and former dissident, communism had authority for many because "it rested on illusions that had accumulated over many centuries"—illusions that had to do with "the happiness of mankind" and "the building of God's kingdom on our planet. It was an ideology that made fanatics out of politicians and warriors out of common people." (*Washington Post*, December 29, 1991, p. A26)

In the end, however, the Soviet rulers destroyed their own authority by ruthlessly suppressing all points of view but the officially approved one. On the one hand, this suppression permitted them to use their interpretation of the past, present, and future to create many "true believers." Even during the height of the purges in the 1930s many of the Soviet people honestly thought that if Joseph Stalin knew what was happening, he would put a stop to it. On the other hand, the Soviet leadership created a web of lies that was so large and complex that it could not be maintained indefinitely. The horrors of collectivization, industrialization, and the purges contradicted the assertions of the leadership and began the process of erosion. Khrushchev's revelations about the crimes of Stalin added to its momentum. The dissident movement and economic decline of the Brezhnev years continued it. And Gorbachev's glasnost finally brought the whole edifice down.

By the end, it had become clear that the Soviet system was largely based on lies and half-truths backed up by the exercise of raw power. As more and more of the people became cynical about their political-economic system and as the system itself began to falter, the Soviet Union slowly began to collapse. Gorbachev's reform was an attempt to reverse that process, to revitalize the Soviet system. The attempt failed. In the words of a labor camp survivor: "Soviet power was based on lies and violence. The whip had to be used continuously and it had to be backed up with lies. As soon as our leaders stopped using the whip, the system began to fall apart. After Gorbachev introduced *glasnost* . . . , and the lies diminished, communism was doomed." (*Washington Post,* December 29, 1991, p. A26) The lies, of course, were the Soviet leadership's basis for legitimacy and the source of its authority. This brings us to the subject of persuasion.

Persuasion

Persuasion is a form of communication. If communication can be defined as "the transmission of information to elicit a response" (Barner-Barry & Rosenwein, 1985, p. 145), then persuasion can be defined as the transmission of information intended to elicit a targeted and voluntary behavioral response. An attempt at persuasion can be judged successful if it causes an appropriate change in behavior. At this point, it becomes necessary to specify what we mean by *behavior.* Here both verbal and physical activity are regarded as behavior—what people say and what they do.

When persuasion is involved, a change in behavior does not stem from simple compliance. Rather, it is based on internalization. (Kelman & Hamilton, 1989, pp. 107–109) The persuasive message has to appeal to some preexisting belief or value held by the target person or group. The relationship between the message and the psychological inclination to think or act in a certain way makes the message persuasive. This inclination can be either intellectual or emotional. Thus, as with authority, the motive for behavior change comes from the conviction that what the individual is being persuaded to do (or not do) is the right and proper thing to do (or not do). Authority in government settings can be backed up by the threat of legitimate force, but persuasion is backed up by the threat of ostracism. In a social context, a person who openly rejects what the others accept may be regarded as a heretic and treated as an outcast.

Simple communication can be verbal or nonverbal (body language), and it is often unintentional. A relatively small change in facial expression, for example, can communicate an enormous amount of information. Thus, we are constantly communicating whenever there is another person who is available to receive the communication. Persuasion, however, is a form of communication that is always a conscious act. The persuader *intends* to communicate something. (Reardon, 1981, p. 24) Less obviously, in persuasion the target person or group is usually (but not always) aware of and participating in the interaction. (Roloff, 1980, p. 30) There is a tendency to regard the target of the persuasive effort as a reacting mechanism. This ignores the way the target's response shapes the message of the persuader.

If you want to persuade someone, you have to base your message on the shared meanings or symbols that make people susceptible to being convinced. Symbols are images that people carry in their heads and use to make sense of the information they get through their five senses. (Edelman, 1971, p. 34) Flags are symbols that evoke complex ideas and emotions in those who view them. The ideas and emotions that a person experiences depend on the meaning that a particular flag has for the person. During the last years of the Soviet Union, the display of pre-Soviet national flags became important to those in the union republics who wanted independence.

One particularly poignant use of the Russian flag as a symbol occurred on the first day of the coup. An American who happened to be in Moscow went to the apartment of some Russian friends. One had had a birthday recently and had been given a flag by a colleague because their joint work dealt "with the tension between Russian spirit and Soviet bureaucracy." The American continues: "This 10-foot length of tricolored fabric has been in the corner of the studio for days, and now Kostya wraps it around his shoulders like a shawl." (*New York Times Magazine,* September 19, 1991, p. 32) Sometimes, Americans talk about excessively patriotic politicians as "wrapping themselves in the flag." Kostya did it quite literally, and the political symbolism was obvious. One of the interesting things about this incident is that, in spite of the fact that the coup was intended to overthrow the *Soviet* government, Kostya chose to express his patriotism and feelings about the coup by wrapping himself in a *Russian* flag. This is particularly notable because resistance to the coup attempt centered on the Russian President, Boris Yeltsin, rather than on the Soviet President, Mikhail Gorbachev.

Shared symbols can be used to convey complex messages with an immediacy and simplicity that makes them powerful tools in the hands of political persuaders. Frequently, symbols evoke myths. A myth is "a belief held in common by a large group of people that gives events and actions a particular meaning; it is typically socially cued rather than empirically based." (Edelman, 1971, p. 14) In the Soviet Union, a complex and sweeping mythology lay at the base of all efforts by the Soviet regime to persuade its people to internalize a common Soviet identity. Supporting that mythology was a Marxist-Leninist ideology that, it was asserted, gave the mythology a "scientific" basis. Part of the job of Soviet education, as well as the system of agitation and propaganda, was to inculcate this mythology. The goal was to create a bedrock of support within the population for the Soviet political-economic system.

Because political persuasion was obvious and pervasive in Soviet life, the relationship between the persuaders' political messages and their symbols usually left little to the imagination. Slogans were everywhere—on billboards, on the sides of buildings, on posters attached to walls. Their content was not subtle. For example, one of the most prevalent read: "Hail to the CPSU!" (*"Slava KPSS!"*) In fact, the symbols were so ever present that they soon became deadening—just part of the landscape. Westerners tended to be amused and, if they stayed there long enough, irritated. Soviet citizens seemed simply to tune them out. The Soviet people, however, were not immune to their subliminal effects. To some extent, the persuaders seemed to succeed in creating and perpetuating the desired political beliefs in at least some of their audience. In retrospect, however, it is clear that acceptance of the CPSU's persuasive message was very superficial among a large proportion of the Soviet people.

The Soviet campaign of indoctrination and misinformation worked reasonably well for a while. Belief in the Soviet Communist Party's mythology and ideology began eroding, however, after the first flush of revolutionary fervor abated. This elaborate web of half-truths and lies never did correspond very well with the reality that the Soviet people experienced in their daily lives. They kept waiting for things to become the way they were "supposed" to be. It never happened. True, there was improvement. After Stalin's death, people stopped getting shot for their ideas (or for no clear reason). Slowly but surely, the standard of living got better—until the Brezhnev "period of stagnation" (*zastoi*). As they waited longer and longer for the promised utopia to materialize, however, the people became more and more cynical, saying: "Communism is like the horizon; it is always receding."

Glasnost cost the mythology and ideology whatever appearance of truth they still had. When people talked about the lies that they thought characterized the Soviet regime, they were talking about this mythology and ideology as well as about the messages of the educational and propaganda systems that perpetrated and embellished them. Thus, by the time the Soviet Union collapsed, most former "true believers" had drawn conclusions similar to those of the senior anchor of Soviet central television: "Only now do I understand that my whole life was devoted to serving a cruel and useless system." He had been part of that system, a key persuader: "The system survived so long thanks to the work of the ideological service of the Communist Party and television. It was a kind of mass hypnosis. They chose me as their spokesman because I was more convincing." (*Washington Post*, December 12, 1991, p. A26) But, in the end, the master persuader was unable any longer to persuade himself—or anyone else.

Exchange

Exchange is the method of social control with which markets are built and on which political compromise is based. Exchange is about individuals offering something to trade and hoping to find a taker. In its simplest manifestation, exchange occurs when two people agree to trade some item, service, or political favor for some other item, service, or political favor. Exchange is a method of control because it is intended to induce a response—to change the behavior of a person or group. Note, however, that exchange occurs only if each party independently and voluntarily concludes that he or she would be better off as a result of the swap. If either party decides otherwise, the deal is off. Thus, exchange is a method of social control based on voluntarism, and the parties to an exchange are motivated by calculations of self-interest.

In 1776, Adam Smith (1937) was among the first to point out the benefits that would naturally follow for the individual and society from using exchange as a basic organizing principle. Markets are the outcome of countless individuals pursuing their self-interest through exchange. Smith used the analogy of the "invisible hand" to communicate the idea that, through exchange, a multitude of actions motivated by self-interest could yield a collectively desirable result. Through markets—structures created as the byproducts of countless exchanges—society could accomplish the task of allocating scarce resources with only limited resort to other control mechanisms (that is, power, authority, and persuasion). With some modification, the same ideas can be applied to politics, where we talk about "trading" votes or the "marketplace" of ideas.

It is important to recognize, however, that exchange cannot do everything that needs to be done in a political-economic system. For example, it cannot be used to meet certain important societal goals. Because exchange is based on self-interested behavior, trades that do not benefit the traders will not be made. Economic markets, for example, will not produce goods unless the enjoyment of them can be restricted to those who "purchase" them. Thus, collective goods (also known as public goods), such as national defense, will never be produced through exchange and markets. The same generally applies to public necessities, such as roads, bridges, canals, and ports—not to mention public education.

Exchange was poorly developed in the Soviet political-economic system. Economically, the Soviet Union functioned officially as a command economy. Production and distribution were centrally planned rather than based on exchange through markets. A massive bureaucracy allocated scarce resources. The bureaucracy was supposed to coordinate the activity of the Soviet economy in order to implement the policies of the CPSU leadership. In some limited areas individual economic activity outside the state command structure was permitted, and the people used an informal barter system to get scarce goods and services.

Exchange relations and market activity were not supposed to exist in the Soviet Union. Centrally planned production and distribution, however, never really worked. To secure the inputs necessary for production, plant managers routinely resorted to arrangements that were illegal or of questionable legality. Also, consumers frequently had to go outside the state-sanctioned system to find goods and services they wanted or needed. A whole set of institutions sprang up to supplement the formal system. These created a rudimentary and extra-legal market economy. The people involved in these types of exchange activities were often those who, along with young adults, found it easiest to adapt to the market reforms begun by Gorbachev.

Because the political system was democratic in name only, it did not have the kind of exchange relationships that usually characterize democratic systems. For example, although there was a legislature (the Supreme Soviet), its members were chosen in noncontested elections and met for only a few days a year to rubber-stamp policies dictated by the Communist Party leadership. There was none of the compromising and vote trading that goes on in the legislatures of fully functioning democracies. To create majorities (at least on a voluntary basis), politicians must wheel and deal. They must trade in votes and favors, much as entrepreneurs trade in goods and services. (Burns, 1978, pp. 19–20, 258)

If there was an ongoing political marketplace anywhere in the Soviet system, it was within the bureaucracy and top leadership, where individuals were forced to bargain over the development and implementation of policies. Thus,

Soviet politics resembled bureaucratic politics more than electoral politics. Now, post-Soviet politicians are being pressured to learn the give-and-take of electoral politics. In many of the successor countries, the result has been government deadlock or confusion, because trading votes and favors is seen as a betrayal of principles. One of the most pressing problems that Gorbachev faced in carrying out his economic and political reforms was people's relative lack of skill and experience in exchange. This remains a problem in all of the successor countries. The creation of viable market economies and democracies requires many people who understand and carry out the exchanges required.

The skills of bargaining and exchange do not come easily. When frustrated, many people fall back on the old way of doing things. For example, when violence was used against the independence movement in Lithuania, the press sharply criticized Gorbachev. In retaliation, he bitterly attacked the journalists who were involved and proposed suspending the new press law,[6] which gave many important protections to the media. (*Washington Post,* January 17, 1991, p. A12) Further, one of the key mistakes Gorbachev made was to have himself appointed to the Soviet parliament, rather than run in a contested election. Subsequently, he had himself appointed to the presidency as well.

Without a popular mandate, he never had the legitimacy that Yeltsin had, both as a popularly elected member of the Russian parliament and as the popularly elected President of Russia. At the time of the failed coup, this difference was crucial. Gorbachev forgot (or never really understood) that an election is an exchange between the candidates and the electorate. The candidate makes promises, and the voters give their votes to the one whose "goods" they wish to "purchase." Not going through the electoral process means that a political leader has not taken part in the exchange relationship that is at the heart of representative democracy. In a crisis like the 1991 attempted coup, this can mean a lack of authority stemming from a lack of the legitimacy that winning a contested election gives a public official.

SOCIAL STRUCTURES, RULES, AND CONFLICT

Every political-economic system—including the international system—uses power, authority, persuasion, and exchange, but their importance, organization, and use vary from system to system. Within political-economic systems, there is an ongoing debate about the appropriate mix and use of these mechanisms of social control. Sometimes the debate is carried out in philosophical terms. More often, the parties involved are concerned about particular problems or policies. Should lethal force (power) have been used in Lithuania? How rapidly and in what way should the old command economy (mainly power but

---

6. O pechati i drugikh sredstvakh massovoi informatsii, *Vedomosti S"ezda Narodnykh Deputatov SSSR i Verkhovnogo Soveta SSSR,* no. 26, June 27, 1990. An English translation of the law appears in *Current Digest of the Soviet Press,* 42(25), pp. 16–20.

with some authority) be converted to a market economy (exchange)? Should an attempt be made to force (power) or convince (persuasion) Armenia and Azerbaijan to compromise (exchange) over the future of Nagorno-Karabakh (a region in Azerbaijan mainly populated by Armenians)?

Societies need mechanisms of social control so that the conflicts that inevitably arise in a world of scarce resources are limited by rules. If they are not, then anarchy and possibly chaos become commonplace. There is little way of predicting how the parties to a conflict will behave in any given situation. One cannot count on peaceful or constructive behavior. This makes preemptive strikes attractive. Thus, the social world becomes more dangerous, because conflicts are likely to escalate into violence.

A social rule structure is, to a great extent, a patterned set of role relationships.[7] The rules give each player a range of permitted behavioral options and specify the penalty for the selection of a forbidden option. They define a player's role. Like members of a football team, different players may have different sets of options according to their position. For example, in American elections incumbents usually have an advantage over challengers, because of important factors such as name recognition and established sources of campaign funding. In the Soviet political-economic system the demands made on party members and the rewards they received were usually greater than the demands and rewards of nonparty members.

The rules that define roles can be based on power, authority, persuasion, or exchange. For example, political-economic systems can have role relationships such as victor/vanquished or exploiter/exploited (power), leader/follower or lawyer/client (authority), propagandist/audience or politician/voter (persuasion), and buyer/seller or legislator/constituent (exchange). Such patterned role relationships are called structures because they serve as the building blocks of the social order. They can emerge spontaneously or be created deliberately. In either case, the result is that conflict proceeds according to some predetermined set of rules.

So far in this discussion, we have treated the rule structures that limit social conflict as all-or-nothing situations: Either the conflict is completely structured by a set of rules, or it is without rules. In the real world, such pure types do not exist (except for trivial cases). Thus, any particular social conflict may be governed by a set of rules ranging from relatively complete (as in a football game) to virtually nonexistent (as in a backyard brawl). What we have is a theoretical continuum ranging from fully structured conflict relationships (rule-bound) to unstructured conflict relationships (rule-less). Real conflicts fall somewhere between these two extremes.

Highly structured conflicts are very rule-bound. The "roles and behavior of the parties to the conflict are prescribed by social norms or laws." (Barner-

---

7. Much of the following discussion is based on Philip Brickman's (1974) structural analysis of conflict relationships. We have made some changes to make the concept more useful for analyzing this case, but the main credit goes to Brickman.

Barry & Rosenwein, 1985, p. 213) "The orientation of parties in fully structured conflict relationships is a moral orientation, involving a concern with the other primarily as a moral agent whose actions are either right or wrong." (Brickman, 1974, p. 12) Highly structured conflicts are almost always the product of explicit design. Through authority and power, patterned role relationships (e.g., courts) are created, and rules (e.g., laws) specify how conflict will be handled in all but the most unpredictable circumstances. Civil and criminal procedural law, for example, make court proceedings highly rule-bound conflicts. When conflicts are highly rule-bound, the people involved can have confidence in their predictions about others' behavior and choose their own actions accordingly. The existence of sanctions to punish those whose behavior violates the rules reinforces this confidence.

Ordinary Soviet trials were less rule-bound than American trials, but they were relatively highly structured. However, during certain periods of Soviet history (e.g., the time of the Stalinist purge trials) and with reference to certain trials of special political significance (e.g., the trials of dissidents under Leonid Brezhnev), the rules were ignored. During the Stalinist purges, which mainly took place in the 1930s, the courts in which the purge trials were held acted arbitrarily. In a series of "show trials" most of the men who had created the Soviet Union were declared "enemies of the people" and were imprisoned or executed. Moreover, this search for "enemies" took on a frenzy that resulted in the arrest and death or imprisonment of thousands of innocent people. Thus, the purges mark a point in Soviet history during which many courts acted in a virtually rule-less way.

In partially structured conflict relationships, there are some limits on what the participants can do, but the limits do not apply to all important aspects of the conflict. "Each party sees the other primarily as a competitive actor rationally pursuing his own self-interest. . . . Intentional or selfish aggression, activated by calculation that this aggression will be rewarded by more favorable outcomes, is an important part of partially structured conflict." (Brickman, 1974, p. 11) Thus, participants are likely to use tactics such as threats, deception, and bribes. American political campaigns are a good example of partially structured conflicts. Participants have to follow reasonably stringent rules governing the way they finance their campaigns. There are, however, no clear rules about the extent to which a candidate can distort an opponent's record.

Partially structured conflicts are sometimes the result of spontaneously generated social structures. Such structures (like markets) result from the independent and simultaneous actions of actors motivated by self-interest (like buyers and sellers), so there are not many explicit rules. Another example is the international system.

The Soviet central economic planning system provides an example of a partially structured conflict process. As a practical matter, it was impossible for the central planners to specify every detail. Thus, they tried "to focus only on the most important commodities and [they delegated to] the lower levels other parts of the planning problem." (Hewett, 1988, p. 129) At the republic or local level, then, the people responsible for economic activity had some leeway to adapt central economic policies to local conditions. They were operating within a partially structured situation. In deciding how to allocate scarce resources, they were partly but not completely limited by orders from above.

Some conflict relationships are virtually unstructured. Because almost no hard-and-fast laws or norms apply, the participants have a lot of room for maneuver. But lack of structure gives rise to great uncertainty and increases the probability of violence. Everyone "sees the other primarily as a [potential] source of threatening or painful stimulation that needs to be escaped, avoided, or destroyed." (Brickman, 1974, p. 9) The options available to the participants are, in theory, practically unlimited. The options available to a political terrorist, for example, are limited mostly by the terrorist's opportunities and creativity. The actions that the targets of terrorism can take to avoid being hurt or killed are essentially unknown, because the terrorist's behavior is highly unpredictable. In fact, "the characteristic features of terrorism are anonymity and the violation of established norms." (Laqueur, 1977, p. 3)

The behavior of the secret police during the Soviet purge period of the 1930s was essentially rule-less. Many refer to it as a period of terror because of the almost total absence of limits on who could be arrested and imprisoned or executed. Certain behaviors were likely to invite the attention of the secret police and their informers; other behaviors were normally harmless. People, however, could never be certain. Persons who knew of nothing they had done wrong were awakened in the middle of the night and hauled off to prison—or worse. There were very few rules that those who wished to avoid being caught up in the hysteria could follow. As a result, many of the people who carried out the earliest purges later became victims themselves.

In summary, extreme uncertainty and even chaos tend to prevail when conflicts are not rule-bound in any significant way. The more rule-bound the social conflict, the greater is the possibility for participants to anticipate at least some of their opponents' moves and act accordingly. Even under moderately rule-bound conditions, conflict can escalate into violence, but it is much less likely to do so than in basically rule-less situations. Finally, highly structured conflict situations can become much like rituals: There is great emphasis on procedures, and the participants have roles that are highly scripted.[8]

DOMESTIC AND INTERNATIONAL SYSTEMS

The domains of domestic affairs and international relations encompass two different types of social system routinely identified and studied in political science and economics. They have typically been treated as different spheres of inquiry. The traditional subfields of political science and economics reflect this split (e.g., comparative politics/international relations and economics/

---

8. In the Brickman schema there is also a related but somewhat different variation: conflict over the rules of conflict. This is revolutionary conflict and is discussed in Chapter 2.

international economics). To analyze the situation in the area of the world that used to be the Soviet Union, we must bridge these traditional lines of demarcation. What distinguishes international systems from domestic systems? What do they have in common? Only within such a framework can we consider the range of possibilities for the future relationships among the former republics of the Soviet Union.

Kenneth Waltz (1979, 1986) offers one of the most frequently cited explanations of the differences between the domestic and international domains. Waltz views domestic politics and international relations in dichotomous terms. International politics is politics in a state of anarchy. There is no source of authority over the nation-state that can enforce rules or arbitrate disputes without the explicit agreement of the parties to the dispute. Political leaders therefore define their countries' interests and defend them to the extent they can, given their power capabilities. In other words, international politics takes place in a "self-help" environment.

Self-help politics, however, is not chaos; it is not rule-less. In the international environment conflict is partially structured. Sovereign states use power to pursue their interests. One eventual result, over time, is the creation of implicit power relationships that limit, or at least inform, the options available to the leaders of these countries. Another result is a formally unorganized situation that has within it a tacit set of limits that partially structure conflict. The bipolar stability of the Cold War is an example. The Soviet Union and the United States independently pursued their national interests, and the result was a rough equivalence in power capabilities (gauged primarily in terms of military might). This balance of power gave their conflict a structure that limited and informed their foreign policy options.

The presence of nuclear weapons served to reinforce this implicit rule structure. In case of nuclear attack, both the US and the USSR had a second-strike capability. The "logic" of mutual second-strike capability means that each actor holds the other's citizens hostage to the potential of a retaliatory nuclear strike. Policymakers and strategists in both countries came to understand which types of weapons systems strengthened and thereby stabilized mutual second-strike capability and which ones, if developed and deployed, could undercut this stability. (Jervis, 1982) In the convoluted logic of nuclear arms, the development of weapons systems that make one country's population centers *less* vulnerable to attack typically spurs another round in an increasingly costly arms race and can encourage the enemy to consider striking first. Such a policy is therefore destabilizing to the rule structure of nuclear deterrence.

In the partially structured environment of superpower relations, however, the rules are implicit and cannot be enforced. Throughout the Cold War between the US and the USSR, occasional episodes of instability occurred during which one or the other adopted policies that were perceived as potential violations of the rules of nuclear deterrence. There was one such episode in the early 1980s. President Ronald Reagan vigorously pursued the Strategic Defense Initiative (SDI). SDI, popularly known as "Star Wars," was described as an "umbrella" that could safeguard the United States from nuclear attack. Soviet leaders were faced with the fact that the United States was pursuing a policy that could potentially make American cities less vulnerable. This raised the specter of a possible American first strike against the Soviet Union. Thus, despite the obvious constraint that potential nuclear holocaust represents, there are no guarantees. In the self-help environment of international relations, nuclear weapons can always be used.

This self-help environment dictates that every state provide for its own security, and the international system is the outcome of these simultaneous and independent efforts. Such a system is necessarily fragile because no authoritative force is charged with safeguarding everyone. Collapse may be brought on by policies adopted and pursued by the same self-interested states that created the international system in the first place. Markets without authority are prone to similar instability. Self-interested buyers and sellers, without government guarantees to the contrary, can violate contracts and thereby can threaten the market structure itself.

In contrast to the anarchy of international politics, Waltz characterizes domestic politics under the rubric of government as hierarchy. A government's authority and monopoly on the legitimate use of force allow people to specialize, develop trust, and become interdependent. Governments establish written (legal) and unwritten (traditional) rules that partially or almost fully structure the conflicts that arise within their domain. Within the jurisdiction of government, individuals can specialize (do what they do best), relying on their ability to exchange goods and services. Thus other people are trusted to meet most of their needs, and they can meet at least one need of many of those others. People can pursue their self-interests through exchange because government exists to guarantee safety, property, and contracts—all of which contribute to the psychological state of trust needed to make such a system of exchange work.

According to Waltz, there is anarchy and there is hierarchy. Politics takes place in one environment or the other—either in the power-driven domain of anarchy or the authority-driven domain of hierarchy. When applied to the Soviet Union, however, this dichotomy is too confining. It is more helpful to view international politics and domestic politics in terms of points on a set of continua. At one end of each continuum is totally unstructured conflict. This can be viewed as an ideal type. Even in Waltz's formulation, the power-driven anarchy of contemporary international relations does not approach this pole. In the international political-economic system, conflict is partially structured.[9] On the other end of each continuum is completely structured conflict. This can be viewed as an ideal type as well. It is approached by Waltz's view of domestic politics under the authority-driven rubric of hierarchy. In the real world, no political system can be completely structured (i.e., rule-bound) or completely unstructured (i.e., rule-less). Moreover, the amount of structure in any political-economic system can vary over time. For example, the Soviet court system was

---

9. For an excellent discussion of anarchy and the structure of world politics, see Wendt (1992).

TABLE 1-1
Political Leaders in the USSR

	Party Office	Government Office
V. I. Lenin		Premier,[1] 1917–24
J. V. Stalin	General Secretary, 1922–53	Premier, 1941–53
N. S. Khrushchev	First Secretary, 1953–64[2]	Premier, 1958–64
L. I. Brezhnev	First Secretary, 1964–66	President,[3] 1977–82
	General Secretary, 1966–82	
Y. V. Andropov	General Secretary, 1982–84	President, 1983–84
K. U. Chernenko	General Secretary, 1984–85	President, 1984–85
M. S. Gorbachev	General Secretary, 1985–91	President,[4] 1988–91

1. "Premier" was the English title used to designate the Chair of the Council of People's Commissars (1917–1946) and the Chair of the Council of Ministers (after 1946).
2. In 1952, the title "General Secretary" was changed to "First Secretary."
3. Until 1990, the English title "President" was used to designate the Chair of the Presidium of the Supreme Soviet (1938–1989) and Chair of the Supreme Soviet (1989–1990).
4. In 1990, a formal executive branch was created by constitutional amendment. It was headed by a president. Gorbachev was its first and only incumbent.

more rule-bound during the Khrushchev era than it had been during the Stalin era. (See Table 1-1.) The amount of structure can also vary with reference to the situation being analyzed. For example, during the Brezhnev era Soviet courts were far more rule-bound when they dealt with ordinary cases than when they dealt with cases involving dissidents. Thus on a practical level, it is more accurate to talk about how much structure can be found in a given political-economic system with reference to a particular situation at a given point in time.

Analyzing the extent to which conflict is structured in any given political-economic system at any particular point in time, however, is insufficient. It is also necessary to assess the kind of conflict being structured. That is why evaluating a political-economic system against a set of continua is important. Thus, each social control mechanism—power, authority, persuasion, and exchange—should be viewed as a continuum. Take power, for example. One of the basic flaws in the Soviet political-economic system was the overreliance placed on power relative to other types of social control. Thus, it is appropriate to ask how rule-bound the exercise of power was with reference to any given situation at any point in Soviet history. The exercise of power, for example, was much more structured (rule-bound) under Khrushchev than it had been under Stalin. One reason for this difference was that Khrushchev was attempting to create a situation in which the Soviet people would not be as subject to the arbitrary use of brute force as they had been under Stalin. To this end, starting with his secret speech in 1956, Khrushchev exposed some of the crimes of Stalin and began a program of de-Stalinization. Combining placement on these continua with an understanding of the mechanisms of social control encourages a much more nuanced analysis of the transformation of the USSR than would be possible with a simple domestic/international relations distinction.

Looking at the mechanisms of social control as being used in a more or less rule-bound way over time offers at least one more advantage. Political scientists tend to bring to their work a bias toward stasis and stability, because it is easier to study a subject that sits still. Most social processes, however, are in constant flux. Why do social scientists act as though social processes are static? Their analytical tools make analyzing a freeze-frame easier than analyzing a moving picture. Even the language of social science reflects this tendency. The term *structure,* for instance, communicates stability and solidity. Structures, however, are patterned role relationships that are fluid and subject to change. In fact, it is fair to say that social structures—unlike physical structures—are always in the process of change.

It is possible to get the flavor of this distinction if you think of a wire with a bead on it. Let the bead represent the Soviet Union. Let the wire represent a continuum ranging from the use of power under highly structured conditions to the use of power under virtually unstructured conditions. Let the situation be the relationship between the Soviet leadership and those who disagree with its policies. During the Stalinist purges, the bead was far over in the direction of unstructured conflict. Few, if any, hard-and-fast rules applied. After Stalin's death and particularly after Khrushchev's secret speech exposing many of Stalin's crimes (at least to the CPSU elite), the bead began moving slowly and fitfully toward the structured side of the continuum. Sometimes it moved forward; often it retreated. Overall, however, the movement was toward more structure—more rule-boundedness in the use of power. With the advent of Gorbachev, the bead began to move more rapidly toward rule-boundedness. When the Soviet Union broke up in 1991, the bead was wavering at a point far closer to the rule-bound end of the continuum than to the point at which it had started in the 1920s.

Any political-economic system can be visualized as a more or less organized structure of wires and beads. All of the beads are constantly moving in varying directions at varying speeds. We can freeze them to capture the state of the system at any particular moment in time. We can also talk about the direction of movement and about momentum. We should not, however, confuse such analyses with the realities of the system. It is constantly in motion. When we make it sit still for purposes of analysis, we are only taking a snapshot in time. When we talk about the direction and momentum of any particular bead, we are abstracting that bead from the whole. In both instances we misrepresent reality unless we allow for the distorting effects of what we are doing.

In the Soviet Union during the Gorbachev era and now in the successor countries, some of the beads are moving very rapidly—so rapidly that observers constantly feel out of breath just trying to keep track of them. It is tempting to wait until the dust settles—until the movement of the beads slows to a more manageable rate. Such an attitude, however, discounts the potential importance and interest of trying to understand the contemporary pattern and momentum of change. In this short book, we cannot make the definitive statement about either this conceptual framework or the analysis it yields. But even though it has limitations and flaws, it captures the real world more accurately than does a simple dichotomy.

The Soviet Union has moved from being a domestic political-economic system to being an international system. The change is not as complete as the Waltz dichotomy would suggest. Russia claims a "special relationship" to the countries that were formerly Soviet republics. Moscow is still actively involved in some of them and very influential in others. This situation is likely to continue into the indefinite future because of the size and potential power of Russia. Thus, at any point in time, it is important to try to determine whether Russia is interacting with the other successor countries in ways that are more or less rule-bound. In addition, with reference to any event or situation, it is important to think about the role played by power, authority, persuasion, and exchange and how rule-bound each social mechanism is in that context.

Human beings play a central role in creating and sustaining any political-economic system. Their natural inclinations and limitations mold the decisions they make. What is it reasonable to expect of them? If the system is to be transformed, how must they change to adapt? The basis for such an analysis is political culture. Thus, because the former Soviet Union is undergoing major political change, it is necessary to identify the characteristics of the most influential political culture that undergirds the change process. Because the Soviet Union was, in essence, a Russian creation and because Russians dominated it, Russian political culture strongly influenced the shape and direction of the Soviet Union. Even Stalin, who was not ethnically Russian, admired Russian culture and espoused the value system it represented. Thus, some knowledge about the basic characteristics of Russian political culture is essential for understanding the Soviet Union and assessing the events that took place after 1991 in the newly independent countries.

REFERENCES

Barner-Barry, C., & Rosenwein, R. (1985). *Psychological perspectives on politics.* Englewood Cliffs, NJ: Prentice-Hall.

Brickman, P. (Ed.). (1974). *Social conflict: Readings in rule structures and conflict relationships.* Lexington, MA: Heath.

Burg, D., & Feifer, G. (1973). *Solzhenitsyn.* New York: Stein and Day.

Burns, J. M. (1978). *Leadership.* New York: Harper & Row.

Dallin, A., & Breslauer, G. W. (1970). *Political terror in communist systems.* Stanford, CA: Stanford University Press.

Doob, L. W. (1983). *Personality, power, and authority: A view from the behavioral sciences.* Westport, CT: Greenwood Press.

Eckstein, H., & Gurr, T. R. (1975). *Patterns of authority: A structural basis for political inquiry.* New York: Wiley.

Edelman, M. (1971). *Politics as symbolic action: Mass arousal and quiescence.* New York: Academic Press.

Gerth, H. H., & Mills, C. W. (1958). *From Max Weber.* New York: Oxford University Press.

Hewett, E. A. (1988). *Reforming the Soviet economy: Equality versus efficiency.* Washington, DC: Brookings Institution.

Hobbes, T. (1962). *The Leviathan.* New York: Macmillan. (Original work published 1651)

Jervis, R. (1982). Security regimes. *International Organization, 36,* 357–378.

Kelman, H. C. (1958). Compliance, identification and internalization: Three processes of attitude change. *Journal of Conflict Resolution, 2,* 51–60.

Kelman, H. C., & Hamilton, L. (1989). *Crimes of obedience: Toward a social psychology of authority and responsibility.* New Haven, CT: Yale University Press.

Kornai, J. (1992). *The socialist system: The political economy of communism.* Princeton, NJ: Princeton University Press.

Kreml, W. (1985). *A model of politics.* New York: Macmillan.

Laqueur, W. (1977). *Terrorism.* Boston: Little, Brown.

Lasswell, H. D. (1958). *Politics: Who gets what, when, how.* New York: Whittlesey House.

Lindblom, C. (1977). *Politics and markets: The world's political economic systems.* New York: Basic Books.

McCauley, M. (1981). *The Soviet Union since 1917.* New York: Longman.

Reardon, K. K. (1981). *Persuasion: Theory and context.* Beverly Hills, CA: Sage.

Roloff, M. E. (1980). Self-awareness and the persuasion process. In M. E. Roloff & G. R. Miller (Eds.), *Persuasion: New directions in theory and research.* Beverly Hills, CA: Sage.

Seaburg, C. (Ed.). (1968). *Great occasions.* Boston: Skinner House.
Smith, A. (1937). *An inquiry into the nature and causes of the wealth of nations.* New York: Modern Library. (Original work published 1776)
Ugolovnyi kodeks RSFSR. (1990). Moscow: Iuridicheskaia Literatura.
Waltz, K. (1979). *Theory of international politics.* Reading, MA: Addison-Wesley.
———. (1986). Reflections on *Theory of international politics.* In R. Keohane (Ed.), *Neorealism and its critics.* New York: Columbia University Press.
Wendt, A. (1992). Anarchy is what states make of it: The social construction of power politics. *International Organization, 46,* 391–425.

· 2 ·

POLITICAL CULTURE: HISTORY, REVOLUTION,
AND REFORM

All of us today are just learning democracy. We are only now forming a political culture.

MIKHAIL S. GORBACHEV *(Time,* June 5, 1989, p. 30)

Russia has russified Communism more than Communism has communized Russia.

ROBERT V. DANIELS (1988, p. 44)

All political-economic systems, including the USSR, are products of their history. But in the case of the Soviet Union this point needs emphasis because of the widely held, albeit erroneous, assumption that the revolutions in February and October of 1917 wiped much of the slate of history clean. Nothing could be further from the truth. The legacy of the past inevitably shaped the course of Soviet history, and its impact continues to reverberate in Russia and the other successor countries.

When Mikhail Gorbachev said that the Soviet people were just learning democracy, he was right—at least in the sense that many of them were trying. When he said that they were only then forming a political culture, he was wrong. They were trying to change one. The Soviet people had inherited a myriad of political cultures, most going far back in time. There was, however, a dominant political culture: the Russian political culture. It was an inheritance from the Russian Empire, and a result of the fact that the Soviet leadership was largely made up of Russians. Even non-Russian Soviet leaders usually embraced Russian political culture—Joseph Stalin, an ethnic Georgian, was a prime example. Thus, as Daniels notes in the chapter epigraph, the Soviet Union's political culture was heavily influenced by pre-Soviet Muscovite and Russian imperial political folkways. What Gorbachev was talking about was the effort to change it enough so that democracy could be planted and flourish in Soviet soil.

Stable democracy was never achieved in the Soviet Union. The question is whether it can be achieved in the diverse set of countries that emerged from the collapse of the Soviet Empire. Right now, the answer varies depending on the successor country in question—not to mention the vicissitudes of fate. In this chapter we examine the Russian political cultural heritage of the overwhelming majority of the leaders of the Soviet Union, as well as a majority of its population. We also consider three turning points in Soviet history with an eye toward the relationship between these events and the Russian political culture that the Soviet Union inherited. The three landmark Soviet experiences are the 1917 revolutions, the Stalinization of the political-economic system, and the reform period that Gorbachev and his associates initiated. First, however, it is necessary to be more specific about how we are defining the term *political culture,* for there is no one generally accepted definition.

In this chapter, *political culture* refers to the subjective orientations of the actors in a political system toward that political system. We expressly reject the definition that includes patterned, overt political behavior, because the broadness of such a definition seriously compromises the analytical usefulness of the concept. (Almond & Verba, 1965; Almond & Verba, 1989; Brown, 1984) Thus, we view behavioral and institutional variables only as indicators of underlying psychological states that we refer to as *assumptions.*

POLITICAL CULTURE

Political culture is both an important and an elusive aspect of political-economic systems. It is important because it forms the context for political-economic ideas and activities. It is elusive because it is abstract and pervasive— something most people do not spend a lot of time thinking about. *Political culture* can be defined as the set of assumptions that members of a society make about politics. People use these assumptions to "order their perceptions and experiences and make decisions." (Vivelo, 1978, p. 17) The assumptions do not require the "persons making them to undertake any action, but they predispose individuals in certain directions; whether they perform these actions will depend on opportunities afforded them by political institutions and by their position in the social structure." (Elkins & Simeon, 1979, p. 133) Political culture exists within a broad general culture; it influences people's ideas about the basic nature of political-economic systems and about their own political-economic system in particular.[1]

People go through life taking their political culture for granted, as they take for granted the air they breathe. They are vaguely aware of it but do not think much about it unless some experience explicitly calls it to their attention. The assumptions that make up a political culture tend to be unexamined. The

---

1. Our thinking about political culture has been heavily influenced by Elkins and Simeon (1979). We acknowledge them here and have limited our in-text citations to direct quotations from their article.

political behavior of a politician or government official who acts in line with the assumptions of his or her political culture is normally regarded as appropriate (though not necessarily desirable). The politician or official is seen as a legitimate political actor. A person whose political behavior is out of line is likely to be regarded as suspect—as an outsider. The same is true of institutions. They must be in fundamental harmony with the underlying political culture.

Thus, political culture is the basis for the political activities of both individuals and institutions. In fact, in the search for that elusive state of mind we call "political culture," valuable clues can be found in the activities and institutions that are considered legitimate by the people within that political-economic system. These clues, of course, must be supplemented by other information—for example, about the origins of widespread behavioral patterns and existing institutions or about the relationship between past political systems and present ones.

Political socialization takes place throughout the life cycle, but the internalization of a political culture tends to take place relatively early in life and becomes more and more resistant to change as people age. Children learn about their political culture primarily from the family, the school, the peer group, and the media. These institutions inculcate certain assumptions. These assumptions gradually become "built into" children's minds as they grow up. Because the assumptions of a political culture are internalized and largely unexamined, they place implicit limits on the alternatives people consider when deciding how to act or when evaluating the actions of others.

Political cultures condition people to think of fewer options than are logically possible. This self-limitation tends to follow general patterns. In American democracy, for example, the idea that government officials should not be "above the law" is central. Thus, breaking the law to win an election or achieve a political goal is not considered an acceptable option. Some politicians do, of course, but if they get caught, their candidacies and political careers usually suffer. Richard Nixon was the only US president to resign from office. Lawbreaking during his 1972 campaign, his alleged involvement in covering it up, and the resulting threat of impeachment forced him from office. In other political cultures, what Nixon did would not have had such a devastating effect on his political career. At the time the Watergate scandal was coming to light, some people in the Soviet Union could not understand what all the fuss was about. Their reaction made sense. In the Soviet political-economic system of the time, the CPSU and government leaders were considered to be above the law. Average Soviet citizens generalizing from their own day-to-day experiences believed that public officials could be expected to routinely ignore the law.

What is considered politically relevant also varies from one political culture to another. In some political cultures the private lives of politicians are considered irrelevant to their fitness for holding government office. In others, private behavior is considered very important. In France, a man who voters know has a mistress is generally not considered unfit to hold public office. In the United

States, in contrast, no politician could openly maintain a mistress. During the 1984 presidential primaries, accusations of adulterous episodes (which fell far short of maintaining a mistress) destroyed the presidential hopes of an early front-runner, Gary Hart. The families of American politicians are also very much in the spotlight. For example, in 1993, the enrollment of President Bill Clinton's daughter in a private rather than a public school attracted media attention and aroused political controversy.

In contrast, the personal lives of Soviet politicians were kept very private. When Gorbachev's wife began to play a more public role, imitating the style of American presidents' wives, she was harshly criticized for behaving in a brazen and inappropriate way. Boris Yeltsin's wife, perhaps learning from this example, decided to play a more traditional role—either not attending or standing quietly in the background at public events.[2]

Political cultures are not monolithic and do not necessarily explain the behavior of any single individual at any specific point in time. Although they account for the basic characteristics of political groups, individual members may or may not share most or all of the assumptions held by other members of a given group. In fact, the range of unconscious assumptions held by a group may be quite broad—particularly if the group is large, like the population of a country. Political subcultures may even be identifiable. In the Soviet case, the most obvious subcultures were those of the many non-Russian ethnic groups that made up the Soviet populace. (White, 1979, pp. 14–15) Many of them are now majority or minority cultural groups in the successor countries.

The important thing is that the members of the larger group have enough basic assumptions in common to sustain a reasonably stable, workable political-economic system. In fact, the assumptions held by a very small number of people may be highly influential—if that group controls key socializing institutions, such as the educational system and the media. Such an elite can consciously and deliberately use such resources to try to persuade others to change their cultural assumptions. More commonly, however, these elites tacitly pass on the political cultures that they inherited by the choices they make. In other words, they teach by example. Those who would make basic changes in a political culture run up against limits. Without the luxury of a great deal of time, they cannot stray too far beyond the traditional assumptions and succeed. Their persuasive attempts are always counterbalanced by stable institutions (e.g., the family) and emotional attachments (e.g., religion or ethnic identification). Because such limiting influences are hard to control, rapid change in a political culture is very difficult to achieve.

Political cultures are not static. Even the most stable are constantly undergoing a slow process of alteration as they adapt to changes in the world. (Harris, 1983, pp. 8–9) Usually this process is so prolonged and subtle that an impres-

---

2. This attitude toward the wives of rulers might be traced back to the ancient custom (changed by Peter the Great) of isolating the women of the court in a part of the palace called the *terem*. Note the similarity between the words *terem* and *harem*.

sion of fundamental stability is conveyed both to the people involved and to those watching from outside. More obvious changes are associated with such things as the replacement of one generation by another. From time to time, though, there are events which have the potential to increase the rate of change dramatically. One such event is revolution.

Revolutions are deliberate attempts to make basic changes in the way a political-economic system works, not just get rid of those currently in power. Because "even abortive or unsuccessful revolutions have a more or less permanent impact on society" (Hagopian, 1974, p. 1), revolutions—whether successful or not—can increase the rate of change in a political culture. The resulting changes may be temporary or permanent. The extent to which they tend to be permanent, as well as the related question of the persistence of the traditional political culture, has been a topic of lively debate among scholars.

No revolution can totally eliminate a previously existing political culture. A revolution can, however, speed up the rate of change. More important, it can reshape aspects of a political culture and in turn also be shaped by them. Thus, to understand the political culture of the Soviet Union, it is necessary to look back in time and identify certain historical patterns indicative of the core assumptions that make up the dominant political culture of the people living in the territory that used to be the Soviet Union. In these lands, various forms of absolutist political rule have been a prominent feature of government and politics for many centuries. In an absolutist system, the powers exercised by the government are unrestrained. There is no rule of law as we understand it. In fact, absolutism is "the opposite of constitutionalism, which provides for government limited by law. . . . [A]n absolutist regime typically defines and determines the scope of its own powers whether or not a constitution exists." (Plano & Greenberg, 1985, p. 1) During most of the Soviet period there was a constitution, but it was ignored when it placed unwanted demands or limits on those in power. Thus, there was a constitution but no constitutionalism.

RUSSIAN POLITICAL CULTURE

In this section, we explore the idea that the absolutist system of rule that the Bolsheviks established was basically in harmony with the dominant Russian political culture. This political culture grew out of the historical experience of the Eastern Slavs, composed approximately of the people of the countries now known as Russia, Ukraine, and Belarus. For most of their recorded histories these lands were dominated in one way or another by the Russians.[3]

Beginning in the fifteenth century, there arose something that can reasonably

---

3. Of course, Kievan Rus with its center in what is now the capital of Ukraine flourished before dominance decisively shifted to Moscow. The interpretation we are using here, however, dates the rise of Russian political culture after the decline of Kiev as the major governing force in the region. (Keenan, 1986, p. 118)

be considered a Russian political culture.[4] For most of its history, Russia had an absolutist government. The rulers had total power over their subjects in that there were no significant restraints on the power they could potentially exercise. Absolutism is frequently associated with the rule of a single individual, but both autocracy and oligarchy can be absolutist. Further, Russian absolutism should not be confused with the absolutism practiced in continental Europe, with its hereditary monarchs. In the West, institutions such as the church and the nobility effectively limited the absolute power of the rulers. In fact, it was the gradual increase in the limits that such institutions placed on monarchs that led to the democratic systems that now prevail in Europe. No such limiting institutions existed in Russia. (Daniels, 1985, pp. 34–35; White, 1979, pp. 40–63) To the contrary, "Russian absolutism was more despotic, more centralized, and more oppressive than any contemporary counterpart in the West. Absolute power, its exercise, and the expectation of its enforcement became the basis of Russian political culture." (Daniels, 1985, p. 35)

The political environment from which Russian political culture developed was not particularly stable. First, there was the influence of the Byzantine Empire, to which the ninth-century rulers of Kievan Rus (the forebears of the Russian rulers) looked when they began to shape their system of rule. The pattern in Byzantium was a despotism with one ruler serving as head of both the state and the bureaucracy of the church.[5] Subsequently, there was the Mongol invasion in the thirteenth century. It was as tribute collectors for the Mongols that the princes of Muscovy became dominant in the region around Moscow, the future heart of Russia.

The Mongols maintained control for almost a century and a half—mostly as "absentee landlords" concerned about little other than that the rent (i.e., tribute) be paid. Finally, in 1480, Ivan III renounced his allegiance to the Mongol khan, and the Mongols "failed to challenge his action seriously." (Riasanovsky, 1984, p. 71) Subsequently, the Muscovite rulers began to expand into the lands that first became Russia and eventually the Russian Empire. The Mongol invasion not only prevented the establishment of other centers of power that might have decisively limited this Muscovite expansion, but it also set an example of the usefulness (at least to those who would rule absolutely) of terror allied with highly centralized administration.

Finally, throughout the establishment of Russia and its expansion into an empire, the Russians were constantly threatened by enemies, both tribal nomads and hostile foreign governments. In response, an absolutist state "had to be accepted to enforce military priorities—that is, to collect the taxes and mobilize the needed armies" that would ensure Russia's survival. (Daniels, 1985, p. 37) This history meant that many of the ethnic groups of the Soviet Union had political histories with one important thing in common: the influ-

---

4. Much of the material in this section is drawn from Keenan (1986). To minimize citations, only direct quotations from Keenan's article will be referenced.
5. This ruler did not exercise theological leadership.

ence of the despotic Mongol approach to rule. Indeed, Stalin, the chief architect of the Soviet system, has been referred to as "Genghis Khan with the telegraph." (Conquest, 1991, p. xvii)

Russian political culture was formed out of the political cultures of three groups that were all living on Russian soil but initially had very separate existences: the peasants, the court, and the bureaucracy. Central to the shaping of Russian political culture was the harshness of the physical setting. It was (and remains) a poor and inhospitable land, most of which is located north of the southern tip of Canada's Hudson Bay. The soil is inferior and acid, the terrain swampy. Winter is "long, dark, and bitterly cold"; spring is "dramatic and destructive with . . . sudden thaws, floods, and ubiquitous mud"; summer is "short and unpredictable." "[O]ne year in seven brought a major crop failure . . . and in the best of times yields were very small." (Keenan, 1986, p. 121) Yet in spite of all this, the inhabitants thrived, creating their own distinctive political culture.

The primary objective of the peasantry was simple physical survival in the face of these daunting conditions. The village, not the individual, was the focus of this effort and minimizing risk the overriding concern. In such an environment, a loner is highly vulnerable and potentially dangerous, because individual actions can threaten the existence of the group. Thus, the norm became to control the individual and make the individual serve the community. To this end, the dominant Russian village culture developed a reliance on institutions that subordinated the individual to the group, a forerunner of the collective. Heads of households participated in a primitive and paternalistic type of majority rule, the outcomes of which were binding on the community. Up to the time of the Bolshevik Revolution in October 1917, most Russians lived in villages and shared this traditional village culture.

The court was historically much less stable in its political culture than was the peasantry. The princes of Muscovy faced a social and political environment as harsh as the natural environment. They were attempting to maintain and extend their rule over a land characterized by poor communications, enormous expanses of impassible territory, sparse settlements, and a lack of urbanization. Under these conditions, it was extremely difficult to establish political control and military security. Like the peasants, however, the Muscovite rulers succeeded in creating a durable political system and eventually an empire that covered approximately one-sixth of the earth's land surface.

The rulers focused their energy on a limited objective: the preservation of the military and political order. Because of a turbulent early history, they were particularly intent on averting chaos and anarchy. Consequently, they avoided the unknown and unpredictable. This meant avoiding risks and innovations, as well as emphasizing sanctions and institutions of control—all to shield them from the consequences of their own perceived weakness. Over time, in its effort to control every aspect of social and political life, the court "developed a tendency to 'overkill' in order to avoid situations in which it might have to deal with uncontrollable outcomes." (Keenan, 1986, p. 131)

At the heart of this control system was an unwavering principle of extreme centralization. All important decisions were made in Moscow by an oligarchy based on the boyar clans, which furnished the nucleus of Muscovite military power. Like the peasants, the main political goal of the boyars was survival, but not mere physical survival. Rather they wanted to survive "as members of a distinct and effective, 'charismatic,' clan, a political and economic unit able to maintain its warrior status and to sustain a princely style." (Keenan, 1986, p. 133) The institution of the Tsar emerged from the need of these warring clans to avoid mutual destruction by building a coalition around the grand prince of Moscow. Like the peasants, the clans created a consensual procedure for policy-making: The elder of each clan represented the clan in councils of state.

Although its origins were earlier, the bureaucracy began to grow significantly in power to fill the administrative needs created by territorial expansion as Muscovy became the Russian Empire. This bureaucracy soon became "a closed hereditary sub-stratum in a society that assigned status and function primarily . . . on the basis of heredity." (Keenan, 1986, p. 137) The bureaucrats were generously rewarded for their services, and their political influence was considerable. This influence, however, was tied to their duties and ceased when a bureaucrat was removed from office due to loss of both income and property.

Thus, the bureaucrats, like the peasants and the courtiers, were motivated by the desire to survive. Decision-making within the bureaucratic culture was hierarchical and individual, rather than collective as it was in the peasant and court cultures. There was an institutionalized chain of command. Bureaucratic control was dependent on the position occupied in the hierarchy, on the level of influence held over government administration, and in many cases, on ties with a powerful clan. In the power games played by the clans clustered around the grand prince and his family, bureaucrats were like chess pieces.

For centuries, then, the Russian game of politics had to do with the acquisition and maintenance of social control to ensure survival. The underlying assumptions were that human beings and their creations, including the political system itself, were frail and prone to corruption and one could not depend on institutions or coalitions. It was very much a Social Darwinist world in which the strong prevailed and the weak either retreated or were eliminated. The boyars who clustered around the grand prince had their clans' client groups as power bases, especially when military power was an issue. But these client groups also made demands on the boyars. At the center was the grand prince himself, born into his role and relinquishing it only at death.

When there was no clear heir to the throne or when the heir was weak, there were outbreaks of chaos. These outbreaks convinced the clans that political stability and survival required the establishment of a single and undisputed dynasty. Thus, a system of political primogeniture was established. "[I]t mattered little, in most generations, who was at the center of this sytem, but it was crucially important that *someone* be, and that the common allegiance to him be at least nominally unconditional." (Keenan, 1986, p. 141, emphasis in the original) In the course of time, the grand prince came to be called *tsar*. The myth of the strong tsar gave the princely clans and the bureaucrats some measure of security in their status and power, as well as protection from each other.

The court in Moscow was the center of all power and authority, so it became important for the representatives of each political interest to maintain a constant presence there. "It was here, in the obligatory all-day sessions of the inner circle, that matters of state were decided and where political decisions, intrigues, and open struggles took place." (Keenan, 1986, p. 143) Until very late in the tsarist period, there was no attempt to codify the rules of government. Those who needed to know them did; those who did not were kept ignorant. Outsiders were fed the myth of the all-powerful tsar and given very little accurate information about how the system actually worked. The fact was that an oligarchy significantly limited what the supposedly all-powerful tsars could do. But this rulership arrangement was still absolutist because the tsar and the boyar oligarchy acted as a unit—the oligarchy being the power behind the throne. Together, they could do pretty much what they pleased without being constrained by other powerful institutions.

As Russia grew into an empire, the court became more and more dependent on the bureaucracy. Consequently, they began to merge. As the importance of the bureaucracy grew, the boyars began to place clan members in posts within the growing administrative structure. In the eighteenth century, in an effort to break the power of the oligarchy and establish a Western type of bureaucratic state, Peter the Great accelerated the tendency toward merger. Thus, in this period both the fortunes of the noble families and the status of individuals within them began to derive—at least in part—from official rank in the state apparatus. The eventual result was an imperial political culture that kept many of the features of the political cultures from which it had evolved.

What basic assumptions seem to have characterized pre-Soviet political culture? First and foremost, the system was and had to be absolutist. (e.g., Glazov, 1985, pp. 222–223) Whether the source of policy was the monarch or an oligarchy working through the monarchy, the rulers had virtually absolute control over their subjects. In practical terms, this meant that average Russians could assume that they owed allegiance to the state and had duties, such as paying taxes and (if they were men) serving in the military. There was no tradition of the common people taking part in policy-making; that was the job of designated (but nonelected) leaders, be they village elders or the tsar and his boyars. The job of everyone else was to do what they were told—and they knew that these orders were backed up by the willingness to use violence. (Daniels, 1988, pp. 42–43) Paternalism was considered a legitimate stance for the rulers to take toward the ruled. Moreover, like some parents, Russian rulers exercised their power and authority in a relatively rule-less way.

The second basic assumption of pre-Soviet political culture was that it was necessary to have a strong ruler (*krepkii khoziain*). This assumption was fostered by the historical experience of foreign invaders and warring clans. The Russians assumed that a strong leader would protect them against threats from the outside, as well as from anarchy and civil war. Fear of chaos is deeply rooted in the psychology of the average Russian. For most of Russian history, the solution seemed to be a strong leader supported by a loyal oligarchy and armed retainers. As Glazov (1985, p. 225) puts it: "The Russian seems to like a regime which does not give him full freedom. From being free and unchained all his troubles begin." This preference was another basis for the people's acceptance of the ruler's right to exercise relatively rule-less authority and power. This absolutist rule was seen as necessary for personal and national survival.

The third assumption of pre-Soviet political culture was that both the populace and their leaders saw the people of the Russian Empire as subjects, not citizens. This reflected the basically pessimistic view of human nature held by peasants, court, and bureaucracy alike. All political subcultures believed that ordinary people could not rule themselves but required someone to take care of them and decide what was best for them. Daniels (1988, p. 47) characterizes this belief as "a deeply misanthropic and paranoid view." At its core, the system was paternalistic, and the father figure was the mythic all-wise and all-powerful tsar. The legitimate role of the tsar was to take care of his "children," the Russian people. "Good tsars" used their power and authority in a relatively rule-bound way; "bad tsars" did not.

The fourth assumption was that survival was an overriding objective. Risks were avoided at all costs. Stability and its attendant predictability were primary goals. Given Russia's harsh and unforgiving climate, as well as its often brutal social order, the people learned that to take chances or to innovate was not usually a good thing. If something worked—no matter how imperfectly—it was best to stick with it. One could devise reasonable ways to deal with known evils. But the unknown evils that innovation might bring could easily turn out to be unmanageable or disastrous. In Russian history, change too often meant uncertainty, risk, and an instability that endangered individual, group, and (potentially) national survival. Thus, there was a premium on social control and a corresponding fear of loss of that control. Authority was a factor, but the primary mechanism of social control was usually the exercise of power, the use or threat of force. Whether power or authority was being exercised, the system tended toward the rule-less end of the continuum.

The fifth assumption was that individual initiative was to be discouraged. If it was seen as an attempt to increase the power or status of an individual or a group, it was treated as a threat to the survival of the system—be it a community or the balance of power in the court. Social and economic creativeness was not prized. Quite to the contrary: Individualism was seen as a threat to the status quo and thus to social control or survival. Nonconformists "ran the risk of severe group sanctions." (Keenan, 1986, p. 158) There was a widespread assumption that the will of the individual *had* to be subjected to the interests of the group or nation. This belief formed the basis for collectivism, as well as the rule of the Communist Party, in the Soviet period.

The sixth assumption was that control was a primary value. Because the people were not trusted to make policy decisions, it seemed necessary for rule to be highly centralized. Geographically, this meant that all roads led to and from Moscow. As the Russian Empire grew, this centralization of power achieved ridiculous proportions. Even fairly routine decisions made at the far reaches of the empire often had to be approved in Moscow—a process that could take months or years. Also, with territorial expansion, the importance of the bureaucracy grew. It became a gigantic organization with tentacles reaching out into the most remote corners of the empire. As its power waxed, the power of the boyar clans waned. More and more, the bureaucracy offered an attractive (and relatively risk-free) career path. Bureaucratic infighting became a "struggle for power and proximity to the Court, under guise of loyal unity and subordination." (Daniels, 1988, p. 43) The people of the Russian Empire learned that in many aspects of their lives success depended in one way or another on how well they dealt with bureaucrats and bureaucracies—both primarily interested in survival and control. This formed the basis for the gigantic bureaucracy that flourished throughout the Soviet period.

The seventh assumption was that this extreme centralization within the context of absolutism made a more formal system of political institutions unnecessary. The political game was based primarily on power, not authority. The rules of the game were few and, for the most part, known only to the participants. Political power and status were determined not by institutional position but by birth, personal contacts, and the balance of power among current political forces. The Russians therefore became accustomed to the fact that there was not necessarily any connection between possession of a particular official position and the political leverage a person wielded. This meant that there was no demand for the rulers to make public the rules and procedures (if any) that were currently in use—or to codify them in any way. As a result, the rule system for the management of political conflict was highly unstructured and, for most practical problems, based on power rather than on authority. "Indeed, for the whole pre-Petrine period, no systematic attempt seems to have been made *by an insider* either to describe or to analyze Muscovite politics at any level." (Keenan, 1986, p. 158, emphasis in the original)

The eighth assumption was that decisions were supposed to be consensual. From both the peasant and the court cultures, the ruling oligarchy had inherited the habit of group decision-making. An elite inner circle clustering around a leader made policy. During the discussion of alternatives, all could speak out and try to convince the others. Once a decision had been made, however, it was declared consensual or unanimous. The alternatives considered or the content of the discussion was normally kept secret. And, more important, the decision held. There was no higher authority to whom the decision could be appealed (such as the electorate in a democracy). This arrangement formed the basis for the decision-making locus and style of the Soviet period.

The ninth assumption was that foreigners were not to be trusted. There was a "fear of revealing to outsiders the content of either political or practical discussions within the ruling class." (Keenan, 1986, p. 162) Anyone associating with foreigners was (at best) suspect or (at worst) punished severely. Glazov (1985, p. 226) attributes to the Russians a tribal mentality involving "the division of the world into 'ours/not-ours.' " An elaborate mythology was constructed to mislead both the common people and foreigners about how the system really worked. From the sixteenth to the twentieth century the operative rule was not to "reveal to nonparticipants authentic information concerning politics, political groupings, or points of discord." (Keenan, 1986, p. 119) Thus, the tradition of conspiratorial and mutually protective silence was created. Also, the realities were masked by misinformation, including the myth of the all-powerful tsar. This practice, in the form of such phenomena as secret laws, closed trials, and disinformation, continued into the Soviet period.

When the Bolsheviks inherited the lands and peoples of the Russian Empire, they inherited a populace that had been deeply imprinted by its long historical experience with absolutism. "Representative institutions . . . were weakly articulated and ineffective; levels of popular participation were low; and governing style was centralized, bureaucratic and authoritarian." (White, 1979, p. 64) The church was clearly subordinated to the state, as was the rest of society. The Russians were true subjects, people who viewed themselves as having no right to participate in their own government in any significant way. They were there to give allegiance to the state and to fulfill their duties to it, not to take part in the making of policy.

Political psychologist Robert Tucker (1971, p. 122) projects an even more extreme picture in his concept of the "dual Russia." In Tucker's schema the state and the people were seen as two different entities, and the absolutist government was seen by the people as "an *alien* power in the Russian land." Thus, the state is conqueror, and society is the conquered; the state controls the society "in the manner of an occupying power." The state is "the organizing and energizing force," and "the population . . . is the passive and subordinate party, tool and victim of the state's designs."

Three landmark periods had—or were supposed to have had—a major impact on the political cultural heritages of the people who made up the Soviet populace: (1) the revolutions of 1917, (2) the imposition of Stalinism, and (3) the Gorbachev reform and subsequent dissolution of the Soviet Union. Each, in its way, was a revolution. To understand these turning points in history, it is necessary to define revolution clearly and to distinguish between revolution and reform. Within the context of the political cultural heritage of the Soviet Union, how much difference did these events make? Before we can answer this question, we must take a closer look at the concepts of revolution and reform.

CONFLICT OVER THE RULES OF CONFLICT

In Chapter 1, we discussed how rule-bound or rule-less various types of political conflict can be. We assumed that there is a general acceptance of the rule structure currently in effect and that people who desire change are interested only in modification of a basically accepted rule structure. Such relatively limited changes are usually considered *reforms*. Sometimes, however, political conflict is over whether the rule structure should be changed in a fundamental way. Changes that alter the basic rule structure prevailing in a political-economic system are usually considered *revolutions*.

In most cases, reform leaves intact most of the overall rule structure, as well as the basic political cultural assumptions on which it rests. In other words, a reform may make a particular political activity more or less rule-bound, or it may alter one or more rules, but the change is at the margins, not at the core. Thus, under most circumstances, reform does not radically speed the process of change in a political culture. In fact, reforms are often viewed as ways to more nearly achieve one or more of the values inherent in the underlying political culture. Gorbachev, for example, in *Perestroika* (1987, p. 31), talks about his reform in this way: "The policy of restructuring [perestroika] puts everything in its place. We are fully restoring the principle of socialism: 'From each according to his ability, to each according to his work.' " Because the desirability of socialism (as a transition to communism) was one of the assumptions the CPSU had tried to inculcate in the populace—and had succeeded in inculcating in Gorbachev—he saw perestroika as a return to basic values, not a radical change.

Revolution, in contrast with reform, has as its goal a pervasive and far-reaching change in the rule structure of a political-economic system.[6] It is a conflict over the rules of conflict that govern the basic institutional structure and functioning of a political-economic system. What we usually think of as historical revolutions occur when revolutionary conflicts lead to a general system breakdown. One of the reasons why there are so many competing definitions of revolution in political science is the failure to distinguish between revolutionary conflict and revolutionary change. Revolutionary conflict arises when two or more parties fight (usually, but not invariably, violently) over whether there should be a basic change in the rule structure of a political-economic system. Revolutionary change is the accomplishment of such a transformation. "It is clear that one can have revolutionary change without revolutionary conflict: a change in the rules may be consensual on the part of everyone involved." (Brickman, 1974, p. 15)

An example of revolutionary change without revolutionary conflict is the writing and ratification of the US Constitution. It replaced the rule system that had prevailed under the Articles of Confederation, and it made a radical change in the way the political game was played in the United States. This change, however, was not forced by events that could be characterized as revolutionary conflict. A failed revolution is an example of revolutionary conflict without revolutionary change. In this case, agents of the status quo defeat the revolutionary challenge, and the rule system stays basically the same. History contains many examples of failed revolutions.

"Neither revolutionary conflict nor revolutionary change need be dramatic, violent, or 'revolutionary' in a more popular sense, though they can be." (Brickman, 1974, p. 15) The major way in which this definition of revolution differs from more traditional political science definitions is that it does *not*

---

6. We take a social psychological approach to defining revolution for two reasons. First, there is little agreement among political scientists on how revolution should be defined. See, e.g., Hagopian, 1974, pp. 45–75; Rejai, 1977, pp. 1–7; Remington, 1992, p. 121; Tilly, 1978, pp. 189–194; Willhoite, 1988, p. 299. Second, this approach offers a useful basis for comparing and contrasting the 1917 revolutions, the imposition of the Stalinist system, and the Gorbachev reform.

require that the revolutionary conflict be violent. Nevertheless, the conflict's essentially rule-less nature invites violence, and events that are labeled "revolutions" tend to involve revolutionary conflict of a violent nature. Obvious examples are the French Revolution and the Russian revolutions. They are frequently used as prototypical examples of revolutionary conflict, and certainly were characterized by considerable violence.

Our definition, however, is oriented toward the potential impact of revolutionary conflict on a society. We ask, "Is this conflict about changing the fundamental rule structure of a political-economic system?" If such revolutionary change happens, the revolution can be said to be successful. If it does not happen, the revolution can be said to have failed. Both a failed and a successful revolution can significantly speed the process of change in a political culture. But a successful revolution, almost by definition, is likely to speed it more.

The 1917 Revolutions

For our purposes, the history of the Soviet Union can be dated from the February and October (Bolshevik) revolutions of 1917.[7] Although it is not possible to go into the reasons for these revolutions in any detail here, it is interesting to note that they came at a time when the tsarist government was violating some basic assumptions of Russian political culture. For example, throughout Russian history, survival—be it of the village or the boyar clan—was a primary value. During the years prior to 1917, the government made a series of decisions that seriously called into question its ability to ensure the survival of the Russian Empire. Most obvious, the government got itself into a war (World War I) for which it was not prepared and, as a result, suffered a series of defeats that took a heavy human toll and demoralized both the army and civilians.

Less obvious but not unrelated was the fact that the entire government was grossly mismanaged. To take one dramatic example, the Tsarina was exercising a great deal of influence on government decision-making, and the chief influence on her was the "Mad Monk" Rasputin. Thus, there was both a threat from the outside and internal misrule. In the face of these conditions, which were evident to all, it was hard to perpetuate the myth of the all-powerful tsar who would ensure the survival and welfare of his subject people. Moreover, the weakness of Tsar Nicholas's response to the external threat and to internal problems also brought to the fore a primitive fear of social chaos—a fear that had long been a feature of Russian political culture.

---

7. The seeds of these revolutions, though important, are outside the scope of this discussion. We encourage interested readers to consult any of the Russian history books cited at the end of this chapter or at other places in this book. For a more revisionist analysis, see Acton (1990). It should also be noted that the USSR did not technically come into existence until 1922. Prior to that, the territory ruled by the Bolsheviks was called the Russian Soviet Federated Socialist Republic (RSFSR), a name subsequently given to the largest of the fifteen Soviet republics.

There were attempts at reform, and it is impossible to know what might have happened if they had been more successful. Because there was no immediate and dramatic change for the better, however, the people—nobility and commoners alike—had to deal with a deeply held cultural fear of innovation. The tendency to return to traditional ways when things went wrong was ingrained—even if the familiar ways amounted to known evils. Another obstacle to reform was the decentralization of power. As the government in St. Petersburg became weaker and less organized, enterprising officials in the hinterlands began to grasp more and more power, thereby contributing to the breakdown of the political-economic system. The decentralization of decision-making also took power away from the noble families, which were accustomed to being part of the ruling oligarchy. The nobility tried to protect its power by, among other things, assassinating Rasputin in the hope of regaining influence over Tsar Nicholas. Such actions only fed the chaos growing within the country.

The February Revolution overthrew the tsarist system of rule and replaced it with a series of provisional governments that fitfully attempted to move toward some sort of democracy. That goal, however, was never reached. During October 1917[8] the provisional government then in place was overthrown and replaced by a Bolshevik government led by Vladimir Lenin and his associates. Certain aspects of those revolutions are instructive in evaluating them as a transition from the Russian Empire to the Soviet Union. Certainly this period was characterized by revolutionary conflict involving considerable violence. But to what extent did this revolutionary conflict lead to revolutionary change?

Undoubtedly, Lenin and his followers intended to use their victory to accomplish revolutionary change. Lenin "saw no general Russian culture to be proud of"; rather he saw Russian political culture and institutions as "despotic and slavish." (Tucker, 1990, p. 43) He regarded cultural change as a primary goal of the revolution. One of the things he feared most was a reversion to the past; he was, however, limited by the internal and external political crises that he inherited. All government institutions were in disarray, and Russia was at war. Both situations were draining the resources and the morale of the Russian people, and the result was considerable dissatisfaction and violent unrest.

The Bolsheviks therefore moved to extricate themselves from World War I by negotiating the Treaty of Brest-Litovsk (1918). This treaty was hardly a triumph for the Bolsheviks. "In addition to Poland and the Baltic regions, Russia lost 27 percent of her sown area, 26 percent of her population, a third of her average crops, three quarters of her iron and steel, and 26 percent of her railway network." (Schapiro, 1984, p. 170) The treaty, however, did free the Bolshevik leadership to devote its attention to the serious breakdown of the social order within the Russian Empire, as well as to the civil war launched by those opposing the Bolshevik takeover.

---

8. This revolution occurred in October, but because of the subsequent adoption of the calendar used by the European countries, the Soviet people celebrated it on November 7 during most of the Soviet period. The Russian Orthodox Church still uses the old calendar.

During this civil war period (1918–21), known as War Communism, repression of internal enemies and summary justice became commonplace features of Soviet communist rule. By 1922, Lenin's health was failing. In 1924, he died. Before his death, many reforms had shown promise of sweeping away the old tsarist absolutism. Much of this tradition, however, remained.[9] In the aftermath of the violence of 1917 and the civil war years, Lenin had begun rebuilding the country in a gradual way. He had instituted the New Economic Policy (NEP) in order "to *revive* trade, petty proprietorship, [and] capitalism, while cautiously and gradually" trying to lay the basis for a transition to socialism. (Lenin as quoted in Tucker, 1990, pp. 29–30, emphasis in Tucker) Lenin envisioned a transition in culture and societal structure that would take as much as two generations.

It is impossible to know what might have happened if Lenin had lived longer. The fact, however, is that he did not. Further, Lenin was succeeded by Stalin, who shared neither his internationalism nor his concern for gradualism. Thus, although the rules of conflict changed in a revolutionary way, many of the changes did not long survive Lenin. For example, NEP was replaced by Stalin's policies of forced industrialization and agricultural collectivization. Thus, the 1917 revolutions marked a period of revolutionary conflict after which Lenin tried to initiate a period of revolutionary change. Lenin's death in January 1924 resulted in the rise of Stalin to the top leadership position. Stalin assumed control over the magnitude, timing, and direction of the institution-building process that followed the establishment of the Soviet Union in 1922, and Stalin decisively shaped the Soviet political-economic system.

Stalin's "Revolution from Above"

Stalin was primarily responsible for the basic institutional framework of the Soviet political-economic system. The changes he wrought were a "revolution from above" because the impetus came from the central leadership, which imposed its will on the populace. Although much of what happened had roots in the Lenin period (particularly in War Communism), Stalin put his own imprint on events and created a Soviet state that was (at the very least) radically different from the Soviet Union that Lenin and his associates had in mind at the time of the October Revolution. As Daniels points out (1988, p. 46), "the Russian Revolutionary experience testifies to the negative effects of an attempt to change a country too far and too fast in ways that run counter to its deep political folkways." Stalin's revolution from above "represented the triumph of old Russian forms of latent political culture."

Lenin was a builder of the Soviet state in the sense that he established the primacy of the Communist Party, but he was cautious in his remodeling of society. "[T]he idea of the construction of socialism as a revolution from above

---

9. For a brief listing, see Tucker (1990, pp. 32–34) or Von Laue (1993, pp. 103–104).

employing repressive means . . . , especially in a terror-enforced collectivization of the peasantry, never entered his mind." (Tucker, 1990, p. 65)[10] It did, however, enter Stalin's, and his role model was the reforming and Westernizing (but despotic) Tsar Peter the Great. Peter had aspired to transform Russia from above but had failed to overcome its social, economic, and political traditions. Stalin intended to succeed. Ironically, however, Stalinism came "to represent the triumph of old Russian forms of latent political culture." (Daniels, 1988, p. 46)

That Stalin appreciated the historical parallels and enormity of what he was doing is clear from the fact that he openly referred to his program as a revolution from above. Moreover, there is no question that Stalin's revolution accomplished much that can be regarded as revolutionary change. At the time of the 1917 revolutions, "Russia was undergoing an extraordinarily rapid change toward Western models in economy, society, modes of thought, and political practices." (Daniels, 1988, p. 44) Lenin took these developments and tried to extend them within the framework of Marxism. At the time of his death, however, the job had only begun, and he did not leave a political heir capable of continuing his task. Stalin, a very different kind of leader, decisively changed the direction in which the Soviet political-economic system was moving.

Stalin's main tools for change were the collectivization of agriculture, forced industrialization, and the purges. The first and second revolutionized the Soviet economic system. The purges removed virtually an entire generation of political leaders—primarily Bolsheviks who had presided over the October Revolution, the period of War Communism, and the early years of Soviet rule. The purges created a power vacuum at the top of the political system. Stalin filled it with persons who professed complete loyalty to him and his policies.

These revolutionary changes were accomplished by the liberal use of terror and violence. From the point of view of Russian political culture, however, the fruits of Stalin's revolution from above turned out to be largely a reversion to the pre-Soviet past. And Stalin's fascination with Russian history, especially with the rule of Peter the Great, suggests that this outcome was not an accident. It was a response to the needs of a country in the throes of a deep crisis. A combination of Stalin's personal ideas and characteristics, the folkways of the country he ruled, and the constraints of the situation itself conditioned Stalin's response to that crisis. The result was revolutionary change, but the resulting rule structure was compatible with the major assumptions of Russian political culture.

During virtually the entire subsequent Soviet period, the system was, and remained, essentially Stalinist. Gorbachev's reform eventually brought about its downfall and the disintegration of the Soviet Union. Thus, it is important to note the continuity between the tsarist and Soviet periods. Within the context of pre-Soviet Russian political culture, Stalin's revolution from above can be seen as a sort of counter-revolution, a reversion to the past. (Reiman, 1987, p. 117) Space

---

10. The major source we have used for information on this period of Stalin's rule is Tucker (1990). We acknowledge this debt here to limit citations to quotations from Tucker's book.

does not permit a fully developed argument to support this assertion. For now, it is sufficient to note briefly how many of the elements of Russian political culture—albeit in modified form—are evident in the political and government order that Stalin created.

First, absolutism was reimposed, along with a cult of Stalin that resembled the myth of the benevolent and all-powerful tsar. But, unlike many of the tsars, who were the tools of oligarchical "powers behind the throne," Stalin was a powerful ruler in his own right—feared even by his closest associates (with good reason). He tried to project a benevolent image to the world both inside and outside the Soviet Union, but it was clear to most that behind the smiling face was an iron fist. His image, like that of the tsars, was both paternal and powerful. Moreover, like the tsars, he claimed and exercised absolute power. This power and his willingness to use it to the fullest allowed him to collectivize, industrialize, and reshape the political system in roughly a single decade. His successors tried to preserve the image of strong leadership, but, like the tsars, they varied greatly in the extent to which they shared their rule with the oligarchy (the CPSU elite, rather than the Russian nobility). None, however, imposed one-man absolutist rule to the extent that Stalin did.

Second, the need to protect the people from outside threats and internal subversion was used to justify the need for a strong ruler. As early as 1925, it was Stalin's view that another international war was inevitable. Because he thought the Soviet Union would certainly be involved, it had to be ready to meet this challenge. His policy of forced industrialization was designed to create a powerful war-oriented heavy-industrial base. The development of consumer-oriented light industries was judged less important and thus was neglected. Collectivization of agriculture was to form the basis for swift industrialization. The purges were designed to create absolute loyalty to Stalin and to the system his policies created. "Subversion" and being an "enemy of the people" were the most common accusations directed at those who fell victim to the purges. The Russian people, given their age-old preoccupation with security, were receptive to these ideas. After all, they shared the memory of numerous invasions over the centuries. The idea that another onslaught by Western (particularly Germanic) forces would take place in the near future was believable. The German invasion during World War II confirmed that idea; later, the stance of the United States and its NATO allies encouraged its perpetuation.

Third, aside from a brief, heady period after the 1917 revolutions (Luke, 1985), the Soviet people continued to be subjects, not citizens. Their rulers continued to view human nature as frail, in need of paternalistic rule. Like Peter the Great, Stalin used the Soviet people to realize his grand plan, ignoring the fact that he was inflicting misery or death on hundreds of thousands. His focus was on his goals. In his view, the end justified the means. (Reiman, 1987, pp. 106–114) The Soviet people found this situation familiar and perhaps natural. As an Italian observer put it: "The people accept their role in the existing order of things, do not dare to imagine an alternative to such an order, and end by considering it natural and unchangeable." (Daniels, 1988, p. 42) They concentrated on doing what they had learned to do best over the centuries: They endured. Taking care to stay out of trouble, they sought what pleasure they could in their private lives, finding solace in small pleasures and, not infrequently, in the bottle. For some, the sacrifices seemed justified by Marxist-Leninist promises that they were building a glorious future for their children and their children's children. For others—perhaps most—it was merely an extension of their age-old status.

Fourth, in Russian political culture conformity was highly valued, and individual initiative that was not officially sponsored was treated as threatening. This norm has always been closely tied to issues of survival. The collectivization of the peasantry reinforced this value with respect to the kulaks or anyone who might be accused of being a kulak. Kulaks were generally the most successful farmers and, as a result of their individual initiative, were singled out for destruction. The message was clear: If you stand out, you may become a target. For most people the purges placed a premium on blending in, on not calling attention to oneself in any way. Finally, forced industrialization treated the Soviet people as interchangeable cogs in a huge industrial machine. Nowhere in this system was there much incentive to innovate or excel, unless the outcome was overfulfilling a state-imposed plan. Even then, in a society that placed a high value on equality, anyone who took risks and surpassed his or her peers was frequently the object of jealousy and anger. That could be dangerous. Individual excellence could land a person in a Siberian labor camp—or worse.

Fifth, the formal government institutions that were established were weak. Lenin instituted a "revolutionary mass-movement regime under single-party auspices." (Tucker, 1971, p. 7) Supreme power rested in the Communist Party of the Soviet Union. Stalin rose to leadership because he was the head of the Party bureaucracy. The Party was the main policy-making organization, and the Soviet government was reduced to carrying out the will of the Party. Although there were several constitutions during the Soviet period, these documents lacked teeth. The Soviet Union was governed by men, not by laws. And no one could ever be sure exactly how the system would work in a particular case. The system was largely rule-less.

The people one could call on for help were more important than any constitutional or statutory rights an individual might theoretically have. Stalin established an absolutist leadership from which there was no appeal. His successors, though somewhat less brutal and capricious, were also relatively unlimited by anything but the power of the other political forces with which they had to contend. As in the tsarist period, policy was a function of the desires of the men (and a few women) holding power, not of any established and authoritative institutional framework or set of laws. Thus, there was no firm legal basis for government authority. In the final analysis, there was only the power that emanated from the barrel of a gun—be that gun real or metaphorical.

Sixth, Stalin, like the tsars, instituted the elements of group or consensus decision-making in an oligarchical setting. Stalin's rule, however, was more autocratic than consensual. After his death, policy-making became more consensual as his successors shrank from the brutality and impulsiveness that had characterized his rule. Instead of the court in Moscow or St. Petersburg, the center for Soviet decision-making was the CPSU Politburo. The Politburo was a group of between ten and fifteen oligarchs at the top of a pyramid of Party committees stretching down to the local level. It was dominated by the General Secretary (initially Stalin), who also headed the Secretariat (bureaucracy) of the Party. These bodies exercised policy-making and supervisory control over the entire Soviet government and economic structure. They overlapped in membership. Thus, those in the Politburo and upper reaches of the Secretariat were just as much an oligarchy behind an absolute ruler as was the group of nobles who stood behind the tsar.

Consensus was theoretically institutionalized in a process called democratic centralism, which involved (at least in theory) "free discussion and deliberation of all issues by the party or involved public until a decision was made." (Laird & Laird, 1988, p. 54) As a practical matter, the Politburo, with significant input from the Secretariat, made all important political decisions. Although the Politburo contained voting and nonvoting members, it was said to operate normally on a consensus basis. And although the General Secretary of the Party was supposed to be just another voting member of the Politburo, in practice he was "more equal" than other members. Once a decision was made, no more discussion was tolerated and everyone was expected to conform. In the process of democratic centralism, centralism was more important than democracy.

Finally, the workings of the Soviet government, like those of the tsarist government, were kept highly secret. Until glasnost, it was not even officially revealed that the Politburo regularly met on Thursdays. And even under glasnost, only a sketchy agenda was published, not a transcript of or reports about the substance of the deliberations. Also, there were secret laws as well as published ones. Generally, the actual workings of the Soviet government were known only to those who needed to know and were kept secret from the general population and, especially, foreigners. Foreigners were treated with much the same suspicion in Soviet Moscow as they had been in tsarist St. Petersburg. They were subjected to travel and living restrictions, as well as surveillance and occasional entrapment.

What Stalin engaged in was, in its essence, an institution-building process involving the creation of (1) a coercive apparatus by which the population could be controlled and (2) a system for extracting and using the material resources of the country to support the state. The Stalinist political-economic system that resulted was "the product of the distinctive Russian political tradition." (Daniels, 1988, p. 47) The revolutions of 1917 had set out to change Russia along Western and Marxist lines. Stalinism was a counterrevolution. The core assumptions of Russian political culture were reinforced, despite changes in political-economic institutions and mythology.

Between the death of Stalin in 1953 and the ascent of Gorbachev to power in 1985, the Soviet leadership repeatedly attempted to reform the system. (Breslauer, 1982) These reforms always revolved around the same issue: how much of Stalin's system should be changed and in what way? No leader ever seriously considered abandoning it completely. (Hammer, 1989; Sakwa, 1990) When Gorbachev came to power in 1985, he knew that most of these reform attempts had been largely ineffective and that radical reform was necessary if the faltering Soviet economy was to be rescued. He intended to save the Soviet Union, not to destroy it. However, his reform—though virtually without revolutionary conflict—created the most revolutionary change of all. The Soviet Union, like the Russian Empire before it, no longer exists. This does not mean, however, that Russian political culture disappeared.

Gorbachev's "Reform"

What Gorbachev set out to do was to overcome the cumulative effects of an increasingly dysfunctional command economy that had stagnated during the regimes of Brezhnev and his two successors in office, Yuri V. Andropov and Konstantin U. Chernenko. (See Table 1-1, p. 27.) He fully realized that this objective could not be met "by timid, creeping reforms." (Gorbachev, 1987, p. 51) Major change was necessary. But, in his eyes, the major change needed to be "an extension and a development of the main ideas of the [Bolshevik] Revolution." (Gorbachev, 1987, p. 50) Although this did not happen, what did happen was genuinely revolutionary: An old order (the Soviet Union) disappeared, and a new order (fifteen successor countries) took its place. In the Gorbachev era, then, we see revolutionary change without revolutionary conflict. Although there was violence, it was seldom used with the aim of implementing change. Rather, it was usually an outgrowth of forces, like nationalism, that were unleashed by glasnost and democratization.

Like Stalin, Gorbachev (1987, pp. 56–57) saw his reform as a revolution from above because "the restructuring effort started with the Party and its leadership." He thought, however, that it was different because it "expressed the fundamental, long-term interests of all the working people; . . . [was] a response to their own thoughts and a recognition of their own demands; and" was supported "vehemently and effectively" by them. Thus, it was "simultaneously a revolution 'from above' and 'from below.' " This might have been what he believed in 1987, but it is more likely that it was what he hoped would be true. With hindsight, it is now clear that Gorbachev began a revolution from above that gradually turned into a revolution from below. Those who launched it and were attempting to guide it lost control of the forces they had released.

Gorbachev's revolution from above spun out of control between 1987 and 1990, because it opened the door to anarchy stemming from "economic dislocation, national and ethnic rivalries and [political] disaffection." (Sakwa, 1990, pp. 362, 366) "By 1990 he was no longer leading from the front . . . , but was overtaken by events and was always one step behind the popular movement." (Sakwa, 1990, p. 390) On December 25, 1991, scorned by his people and shamed by the failed August coup, he stepped down from his office as President, and the Soviet Union disappeared as a political-economic system. The dissolution of the Soviet Union as a geographical entity is about as revolutionary as a change can be. Let us try to put these changes into the context of Russian political culture.

First, the Gorbachev reform was conceived as a process that would move the people of the Soviet Union away from absolutism and toward democracy. Certainly, it did lead to a significant increase in political participation, which ranged from discussion to violence. Gorbachev linked the idea of democracy to the idea of socialism but was never able to convey a clear idea of what the new system would look like and how it would work. Like most revolutionaries, he was clearer about what had to be eliminated than about what would replace it. (Sakwa, 1990, p. 389) Perhaps more important, he did not anticipate and prepare for the serious problems that arose as a result of the reform process. The rapid growth of virulent nationalism is the most obvious example. He did not anticipate it or appreciate its importance when it did arise; thus, he was unable to deal with it effectively. (Kaiser, 1992) Democracy is ill equipped to deal with nationalist extremism and violence. Absolutism had simply crushed nationalist movements.

Second, to get rid of absolutism, it was also necessary to destroy the institution of the absolute ruler. The cult of the supreme leader had to go the way of the myth of the benevolent and all-powerful tsar. Thus, very early in the process, glasnost served primarily to expose the evils of the Stalin period and to tie those evils to the leadership of Stalin. The process of demythologizing Stalin had begun with Khrushchev, but that effort had centered on elimination of the cult of Stalin (*kul't lichnosti*). It had not challenged the need for a strong ruler or the paternalistic orientation of Soviet rule. Glasnost completely demolished the Stalin mystique. At the same time, it placed all of the other past leaders of the Soviet Union in a more historically accurate perspective. Only the mystique of Lenin, the founding father, was left in place—temporarily.

As glasnost became institutionalized, however, it was only a matter of time before historians and writers began to turn their attention to the Soviet Union's "founding father" and to find in him the roots of much that had gone wrong with the system. Thus, the last great Soviet father figure was demythologized, and the idea of an elected, constitutionally limited leader—a fallible human being—was substituted. The first prominent example was Boris Yeltsin, the popularly elected President of the Russian Republic and the charismatic leader of the forces defeating the 1991 coup attempt. His popularity, however, was based on the people's perception of him as a strong leader. So beneath the surface still lingers the idea that a strong leader is needed—which is not surprising given the magnitude of the economic and other problems currently facing the Soviet successor countries.

Third, Gorbachev encouraged the Soviet people to stop thinking of themselves as subjects and to begin to act like citizens—people with rights and duties who are active participants in the policy-making process. Also, he extended the idea of popular government not just to the political system but to the economy as well. Thus, the first contested elections were not government elections but elections of factory directors by factory workers. Gorbachev wrote (1987, p. 44), "we should rely . . . on the active participation of the widest sections of the population in the implementation of the reforms planned; that is, on democratization and again democratization." This was an unrealistic expectation given the fact that the people in question had little or no tradition of popular participation in government or, for that matter, in the economy. From time immemorial they had been accustomed to leaving their fates in the hands of their political leaders. It is not surprising that most of them sat back and waited for Gorbachev to make their lives better. When things got worse, they denounced and blamed him and withdrew their support.

Fourth, personal and national survival had always been a high priority. As the reform progressed, the people saw ethnic violence and economic crises threatening the security they had under the old system. The reformers appeared to have lost the ability to ensure even the most basic elements of personal and national security. Material goods became scarcer, and the value of savings and paychecks dwindled at an alarming rate. They did not know how to fend for themselves in the new social order, and the heady feeling of freedom that had prevailed in the first years of the Gorbachev era gave way to a grim battle for personal survival. Those who did best were (1) members of the Party elite who drew on the resources of the CPSU to establish themselves in capitalist ventures; (2) those, like black-marketeers, who had been on the margins of the old society and had learned to take care of themselves in a competitive atmosphere; and (3) the always adaptable young, who were willing and able to learn quickly and scramble for a place in the new system. The majority were left bewildered and wondering if they would survive. Many of those who managed to make the transition did not like it. A Communist Party official turned capitalist complained, "What is difficult is that there is . . . no ideal at all that could bring people together for the good of society. . . . Now each person just paddles his own canoe. This I do not like." (*Washington Post*, August 3, 1992, p. A1)

Under Gorbachev's leadership the Soviet Union became less and less able to claim superpower status; its economic and other problems were too great. This change was a blow to the pride of most Soviet citizens and raised questions about Soviet vulnerability. Moreover, as the various nationality groups began to call more insistently for increased sovereignty or outright independence, the specter of Soviet disintegration loomed. Much of Gorbachev's energy during his last years in office was directed toward trying to hold the union together by means of a renegotiated treaty among the newly militant subunits of the country. In fact, the 1991 coup was timed to prevent the signing of a new union treaty. The coup destroyed any remaining hope that the Soviet Union would be able to function effectively as a political-economic unit. Finally, the republics decided to take on themselves responsibility for their own survival and welfare, seceding from the union and, in the process, destroying the USSR.

Fifth, one of the cornerstones of the reform was the notion that the reformers could "rely on the initiative and creativity of the masses." (Gorbachev, 1987, p. 44) The masses, however, had always been actively discouraged from risk-taking and innovation. To expect a people with a history of being punished (often severely) for individual initiative and creativity to change immediately— or even quickly—was also unrealistic. In the words of a newly fledged Soviet businessman: "What do you expect? The command-administrative system . . .

killed all individual initiative and enterprise and made us all completely inert."
(*Washington Post,* November 20, 1989, p. A18)

Sixth, Gorbachev tried to move the Soviet Union from rule that was extremely centralized to rule that was much more diffused, both geographically and institutionally. As part of this effort, he attempted to establish a set of entirely new government institutions (such as a popularly elected parliament and chief executive) in which policy could be made openly. The underlying goal was to establish participatory democracy and the rule of law. But the reformers' ambivalence about this radical change was reflected in the institutions they established. For example, the new Soviet parliament was supposed to be popularly elected, but at least one-third of its members were selected by social organizations—a process of appointment rather than a contested election. Even in elections that were supposed to be contested, many Party candidates ran unopposed. Also, although Gorbachev was elected the first (and last) constitutional president of the Soviet Union (Art. 127, adopted in 1990), he chose to be elected by the parliament rather than by the people. In the long run, this decision hurt him because he could claim no popular mandate for his policies. Thus, despite some movement toward establishing stronger and more open political institutions, the reformers were unable to make a complete break from the past.

Also, although there was an attempt to establish a state in which the rule of law (rather than the whims of rulers) prevailed, the new system was more form than substance. For example, one of the features of the pre reform Soviet system was "telephone justice." A Party official could control the outcome of a trial by simply phoning the judge. A highly placed Moscow lawyer affirmed that the practice continued, although the people making the phone calls were more likely to be part of the reform government. His wry comment was: "As long as there are telephones there will be telephone justice." (personal communication, September 16, 1991) He also quoted the reform mayor of Moscow as saying: "If the judges make decisions we don't like, we will fire them." The lawyer sadly observed that it had taken a long time to get the mayor to understand that this policy was dangerous. This attitude toward judicial independence makes sense, because it was completely consistent with Russian political tradition, and even the most avid reformers were socialized to a system that reflected its absolutist heritage. Finally, a deep pessimism was reflected in this observation by another prominent attorney: "My generation will not live long enough to see independent courts in the Soviet Union." (personal communication, September 16, 1991)

CHANGING POLITICAL CULTURE

Because political culture is mostly an internalized set of assumptions, attempts from above to impose a new political culture usually result in an unstable status quo that is highly subject to disintegration. Until new assumptions become widely internalized, compliance is the best that can be expected. Compliance, however, is fragile and tends to disappear as times get more difficult. If an authority-based political-economic system is to replace a power-based political-economic system, the people must internalize a new set of norms. Such socialization is a monumental task when the old political culture has been around for centuries. Also, if a democratic political culture is the goal, the scope of the change needed is daunting. Gorbachev tried to accomplish this change quickly and failed. The USSR's power-based political-economic system was in harmony with its leaders' and its people's inherited political traditions and, as a result, was much less fragile than the reforms of Gorbachev and his associates.

If the successor countries are to become stable democracies, it will be necessary for their people to internalize the assumptions necessary for successful democracy and to make a fundamental change away from their inherited political culture. To say that making this change is not easy is a gross understatement. It may be possible on a widespread basis only after substantial socialization efforts and generational change. That means that democracy has to be a long-term rather than a short-term goal. The best that the new leaders of the successor states can do (assuming they want to move toward stable democratic systems) is to begin the process of resocialization.

The dominance of Russian political culture facilitated the transition from the rule of the Russian Empire to the rule of the Soviet Empire. There was no strong nonabsolutist, participatory political culture among the major ethnic groups in the Soviet Union. Pre-Soviet Russian political culture did exert a powerful influence on Soviet political culture. In fact, after reading Keenan's article on Russian political culture, Daniels (1988, p. 39) made this observation about the relationship between the Russian and Soviet patterns of political behavior: "the correspondence is so close that one finds it hard to believe that Keenan did not have the Soviet regime in mind when he constructed his image of Muscovite politics. But in any case, the resemblance between the two epochs implies a powerful carryover of ancient prerevolutionary ways into the postrevolutionary mentality." And, it should be added, much that happened during the years of Soviet rule reinforced this mentality.

In both the Russian and the Soviet past, crises have tended to cause the elimination of any new, Westernizing elements that were being introduced into the political-economic system. The oldest and deepest elements of Russian tradition have persisted—usually taking refuge in new institutions. Now Russian political culture is in crisis, and Western democratic ideas are being promoted as replacements for both ancient and recent ways of thinking. Will the geographical and political fragmentation that characterizes this revolution result in a rapid political cultural change throughout the former USSR? Or will the cultural heritage of these people again take on new forms and prevail? The jury is still out, and the wait for a verdict may be very long.

REFERENCES

Acton, E. (1990). *Rethinking the Russian Revolution.* London: Edward Arnold.

Almond, G. A., & Verba, S. (1965). *The civic culture: Political attitudes and democracy in five nations.* Boston: Little, Brown.

———. (Eds.). (1989). *The civic culture revisited.* Newbury Park, CA: Sage.

Breslauer, G. W. (1982). *Khrushchev and Brezhnev as leaders: Building authority in Soviet politics.* London: Allen & Unwin.

Brickman, P. (Ed.). (1974). *Social conflict: Readings in rule structure and conflict relationships.* Lexington, MA: Heath.

Brown, A. (Ed.). (1984). *Political culture and communist studies.* Armonk, NY: M.E. Sharpe, Inc.

Conquest, R. (1991). *Stalin: Breaker of nations.* New York: Penguin.

Daniels, R. V. (1985). *Russia: The roots of confrontation.* Cambridge, MA: Harvard University Press.

———. (1988). *Is Russia reformable?* Boulder, CO: Westview Press.

Elkins, D.J., & Simeon, R. E. B. (1979). A cause in search of its effect, or what does political culture explain? *Comparative Politics, 11,* 127–145.

Glazov, Y. (1985). *The Russian mind since Stalin's death.* Boston: Reidel.

Gorbachev, M. (1987). *Perestroika: New thinking for our country and the world.* New York: Harper & Row.

Hagopian, M. N. (1974). *The phenomenon of revolution.* New York: Dodd, Mead.

Hammer, D. P. (1989). Gorbachev's political agenda: The historical background of the reform program. In J. S. Zacek (Ed.), *The Gorbachev generation: Issues in Soviet domestic policy* (pp. 1–21). New York: Paragon House.

Harris, M. (1983). *Cultural anthropology.* New York: Harper & Row.

Kaiser, R. G. (1992). *Why Gorbachev happened.* New York: Simon and Schuster.

Keenan, E. L. (1986). Russian political folkways. *The Russian Review, 45,* 115–181.

Laird, R. D., & Laird, B. A. (1988). *A Soviet lexicon: Important concepts, terms, and phrases.* Lexington, MA: Lexington Books.

Luke, T. W. (1985). *Ideology and Soviet industrialization.* Westport, CT: Greenwood Press.

Plano, J. C., & Greenberg, M. (1985). *The American political dictionary* (7th ed.). New York: Holt, Rinehart and Winston.

Reiman, M. (1987). *The Birth of Stalinism: The USSR on the eve of the "second revolution."* Bloomington: Indiana University Press.

Rejai, M. (1977). *The comparative study of revolutionary strategy.* New York: McKay.

Remington, T. F. (1992). Reform, revolution, and regime transition in the Soviet Union. In G. Rozman (Ed.), *Dismantling communism: Common causes and regional variations* (pp. 121–151). Washington, DC: Woodrow Wilson Center Press.

Riasanovsky, N. V. (1984). *A history of Russia* (4th ed.). New York: Oxford University Press.

Sakwa, R. (1990). *Gorbachev and his reforms, 1985–1990.* Englewood Cliffs, NJ: Prentice-Hall.

Schapiro, L. (1984). *The Russian revolutions of 1917: The origins of modern communism.* New York: Basic Books.

Tilly, C. (1978). *From mobilization to revolution.* Reading, MA: Addison-Wesley.

Tucker, R. C. (1971). *The Soviet political mind: Stalinism and post-Stalin change* (Rev. ed.). New York: Norton.

―――. (1990). *Stalin in power: The revolution from above, 1928–1941.* New York: Norton.

Vivelo, F. R. (1978). *Cultural anthropology handbook.* New York: McGraw-Hill.

Von Laue, T. H. (1993). *Why Lenin? Why Stalin? Why Gorbachev? The rise and fall of the Soviet system.* New York: HarperCollins.

White, S. (1979). *Political culture and Soviet politics.* New York: St. Martin's Press.

Willhoite, F. H. (1988). *Power and governments: An introduction to politics.* Pacific Grove, CA: Brooks/Cole.

Wishnevsky, J. (1992). Antidemocratic tendencies in Russian policy-making. *RFE/RL Research Report, 1*(45), 21–25.

· 3 ·

UNRAVELING THE PARADOX OF THE SOVIET UNION: THE LEGACY OF EMPIRE IN THE ERA OF THE NATION-STATE

> *"Force always thinks itself indomitable," Lily went on. "But in fact it is a very precarious sort of power, because to expend force requires the use of resources, energy, human lives. Force is extremely expensive to use. . . . [N]o system of domination can survive if it is actually required to use force every time it wants to be obeyed."*
>
> STARHAWK (1993, p. 441)

> *As a historian, I can see that all great empires collapsed when the center was dying and the periphery became stronger. It looks as if that is what we have now.*
>
> VALERY TISHKOV[1] (Solchanyk, 1990, p. 19)

Because prerevolutionary Russia and the postrevolutionary Soviet Union were empires, Russian political culture was the dominant political culture in a vast multicultural territory. The term *empire* designates a relationship of dominance and subjugation between an imperial center and its periphery. In an empire, "one state controls the effective political sovereignty of another political society." (Doyle, 1986, p. 45) Although this definition needs exploring, there is no doubt that, according to it and most other definitions, the Soviet Union was an empire. The "state" in Doyle's terms was European Russia and the "other political societies" were the non-Russian union republics plus the Russian republic east of the Urals. The imperial center of rule was Moscow. Our purpose in this chapter is to examine this thing called empire and to analyze its relevance to the former Soviet Union.

---

1. At the time of this statement Dr. Tishkov was Director of the Institute of Ethnography of the USSR Academy of Sciences.

The words *empire* and *imperialism* stem from the Latin word *imperatum* and capture different aspects of the same phenomenon. Both have been defined as relationships of dominance and subjugation. Both involve the exercise of power as a means of control. There is, however, a basic difference: The term *imperialism* describes a process, and *empire* describes a product of that process. Thus, Benjamin Cohen (1973, p. 16) defines imperialism as "any relationship of effective domination or control, political or economic, direct or indirect of one nation over another." Imperialism thus is the process of seeking or maintaining a relationship of dominance and subjugation between political units.

Empire is the product of established relationships of dominance and subjugation in cases "where all the units, save one [the imperial center] lose their autonomy and tend to disappear as centers of political decisions." (Aron, 1966, p. 151) For a cluster of political units to be an empire, the imperial center must exercise effective sovereignty over the subordinate peripheral units. Sovereignty is "the supreme [control] of a state, exercised within its boundaries, free from external interference." (Plano & Greenberg, 1985, p. 24) But relationships of dominance and subjugation between nations—that is, imperialism— do not necessarily result in empire. From such relationships, hegemony can alternatively develop.

Hegemony exists when one country operates internationally from such a position of superiority that subordinate countries "despair of modifying the status quo, and yet the hegemonic state does not try to absorb the units reduced to impotence ... it does not aspire to empire." (Aron, 1966, p. 152) For example, hegemony characterized the relationship between the USSR and Finland for decades and could conceivably characterize future international relations between Russia and some of the other former republics of the Soviet Union.

In both empire and hegemony, the dominant country tends to justify its dominance in ideological and mythological terms, attempting to gain the legitimacy necessary for authority. The Soviet Empire used Marxism-Leninism and a corresponding mythology to justify its dominance over the non-Russian people. Marxism-Leninism justified "the continued existence of a transformed Russian empire and of a highly centralized and coercive state." Because of its emphasis on class as a factor transcending national differences, Marxism-Leninism "undercut any claims for independence by national groups" and "justified Moscow's nihilistic approach to all cultures ... reducing ethnicity to a curiosity by means of the formula 'national in form, socialist in content.' " (Goble, 1990, p. 98) As belief in Marxism-Leninism began to erode under the onslaught of the realities of daily Soviet life and, later, glasnost, nationalism stepped into the void to challenge the primacy of Communist Party rule.

The concept of empire captures the essence of both the Soviet Union and the Russian Empire. Viewing an empire as a social, political, and economic structure embodying distinctive patterns of control relationships will bring into sharp focus the inherent instability of the Soviet political-economic system. It will also highlight the challenges and difficulties that Soviet leaders confronted in their efforts to transcend empire through the building of a Soviet nation-state. Finally, appreciating the legacy of empire—both Russian and Soviet—will contribute to a better understanding of contemporary nationalism and its dynamic impact on relations within and between the countries that formerly were republics of the Soviet Union.

Before we discuss the Soviet Empire, however, we must provide some information about how that empire was created. The Soviet Empire was, in large measure, the Russian Empire with a new set of rulers and a new mythology and ideology. The boundaries were almost identical (see Maps 3-1 and 3-2), as was the basic system of absolute rule from Moscow. Also, the creation of both empires was the work of the Russians. Even today, many Russians think that the other fourteen former union republics should rightfully be under the control of Russia. Russian philosopher Yurii Borodai, for example, stated in 1992: "I can say frankly that I am an imperialist. . . . I believe in the resurrection of the Russian empire." (Tolz, 1993, p. 43) This belief is a major factor in contemporary Russian nationalism and will continue to affect Russia's success or failure in building a nation-state rather than another empire.

THE CREATION OF THE RUSSIAN EMPIRE

The USSR, like all other political-economic systems, was a product of its history. This point needs to be emphasized because of the widely held but erroneous assumption that the Bolshevik Revolution of 1917 wiped the slate of history clean. Nothing could be further from the truth. Russian political culture intertwined with the legacy of empire to shape the course of Soviet history, and their impact continues to reverberate in Russia and in the other former Soviet republics.

The center of the Russian Empire was first Moscow; then, in the early eighteenth century under Peter the Great, it became St. Petersburg. The Bolsheviks moved the center back to Moscow, where it remained until the fall of the Soviet Union. Moscow's role was pivotal because the princes of Muscovy had led the effort to end the subjugation by the Mongols from the thirteenth to the fifteenth century. The society that consolidated during this period eventually incorporated European Russia—Russia west of the Ural Mountains. Moscow became its political, economic, and cultural hub.

Until Peter the Great turned Russia's attention toward the West at the beginning of the eighteenth century, Russian society was largely cut off from the societies of western Europe. Before the Mongol conquest, an Eastern Slavic culture had developed in the territory now occupied by much of modern Russia west of the Urals, as well as Ukraine and Belarus. Historians label this the Kievan period in recognition of Kiev's prominence during that time. Outside influences on Kievan Rus came largely from the Byzantine Empire, not from feudal Europe. The Mongol invasions in the thirteenth century effectively isolated the various groups of Eastern Slavs and precipitated the evolution of separate societies in Ukraine and Belarus. These societies were rejoined with

MAP 3-1 The Russian Empire in 1914

Russia through imperial acquisition during the seventeenth and eighteenth centuries.

Russia was shaped by factors and influences alien to the European experience. The bitter climate coupled with the oppression and isolation imposed by the Mongols spawned pessimistic expectations about life and about the world. These, in turn, generated enduring assumptions about the outside world that help to explain Russia's drive to empire. Specifically, the Russians were obsessed with security—both national and personal—and thus with defending themselves against foreign invasion. Military power was all-important to them. The unquestioned acceptance of this priority had profound implications for governance. Robert V. Daniels (1985, p. 26) writes, "Russia became committed to the proposition that military power was the country's supreme priority and that all of its energies and resources needed to be coordinated to that end through the agency of an all-powerful government." Moreover, as if following the strategic adage "The best defense is a good offense," Russia practiced territorial expansion to achieve its desired end: security.

Direct annexation of non-Russian territory and populations by the princes of Muscovy began shortly after the overthrow of Mongol domination. In 1547, Ivan IV (Ivan the Terrible) crowned himself tsar and initiated a campaign of conquest to both the east and the west. In the west, he was thwarted by the Poles and the Swedes in the protracted Livonian War. But to the east, he achieved considerable success. He defeated the heirs to the Mongols, the Muslim Tatars, then pressed down the Volga River to the Caspian Sea. Subsequently, he moved across the Ural Mountains and launched an unprecedented period of eastward exploration and conquest, which culminated in 1639 when Russian forces reached the Pacific Ocean. Within a century, Russia had annexed the entire northern third of Asia.

MAP 3-2 The Soviet Union in 1922

From the mid-seventeenth until the early nineteenth century, Russia turned its quest for territory to the west. During this period, land was acquired primarily at the expense of the large but disorganized kingdom of Poland. In the mid-seventeenth century the Russians conquered what is now the northeastern portion of Ukraine, including the city of Kiev. Under Peter the Great, Russia defeated the kingdom of Sweden, which at that time extended to the Baltics. As spoils of war, Russia obtained the site on the Gulf of Finland where St. Petersburg was later built, as well as the territory that is now Estonia and a portion of Latvia.

During the reign of Catherine the Great, as a result of three partitions of Poland, Russia acquired Belarus, the rest of Latvia, and most of Ukraine and Lithuania. Catherine also extended the empire to the Black Sea, including the Crimean peninsula. Then, during the Napoleonic period, present-day Moldova was seized from the Ottoman Empire, and Sweden was forced to cede Finland to Russia. At the Congress of Vienna (1814–15), where the Great Powers of Europe negotiated a settlement after the Napoleonic Wars, Russia acquired dominion over Poland. Next, Russia turned its expansionary zeal once again toward Asia. Between 1761 and 1878, Russian forces seized most of contemporary Georgia, Armenia, and Azerbaijan. During the mid-nineteenth century, Russia pushed across the deserts of Central Asia to conquer the Kazakh nomads and the peoples of what are now Turkmenistan, Uzbekistan, Tajikistan, and Kyrgyzstan. In the Far East, Russia seized from China the sparsely populated territory where the present-day port city of Vladivostok is located.

Just a few decades before the Bolsheviks seized power in 1917, the Russian Empire reached its fullest extent. It stretched across eleven time zones and covered one-sixth of the earth's land surface. More important, however, from the standpoint of empire, it exercised dominion over numerous distinct ethnic groups, each with its own culture, traditions, and language. We explore the ethnicity issue and the problem it presented (and still presents) for nation-building in the next chapter. Here, let us say only that from the sixteenth to the twentieth century Russia was an ever-expanding empire.

From the sixteenth century to 1905, absolute monarchs ruled Russia. A state administrative and coercive apparatus enforced their claims to absolute power. Indeed, there existed a synergism between absolutism and state-building: Absolutism fostered the drive toward state-building: state-building in turn supported the exercise of absolute power. When the revolutions of 1917 and the ensuing civil war brought this vast territory under Bolshevik rule, conditions were ripe for the creation of a Soviet Empire.

THE NATURE OF EMPIRE AND THE SOVIET EMPIRE

To understand empire as a social structure, it is necessary to identify and examine its component elements. Empires consist of a dominant center and a subordinate periphery. Control by the imperial center is usually absolutist, and this absolutism is typically justified by a legitimating ideology, mythology, or both. The coercive and administrative apparatus of the imperial center enables it to establish and maintain control over the periphery. Let us examine each of these three elements to see how they work together to create an empire.

Characteristics of the Center and the Periphery

For a political-economic system to be identified as an empire, its center and periphery must be clearly differentiated. The center and the periphery must have separate and distinct populations distinguishable from one another in culture, social structure, and geography.

Ethnic, religious, and linguistic differences typically mark the populations of a center and a periphery. On a fundamental level, "the traditional ways of thinking, evaluating, and behaving transmitted from generation to generation" (Doob, 1983, p. 39) are different in the center and the periphery. This was certainly true in both the Soviet Union and the Russian Empire. European Russia was the imperial center of each, and Moscow was its ruling core.[2] Under the auspices of the leadership in Moscow, European Russia extended its dominion over the broad expanses of eastern Europe and Asia, enveloping well over a hundred distinct cultural groups. In doing so, it brought to a multitude of other distinct cultures the mentality of Russian political culture.

---

2. As noted previously, Peter the Great (r. 1682–1725) moved the imperial center to St. Petersburg. After the revolutions of 1917, however, it was moved back to Moscow and remained there until the demise of the Soviet Union in 1991. To avoid confusion, we regard Moscow as the imperial center—as it was during practically all of the Soviet period.

In an empire, the imperial center and periphery also have separate and distinct societies. A society exists wherever there are "rules and customs governing human relations in a specific area." (Doob, 1983, p. 39) In every society, specific formal and informal rules of conflict guide the behavior of the population. These rules establish a social order, which is embodied in institutions. In a society, there are identifiable leaders and elites. The criteria for leadership or elite status are peculiar to each society. A society with reasonably well-established laws, customs, institutions, and elites is able to regulate and govern itself. When absorbed into an empire, peripheral societies lose their ability to regulate and govern themselves; the imperial center takes effective political sovereignty away from the periphery and imposes its own rule system.

The Russian leadership was much less able to totally dominate the periphery than was the Soviet leadership. The determining factor was technology. Travel and communication were much more rapid in the Soviet Union than they had been in the Russian Empire. As a result, the Soviet leadership in Moscow could more easily dominate the peoples of the periphery. Also, the Soviet Communist Party exerted much more effort than the tsars to impose the Russian language and culture, as well as a common mythology based on Marxism-Leninism. The Russian imperialists never made a concerted effort to shape their vast territory into a relatively homogeneous nation. The Soviet leadership, however, did try to create a Soviet people and a Soviet culture out of the widely diverse ethnic groups it had inherited.

The imperial center and periphery occupy separate territories. The territory of the periphery may or may not border on the territory of the imperial center. The geographical relationship between the center and the periphery is very significant. If the center and periphery are next to each other, integrating the various cultures and societies of the periphery with the culture and society of the center is simplified. Moreover, in a geographically contiguous empire, ties are more likely to develop among the various societies of the periphery, particularly among the local elites of the peripheral societies. (Motyl, 1992)

Both the Russian Empire and the Soviet Union were geographically contiguous empires. The Russian Empire was broken up into territories for administrative purposes, but there were no sharp boundaries between politically distinct units. The Soviet Union changed this arrangement when it chose a formally federal structure of government. To placate the various ethnic groups that desired independence after the 1917 revolutions, the young Soviet government established a set of republics which were promised considerable home rule. In addition, because these republics encompassed various nationalities, many were further divided into territorially distinct political subunits.

The Soviet federal structure, however, was more theoretical than actual. Although some decisions were made in the peripheral republics and their subunits, the most important policy-making took place in Moscow. The peripheral peoples were supposed to participate freely in the choice of their leaders and in the consideration of policy alternatives that would affect them. But once a leader had been chosen or a policy had been set, they were bound to follow the leader or policy without question. Although some Soviet leaders came from the ethnic groups of the periphery, they were greatly outnumbered by the Russians and tended to be people who could function comfortably within the dominant political culture. Thus, the Soviet leadership in Moscow could and did make vital choices with little or no consideration of the preferences of the peoples of the periphery.

Geographical contiguity permitted the Soviet leadership to attempt to create one unified Soviet people. If this goal had been reached, the Soviet Union might have been able to move gradually from an empire based on power to a nation-state based on authority. Such a development would have been in line with the Marxist idea that, under the right conditions, the unity of the working class would transcend ethnic and cultural divisions.

What actually happened was that the ethnic and cultural loyalties of the peripheral peoples were suppressed but remained strong beneath the surface. Moscow's attempts to impose a Soviet culture that was largely Russian encouraged ties among the peripheral peoples which were based on their resentment of Russian domination and of their own lack of effective sovereignty. Hatred of the Russians was the only unifying force among many ethnic groups on the periphery. Simmering beneath the surface, in addition, were age-old hostilities between non-Russian peoples. After all, they had been neighbors for centuries, and there were many accumulated resentments and hostilities.

This discussion of territorial contiguity calls attention to an important characteristic of an empire's social structure: its inherent instability. Empires are naturally prone to decay. One strategy for overcoming this tendency is to forge a unified entity—a single nation—out of an empire. *Nation* is a relatively modern concept of identification. It is typically associated with a sizeable group of people who share a common cultural heritage. Central to the concept of nation is the idea of a political community that bonds its members to one another and helps to legitimate the exercise of authority by nationally sanctioned elites.

The process through which such a community is forged is nation-building. Inevitably, the result of successful nation-building in an empire is the transformation of the empire into a more closely knit political-economic entity. Without successful nation-building, empires eventually decay and stagnate, or they disintegrate altogether. In this context, it should be remembered that the subsequent rule of Leonid Brezhnev was called a "period of stagnation" (*zastoi*) and the rule of Mikhail Gorbachev[3] ended in the disintegration of the Soviet Union.

Because the control that the center exercises over the periphery is based on power, a successful transition from empire to nation-state is always difficult to achieve—even when geographical contiguity facilitates the process. The failure of the Soviet nation-building effort was a major reason for the ease and rapidity with which the Soviet Union disintegrated.

---

3. The interval between these two was filled with the short and largely ineffective leadership of Yuri Andropov (1982–84) and Konstantin Chernenko (1984–85).

Control in an Empire

Social control in an empire stems from coercion. Because there are no well-established authority relationships between the center and the periphery, maintaining effective control over distinct territories, populations, and societies requires a disproportionate reliance on power. It also requires coordination and centralization. Without effective control from the imperial center, the centrifugal tendencies inherent in empire cannot be contained.

Power can be exercised in two different ways: coercively and administratively. First, the power-wielder can alter subjects' behavior by means of force. Subjects comply because of the threat of immediate punishment. Within the Soviet Union the two most important organizations that specialized in the exercise of force in internal affairs were the KGB and the MVD. They were backed up by military units stationed throughout the Soviet Union.

The KGB (Komitet Gosudarstvennoi Bezopasnosti) functioned as a secret police with informers throughout the population. Its parent organization was the MVD (Ministerstvo Vnutrennikh Del), the internal police force of the Soviet Union. Before 1954, the KGB was part of the MVD. After they were separated, the KGB dominated the MVD.[4] In the context of empire, the most important subunit of the KGB was the Fifth Directorate, which was charged with infiltrating ethnic, political, and religious groups in the Soviet Union. The job of Fifth Directorate operatives was to uncover and eliminate dissent and subversion. Also significant were the Second Directorate and the Seventh Directorate, which had somewhat different missions but were basically responsible for monitoring the activities of the Soviet people.

The MVD was the more visible organization and performed many duties associated with police work in Western countries. MVD officers investigated crimes and arrested criminal suspects, maintained public order, controlled traffic, and ran the prison system. But some of their activities were very different from those of police officers in the West. For example, every Soviet citizen had to carry an internal passport containing personal information. Most important was information about where a person worked and lived. The MVD administered this system, identifying and dealing with individuals who were not where their internal passports and other documents said they should be.

The KGB controlled the MVD by the placement of KGB people in key MVD positions. (Yasmann, 1991, p. 15) In 1991, the Law on the Organs of State Security[5] gave the KGB official functional supervision of all MVD activities. The KGB also wielded power over other key organizations that were military

---

4. The organizations responsible for internal security underwent many changes in name and organization during the history of the Soviet Union. To keep the discussion from getting too complicated, we focus on the KGB and the MVD, which were the two most important internal security organizations during the periods of stagnation and disintegration.

5. Zakon ob organakh gosydarstvennoi bezopastnosti v SSSR, 1991, Articles 9, 13, 14, *Vedomosti S"ezda Narodnykh Deputatov SSSR i Verkhovnogo Soveta SSSR*, no. 22, May 29, 1991.

in nature, such as the Border Guards. Most important, it had a direct tie to the CPSU. Prior to the 1991 law, this tie was described in a secret law passed in 1959, which stated: "The KGB is a political working organization of the CPSU. . . . All important questions relating to KGB activity are decided in advance by the Central Committee of the CPSU and enforced by KGB orders." (Yasmann, 1991, p. 13) This provision did not appear in the 1991 law, but in practice the situation did not change, for all KGB officers were carefully selected CPSU members.[6]

The second way in which power can be exercised is by administratively manipulating people's activities and the quality of their lives. Acting in this way, power-wielders in large measure can compel people to live as they want them to live. The source of this type of power lies in the benefits the power-wielders have to distribute. The benefits can be given as rewards or withheld as punishment. And they can be things that greatly affect a person's quality of life—such as a decent job and an adequate place to live. Anthony Giddens labels this capacity to alter outcomes through control over people's activities and the quality of life "administrative power." According to Giddens (1985, p. 47), administrative power is "based upon the regulation and co-ordination of human conduct through manipulation of the settings in which it takes place." The Communist Party carried out this exercise of power mainly through its local and regional Party committees and its bureaucracy (apparat). These organizations supervised and directed the activities of the government bureaucracy and, thus, exercised considerable control over the lives of the people.

To understand how this system worked, we need to take a look at the basic political and governmental organizations of the Soviet Union. Ultimately, the CPSU was responsible for creating, modifying, and maintaining the Soviet political-economic system. Every organization—from government ministries to trade unions to stores and restaurants—was a creature of the CPSU. In addition, the Party decided who would occupy the key positions in Soviet society. The top, or nomenklatura, positions included not just important government posts but also others such as the editors of newspapers and the directors of large industrial enterprises. (Harasymiw, 1969; Vozlensky, 1984)

At the heart of this administrative power structure was the Politburo of the CPSU—the major policy-making body of the imperial center. Closely connected to it was the Secretariat—the major administrative body. Working in concert, these two controlled a hierarchy of Party committees and Party bureaucracies that stretched down through the republican, regional, and local levels to the primary Party organizations—the basic face-to-face units to which all Party members belonged. At all of these levels, the Party committees and the apparat worked together to supervise and control all of the activities of the Soviet government, economic, and social organizations. Thus, the imperial center

6. For a more detailed description and analysis of the KGB, see Knight (1988).

maintained political and administrative power over the periphery. And this complex of organizations was largely composed of Russians or Russified indigenous people.

It requires a tremendous commitment of human and material resources for such administrative power to be sustained—especially over the wide expanse of territory that constituted the Soviet Union. Thus, we can distinguish between the claim to absolute power, which all empires make, and the actual capacity to maintain such rule. The sustained exercise of imperial power requires information and resources in huge amounts. Without information, rulers cannot rule. What Anthony Giddens (1985) calls "surveillance" is an essential component of administrative control in any government, but its importance in imperial regimes cannot be overstated. The continued existence of the Soviet Empire depended on the ability of the security forces to carry out surveillance and maintain order and on the ability of the CPSU and its apparat to gather information and coordinate the conduct of its subjects.

Imperial regimes also require an abundant supply of material and financial resources. Of course, all governments need resources, but this requirement increases in proportion to the extent to which power has to be wielded. The source of many of these material and financial resources is the periphery. Imperial rulers use these resources to impose and maintain their rule through both direct and indirect means. They require a well-developed administrative and coercive apparatus. Imperial regimes, in other words, need a state.

The State in an Empire

Americans use the word *state* in a way that is unusual in the world of scholars and diplomats. In the United States, *state* designates a major territorial subdivision of the federal system. This use of *state* can be explained by reference to early American history.

During the period between the writing of the Declaration of Independence in 1776 and the ratification of the Constitution in 1788, the thirteen former colonies actually fit the definition of *state* used by the diplomatic and scholarly world: a political entity "occupying a definite territory, having an organized government, and *possessing internal and external sovereignty*." (Plano & Greenberg, 1985, p. 24, emphasis added) The American states were only loosely bound together by the Articles of Confederation. The label *state* was retained in the Constitution, but only to denote the major subdivisions of the United States. (Wood, 1969) The American states lack the essential characteristic of a state: virtually unlimited sovereignty. Thus, since 1788, the real American state has been the United States itself.

Internal sovereignty and external sovereignty are significantly different concepts. Let us start with the latter. The international community of established states confers external sovereignty when it accepts the right of an existing government to make decisions for the people who live within its territorial jurisdiction. In theory, a grant of external sovereignty means that other states cannot claim any part of its territory.[7] The population can have whatever kind of government and economic system it wants (although this choice is not necessarily made democratically). However, given the fact that politics in the international domain takes place in a self-help environment where "might makes right," the leaders of states choose the extent to which they will honor and defend their own recognition of external sovereignty. Clearly, the Soviet Union's unwillingness in the years after World War II to honor the external sovereignty of the states of eastern Europe and the West's reluctance to defend it, effectively made eastern Europe part of the USSR's "outer empire."[8]

Viewed from the standpoint of external sovereignty, a state exists when the international community recognizes that a government has the right to exercise control over a given territory and its inhabitants. However, viewed from the standpoint of internal sovereignty, a state is the administrative and coercive apparatus that ensures the effective exercise of such control. Internal sovereignty implies the ability to exercise monopoly control over the means of violence, as well as hierarchical control over the administrative apparatus.

In an empire such control emanates from the imperial center. (Doyle, 1986; Lichtheim, 1971) Defined separately from the societies over which it exercises control, the imperial state is "a set of administrative, policing, and military organizations headed, and more or less well coordinated, by an executive authority." The state apparatus works to extract resources from the societies under its control, and these resources, in turn, are used "to create and support administrative and coercive organizations." (Skocpol, 1979, p. 29) In the Soviet Union, internal sovereignty was exercised primarily through the KGB, the MVD, and the apparat of the CPSU.

Empire, as a political form, predates the development of the modern nation-state. A sovereign territory may be a state (as were both the Russian Empire and the Soviet Union) without being a nation-state. The latter implies a single society, the nation. In a nation-state, internal sovereignty is largely achieved through authority and thus the need to rely on coercion and administrative control is reduced. Empires by definition encompass more than one society. Thus, within an empire the critical issue of legitimacy looms large. The imperial center typically claims that its control over the periphery is legitimate, but this claim is difficult to sustain because the vast majority of subjugated peoples usually believe otherwise. Thus, in an empire, the coercive and administrative apparatus of the state is crucial in holding the empire together. All empires, ancient or otherwise, have exercised considerable control over their domains. At a minimum, they initially use armed force to conquer their subject peoples

---

7. Of course, states may disagree about where their border should lie. Efforts to change borders frequently take the form of an armed invasion of one state by another and are regarded by the international community as interstate warfare.
8. See Barkin and Cronin (1994) for an illuminating examination of the sovereignty concept in international relations.

and societies. Once their rule is stabilized, they use coercive and administrative power to extract resources from the peripheral societies.

The political elites of the Russian Empire were particularly able state-builders. This ability made their claims to absolute power compelling. Correspondingly, it was their failure to maintain strong central control via the coercive and administrative organizations of the state which, after the 1917 revolutions, made the splintering of the empire possible. Nevertheless, after the initial civil war period (1919–21) ended and the territorial boundaries of Bolshevik rule stabilized, these boundaries did not differ greatly from those of the Russian Empire. From that point on, the international community came to recognize the Soviet Empire as a sovereign state.

IMPERIAL DECAY AND THE SOVIET EMPIRE

Thus, we come to the paradox of the Soviet Union. The only way to sustain imperial rule is for the center to use power to keep the periphery subjugated. The paradox stems from the fact that the steps taken to sustain imperial power undermine the possibility of establishing authority as the foundation for rule. Converting an empire into a modern nation-state becomes impossible. The Soviet Union spawned an enormous coercive and administrative apparatus. It was useful for establishing and maintaining the Soviet state, which, in turn, was the mechanism that generated the resources that enabled the center to hold the empire together. At the same time, however, the exercise of internal sovereignty through the coercive and administrative apparatus undermined the Soviet leadership's effort to build a single Soviet society—that is, a nation—that could have been the basis for the conversion of the Soviet Union from an anachronistic empire to a modern nation-state.

Although the state facilitates the domination of the center in an empire, it also demonstrates the pathologies inherent in rule by power. Ironically, the imposition and maintenance of political control by power lead to the decline of the state. An understanding of the paradox of imperial decay is necessary to an appreciation of the centrifugal forces at work in the Soviet Empire—the centrifugal forces that eventually tore it apart.

Pathologies of Empire

A basic pathology of empire stems from the fact that an empire is a political-economic system based almost exclusively on power. Coercion is the main force binding the periphery to the center. However, "whereas coercion is most effective in securing short-term compliance, it is least effective in securing subjective commitment over long periods." (Dallin & Breslauer, 1970, p. 3) For the long haul, social control based on authority is much more effective. Those who create empires intend them to last indefinitely, but this goal is unattainable because—sooner or later—the imperial center is forced to deal with the fact that rule by power is highly unstable. To counter this instability, the center must devote enormous energy and resources to maintaining its coercive dominance and in doing so feeds other pathologies of empire.

The maintenance of an empire normally requires that the center have two resources to guide and fortify its rule: (1) accurate information about what is going on in all parts of the empire, and (2) material and financial resources to sustain the power of the center and its control apparatus. The information is obtained and the resources are extracted by administrative agents who are sent out from the center to the societies of the periphery. Ideally, imperial agents have no loyalty except to the leadership at the center and faithfully transmit information and transport resources, retaining for themselves only their wages.

In the Soviet Union, most of these agents were Communist Party officials and officers of the internal security apparatus (who were usually also Party members). In addition, most of the commanding officers of the military forces stationed throughout the periphery were Russian and carefully selected by the CPSU. The members of local, especially non-Slavic, ethnic groups were normally assigned to military duty outside of their home territories. Thus, the military could serve as a backup for the internal security forces in the event of a violent or potentially violent situation.

These nonindigenous agents were frequently rotated in and out of their posts on the periphery. Those frequent transfers created a problem. An imperial agent without ties to or practical knowledge of the region to be administered is seriously hampered in obtaining the requisite information and resources. An agent familiar with the region is usually a much more competent information gatherer and resource extractor. Thus, frequent transfers mean that the loyalty of an agent from the center is guaranteed but the short-term ability of that agent to perform the necessary duties is jeopardized. This, in turn, compromises the center's ability to make and implement appropriate policies.

The obvious solutions to this problem are either to allow the imperial agents to establish roots in the periphery or to co-opt agents from among the indigenous people. Both solutions, however, have long-term consequences for the exercise of strong central control. If the agents view or come to view the region as their own, they will be tempted to put their interests and the interests of their region ahead of the interests of the imperial center. If they do so, the flow of information and resources from the periphery to the center becomes disrupted, and imperial rule is compromised. Under such circumstances, only information that enhances the reputation of the agent is passed on, and only resources that cannot be siphoned off are transferred to the center. The outcome, over time, is that the rulers at the imperial center receive diminishing amounts of accurate information and needed resources.

What is the solution to this problem? The imperial leadership might purge the local agents and replace them with new ones from the center. That move, however, will only put the center back where it started—with agents who know relatively little about the area to which they are assigned. Alternatively, the central leadership might decide to send additional agents to the region to supervise the ones already there. But in all likelihood, this choice will simply add another layer of inefficiency and corruption to a control structure that is probably already inefficient and corrupt.

Under Soviet rule—particularly after Stalin's death—the leadership in Moscow placed indigenous people in positions where they were highly visible but exercised little real power. The agents of the imperial center, though less visible, were much more powerful than the indigenous officials. The head of each union republic's Party organization, for example, was traditionally a member of the local dominant ethnic group. The position of Party First Secretary would seem to give that person great power, for in the periphery—as in the center—it was the Soviet Communist Party that ruled, not the government. The person serving directly under the indigenous Party First Secretary, however, was an agent of the center—usually a Russian. And it was this seemingly subordinate Party Second Secretary who, as a practical matter, controlled the administrative and coercive apparatus in the republic. (Miller, 1992) The issue of loyalty to the center was handled by limiting the length of the assignments of these imperial agents. Similarly, the organs responsible for internal security were dominated by Russians. For example, the top leader of the KGB in the union republics was traditionally Russian. (Connor, 1992, p. 38)

Alexander Motyl (1992, p. 26) concludes that the only option available to emperors who wish "to reestablish equilibrium between their imperial ambitions and the information and resources they possess to fulfill those ambitions is to *deabsolutize*" their rule (emphasis in the original). Emperors must embark on a purposeful strategy whereby policy-making becomes more widely shared. In the Soviet Union, Stalin's death was followed by a greater willingness on the part of the Soviet Party leadership to share power with other entities, such as government ministries. More power also devolved to the local agents of the imperial center. This process reached its culmination during the rule of Brezhnev, who placed a premium on maintenance of the status quo. (Burg, 1990, pp. 25–26)

In effect, Brezhnev bought his own security in the office of CPSU General Secretary by looking the other way as his central and peripheral leadership apparatus grew secure in their posts and, not coincidentally, "rich with the pickings of office." (McAuley, 1992, p. 79) More than any previous leader, Brezhnev also placed his close friends and relatives in powerful and lucrative positions.

Personnel turnover declined, and key officials began to "identify with the interests of the sector for which they were responsible." (McAuley, 1992, p. 82) Increasingly, they began to misuse the resources they controlled. As they gained more autonomous power, they became more susceptible to bribery and other forms of corruption. In the regions, the local elite often became part of this arrangement. "[A]lthough the system might appear monolithic, Moscow centered and controlled, under the surface local elites had formed and were becoming increasingly used to acting in their own interests. This entailed defending regional or republican interests against what they perceived as an ineffective and uninspired central leadership, but one which might still intervene in a wholly arbitrary manner." (McAuley, 1992, p. 83) Even this threat, however, was not as intimidating as it had been in the Stalinist era.

Members of the Party elite who came into power after Stalin's death had learned two important lessons during the purges: First, there was a limit to what could be accomplished through terror. Second, once begun, terror could become self-sustaining and eat its own. As a result, there was an increasing reluctance to use terror except in very limited ways, such as against troublesome dissidents. The government lost its Stalinist capacity for brutality and increasingly tried to substitute persuasion. This change did not escape the notice of the subject peoples of the empire. (Cullen, 1993)

A number of consequences follow from the partial decentralization of power. On the positive side, it reduces the amount of information and resources the center needs to remain in power, and it discourages the ascent of rivals for the "throne." It also works to relieve the problem of too few people trying to make policy for a huge and diverse territory. The strategy, however, also unleashes a host of debilitating consequences for imperial rule.

By design, it extends decision-making authority beyond the central leadership to include other elites—some of them indigenous—and thereby transforms the relationship between the imperial center and the periphery. Before, the central leaders exercised exclusive hierarchical control over their agents in the periphery. With decentralization, the imperial center relinquishes some of its control to key agents in the periphery. In effect, the elite splits into a center-based imperial faction and a periphery-based one. The repercussions are far-reaching.

As we mentioned above, agents who begin to identify more with the region than with the center are likely to siphon off resources to enrich themselves and their region. This usually leads to corruption, which in turn erodes some of the key beliefs that justify the existence of the empire. For example, the myth of imperial infallibility, a legacy of the Russian Empire, became strained when it was extended to include the obviously fallible mortals acting as imperial agents in the periphery—particularly those who were known to be corrupt.

A notorious example of corruption is the cotton affair. During the Brezhnev era, corruption was widespread in Uzbekistan. The top leadership—both indigenous and imperial—was deeply involved. Uzbekistan officials sent false information to the center. They claimed that they had produced and shipped to state purchasing agents millions more tons of cotton than they actually had. This deception allowed them to divert billions of rubles into the illegal economy. In addition, "bribes to conceal false production figures were the rule, . . . offices were regularly bought and sold [and] those yielding the highest profits from bribes sold for the highest price." (Cavanaugh, 1992, p. 7) The cotton affair involved numerous top officials of the Party and the government, including the Party leaders of seven of the twelve autonomous regions of Uzbekistan and Brezhnev's son-in-law.

Between 1984 and 1988, approximately fifty-eight thousand senior officials were dismissed. The minister in charge of cotton production was sentenced to death for accepting huge bribes and defrauding the Soviet government by falsifying production figures. At the center of this corrupt network was Uzbek Party First Secretary Sharaf Rashidov, who held his post from 1959 to 1983. During this period, he constructed an alliance between the local Party organization and major figures in the illegal economy. After Uzbekistan became independent, however, the story of the cotton affair was given a nationalist spin. Most notably, Rashidov was rehabilitated and declared "a national hero who did all he could to advance Uzbekistan's interests in opposition to the excessive demands of the center." (Cavanaugh, 1992, p. 9)

Such situations affect an empire in two important ways. First, they undermine the authority relationships within the empire's administrative hierarchy. Leaders in the periphery may come to question the basis of their loyalty to the center. As this happens, opportunities to advance personal ambitions or local interests at the expense of imperial interests will become more attractive, especially when the top leadership has a policy of looking the other way—as did Brezhnev and his immediate entourage. Second, "[a]n empty ideological space will emerge at the center of the polity" (Motyl, 1992, p. 26), a space that renders local elites susceptible to the appeals of other "anti-empire" ideologies, most notably nationalism. (Goble, 1990) Erosion of the beliefs that justify imperialism and the growth of nationalism undermine the center's efforts at building a homogeneous society that could be the basis for the empire's evolution into a nation-state. Only by forging a single society out of the many societies that constitute an empire can the centrifugal forces of imperial decay be circumvented. In the Soviet Union, Marxism-Leninism was not a strong enough force to unite the center and the periphery.

A split in the imperial elite between the center and its agents further increases the autonomy of the agents. As their autonomy and attachment to the place in which they are located grow, the agents increasingly turn their attention to regional interests. As a result, these interests attain a coherence and a legitimacy they did not have before. Meanwhile, officials at the imperial center are more free to focus on politics and intrigues within the center itself. This outcome is hardly surprising, for decentralization limits the central leadership's control over the far reaches of the empire. The central leadership increasingly becomes viewed as the ruler of the metropolitan center and its population.

This ongoing process of imperial decay provides opportunities for regional nationalist elites to assert their own interests and to forge coalitions against the center with the increasingly disaffected imperial agents. Here it is important to recall a characteristic of societies in the periphery that we mentioned earlier. Peripheral populations are societies in their own right, complete with traditions, customs, *and their own leaders and elites.* Subjugated under empire, local elites are compelled to surrender much of their ability to exercise control over their own societies. But as imperial decay sets in, local elites seize opportunities to advance their own interests and those of their followers. Initially, self-interest motivates imperial agents and local elites to forge coalitions, as in the Uzbek cotton affair. Over time, however, as the myths and ideology of the center deteriorate, these coalitions gain a more normative justification.[9] Although this process can have a number of outcomes, nationalism typically is the outcome most appealing to peripheral societies.

Nationalism is a predominantly psychological phenomenon. It emerges among individuals who recognize themselves as part of a distinct political and social community or nation. Thus, nationalism is "the affiliation of [such] individuals to a set of symbols and beliefs emphasizing communality among the members of a political order." (Giddens, 1985, p. 116) Paramount among the beliefs peculiar to nationalism is "the belief that nations should have political sovereignty." (Motyl, 1992, p. 27) Not surprisingly, regional elites frequently use nationalism to further and to legitimate their own aspirations to self-rule. Thus, the forces of nationalism can—and in the Soviet Union did—thwart the efforts of the central leadership to move toward building a nation-state. Given these developments, it is not surprising that one of the major forces that destroyed the Soviet Union was nationalism.

Highly centralized rule contributes to imperial decay in yet another way. It engenders crises of succession. In highly centralized regimes, succession is seldom peaceful and never routine. Replacing very powerful rulers can spark wars of succession. In the absence of outright war, succession minimally creates periods of extreme instability, which in turn compromises effective rule. Succession struggles squander state resources and render the center, at least for a time, incapable of overseeing the periphery. This kind of faltering was evident during the last years of the Soviet Union.

Long before he died, Brezhnev had become physically and mentally incapable of effective personal rule. There was, however, no mechanism of succession that could replace him with a top leader who could be vigorous and competent. In addition, Brezhnev had tied his own retention of the general secretary's post to the job security of most of the Soviet elite. This tactic gave his subordinates considerable incentive to keep him in office as long as possible: A new ruler could threaten the self-interest of many in the elite. Thus, the Soviet Union virtually ground to a halt waiting for Brezhnev to die. The key leaders of the Party and state gradually became a gerontocracy, a ruling elite composed of the elderly. When Brezhnev did finally die in 1982, the gerontocracy was able to keep the choice of his successor within its own ranks. The elderly leadership replaced Brezhnev with two successive sickly old men: (1) Yuri Andropov (General Secretary from 1982 to 1984), who spent almost half of his tenure in office terminally ill and incapacitated; and (2) Konstantin Chernenko, (General Secretary from 1984 to early 1985), who did not have the talent or the vigor to lead effectively and who died shortly after assuming office.

A gerontocracy, by definition, is unable to remain in power for an extended period of time. Finally, in March 1985, the elderly leadership was forced to permit a younger generation to take power. The post of general secretary was

---

9. Self-interest and corruption do not necessarily vanish. Indeed, they tend to remain but may take on somewhat different justifications or forms.

passed to a person who was in his early fifties and was vigorous and able to truly lead. Mikhail Gorbachev, the new General Secretary, began with a whirl-wind of activity designed to get the Soviet Union moving again. The implementation of his reform plans was helped by the fact that the members of the gerontocracy quickly began to lose power through death or retirement.

Let us review the pathologies of empire that we have outlined so far. Empire is a type of rule that cannot be realized in its ideal form. Even when sustained by a well-developed coercive and administrative apparatus, imperialist rulers eventually confront the fact that their rule is critically compromised by an inability to muster sufficient information and resources to maintain absolute control. Sooner or later, they decide that the only way to preserve the empire is to decentralize imperial decision-making. This strategy unleashes consequences that foster rather than inhibit the process of imperial decay. Add the fact that succession crises waste resources and compromise ruler effectiveness, and we have a good-sized list of pathologies associated with imperial rule. The net impact of these pathologies is the deterioration of the state—the vehicle for control in an empire.

State Decline

It is indeed ironic that the means by which imperial control is exercised should be the casualty of its exercise. Imperialism leads to a fragmentation of the state control apparatus, which worsens the ongoing problem of inefficient accumulation of information and resources. These are mutually reinforcing processes, and they ultimately compromise an empire's effectiveness as an international actor. Alexander Motyl (1992), for example, thinks that the ability of territorially contiguous empires to withstand the military pressures of nation-states is likely to diminish over time. State decline, therefore, renders an empire vulnerable to both internal decay and external threats.

Few alternatives—either domestic or international—are available to an imperial center seeking to reverse the process of state decline. Imperial leaders have historically pursued some combination of the following strategies to halt the decline of their status in the international state system and to fend off external threats: (1) alliances, (2) territorial expansion, (3) enhancing prestige, (4) economic mobilization to increase war-making capability, (5) strategic withdrawal. (Motyl, 1992)

Alliances with other international actors may temporarily remedy a strategic imbalance that has increased an empire's external vulnerability. But alliances do nothing to address the true cause of state decline: imperial decay. Moreover, aligning with a powerful ally may reinforce the empire's second-rate status within the international pecking order of states. Powerful rulers cloaked in myths of infallibility and destiny cannot abide second-tier status. The super-power status of the Soviet Union was a source of great pride. Loss of that status has led many to adopt right-wing Russian nationalist positions, arguing that Russia should strive to recapture not only its former glory but also some or all of its imperial territory. At this point, however, the military and economic weakness of Russia makes a successful policy of conquest unlikely.

Eliminating external threats by expanding frontiers does little to redress the problem of an empire in decline. In fact, territorial expansion compounds the problem. It diverts limited resources to the expansion effort, and it increases the size of the periphery and thus further strains the administrative and coercive apparatus. The war in Afghanistan, for example, turned out to be the Soviet Union's Vietnam. The Soviet leadership expended enormous resources needed elsewhere in the economy, yet they still could not win. This course of action aggravated other problems, which led to the Soviet Union's downfall.

Depending on the tactic employed, seeking enhanced prestige can be a relatively cost-effective way to mask temporarily the debilitating effects of imperial decay. Into this category go bellicose threats and opportunistic actions intended to add credibility to an empire's deterrent posture. An example is the Soviet downing of a Korean passenger airliner in 1983. Despite an international outcry condemning the Soviet reaction to the accidental violation of its airspace, the USSR used the occasion to enhance its reputation as an actor not to be trifled with in the international community. In fact, throughout its post–World War II history, the Soviet Union was particularly effective at periodically enhancing its prestige. Its success was partly due to its ability to control the information that reached the rest of the world and to its use of technological feats, such as the detonation of an atomic bomb in 1949 and the launching of Sputnik in 1957, to increase its international prestige.

Economic mobilization to increase war-making capability does little to reverse the long-term trend of imperial decay and state decline. Indeed, economic mobilization of this kind tends to accelerate the process, for at least two reasons. First, although economic mobilization for military purposes generates jobs, it diverts resources away from the production of consumer goods, which are an essential component of improved living standards for the population. As access to the basic amenities of life dwindles or fails to improve, popular dissatisfaction grows. Second, economic mobilization to increase military capabilities triggers a similar mobilization by potential international adversaries who may be better equipped economically to engage in a protracted arms race. The diversion of limited resources continues, and popular dissatisfaction grows, undermining the center's already tenuous claims to legitimacy. In this sense, the United States did not win the Cold War; rather, the Soviet Union lost it.

Finally, the rulers of declining empires sooner or later consider strategic withdrawal or disengagement from parts of the periphery as a way to reverse the process of decay. The logic driving this option is obvious. If the rulers can free up resources, they can concentrate their efforts on rehabilitating the most important (in their opinion) parts of the empire. It is unusual for imperial rulers to withdraw abruptly from a region. They typically grant increasing levels of autonomy to designated regions. This move, however, only stimulates regional elites to redouble their efforts to achieve increased sovereignty or even independence. The center must then enlarge (rather than reduce) resource commitments to maintain control in the rest of the periphery. This strategy could be seen in the Soviet treatment of its eastern European satellites over time. When Hungary and Czechoslovakia challenged Moscow's rule in 1956 and 1968, the Soviet leadership sent in the military. By the 1980s, however, the Soviet Union was not as ready to send in troops. Instead, it tried to control the Polish rebellion by using persuasion backed by the threat of force.

Imperial decay and international decline are the fate of empires. Efforts to offset the trend toward international decline accelerate the process of imperial decay. Stagnation and instability, therefore, eventually characterize empires and make them increasingly vulnerable to systemic crises. Such crises can be triggered by natural disaster, international war, problems of succession, or efforts to reform. Whatever the cause, systemic crises threaten the very survival of an empire. By 1991, the Soviet Union was in such bad shape that it could not recover from a failed coup.

CAN EMPIRES BE TRANSFORMED?

We have outlined a rather negative prognosis for empires. The dynamics of imperial dominance and subjugation breed pathologies of governance that doom empires to decay, stagnation, and ultimate collapse. But could there be an alternative outcome?

Nation-building, the process whereby people come to identify themselves as part of a political community, might produce a transformation: The distinction between center and periphery would disappear, and peripheral populations would come to identify themselves as part of a unified society. Integral to this transformation would be the creation of authority relationships. With the establishment of such relationships, authority rooted in legitimacy would supplant power as the primary control mechanism operating in the political-economic system. A social contract between the governed and their government would replace the oppression of the ruled by the rulers, and the outcome would be a modern nation-state.

The Soviet leadership tried to unite the various peoples of the Soviet Empire into a single Soviet people (*sovetskii narod*). Had this effort succeeded, the Soviet Union might have been able to become a modern nation-state. The rapidity with which the Soviet Empire collapsed is a good indication that the leadership failed. The magnitude of the task and the leadership's failure to accomplish it were a function of the failure to superimpose a Soviet identity over the ethnic identities of the peoples of the periphery. Thus, we now turn to the problems posed by the extreme ethnic diversity of the Soviet Union and the efforts of the Soviet leadership to mold these diverse peoples into a common nation.

REFERENCES

Aron, R. (1966). *Peace and war: A theory of international relations.* New York: Double-day.

Barkin, J. S. & Cronin, B. (1994). The state and the nation: Changing norms and the rules of sovereignty in international relations. *International Organization, 48,* 107–30.

Burg, S. L. (1990). Nationality elites and political change in the Soviet Union. In L. Hajda & M. Beissinger (Eds.), *The nationalities factor in Soviet politics and society* (pp. 24–42). Boulder, CO: Westview Press.

Cavanaugh, C. (1992). Uzbekistan reexamines the cotton affair. *RFE/RL Research Report, 1*(37), 7–11.

Cohen, B. (1973). *The question of imperialism.* New York: Basic Books.

Connor, W. (1992). Soviet policies toward the non-Russian peoples in theoretic and historic perspective: What Gorbachev inherited. In A. J. Motyl (Ed.), *The post-Soviet nations: Perspectives on the demise of the USSR* (pp. 30–49). New York: Columbia University Press.

Cullen, R. (1993). *Twilight of empire: Inside the crumbling Soviet bloc.* New York: Atlantic Monthly Press.

Dallin, A., & Breslauer, G. W. (1970). *Political terror in communist systems.* Stanford, CA: Stanford University Press.

Daniels, R. V. (1985). *Russia: The roots of confrontation.* Cambridge, MA: Harvard University Press.

Doob, L. W. (1983). *Personality, power, and authority: A view from the behavioral sciences.* Westport, CT: Greenwood Press.

Doyle, M. W. (1986). *Empires.* Ithaca, NY: Cornell University Press.

Giddens, A. (1985). *The nation-state and violence.* Berkeley: University of California Press.

Goble, P. A. (1990). The end of the "national question": Ideological decay and ethnic relations in the USSR. In S. Woodby & A. B. Evans, Jr. (Eds.), *Restructuring Soviet ideology: Gorbachev's new thinking.* Boulder, CO: Westview Press.

Harasymiw, B. (1969). Nomenklatura: The Soviet communist party's leadership recruitment system. *Canadian Journal of Political Science, 2,* 505–512.

Knight, A. (1988). *The KGB: Police and politics in the Soviet Union.* Winchester, MA: Allen & Unwin.

———. (1992). The political police and the national question in the Soviet Union. In A. J. Motyl (Ed.), *The post-Soviet nations: Perspectives on the demise of the USSR* (pp. 170–189). New York: Columbia University Press.

Lichtheim, G. (1971). *Imperialism.* New York: Praeger.

McAuley, M. (1992). *Soviet politics: 1917–1991.* New York: Oxford University Press.

Miller, J. H. (1992). Cadres policy in nationality areas: Recruitment of CPSU first and second secretaries in non-Russian republics. In R. Denber (Ed.), *The Soviet nationality reader: The disintegration in context* (pp. 183–209). Boulder, CO: Westview Press.

Motyl, A. J. (1992). From imperial decay to imperial collapse: The fall of the Soviet empire in comparative perspective. In R. L. Rudolph and D. F. Good (Eds.), *Nationalism and empire: The Hapsburg empire and the Soviet Union* (pp. 15–43). New York: St. Martin's Press.

Plano, J. C., & Greenberg, M. (1985). *The American political dictionary* (7th ed.). New York: Holt, Rinehart and Winston.

Skocpol, T. (1979). *States and social revolutions.* New York: Cambridge University Press.

Solchanyk, R. (1990). Roman Szporluk and Valerii Tishkov talk about the national question. *Report on the USSR, 2*(22), 19–24.

Starhawk, (1993). *The fifth sacred thing.* New York: Bantam.

Tolz, V. (1993). The burden of the imperial legacy. *RFE/RL Research Report, 2*(20), 41–46.

Vozlensky, M. (1984). *Nomenklatura: The Soviet ruling class.* New York: Doubleday.

Wood, G. (1969). *The creation of the American republic.* Chapel Hill: University of North Carolina Press.

Yasmann, V. (1991). Law on the KGB published. *Report on the USSR, 3*(31), 12–18.

· 4 ·

ETHNICITY, NATIONALISM, AND NATION-BUILDING

A unique union of republics is the result of the efforts of many generations of Soviet people. On its banner is inscribed the internationalist unity of the working people of all Soviet nations and nationalities, the right of nations to self-determination, revival and advancement of national cultures, accelerated progress of formerly backward national regions, and elimination of strife between nations.

Nineteenth All-Union Conference of the CPSU
(1988, p. 146)

Those words sound great, and the "unique union of republics" they describe might even have been great—if it had ever existed. After the October Revolution in 1917, the Bolsheviks gradually gained control over most of the multi-ethnic territory of the former Russian Empire. The Communist Party of the Soviet Union tried to build a new nation-state in which people's primary loyalty would be to the Soviet Union, no matter what their ethnic roots. The rapid disintegration of the USSR in 1991 showed dramatically that the CPSU had failed. In this chapter we explore the ethnic diversity of the Soviet Union. An appreciation of this diversity is essential for a proper understanding of why the Soviet leadership failed to create a common Soviet identity and why nationalism tore the Soviet Union apart.

Because England, France, and many of the other countries with which we are most familiar went through their initial nation-building phases centuries ago, we tend to look on such countries as being fixed and eternal. The borders of France, for example, seem natural; the people who live within them are French, and the people who do not are Belgian, German, or some other nationality. It seems as though France has always been as it is today and will always remain that way. Many wars, however, have been fought over the issue of preserving "natural" or "proper" national boundaries. The Gulf War, for example, was fought in 1991 to restore the boundaries of Kuwait to what they had been before the Iraqi invasion. Nation-building, however, is not easy—nor is it ever complete.

NATION-BUILDING AND THE PSYCHOLOGY OF NATIONALISM

What do we mean by the term *nation-building?* It is "the process whereby the inhabitants of a state's territory come to be *loyal* citizens of that state." (Bloom, 1990, p. 55, emphasis in the original) This definition raises a question: What is the difference between a nation and a state? As we discussed in Chapter 3, a state is a political entity "occupying a definite territory, having an organized government, and possessing internal and external sovereignty." (Plano & Greenberg, 1985, p. 24) If that is a state, then what is a nation?

The word *nation* commonly designates "any sizable group of people united by common bonds of geography, religion, language, race, custom, and traditions," which has "shared experiences and common aspirations." (Plano & Greenberg, 1985, p. 17) There is also a political aspect to nationhood. Paul Brass (1992, p. 20) calls attention to this dimension when he defines nation as "a particular type of ethnic community, . . . an ethnic community politicized, with recognized group rights in the political system."

When almost all of the people living within a state identify themselves as members of a common nation, a nation-state exists—the nation and the state assume a common identity in most people's minds. An example is France, where the overwhelming majority identify themselves as French. Many states, however, are multinational—that is, they are home to more than one large national group. An example is Switzerland, which is roughly divided into a major German-speaking area, a major French-speaking area, and smaller areas where Italian and other languages are spoken. Because we are about to consider the case of the USSR and its successor countries, it is important to note that a stable and prosperous state can unite a multinational territory.

In recent history, a number of states were created before nations. In such cases the challenge has been to build and maintain a common national identity among the people inhabiting the territory of the state. The new Soviet government faced this task after the October Revolution, and the fifteen successor countries are facing it now. Creating a new nation usually requires the destruction of one or more old national identities. (Connor, 1972) The Soviet leadership created a formidable and pervasive system of political persuasion designed to create the "new Soviet person" (*novyi sovetskii chelovek*) who identified himself or herself first and foremost as "Soviet" and only secondarily as Ukrainian or Armenian. The individual's fundamental loyalty was intended to be to the Soviet state and to the Soviet people (Szporluk, 1990, pp. 7–8)

Had this task of nation-building been accomplished successfully, the Soviet Union would probably still exist. The main force that tore the Soviet Union apart was the fact that most of its people continued to identify more strongly with their ethnic groups than they did with the Soviet Union. This was the result of a complex of factors, including the way in which the new Soviet state chose to organize itself politically after the 1917 revolutions, as well as the way in which it treated the ethnic groups within its territory.

The Soviet successor countries are now faced with carrying out a similar nation-building process. None of them is ethnically homogeneous; all of them are dealing with various degrees of multinationality. For example, at the time of the last Soviet all-union election, in 1990, the ethnic breakdown in the union republics ranged from Armenia, which was 94 percent Armenian, to Kazakhstan, which was only 39 percent Kazakh. (*Washington Post*, February 25, 1990, p. A20) Significant population shifts have occurred since then—most notably, Russians returning to Russia from the other former union republics. (Marnie & Slater, 1993) But this movement of people has not created anything resembling ethnically "pure" successor countries. All have significant minorities, many of which are resentful of what they see as domination by the titular ethnic group.

As a result, the dominant national group in each successor country must find some way to persuade minority nationalities to develop a primary loyalty to the new political entity that inherited the territory of a former union republic. Significant problems have already emerged. In Russia by 1992 ethnic divisions and dissatisfactions posed so great a problem that the various nationalities signed a treaty of federation in order to preserve the unity of the new Russian state. (*Washington Post*, April 1, 1992, p. A25) At the same time, in Georgia the Georgians and Ossetians were engaged in a shooting war over the issue of Ossetian self-rule. Nearby, the Armenians and Azeris[1] were fighting a war that started when the Armenians began trying to unite the Armenian nation under one Armenian-ruled state—a goal involving the annexation of Nagorno-Karabakh, a largely Armenian-populated part of Azerbaijan.

So, a major task facing most of the former Soviet republics is to create among their citizens a new national loyalty that transcends the ethnic differences within their populations. According to William Bloom (1990), the key to nation-building is to create a unifying psychological identity among people who currently identify with the various nations or ethnic groups within a state. How is this process of identification to be accomplished? First, the inhabitants of the state must see the state as offering protection against external and internal foes. Second, the inhabitants must be confident that significant benefits will result if they give their primary loyalty to the state. Because nation-building is not a one-time endeavor but a continuous process, there may be periods of time during which one or the other of these factors is more important.

The bond between nation and state is psychological. It depends more on perceptions and emotions than on facts and logic. Both the state and the nation are defined in terms of inclusion and exclusion. Statehood requires a certain mind-set: The people of a territorial unit must accept the fact that a given regime exercises control over them. They do not have to like this fact; they

---

1. Azeris are the majority ethnic group in Azerbaijan. They are also referred to as Azerbaijanis.

simply have to accept it. Most of the nations on the periphery of the Soviet Union did not like being ruled by Moscow, but they accepted the situation because they believed they could not change it. States are built on positions of relative power. Nation-states require a stronger psychological bond. The identification of a large majority of the people with their nation-state is what gives the rulers of a nation-state their legitimacy and thus their authority.

Identification occurs when individuals adopt the behavior, values, and attitudes of people who are important to them—in the case of national identification, the leaders or "typical" members of their ethnic group. Group identification has two basic conponents: "(1) a self-awareness of one's membership in a group; and (2) a feeling of psychological closeness to the group." (Conover & Feldman, 1984, p. 154) Through socialization, ideas are learned and eventually internalized. That is, they become so basic to the personality that "they are intrinsically rewarding, . . . useful for solving a problem or . . . congenial to the person's needs." (Barner-Barry & Rosenwein, 1985, p. 62; Kelman & Hamilton, 1989, pp. 107–109) Behavior that expresses them is satisfying because such behavior is seen as being "good," as having unquestionable merit. Nation-building is the process of creating and maintaining such a mentality among the population of a state. It leads to the attitude that citizens of the state are "us" and everyone else is "them." This ingroup-outgroup distinction is at the core of nationalism. (Larsen et al., 1992, pp. 310–311) When it encompasses a state that occupies roughly the same territory as the nation in question, it lays the foundation for a nation-state. Nationalism was the most powerful force that tore apart the Soviet Union.

People disagree about whether nationalism is good or bad. (Forbes, 1985) "Good" nationalism tends to be equated with patriotism, "bad" nationalism with ethnocentrism or xenophobia. In ordinary times, nationalism can be a source of personal satisfaction and psychological stability. In a crisis, it can mobilize a population to solve a common problem or confront a common enemy. Comparison of the characteristics of "us" and "them" plays a central role in ethnic imagery. (White & Prachuabmoh, 1983, p. 30) Thus, nationalism can shade into ethnocentrism when it involves the conviction that one's own ethnic group and culture are inherently superior to all others. It can also shade into xenophobia when it involves an unrealistic fear or distrust of "foreign" people or countries.

In the Soviet Union, the task of blending its many ethnic groups to create a common Soviet nationality was formidable. The Soviet Union, like the Russian Empire before it, was a mosaic of ethnic groups divided by language, culture, history, religion, and even alphabet. Most groups never lost their primary identification with their own people. Their attachment to the Soviet Union was either superficial (with little or no internalization) or perfunctory—simple compliance motivated by the power wielded by the Communist Party. Three major factors contributed to the failure of the CPSU to build a firm Soviet national identity: (1) the creation of political subdivisions on an ethnic basis; (2) age-old fears and hatreds among the ethnic groups living in the Soviet Union; and (3) the domination of the Soviet leadership by one ethnic group, the Russians.

ETHNICITY AND THE CREATION OF THE SOVIET STATE

After the Communist Party consolidated its control over the Soviet Union, the borders of the new state were not much different from the borders of the Russian Empire. Under tsarist rule, the subject nationalities had very little control over their territories. They were politically submerged in Russia and subjected to an oppressive rule by Russians. During the nineteenth century, the tsarist government adopted more and more policies intended to destroy the national cultures of its subject populations. This harsh rule "provoked ever greater resentment and the growth of national consciousness and resistance." (Nahaylo & Swoboda, 1989, p. 14)

After the fall of the old regime, the Soviet Union became the world's largest multiethnic state. One reason why the Bolsheviks were able to gain control over most of the old Russian Empire was that they promised oppressed and angry ethnic groups more respect and self-determination than they had enjoyed under tsarist rule. Before Lenin became leader of the new Soviet Union, he had already gone on record as a champion of each nationality's right to determine its own destiny. He was convinced that the solidarity of the proletariat of all nationalities and the obvious (to Lenin, at least) disadvantages of fragmentation into small states would ensure the ultimate unity of any communist state on Russian soil. He pointed to Switzerland as a good example of how the nationalities problem could be solved without breaking up a state.

Immediately after the October Revolution, Lenin's new government proclaimed in the "Declaration of the Rights of the Peoples of Russia" that the Soviet Union's policy would be governed by the following principles:

1. The equality and sovereignty of the peoples of Russia.
2. The right of the peoples of Russia to free self-determination including secession and formation of independent states.
3. The abolition of all national and national-religious privileges and restrictions of any kind.
4. The free development of national minorities and ethnic groups populating the territory of Russia. (Nahaylo & Swoboda, 1989, pp. 18–19)

Over the next few years, however, the practice of the new Soviet government was only superficially in accord with these principles.

By the end of 1918, there were at least thirteen new states within the territory of the former Russian Empire. Moreover, the new Soviet government officially recognized many of them. At this point in history, it was in the self-interest of the new Bolshevik government to gain the goodwill of as many nationalities as possible. It was fighting a civil war with the White Army, which was trying to wrest control of the country from the Bolsheviks. The White forces were concentrated almost entirely in non-Russian areas. The fact that the Whites followed a policy that would not permit succession by minorities allowed the Bolsheviks to court these nationality groups by promising them self-determination. (Connor, 1992, pp. 16–17) In the words of Stalin, the Whites "offered to the oppressed peoples a prospect of further oppression, and the oppressed peoples were obliged to come forward and embrace us, seeing that we unfurled the banner of the liberation of these oppressed peoples." (Connor, 1992, p. 17)

At the same time, however, the Bolsheviks began to change the meaning of self-determination. The right to self-determination of nations became the right to self-determination of the proletariats within those nations. Because the Communist Party was the only group that could speak for the proletariat, it was empowered to make key decisions about the self-determination of nations. Thus, the welfare of the new Communist Party–ruled Soviet Union became more important than the self-determination of nations when these two principles clashed. By the end of the civil war period, the Soviet government (by using cooperative local Communists, as well as force where necessary) had managed to return most of the seceded nationalities to the Soviet Union.

After that point there was no meaningful right to secede from the Soviet Union—even though this right was theoretically guaranteed by the Soviet constitutions in force throughout most of the Soviet period. The official political structure chosen for the USSR was a federal structure. Under ordinary circumstances, a federation has a system of government that divides internal sovereignty between a central government and the governments of its major subdivisions. Each level has a sphere of government authority within which it can rule its citizens, using its own officials and laws. Each is supreme within its own sphere of authority. The United States and its fifty states make up a federal system of government.

In contrast, a unitary system of government has a central government that is supreme over both regional and local governments. Each of the fifty US states is a unitary government in the sense that each has complete control over both the structure and the functioning of its political subdivisions, such as counties, townships, or cities. In other words, all American local jurisdictions are creatures of the state that created them and within which they are located. The states, however, are not creatures of the federal government, which they both preceded and created.

Adoption of a formal federal structure by the new Soviet Union allowed the major nationalities that had tried to establish independent states to enter the Soviet fold as "sovereign" union republics. These union republics were the major political subdivisions within the formal federal structure of the USSR.[2] Similarly, many of the smaller nationalities were given the lesser status of autonomous republic or autonomous province (*oblast'*)—a formal status that appeared to give them significant self-rule. Thus, Lenin and his fellow Bolsheviks established a state that was federal in form. Under the rule of the highly

---

2. The fifteen Soviet successor countries used to be the fifteen union republics or, more formally, Soviet Socialist Republics (SSRs).

centralized CPSU, however, it became unitary in practice.[3] And, very quickly, this unitary state took on the characteristics of an empire.

The Communist Party of the Soviet Union subjected all of its regional and local organizations to the strict control of the central Party apparatus. Although important decisions could and were made at the lower levels, they had to be in conformity with the policies of the central leadership in Moscow. Regional and local self-rule existed (1) to implement central policies in ways that took into account the peculiarities of the region or locality and (2) to establish policy within issue areas considered sufficiently unimportant by the central authorities. If a regional or local policy became important to Moscow, the central authorities would not hesitate to move in and take over—even when regional or local authorities objected. Thus, the federal structure of the Soviet Union had little practical meaning. The center ruled, and the periphery was expected to obey.

Because the federal subdivisions were established on roughly the same territory as the national homelands of most of the country's important nationalities, there was never any possibility that Soviet nation-building could be aided by an American-style "melting pot." The members of a majority of the various ethnic groups remained relatively isolated from each other by geography, language, and culture.[4] There was much less of the intermingling and intermarriage of the members of these ethnic groups than there has been in the United States. Of equal importance was the fact that the new citizens of the Soviet Union were not newcomers to a strange land, as most Americans were. Rather, a majority continued to live where their ancestors had lived for hundreds— even thousands—of years. Thus, there was no opportunity to leave behind the prejudices and animosities that had existed between adjacent ethnic groups since long before the creation of the Soviet Empire and, in many cases, the Russian Empire.

THE UNEASY COEXISTENCE OF THE SOVIET NATIONALITIES

Central to the nationalities problem in the Soviet Union and to the situation facing its successor countries are the number and diversity of ethnic groups in that part of the world. The territory of the former Soviet Union is huge. Estimates of the number of ethnic groups vary from report to report, because different criteria are used by different people to draw boundaries between similar—but not identical—peoples. Thus, depending on the source, there are

---

3. During a trip to Lithuania in 1990, Gorbachev acknowledged the fact that the USSR was not a federation: "[W]e have not lived in a federation. We have lived in a unitary state with its own realities." (Girnius, 1990, p. 5)

4. Two notable exceptions were the Jews, who were much more geographically dispersed than the other nationalities, and the Russians, many of whom moved to other ethnic areas for economic or social reasons.

between 100 and 150 ethnic groups within the territory of the former Soviet Union. According to Boris Yeltsin, there are "130 peoples and nations" in the Russian Federation alone. (*Washington Post*, June 12, 1992, p. A28)

The Soviet state based its federal structure on these preexisting ethnic groupings. It had fifteen union republics, twenty autonomous republics, eight autonomous provinces (*oblast'*) and ten autonomous areas (*krai*). The establishment of these fifty-three political subdivisions gave a large number of ethnic groups at least the illusion that they had some control over their own destinies. More important in retrospect is the fact that this arrangement maintained a psychological focus for the national loyalties of these people. This focus made the job of building a Soviet national identity more difficult and complex.

Many of the ethnic groups are quite small. The seventeen largest include over 90 percent of the Soviet population. (See Table 4-1) Of those seventeen groups, fifteen were given their own union republics. The other two, the Jews and the Tatars, did not manage to achieve union republic status because they lacked the necessary population concentrations. At the time of the 1917 revolutions, the Tatars were separated into two major clusters, one around Kazan on the Volga River and the other far away on the Crimean peninsula. Because the Tatars were considered too dispersed to be given a union republic of their own, each Tatar group was given the lesser status of an autonomous republic.[5] The Jews were even more scattered than the Tatars. In the early 1930s, the Soviet government created the Jewish Autonomous Province in the far eastern part of Siberia. But few Jews ever moved there, preferring to remain in the more urbanized European part of the Soviet Union.

At the time of the last Soviet census, in 1989, several ethnic groups had significantly larger populations than the titular nationalities of some of the union republics (see Table 4-1). Most notable were the Tatars, who had a larger population than ten of the titular nationalities. Also notable is the fact that the Jewish population was comparatively much smaller than it had been at the birth of the Soviet Union. The decrease is largely due to World War II and the substantial emigration of the Jews to Israel and to the West in the 1970s and 1980s.

Basing the federal structure of the Soviet state on ethnic criteria had another troublesome effect on the Soviet Union's nation-building efforts. It helped to perpetuate the interethnic rivalries and hostilities of the past. The way in which the boundaries of the subdivisions were drawn, as well as differences in the way in which the nationalities felt they were being treated by Moscow, aggravated underlying problems in the relationships among the nationalities.

For example, within the Union Republic of Azerbaijan was an enclave of about 4,400 square kilometers called Nagorno-Karabakh (see Map 4-1). A large majority of the population was Armenian. Azerbaijan had been willing to return

---

5. In 1944, the autonomous republic of the Crimean Tatars was dissolved because of their alleged collaboration with the Nazis. The Crimean Tatars were subsequently deported to other parts of the USSR and have only recently begun to return to the Crimea in significant numbers.

TABLE 4-1
Largest Ethnic Groups in the USSR, 1989 Census (by thousands)

	Population	Percentage of total	Cumulative percentage
USSR total	285,743		
*Russian	145,155	50.8	50.8
*Ukrainian	44,186	15.5	66.3
*Uzbek	16,698	5.8	72.1
*Belorussian	10,036	3.5	75.6
*Kazakh	8,136	2.8	78.4
Tatar (incl. Crimean)	6,921	2.4	80.8
*Azeri	6,770	2.4	83.2
*Armenian	4,623	1.6	84.8
*Tajik	4,215	1.5	86.3
*Georgian	3,981	1.4	87.7
*Moldavian	3,352	1.2	88.9
*Lithuanian	3,067	1.1	90.0
*Turkmen	2,729	.9	90.9
*Kirgiz	2,529	.8	91.7
German	2,039	.7	92.4
Chuvash	1,842	.6	93.0
*Latvian	1,459	.5	93.5
Bashkir	1,449	.5	94.0
Jewish	1,449	.5	94.5
Mordovan	1,154	.4	94.9
Polish	1,126	.4	95.3
*Estonian	1,027	.4	95.7

*Titular nationalities of union republics.
Source: *Narodnoe Khoziaistvo SSSR v 1990 g.: Statisticheskii ezhegodnik.* (1991). Moscow: Finansy i Statistika, p. 77.

Nagorno-Karabakh to Armenia in 1920, when both became part of Soviet Russia. It is said that Stalin, who was Commissar for Nationalities at the time, decided to leave it in the Union Republic of Azerbaijan because he was concerned about access to the vast oil reserves of Azerbaijan. (Richards, 1990, p. 141) Under Gorbachev, the Armenians tried to get the territory back, but by that time the Azeris were in no mood to let that happen. The leadership in Moscow sided with the Azeris, and the result was the bloody Armenian-Azerbaijani War.

The depth and bitterness of interethnic animosities were masked by the nature of Soviet rule. In particular, the rigid limits on speech and other forms of expression that the USSR imposed on its subjects stifled any display of resentment or anger. As a result, even solvable interethnic problems remained unsolved and smoldering under the surface. By refusing to look very far beneath superficialities (or to let anyone else do so), Moscow was able to give the impression that ethnic problems were being solved as the people of the USSR moved toward a common Soviet identity. Glasnost changed all that.

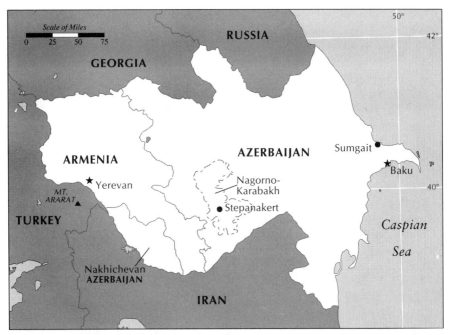

MAP 4-1 Armenia and Azerbaijan

Glasnost was never intended to unleash a storm of pent-up nationalist complaints, accusations, and demands, but it had that effect. Gorbachev was "the first Soviet leader since Lenin without any experience in a non-Russian region . . . and the first . . . not to have written an article or given a speech about nationality issues before coming to power." (Goble, 1990c, p. 100) Perhaps for this reason, he never seemed to grasp the full significance of this issue. He did not anticipate how explosive the combination of glasnost, democratization, and nationalism would be. Moreover, when the problems became apparent, he failed to develop an effective policy to deal with the challenge. (Burg, 1990; Motyl, 1992)

Much of the anger of the peoples of the periphery was directed at Moscow and the political domination of the Russians. Also, however, glasnost and democratization loosened the limits on expression and exposed old hostilities and fears between neighboring ethnic groups with long-standing enmities. Some of these could be traced back to the pre-Soviet historical experience; some stemmed from decisions made during the Soviet period. The case of Armenia and Azerbaijan illustrates both the pre-Soviet and the Soviet elements in interethnic hostilities.

The forebears of the present-day Armenians and Azeris have lived in Transcaucasia for many centuries. The first Armenian state was founded in 109 B.C.E. and extended from the Mediterranean Sea to the Black and Caspian seas. The Azeris can trace their roots back to before the eleventh century. A fundamental difference between them is religion: The Azeris are Muslims, and the Armenians are Christians. The Armenians officially adopted Christianity as a state religion at the beginning of the fourth century. The conversion of the ancestors of the Azeris to Islam began in the eleventh century, when they were invaded by the Islamic Seljuks. Associated with this religious difference, of course, are many cultural differences.

Before the Russians annexed these territories to the Russian Empire in the first half of the nineteenth century, the Muslims had ruled over the Christians for many centuries. Under the rule of the Russian Empire, the Armenians acquired a large share of the key economic and political positions in the area. This situation continued under Soviet rule. The growth of Armenian political and economic power during the Russian and Soviet periods was seen differently by the Armenians and the Azeris.

The Armenians saw their gains as the reward for superior education, skills, and effort. They viewed the Azeris as a backward people and had little respect for them. The Armenians' attitudes were influenced by their memories of having lost three-fourths of historically Armenian territory to Muslim Turkey. When Nagorno-Karabakh was made part of Soviet (Muslim) Azerbaijan, old wounds were reopened. There was also a fear of genocide, stemming from the 1915 massacre of approximately 1.5 million[6] Armenians by the Ottoman Turks and the 1918 massacre of 20,000 Baku Armenians by the Azeris. (Suny, 1992, p. 493)

The Azeris considered the superior position of the Armenians to be the result of official favoritism during the period of tsarist rule that continued into the period of Soviet rule. They felt that Armenian claims to parts of Azerbaijan heavily populated by Armenians were the first step in an Armenian plan to take control of the entire area. Both the Turks and the Azeris claimed that the killing of Armenians in 1915 was the Armenians' own fault and, in any case, was not as extreme as the Armenians claimed. (Suny, 1992)

The trigger for the Armenian-Azeri violence that erupted during the Gorbachev era was the disputed territory of Nagorno-Karabakh.[7] Karabakh is a mountainous territory in western Azerbaijan which is close to, but does not touch, the eastern border of Armenia (see Map 4-1). Armenians ruled it until the early nineteenth century, when it became part of the Russian Empire. During tsarist rule it developed closer administrative links to the area that subsequently became Soviet Azerbaijan. After the October Revolution the Armenians in Karabakh wanted to become part of the Union Republic of Armenia, but they were forced to remain in Azerbaijan.[8] Thus, for virtually all of the

---

6. This figure is disputed by the Turks, as are most of the beliefs the Armenians hold with respect to this particular incident in the common history of these two countries. To appreciate the magnitude of what the Armenians believe to be true, it should be noted that the 1989 Soviet census showed a total Armenian population of 4.6 million (see Table 4-1).
7. Although the Western media usually use the full name, the Armenians call the territory Karabakh, and we too will do so in the following discussion.
8. There was a short period after the Communist takeover when the new Soviet government promised Karabakh that it would be joined with Armenia. There are several versions of the reasons why this did not happen (one of which has been given previously). For purposes of this discussion,

Soviet period Karabakh was an enclave within Azerbaijan and had the status of an autonomous province.

This was an unusual situation in the Soviet federal order. No other autonomous national region with an ethnic majority that was the same as that of a neighboring union republic was kept separate from that republic. To a Westerner looking at a map, Karabakh's status might seem to make sense, because Karabakh appears as an island surrounded by Azerbaijani territory. But having geographically separate pieces of land belong to the same union republic was not unprecedented in the Soviet federation. For example, Nakhichevan, which was also part of Azerbaijan, lay west of Armenia and did not touch any part of Azerbaijan (see Map 4-1). Similarly, the Russian republic had an enclave around the city of Kaliningrad, which was between Lithuania and Poland— completely separate from the rest of Russia.

In addition, Moscow had changed other borders between Soviet republics. Between 1921 and 1980 "there were ninety interrepublican territorial transfers that were large enough to be registered in central government gazettes and a far larger number . . . that were too small to be included there." (Goble, 1990b, p. 20) Forty-five of them took place after 1930 and three between 1971 and 1980. Thus, it was not unreasonable for the Armenians to think that the fact that Armenians constituted an overwhelming majority in the population of Karabakh entitled Karabakh to become part of Soviet Armenia. The reform position of Gorbachev raised their hopes because a large number of these border changes had taken place during politically permissive times.

Over the years, as the Azerbaijani rulers tried to minimize the use of the Armenian language and to suppress Armenian culture, tension increased. Contacts with Armenia were discouraged. The Armenians believed the Azeri rulers were investing more heavily in the economic growth of Azeri-dominated parts of the union republic than in Karabakh. Although Azeris continued to live in Karabakh and Armenians continued to live in Azeri-dominated regions, there was very little social mixing and almost no intermarriage. Each group retained its separate identity.

After the death of Stalin, Armenian nationalism began to intensify. At that point, there were three major issues: (1) the 1915 genocide by the Ottoman Turks and Armenian determination that it would never happen again; (2) the preservation of the Armenian national culture and language (including its unique alphabet); and (3) the annexation of Karabakh by Armenia. During the 1960s and 1970s there were appeals to Moscow and scattered incidents of violence, but Moscow chose to stay relatively detached from the problem. When Gorbachev became General Secretary and instituted his policy of glasnost, the Armenians found more outlets for their pent-up frustration. To their earlier set of key issues was added growing concern about environmental pollution and the corruption of the Armenian Communist leadership.

---

it is sufficient to note that Karabakh remained under the jurisdiction of Azerbaijan and that this arrangement violated the right to self-determination of a majority of the inhabitants of Karabakh.

Then a series of steps triggered the war that soon engulfed Karabakh and spilled over into places like Sumgait and Baku, on the Caspian Sea in Azerbaijan. In January 1988, the Karabakh Armenians formally petitioned Moscow for a referendum in Karabakh to determine whether its status should be changed. During February, demonstrations were held in Stepanakert (the capital of Karabakh) and Yerevan (the capital of Armenia). On February 20, the Karabakh Soviet of People's Deputies voted 110 to 17 to ask for annexation to Armenia. Moscow found itself in a no-win position, because a decision for either Azerbaijan or Armenia would be seen as unreasonable favoritism by the loser. The Politburo decided to leave things the way they were. It also replaced an unpopular Karabakh leader, sent troops into the area, and called for calm. That was not enough, however. Demonstrations and violent incidents escalated. On February 28, a riot started in Sumgait. During the two days it lasted, at least thirty-one people were killed—mostly Armenians—some brutally.

Although the reasons for these riots were, and remain, unclear, they triggered Armenian fears of genocide at the hands of the Turkic peoples surrounding them. Both sides began to take more extreme and inflexible positions, and any hope that the Karabakh situation could be settled peacefully began to fade. Slowly but inexorably, the dispute escalated to out-and-out war between Armenia and Azerbaijan. The leadership in Moscow, which had more than enough troubles of its own at that time, was unable to stop the fighting. After the disintegration of the Soviet Union, other members of the international community, as well as the Commonwealth of Independent States (CIS), began to become involved. As of mid-1994 the international community had been unable to come up with a viable solution that would at least stop the violence. (Fuller, 1992; Fuller, 1994a; Fuller 1994b; *Washington Post,* March 13, 1994, p. A27)

The fighting between Armenia and Azerbaijan has deep pre-Soviet roots. On the Armenian side, there is powerful resentment over centuries of domination by the Muslims. Added to this resentment is fear that the long-term agenda of the Azerbaijanis and the Turks includes the elimination of Armenians in that part of the world. This fear is fueled by the Armenians' frequent evocation of the 1915 massacre; memories of 1915 also give added urgency to the Armenians' desire to be able to guarantee the safety of Armenians in Karabakh.

The Azeris also have memories of centuries of Muslim rule. The memory of their past power makes it hard for the Muslim Azeris to accept the economic and political prominence that the Armenians acquired under tsarist and Soviet rule. Azeris fear that the Armenian agenda includes taking Azeri territory (starting with Karabakh) and eventually gaining political control over all of the lands where the Azeris now live and over which they rule. Added to this fear is the normal reluctance of any country to give up part of its territory to a historical enemy. Fighting to defend its territory is a basic function of any state.

Soviet policy worsened the underlying tensions inherited from the pre-Soviet period. The decision to allow Karabakh to become part of the Union Republic of Azerbaijan instead of the Union Republic of Armenia might have seemed expedient at the time. In the long run, however, it sowed the seeds of violence. The prominence of Armenians in the CPSU during most of the Soviet period made it seem to the Azeris that Moscow was biased in favor of the Armenians. Armenian prominence in the Party also fostered resentment toward both the leadership of the Soviet Union and the neighboring Armenians. The final and arguably the most important factor contributing to the outbreak of violence was the failure of the CPSU leadership to appreciate the depth of Azeri-Armenian hostility or the potential for uncontrollable violence inherent in the Karabakh problem.

The case of Armenia and Azerbaijan is a dramatic example of interethnic enmity preventing normal relations among the Soviet successor states, but there are many similar cases. Some involve problems that cross the borders of the newly independent countries, as does the Armenian-Azerbaijani dispute. Others involve problems that are internal to one or more of the successor states. An example of the latter is the ongoing hostility between Georgians and Abkhazians. The latter are a tiny minority in western Georgia that wants to be independent from Georgia—despite the fact that Abkhazians constitute only 18 percent of the population of the former Abkhazian Autonomous Republic. (*Washington Post*, July 3, 1993, p. A20) The only safe generalization is that ethnic loyalties create problems that do not go away either quickly or easily. These problems will seriously interfere with the nation-building efforts of the successor countries and may even precipitate disputes that could escalate into additional violence—as they already have done in Armenia, Azerbaijan, and Georgia.

The most obvious potential for confrontation involves the border issue. Should the present borders between and within the former union republics remain as they were under Soviet rule? Or should they be redrawn to take into account the wishes of ethnic groups within the successor countries or ethnic groups split by the borders of the Soviet union republics? Also at issue is the relationship between the various nationalities and the Russians who dominated them first in the Russian Empire and subsequently in the Soviet Empire.

THE RUSSIANS: ELDER BROTHER OR COMMON ENEMY?

Basic to understanding ethnic and nation-building problems in the former Soviet Union and its successor countries is an understanding of the implications of two facts: (1) The Soviet Empire was a direct descendant of the Russian Empire. (2) The political leadership of both the Russian Empire and the Soviet Empire was dominated by Russians. The Russians are subject to many of the same historical fears and hatreds as the other ethnic groups in the former Soviet Union. In addition, the Russians have a set of problems associated with their historical dominance in the region. (Szporluk, 1992)

The advent of glasnost and subsequent events made the Russians a target of anger, criticism, and demands for change. In addition, the disintegration of the

Soviet Union caused a profound identity crisis among many Russians who identified with the Soviet Union and did not see it as imposing an alien rule. As an 18-year-old university student put it:

> We don't even know who we are anymore. They tell me I'm a "Russian" now. What does that mean? Does it mean that my parents, who live in Uzbekistan, are foreigners? Will I need a visa to visit them: I think of myself as Soviet. I know nothing about Russia. In school, our history lessons began with the revolution and 1917. I am all for the changes in this country, but I am completely confused. What does it mean—"Russian?" (*Washington Post,* December 30, 1991, p. A1)

The non-Russian peoples of the Soviet Union had a point of view similar to that of the bewildered student but a different emotional reaction. For example, a British visitor to Azerbaijan reported: "The words Soviet and Russian were treated as though they were synonymous. People saw their rich country as having been robbed of oil, poisoned with insecticides and given nothing in return." (Richards, 1990, p. 127; also see Szporluk, 1990, p. 17) Even outside the Soviet Union, people routinely said "Russia" when talking about the Soviet Union.

The student's parents were probably in Uzbekistan because under both the tsars and the CPSU many Russians moved into non-Russian areas of the Russian Republic and the other union republics. As of 1991, the percentage of Russians living in the non-Russian union republics ranged from 2 percent of the total population of Armenia to 38 percent of the total population of Kazakhstan. (*New York Times,* August 29, 1991, p. A19) In almost all of the major ethnic subdivisions of the Soviet Union, there was a significant Russian presence, and the Russians' status as the dominant Soviet nationality frequently caused resentment.

Now, in the post-Soviet era, people fear that the presence of a significant number of Russians could lead to Russian Federation interference in the affairs of the other successor countries. This fear is not unrealistic. Discrimination against Russian minorities in the successor countries and concern for their safety provoke anxiety among many Russians, and some of them advocate armed intervention by the Russian Federation if the situation warrants it. Moreover, this posture has won official sanction in Russian foreign policy. The Russian Federation has claimed the right to protect Russians in the other former union republics.

The Russians had dominated all of the other nationalities under tsarist rule and continued to do so under Soviet rule. (Szporluk, 1990) Many scholars argue that Soviet rule was much more oppressive than tsarist rule. For example, historian Richard Pipes (1992, p. 80) asserts: "From the point of view of self-rule the Communist government was even less generous to the minorities than its tsarist predecessor had been: it destroyed independent parties, tribal self-rule, religious and cultural institutions." Most of the agents of this oppressive rule were Russians.

Moreover, under both regimes, Russians were encouraged to move to non-

Russian regions in order to help Russify the other nationalities. This population shift put Russians in a unique position. In the union republics (and in other ethnically based political subdivisions), the titular nationality was usually the primary ethnic group, and all other ethnic groups were subordinate. The Russians, however, though a minority, could not be treated as subordinate. Russians were officially the dominant ethnic group throughout the USSR and did not hesitate to claim their status as the senior partner in ethnic relations, no matter where they happened to be located. (Karklins, 1986)

In some union republics, the titular nationality regarded the influx of Russians as a threat to its national identity. Particularly in Kazakhstan and Latvia, the titular nationality felt itself being engulfed by the large number of Russians in the population. Russification, however, was not a matter of mere numbers. The incoming Russians were likely to lay claim to preferred social, economic, and political positions. Thus, the indigenous people felt that they were being made into an underclass. Because of their relative powerlessness, they tended to respond with minor hostile acts directed at individual Russians. For example, Russians were often treated rudely in public places or made the butt of jokes. (Karklins, 1992, pp. 53–54)

A major battleground was language. (Anderson & Silver, 1990; Denber, 1992, pp. 321–386; Dunlop, 1986) In the multiethnic Soviet Union there was no common language. The Soviet people not only spoke a host of native languages but wrote their languages in several different alphabets. Early in the Soviet period, the Communist leaders introduced a common language, Russian, in all parts of the Soviet Union. This policy was practical in the sense that widespread knowledge of one language can lessen the communication problems that naturally arise in a multiethnic country. Many, however, saw only the symbolic significance of Russian as the common language.

The Russians believed that Russian was the most advanced language—the language of science and technology. They regarded linguistic Russification as the best and most practical solution to the problem of interethnic communication. (Anderson & Silver, 1984) However, if Russian was the common language of communication and commerce and if Russian was taught to all schoolchildren, other languages were likely to fall into disuse and die out. The way the Soviet leadership carried out this policy of bilingualism showed great insensitivity to the cultural and symbolic functions of indigenous languages.

The purges of the 1930s also decimated the cultural and literary elite of the non-Russian, as well as the Russian, peoples. Nahaylo and Swoboda (1989, p. 78) refer to the purges as the "beheading of the non-Russian nations." The purges delivered an additional blow to the continuity and status of the native languages. After the purges, fewer and fewer books were published in non-Russian languages, and those that were published tended to be of inferior quality. Sometimes the local alphabet was not even respected. By 1930, the Latin alphabet had replaced the Arabic script in the Muslim areas. Then, between 1938 and 1940, the Russian alphabet (Cyrillic) replaced the Latin alphabet. The effects that such changes can have on local culture and learning are obvious.

In Armenia and Georgia the native language and alphabet were allowed to remain untouched, but Moscow insisted that students learn Russian in school. Everywhere outside the Russian Republic people had to face the issue of what language to use in everyday life. Non-Russians who wanted to get ahead were forced to be bilingual. The Russians did not experience the same pressure to be bilingual, and many were not—even when they were living permanently in a non-Russian-speaking union republic.

Estonia is a good example. Starting in the 1940s after Estonia's annexation to the Soviet Union, the Estonians were subjected to a concerted campaign by the central authorities to increase the use of Russian at the expense of Estonian. This campaign continued until the 1980s, with "resources . . . systematically and increasingly diverted from teaching and publishing in [Estonian] to bolstering the Russian tongue." (Kionka, 1991, p. 21) Estonian schoolchildren were given more training in Russian than in Estonian.

The central authorities argued that this policy promoted bilingualism. From an Estonian point of view, however, the goal seemed to be the gradual replacement of Estonian by Russian. Thus, in 1989 the Estonians used their new freedom under Gorbachev to pass a law making Estonian the official language of the republic. The law gave all state workers four years to become competent in Estonian. Many Estonians hoped that this law, together with other new laws on citizenship and immigration, would discourage Russians from moving to Estonia and perhaps even encourage some to return to Russia.

The language law caused much resentment among Russians living in Estonia. Although Russians constituted more than 30 percent of the Estonian population[9] (*Washington Post*, September 3, 1991, p. A12), only 14 percent had bothered to learn Estonian. (Kionka, 1991, p. 22) One Russian holding a government position in Estonia remarked, "There was never any reason to learn Estonian. Who would have ever thought we would be anything but a part of the Soviet Union." (*Washington Post*, September 30, 1991, p. A13)

That quotation illustrates two beliefs: (1) that Russian was the only language necessary for living in any part of the Soviet Union and (2) that there was no need for a Russian-speaker living in Estonia and holding an important government office there to try to communicate with Estonians in their native language. This attitude was common because most Russians could, in fact, manage quite well without knowing Estonian. Most lived in the industrialized northeast, where they constituted 96 percent of the population of Narva, the region's most important city. Even in Tallinn, the Estonian capital, 51 percent of the population were Russians. They lived in Russian enclaves, shopped in Russian stores, and sent their children to Russian schools. It was easy for them to ignore the Estonians and their language.

All over the Soviet Union, the language issue caused a great deal of friction

---

9. This is a Soviet estimate. The Estonian government placed the figure higher, at 40 percent. (*Washington Post*, September 30, 1991, p. A17)

between Russians and non-Russians. Language usage became a battleground where the chief weapon was passive aggression. Indigenous people would pretend that they did not understand or speak Russian. "When in the Ukraine, speak Ukrainian." Less often, but occasionally, language disputes resulted in violence. For example, a Russian was reportedly murdered for refusing to reply in Tuvinian to a question asked in Tuvinian.[10] (*Washington Post*, October 7, 1990, p. A1) Russians facing such behavior often reacted with confusion or hostility, because it seemed obvious to them that Russian was the most practical common language. After all, a majority of the population of the USSR was Russian. Because they did not encounter comparable problems, many found it hard to sympathize with the position of the non-Russians.

Thus, we have a picture of the Russians as a colonizing ethnic group. Although the goal of much Soviet policy was to create a new Soviet identity among the peoples of the Soviet Union, policies were based on assumptions about the superiority of Russians and things Russian. Reinforcing this mind-set was the conviction that the way to make the Soviet Union into a modern nation-state was to eliminate all but the most superficial ethnic differences. The Soviet leadership, however, never came close to achieving this goal. As soon as glasnost permitted, ethnic loyalties and nationality rights began to be asserted all over the Soviet Union. From the Baltic republics, which wanted complete independence, to the Central Asian republics, which wanted more self-rule, virtually all of the major (and some of the minor) nationalities demonstrated the extent to which they had not been either Russified or Sovietized. Very clearly, their primary loyalty was still to their ethnic groups. Was this also true of the Russians?

As of the last Soviet census, in 1989, over 25 million Russians (17.4 percent) lived outside the Russian Republic. (*Narodnoe Khoziaistvo SSSR v 1990 g.*, 1991, p. 81) During the years before and after the breakup of the USSR, many of them became refugees returning to Russia. In Russia, however, grossly overcrowded housing conditions and serious scarcities in virtually all consumer goods made the returning Russians less than totally welcome. A Russian oil worker who had fled Tajikistan said sadly: "We believed in the slogan of friendship between peoples. We did our internationalist duty for 32 years. Now we find ourselves without a home and without a homeland. Nobody seems to want us." (*Washington Post*, October 7, 1990, p. A35; see also Marnie & Slater, 1993)

As that quotation shows, the gradual collapse of the Soviet Union had an effect on the Russians that was different from its effect on other ethnic groups. They did not see themselves as oppressors or the indigenous people among whom they lived and worked as victims. Most Russians thought they had left Russia to bring the benefits of their skills and education to the non-Russian people, and many developed a genuine affection for the lands where they

---

10. Tuva was an autonomous republic on the border between the USSR and Mongolia.

settled. In short, they saw their presence in the non-Russian areas as the result of altruism and mutual advantage, not oppressive colonization.

The Russians had a sort of dual identity. They thought of themselves as Russians, but within that identity was a large element of imperial consciousness—Soviet identity was an extension of Russian identity. (Anisimov, 1991; Hosking, 1991) Being criticized by the other national groups and ignominiously forced out of parts of the Soviet Union that they regarded as part of a larger Russia gave new impetus to a resurgence of Russian nationalism that had begun in the mid-1960s. (Spechler, 1990, pp. 282–287) Formerly, Russian nationalism had been bound up with the preservation of the empire. Now Russians began to focus on the belief that they had made great sacrifices for the development and welfare of the non-Russian nationalities and that they were resented instead of appreciated. Thus, they began to ask, "Who needs an empire?" (V. Shlapentokh in *The Washington Post*, April 29, 1990, p. D2)

Many Russians were hurt and angry because of the hostility and demands of the other nationalities. They were also resentful because of the economic deprivations they believed they had endured. To some extent (estimates of how much differ), they saw their economic deprivation as stemming from the aid they gave to the rest of the Soviet Union. In 1990, Russia was subsidizing the other union republics at a cost of approximately 70 billion rubles a year. (*The Economist*, October 20, 1990, p. 10) For example, in 1990 Russia sold oil to the other Soviet republics at about 45 percent of the world market price, but it bought color television sets from other republics at 438 percent of the world market price. (*Washington Post*, April 29, 1990, p. A8)

Russia is rich in natural resources, the proceeds of which were used to finance projects and activities all over the Soviet Union. Thus, it is not surprising that one form of Russian nationalism was exemplified by calls for "economic sovereignty," the right of the Russians to use their wealth to help themselves rather than the other ethnic groups—at least those located outside Russia. In fact, during the economically bruising Gorbachev years, the Soviet economist Vladimir Kvint pointed out that it might be economically wise for Russia to secede from the Soviet Union. (*Forbes Magazine*, February 19, 1990, pp. 103–108)

The first person to suggest that the Russians might be better off without the Soviet Empire was Alexander Solzhenitsyn in 1973. (Hosking, 1991) He pointed out that the empire was ruled not by the Russian nation but by the Communist Party. At the time, his ideas were dismissed. They did not come to the fore again until the late 1980s, when the Russians began to perceive themselves as exploited and impoverished by the demands and needs of the other Soviet republics.

The first major Russian nationalist movement was the anti-Semitic fringe movement *Pamyat'* (Memory). Later, moderate Russian nationalist organizations began to arise. One of them, Memorial, had a more balanced view, acknowledging that the Russians had been both oppressors and victims. As its name suggests, however, Memorial was most interested in shedding light on the past. As a result, other organizations sprang up to represent Russian nationalist interests.

Initially, Russian nationalist political movements were not able to mobilize the Russian people as effectively as many of the other national fronts had mobilized non-Russians. The main problem was that the Russians, unlike the non-Russians, had no common enemy or single vision. (Hosking, 1991) One of the most successful Russian movements was Democratic Russia, which was instrumental in Yeltsin's rise to power and the defeat of the August 1991 coup. At the time, it envisioned itself not as a party or even a proto-party but as an umbrella movement facilitating the coordination of many smaller parties. As might be expected under the circumstances, it was too split internally to put forth a coherent political program for the future of Russia. Yeltsin tried to dampen Russian nationalist sentiment in his effort to build a viable multiethnic Russian Federation: "The Russian state," he said, "having chosen democracy and freedom, will never be an empire, nor an older or younger brother. It will be an equal among equals." (Hosking, 1991, p. 8)

Especially after the coup, however, the pain and anger of the Russian people opened the way for political movements with less benign slogans and goals. One was the Liberal Democratic Party led by Vladimir Zhirinovsky. Zhirinovsky was catapulted to fame when he ran against Boris Yeltsin in the 1991 Russian presidential election and won more than 6 million votes. In the December 1993 parliamentary election his importance increased when his party won the second largest number of seats in the lower house of the new Russian parliament. This victory made the Liberal Democrats the strongest party in an antireform coalition.

Most commentators saw this outcome as a protest against the hardships of the Yeltsin economic reform. Zhirinovsky's nationalist appeal, however, could not be ignored. "[T]he essence of Zhirinovsky's political platform [was] that the Russians were discriminated against throughout the Soviet period, often living in worse conditions than the relatively privileged non-Russians." (Tolz, 1994, p. 7) Some observers compared him to Hitler, and his rhetoric seemed to support the comparison. For example: "I'm a dictator. What I am going to do is bad, but it is good for Russia," and "If you do vote for me, I'll make you obey my orders. And you'll be happy, all of you. This country needs a tough military regime and a secret police." (*Washington Post*, December 30, 1991, p. A10) This message appealed to those who thought that Russia needed an autocratic ruler and who compared the current situation to other "times of trouble" in Russian history.

These developments gave rise to a Russian imperial nationalism. As one extreme nationalist leader put it: "The basic principle that links these [nationalist and antireform] organizations is statism—a desire to preserve and develop the millennium-old tradition of [Russia as a] great power." (Torbakov, 1992, p. 11) People gravitating to this movement tend to be imperialist, anti-Western, and antidemocratic. Many think—however unrealistically—in terms of a Russian sphere of influence that would encompass all of Europe and Asia.

Finally, it should be noted that during the last few years of the USSR, more and more Soviet citizens (including Russians) began to think that their troubles were attributable to the social and political order under which they lived, not to any individual or ethnic group. Poll respondents from all over the Soviet Union increasingly blamed their troubles on the Moscow leadership and the Soviet system, instead of on the Russians or any other ethnic group. Correspondingly, more and more Russians began to cast their lot with the indigenous people among whom they lived, joining non-Russian popular fronts and expressing support for the independence of the non-Russian republics. (Goble, 1990a)

Russia still dominates the land mass that was the Soviet Union. It is by far the largest of the successor countries—like the old Soviet Union, stretching from eastern Europe to the Pacific. It has inherited many of the trappings of Soviet power, such as the Soviet seat on the United Nations Security Council. If the Commonwealth of Independent States, which to date has played a relatively minor role in the politics of the region, ultimately fails to provide a strong unifying political force, the Russian Federation will be treading a thin line. (*Literaturnaia gazeta,* April 29, 1992, p. 11) It wishes to maintain good relations with the other successor countries in what it calls the "near abroad" (*blizhnee zarubezh'e*) and perhaps even play a leadership role, which it thinks it deserves because of its size and power. But any government in Moscow needs to be responsive to the wishes of the Russian nationalists concerned with the status of Russians in the "near abroad." These Russians feel entitled to remain where they are, but they look to Russia for aid and protection. Slowly and tentatively Russia is trying to decide what kind of a country it will become.

NATION-BUILDING: PAST AND FUTURE

It is possible to create a state by means of power politics, but the stability of such a state over time depends on whether a psychological nation has been built. (Bloom, 1990, p. 56) As we consider the territory and people that once made up the Soviet Union, it is necessary to look both backward and forward. The fragments of the Soviet Empire have declared themselves separate and independent states. To what extent is each of them likely to succeed in the task of nation-building?

It is clear that the Soviet leadership was never able to destroy old national identities sufficiently to be able to replace them with a viable Soviet identity. (Connor, 1972) They were most successful with the Russians, but only because their concept of a Soviet identity was so closely tied to their concept of a Russian identity. To create a Soviet nation from all the varied ethnic groups in the Soviet Empire, the CPSU, at a minimum, would have had to do two things: (1) persuade the people that their national loyalties were no longer worth clinging to and (2) offer them a more attractive alternative embodied in a Soviet nation.

In retrospect, it seems that the process of persuasion concentrated on the latter more than on the former. After all, Marxism was an internationalist ideology. It assumed that people's position in society was more important than their ethnic identity or national loyalty. Accordingly, it was easy for the CPSU leadership (including Gorbachev) to suppose that as Soviet citizens became more and more aware of what they had in common, their nationalist passions and loyalties would spontaneously fade and disappear. This major miscalculation led to another. The Soviet leadership thought that a Soviet national identity could be inculcated quickly if information was tightly controlled and if the process of persuasion was pervasive and carefully orchestrated. As a nation-building effort, this strategy only appeared to succeed—contrary voices were being suppressed. In fact, many of the actions that the Soviet regime undertook in its attempt at nation-building had an effect opposite to the intended effect: They tended to strengthen national loyalties.

Members of the various ethnic groups looked at their neighbors, remembered past slights—or worse—and found it difficult to regard those others as "us" rather than as "them." Ironically, many of the actions that the Soviet regime took to make such groups behave as though they were a single people only served to call their attention to their differences. Moreover, many of them saw these differences as irreconcilable. Because all but the mildest expression of ethnic identity[11] was unacceptable to leaders who used ample amounts of force to rule, the various ethnic groups had to pretend that the differences did not exist or, at least, did not matter. But this pretense did not prevent resentments from building up. It led to a multitude of covertly expressed hostilities, which magnified the importance of the differences and fed the notion that they were irreconcilable.

Also, the new Soviet identity being pushed on the non-Russians was too Russian in form and content. An eclectic identity reflecting the diversity of the peoples of the USSR was never tried—and, in all fairness, might have been impossible to achieve. Soviet nation-building, then, was inextricably intertwined with Russification. This made it unattractive to many of the other ethnic groups, especially those (like the Ukrainians) who placed great importance on being different from the Russians and had done so for hundreds of years. Becoming one national unit, particularly when doing so seemed to mean being "more Russian," held little allure.

Some of the non-Russian groups, like the Turkic people, were not even Slavic. Like most colonial peoples, they wished to keep their own cultures, languages, and alphabets. Many non-Slavic groups, such as the Central Asians and Jews, were victims of prejudice[12] and anti-Semitism. Reinforcing this was the overt or covert clash between their religious heritages (which were often inextricably intermingled with their cultural heritages) and the militant atheism of the Soviet state. Finally, many of the non-Slavic groups had cultures that were radically different from Russian culture. For them, becoming more Soviet meant changing to an extent that was virtually impossible—at least in the short

---

11. Groups that dressed in national costume and entertained with ethnic songs and dances were encouraged by the regime as a harmless form of national expression. For foreigners, they were a delight. Members of the ethnic groups involved sometimes regarded them with less enthusiasm.
12. European Russians often regarded the darker peoples of Asia in much the same way as racist Americans regard African-Americans.

run. Although the Soviet regime occasionally showed some recognition of this problem, policies like imposing a uniform school curriculum undermined any efforts that the central authorities made to be sensitive to the importance of ancient traditions.

Furthermore, Soviet efforts at nation-building failed to meet the two crucial prerequisites that we mentioned at the beginning of this chapter. The inhabitants of a state must believe that the state offers them the best protection against external and internal foes. The inhabitants must also believe that they will receive significant benefits if they give their primary loyalty to the state.

The Soviet state only partially succeeded in assuring its diverse peoples that the state would keep them secure. True, the Soviet military (after faltering initially) repulsed the Germans during World War II, but the effect of this victory on the non-Russian nationalities was limited because both rhetorically and symbolically it was presented as more a Russian victory than a Soviet one. Also, many non-Russian nationalists (notably the Ukrainians) collaborated with the Nazis, who promised them independence from the Soviet Union if the Germans won.

During the Cold War, the mighty Soviet military machine seemed to ensure the safety of the Soviet people from their Western enemies. Curiously, however, very few Westerners were treated as enemies by ordinary Soviet citizens. Americans who lived in the Soviet Union during that time usually found themselves to be the objects of curiosity and friendliness. Rather than fearing and hating the people of the United States, the Soviet people, whatever their nationality, seemed eager to find common threads in the Soviet and American cultures and to imitate the American way of life. The Soviet leadership devoted an enormous amount of national wealth to supporting its defense against Western "imperialism." The price for security from external enemies was the relative impoverishment of the consumer sector and a standard of living (for all but the most privileged Soviet citizens) that was extremely low in comparison with living standards in other industrialized countries.

Internal security—security within the Soviet Union—was another matter. No individual or ethnic group could feel secure *from the state*. Beginning in the 1920s, the Soviet state was responsible for the starvation, exile, imprisonment, and execution of a multitude of its population. Not only individuals but entire ethnic groups were victims. These events were constant reminders that the Soviet state could not be depended upon to guarantee the security of its people from threats within its borders. The state actually posed the main threat to personal and group security, and the Soviet people were acutely aware of this fact. To some extent, they could avoid problems by behaving in the "proper" way. But proper behavior was no guarantee of security under a capricious ruler, be he the supreme leader in the Kremlin or the chairman of the local Party committee.

This brings us to the second prerequisite for successful nation-building: The leaders and institutions embodying the state must be perceived as acting beneficently toward the individuals and ethnic groups that make up its population.

Obviously, if the state poses a threat to the physical well-being of individuals and groups, there is a problem. There was also the additional problem of the negative effect of the economic system on the lives of the Soviet people. The state ran the entire economy, so the USSR had no private sector in the Western sense. Thus, workers' resentments against unfair and uncaring employers became resentment directed at their rulers. Consumers' resentments about scarce, overpriced, and shoddy goods also became resentment directed at the rulers.

Most Soviet citizens had little reason to regard the Soviet leadership as a beneficent provider of jobs, goods, and services. They were guaranteed a low level of economic welfare but had little opportunity to better their lot significantly. In contrast, those who ruled lived very well (by Soviet standards), and most ordinary Soviet citizens were aware of the disparity.

Thus, if the Soviet state succeeded in creating a Soviet national identity, that national identity was—more often than not—little more than skin deep and very fragile. Although some Soviet citizens (especially many Russians) internalized loyalty to the Soviet state, most people simply went through the motions, complying with the demands made on them in order to create a decent life. The Soviet state, they assumed, would last into the indefinite future—whether they liked it or not—so it was expedient to accommodate and make the best of their situation.

The loyalty of those Soviet citizens who had a reasonably firm identification with the Soviet state was put to a stern test in the 1980s. Before the death of Brezhnev it was clear that the economy was faltering badly. The Soviet people had become accustomed to a standard of living that was rising (albeit slowly); now it began to fail. The economy was stagnating and the leadership seemed unable to get it moving again.

Perestroika was, first and foremost, a plan for reinvigorating the Soviet economy. Glasnost was part of an effort to mobilize popular support for economic renewal. Instead of improving under perestroika, however, the economy went into a rapid decline, and the revelations of glasnost shocked even the most committed Soviet loyalists. The result was a more and more acute sense of dissatisfaction, which made the increasingly visible nationalist movements more attractive. The vast, bureaucratic Soviet state had failed the people. Perhaps smaller nation-states could be more responsive to their needs and thus would be objects more worthy of their loyalty. For the 100-plus ethnic groups in the Soviet Empire, the time seemed ripe for more national sovereignty or perhaps even independence.

To summarize, the Soviet people lived within a state that demanded loyalty to a regime that was led primarily by Russians (or their agents) and that tried to impose basically Russian ways. Soviet citizens were asked to be loyal to political institutions that constantly threatened their personal and group security. And the Soviet state gave them few of the good things of life. Instead, it constantly asked them to sacrifice for a glorious future that never seemed to arrive. Gorbachev's pleas to work hard for perestroika sounded suspiciously familiar. His listeners were profoundly cynical. They had heard it all before—

from Stalin, from Khrushchev, from Brezhnev, and from Kosygin.[13] For a while, glasnost made it seem as though this time things might be different. When deterioration rather than improvement resulted, all but the most optimistic lost patience with the Kremlin leadership once and for all. Having given up on their Communist leaders in the Kremlin, they began looking closer to home for leadership.

Most of the leaders of the Soviet state, as absolutist rulers, never fully appreciated the extent to which they had failed to build a viable Soviet nation and what that failure might mean for the future. Of those who did see dark clouds on the horizon, most appeared too ideologically blind (Goble, 1990c; Hill, 1992) or arrogant to get the message and do something about it while there was still time. Perhaps they thought that brute force could sustain Party rule forever. Force, however, cannot sustain a state indefinitely. Among the populace, there must be a bedrock of psychological identification and internalization supporting loyalty. Sooner or later an empire must become a nation-state if it is to survive in the contemporary world. The Communist Party of the Soviet Union got compliance from most of the people most of the time, but mere compliance will only get you so far. In the case of the Soviet Union, it is clear that no successful nation-building effort could have been undone so rapidly and so completely.

Now the Soviet Union has broken up into fifteen separate countries. If they are to remain independent, they will have to solve the problems of nation-building. Because all of them are multiethnic to a greater or lesser degree, they will inherit many of the same nation-building problems faced by the Soviet Union. On the other hand, with the possible exception of the Russian Federation, they do not face the issues of sheer size and diversity that the Soviet Union faced.

As we watch them go through the process of nation-building, there are some things that are particularly important to keep in mind. First and foremost is the fact that not all of the successor countries are at the same point in their nation-building process. They vary greatly in the extent to which their populations already had some significant sense of national identity when they got their independence. Some were much further along than others. Related to this is the history of the majority nationality in each newly independent country, its attitudes, and its proportion in the population. Also significant are differences in the way the majority ethnic group has treated minority ethnic groups. Finally, there is great variation in the hopes and fears of each ethnic group. Are the expectations of different ethnic groups compatible or incompatible? Are the expectations of the majority attractive to minorities? Or do they evoke resentment or fear? Let us consider two examples, Lithuania and Moldova.

The Lithuanian people can look back on a long and at times glorious his-

13. Leonid Brezhnev and Alexei Kosygin came to power as joint leaders in 1964. Brezhnev was leader of the CPSU, and Kosygin was head of the government. This brief experiment with collective leadership was relatively short-lived. Brezhnev soon emerged as the top leader.

tory. In the fourteenth century, Lithuania was Europe's largest country, stretching from the Baltic Sea to the Black Sea. The Lithuanian language is an ancient one that many scholars think is (along with Latvian) closest to Proto-Indo-European.[14] (Clemens, 1991, p. 17) In more recent times, it was the union republic that led the way in demanding independence from the Soviet Union. Moscow's attempts to bully the Lithuanians into giving up their demands gave the fledgling Lithuanian nation a unifying external threat and martyrs to its cause. The population of contemporary Lithuania is approximately 80 percent Lithuanian. None of its minority ethnic groups comprises more than 10 percent of the population. Lithuania is well along in the nation-building process, and the prognosis for its future as a nation-state is excellent.[15]

At the time the Soviet Union disintegrated, the Moldavian Republic[16] was at the opposite extreme from Lithuania. It was a political unit without a clear identity except as a union republic in the Soviet Union. It had been artificially created on territory taken from Romania by Hitler and given to Stalin in their 1939 pact. The language that the Soviets called Moldavian is, with relatively minor differences, the same as Romanian. From early in its movement toward independence, many of its prominent nationalist leaders and a large proportion of its people called for reunification with Romania. One major factor discouraged immediate reunification after the disintegration of the USSR. Among the newly freed satellite countries of eastern Europe, Romania was notable for being in unusually bad shape economically and politically. The impact of reunification on Moldavia at that point would have been disastrous, and many of its leaders realized this. Thus, they proclaimed the independent state of Moldova.

From the start, the Moldovan nation-building effort was hampered by powerful divisive forces. First, there continued to be a substantial block of support for eventual reunification with Romania. They were not interested in creating the psychological prerequisites for a separate Moldovan nation-state. Second, there were significant segments of the population which did not want to be part of Moldova whether or not it stayed independent; they wanted independence from Moldova. In August 1990, ethnic Turks in Moldova claiming that the ethnically Romanian majority was discriminating against them tried to set up the Gaugauz Soviet Socialist Republic. Shortly afterward, the Russian and Ukrainian minorities created the Dniester Soviet Socialist Republic along the border between the Moldavian SSR and the Ukrainian SSR (see Map 4-2). These Slavic minorities feared reunification with Romania in the long run and

---

14. Proto-Indo-European is the root from which the languages of the Indo-European group are thought to have sprung. Both Russian and English are Indo-European.
15. Of course, other factors may affect this prognosis, but in this discussion we focus on the potential of the successor countries to carry out a successful nation-building process, and we hold other variables constant. In Chapter 9 we present a more complex analysis of the potential for Lithuania (and Moldova) to establish a stable democracy.
16. While it was part of the Soviet Union, Moldova was called the Moldavian Soviet Socialist Republic.

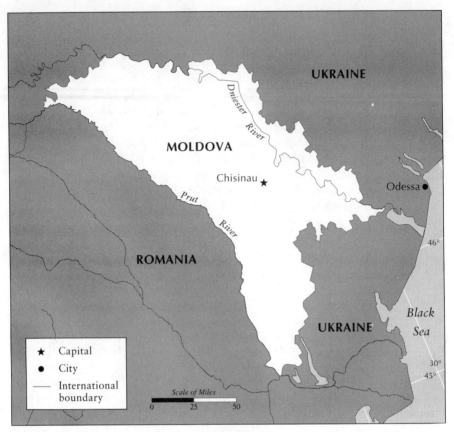

MAP 4-2 Moldova

Source: Modified from RFE/RL Research Report, 1 (36), 42.

discrimination in the short run. Some of their leaders talked of annexation to Ukraine.

Although the August 1991 coup gave Moldova its independence and a new name, it also polarized these ethnically divisive forces. In some cases, violence erupted. This fragmented situation did not last, however. Through an elaborate process of bargaining and compromise, the leaders of Moldova managed to unite all of these forces—except for those involved in the Russian insurrection on the east bank of the Dniester River—into a "government of national consensus." This government continued to try to win the support of the east-bank Slavs, primarily Russians.

Thus, although Moldova had a much greater problem with ethnic diversity than did Lithuania, it made a promising start toward overcoming that obstacle to nation-building. It is impossible to know whether this effort will be successful in the long run. In the short run, the outcome will depend on the extent to which Russian nationalists in the Russian Federation continue to support the Dniester Republic's government and whether Russian troops remain there.

As we consider the nation-building now taking place in the countries that were once part of the USSR, a series of questions can help us analyze their prospects. The answers, of course, will differ from one country to another. The questions are similar to those previously posed in this chapter: (1) How well does the successor country handle threats to the security of its people? (2) How well does the successor country provide for the welfare of its people? The answers to these questions (and to related ones that are discussed below) do not depend entirely on any objective situation. Rather, what is important is the combination of the objective situation and the perceptions of the people—whether or not their perceptions are accurate.

With regard to national security, an obvious question is whether the new country has one or more significant external foes. The related question, of course, is: How well is the new country dealing with the threat posed by its enemy or enemies? Put another way, does the new country have relatively peaceful and cooperative relations with its neighboring states? Second, is there a significant security threat within the country? The existence of even one seriously disaffected minority is crucial, as is its willingness to use force against the majority—and, of course, vice versa. How willing are the country's leaders to use violent or illegal means to deal with opposition?

With regard to providing for the welfare of the people, one important question is how economically strong and self-sufficient was the new country when it became independent. Because of the dismal state of the Soviet economy at the time of its disintegration, none of the successor countries emerged with an economy that was in very good shape. They also differ greatly in economic potential. Because Soviet economic policies created an enormous degree of interdependence among the Soviet republics, another important question is: How well has the country handled the fact that economic independence from the other successor countries is, in the short run, impossible? And because they differ greatly in their potential for independent economic viability, questions must be asked about such factors as natural resources, the skills and dedication of the work force, and the condition of the infrastructure.

Another set of questions seeks to shed light on the strength and wisdom of the new country's political leaders. Obviously, the quality of leadership is not unrelated to the other issues we have discussed. It does, however, have its own dimension. The most important is the degree of political stability that the leaders manage to achieve and the form of government that they establish for the long run.

When these countries became independent, they all asserted that they wanted to become democracies. Whether they eventually will achieve this objective is an open question. Some, like Lithuania, embarked on political independence with an experienced set of leaders, a high degree of political stability, and reasonably democratic institutions. During its first two years of full independence, Lithuania peacefully elected a new parliament and president. In both instances the winner was the former Communist Party of Lithuania. Nevertheless, the newly elected officials took office without incident and proceeded to rule with only peaceful opposition.

Georgia, in contrast, started out with an elected leadership and reasonably democratic institutions, but neither lasted for long. Very rapidly, Georgia disintegrated into political turmoil and violence. Whether the Georgians can find their way to some sort of viable democratic political system and what will happen if they do not remain open questions.

Nation-building is a dynamic process. A stable national identification and loyalty must be created, sustained, and nurtured. The stronger they are, the less likely they are to fade away under adversity. Thus, the nation-building effort must be centered on some system of ideology, mythology, and symbolism that transcends ethnic divisions and forges a common bond among the diverse peoples making up the emerging nation-state. The system that the Soviet leadership chose was based strongly on Marxism-Leninism. The system that most of the successor countries have chosen centers on nationalism, even though they are not ethnically homogeneous. Because most of them have significant ethnic minorities, they face some of the nation-building problems that challenged the Soviet Union. If they are to become nation-states, they must find a way to unite their people around a common source of national identity.

The Soviet Union chose Marxism-Leninism. Although it is usually considered an ideology, in the hands of the CPSU it took on the characteristics of myth and became a source of symbols and rituals. The effort to fashion a Soviet identity that transcended ethnic differences failed. Nevertheless, an understanding of what it was, how it worked, and why it failed can provide the basis for an informed perspective on the nation-building efforts of the newly independent countries.

REFERENCES

Anderson, B. A., & Silver, B. D. (1984). Equality, efficiency, and politics in Soviet bilingual education policy, 1934–1980. *American Political Science Review, 78*(4), 1019–1039.

———. (1990). Some factors in the linguistic and ethnic Russification of Soviet nationalities: Is everyone becoming Russian? In L. Hajda & M. Beissinger (Eds.), *The nationalities factor in Soviet politics and society* (pp. 95–130). Boulder, CO: Westview Press.

Anisimov, E. (1991). *Imperial consciousness in Russia*. Presented at the Kennan Institute for Advanced Russian Studies, Washington, DC.

Barner-Barry, C., & Rosenwein, R. (1985). *Psychological perspectives on politics*. Englewood Cliffs, NJ: Prentice-Hall.

Bloom, W. (1990). *Personal identity, national identity and international relations*. Cambridge, England: Cambridge University Press.

Brass, P. R. (1991). *Ethnicity and nationalism: Theory and comparison*. London: Sage.

Burg, S. L. (1990). Nationality elites and political change in the Soviet Union. In L. Hajda & M. Beissinger (Eds.), *The nationalities factor in Soviet politics and society* (pp. 24–42). Boulder, CO: Westview Press.

Clemens, W. C. (1991). *Baltic independence and Russian Empire*. New York: St. Martin's Press.

Connor, W. (1972). Nation-building or nation-destroying. *World Politics, 24*, 319–355.

———. (1992). The Soviet prototype. In R. Denber (Ed.), *The Soviet nationality reader: The disintegration in context* (pp. 15–33). Boulder, CO: Westview Press.

Conover, P. J., & Feldman, S. (1984). Group identification, values, and the nature of political beliefs. *American Political Quarterly, 12*(2), 151–175.

Denber, R. (Ed.). (1992). *The Soviet nationality reader: The disintegration in context*. Boulder, CO: Westview Press.

Dunlop, J. B. (1986). Language, culture, religion and national awareness. In R. Conquest (Ed.), *The last empire: Nationality and the Soviet future* (pp. 263–289). Stanford, CA: Hoover Institution Press.

Forbes, H. D. (1985). *Nationalism, ethnocentrism, and personality*. Chicago: University of Chicago Press.

Fuller, E. (1992). Nagorno-Karabakh: Internal conflict becomes international. *RFE/RL Research Report, 1*(22), 1–5.

———. (1994a). Russia, Turkey, Iran, and the Karabakh mediation process. *RFE/RL Research Report, 3*(8), 31–36.

———. (1994b). The Karabakh mediation process: Grachev versus the CSCE? *RFE/RL Research Report, 3*(23), 13–17.

Girnius, S. (1990). Gorbachev's visit to Lithuania. *Report on the USSR, 2*(4), 4–7.

Goble, P. (1990a). Soviet citizens blame system for ethnic problems. *Report on the USSR, 2*(26), 5–6.

———. (1990b). Can republican borders be changed? *Report on the USSR, 2*(39), 20–22.

———. (1990c). The end of the "nationality question": Ideological decay and ethnic relations in the USSR. In S. Woodby & A. B. Evans, Jr. (Eds.), *Restructuring Soviet ideology: Gorbachev's new thinking* (pp. 97–105). Boulder, CO: Westview Press.

Hill, R. J. (1992). Ideology and the making of a nationalities policy. In A. J. Motyl (Ed.), *The post-Soviet nations: Perspectives on the demise of the USSR* (pp. 50–78). New York: Columbia University Press.

Hosking, G. (1991). The Russian national revival. *Report on the USSR, 3*(44), 5–8.

Karklins, R. (1986). *Ethnic relations in the USSR: The perspective from below.* Boston: Unwin Hyman.

Kelman, H. C., & Hamilton, F. L. (1989). *Crimes of obedience: Toward a social psychology of authority and responsibility.* New Haven, CT: Yale University Press.

Kionka, R. (1991). Are the Baltic laws discriminatory? *Report on the USSR, 3*(15), 21–24.

Larsen, K. S., Killifer, C., Csepeli, G., Krumov, K., Andrejeva, L., Kashlakeva, N., Russinova, Z., & Pordany, L. (1992). National identity: A new look at an old issue. *Journal of Social Behavior and Personality, 7*(2), 309–322.

Marnie, S., & Slater, W. (1993). Russia's refugees. *RFE/RL Research Report, 2*(37), 46–53.

Motyl, A. J. (1992). The sobering of Gorbachev: Nationality, restructuring, and the West. In R. Denber (Ed.), *The Soviet nationality reader: The disintegration in context* (pp. 573–595). Boulder, CO: Westview Press.

Nahaylo, B., & Swoboda, V. (1989). *Soviet disunion: A history of the nationalities problem in the USSR.* New York: Free Press.

Narodnoe khoziaistvo SSSR v 1990 g.: Statisticheskii ezhegodnik. (1991). Moscow: Finansy i Statistika.

Nineteenth All-Union Conference of the CPSU. (1988). *Documents and materials.* Washington, DC: Embassy of the USSR.

Pipes, R. (1992). The establishment of the Union of Soviet Socialist Republics. In R. Denber (Ed.), *The Soviet nationality reader: The disintegration in context* (pp. 35–86). Boulder, CO: Westview Press.

Plano, J. C., & Greenberg, M. (1985). *The American political dictionary* (7th ed.). New York: Holt, Rinehart and Winston.

Richards, S. (1990). *Epics of everyday life: Encounters in a changing Russia.* New York: Penguin.

Solchanyk, R. (1993). Ukraine's search for security. *RFE/RL Research Report, 2*(21), 1–6.

Spechler, D. R. (1990). Russian nationalism and Soviet politics. In L. Hajda & M. Beissinger (Eds.), *The nationalities factor in Soviet politics and society* (pp. 281–304). Boulder, CO: Westview Press.

Suny, R. G. (1992). Nationalism and democracy in Gorbachev's Soviet Union: The case of Karabakh. In R. Denber (Ed.), *The Soviet nationality reader: The disintegration in context* (pp. 485–507). Boulder, CO: Westview Press.

Szporluk, R. (1990). The imperial legacy and the Soviet nationalities. In L. Hajda & M. Beissinger (Eds.), *The nationalities factor in Soviet politics and society* (pp. 1–23). Boulder, CO: Westview Press.

———. (1992). Dilemmas of Russian nationalism. In R. Denber (Ed.), *The Soviet nationality reader: The disintegration in context* (pp. 509–543). Boulder, CO: Westview Press.

Tolz, V. (1994). Russia's parliamentary elections: What happened and why. *RFE/RL Research Report, 3*(2), 1–8.

Torbakov, I. (1992). The "statists" and the ideology of Russian imperial nationalism. *RFE/RL Research Report, 1*(49), 10–16.

White, G. M., & Prachuabmoh, C. (1983). The cognitive organization of ethnic images. *Ethos, 11*(1/2), 2–32.

· 5 ·

THE MYTHOLOGY OF THE SOVIET UNION

[I]f a myth is to be a practical argument, the chief condition for its success is that it be understood as a true narrative of events. If it is regarded as a pack of lies, it . . . will fail as an explanation and it will lack prescriptive force.

HENRY TUDOR (1972, p. 123)

Marxism-Leninism was a . . . myth. . . . Many ingredients recommended this myth to the condition of Russia. . . . The preservation of the myth was the central condition for Communist survival.

THEODORE H. VON LAUE (1993, pp. 93, 95)

Human beings are myth-making animals. As far back in history as anyone can trace, people have been creating and using myths. This fact alone indicates that mythology fills some basic and continuing human need. When most people think of myths, however, they tend to think of them as fantastic stories concocted by primitive people who needed some way to explain what they found bewildering in the world around them. Most of us are quite sure that we do not have or need myths because we have science to look to for explanations. (Parenti, 1994, p. vii; Wolin, 1985) Even though there is much that we still do not understand about our world, the scientific method gives us confidence that, in time, research will bring us understanding. We like to think of ourselves as rational, logical beings who will be able—sooner or later—to figure things out. Nothing, however, could be farther from the truth than the notion that we live in a myth-free world.

In the modern world, a myth is "a widely accepted belief that gives meaning to events and that is socially cued, whether or not it is verifiable." (Edelman, 1977, p. 3) We all embrace myths about ourselves and our world, but we usually do not call these beliefs myths or even recognize them as such. We need myths to help us

An earlier version of this chapter was published as: C. Barner-Barry & C. Hody (1994). Soviet Marxism-Leninism as mythology. *Political Psychology, 15* (4), pp. 611–632.

to understand ourselves and our place in the world. The Star Trek character Worf expressed this idea clearly when he said: "These are our stories. They tell us who we are." (Star Trek: The Next Generation, Birthright II)

Political myths are tales that help people to make sense of their political past, present, and future. (Nimmo & Combs, 1980) They can also persuade people to act in certain ways, and for this reason they can be powerful aids in the imposition of social control on a population. When political myths are successful in their persuasive role, people do not think of them as myths. They believe them to be true.

And they may be. The truth or falsity of a myth is not what gives it its psychological persuasiveness. Most myths about the modern world combine fact and fiction. When people internalize a myth, along with its attendant values, they accept its persuasive influence and act on that basis. They find their actions and attitudes to be "intrinsically rewarding" because they are "congruent with" their value system. (Kelman, 1958, p. 53) Myths play a persuasive role in life because of their characteristics and functions.

CHARACTERISTICS AND FUNCTIONS OF MYTHS

According to Nimmo and Combs (1980), modern myths have five basic characteristics.[1] The first is believability. It does not matter if myths are true, partly true, or blatantly false. What matters is that perfectly reasonable people believe them to be true. According to Soviet mythology, Lenin was a wise, benevolent, and heroic leader. Because Lenin died before the Soviet Union took on a relatively stable form and because of the way the official historians presented Lenin and his life, Soviet citizens found it easy to believe that Lenin was one of the truly great and good figures of history. Thus, right up to the collapse of the Soviet Union (Smart, 1990), Lenin served as a believable mythic hero for the Soviet people—because he had led the Bolshevik Revolution and because the Communist Party leadership carefully controlled information about him as part of its use of persuasion as a social control mechanism.

The second characteristic of myths is that they are created through a social process. A myth can emerge from a group of people spontaneously—seemingly without conscious direction. Most of the major Soviet myths, however, were cultivated, if not created from scratch, by the Soviet leadership. Again, we can use Lenin as an example. After the 1917 October Revolution, Lenin was hailed as the single most important person bringing about the victory of the "people" over their "oppressors." In those first heady days after the Bolshevik victory, many believed in a certain and glorious communist future, and they began to endow Lenin with mythic qualities—to make him a mythic hero. (Tumarkin, 1983, pp. 64–111) After Lenin's death, and particularly after Stalin's death,

---

1. In their book they list six. Because the sixth characteristic is qualitatively different from the other five, we discuss it separately later in this chapter.

the Soviet leadership took specific measures to encourage and strengthen Lenin's mythic status. The result was a cult of Lenin that was "the collective construction of a credible reality." (Nimmo & Combs, 1980, p. 17; Tumarkin, 1983) Long after glasnost had led to the discrediting of other Soviet leaders, belief in the mythic qualities of Lenin persisted. In 1988, one member of the CPSU's Central Committee put it this way: "For me, Lenin was the man who provided us with our Soviet Union and all that we became—an advanced country. The mistakes were not Lenin's. The mistakes came in carrying out Lenin's line. . . . I tell you straight that we have a genius in Lenin." (*Washington Post,* November 1, 1988, p. 27)

The third characteristic of modern myths is dramatic structure. A myth is a story with a beginning, a middle, and an end. Lenin's life furnished just such a story. There he was, a normal boy growing up in an ordinary upper-middle-class family. Then his beloved and brave older brother got involved in revolutionary activities in St. Petersburg and was executed by the evil tsarist regime. Radicalized by this event and by the blatant discrimination he experienced as the relative of a convicted anarchist, Lenin selflessly decided to sacrifice all and devote his life to the cause for which his brother had died: overthrowing the evil tsarist regime. After many struggles, Lenin emerged triumphant—a savior of the common people of Russia. Soon afterward, he was the victim of an assassination attempt, which hastened his premature death. What more dramatic story could one wish?

The fourth characteristic of a story that has attained mythic status is that it is seldom questioned. Lenin became an object of unquestioning, almost religious, veneration. The Lenin mausoleum in Red Square became a "holy shrine" to which people made pilgrimages: "To this ritual centre both individual persons and society (in the form of its representative groups) [came] to draw moral strength at crisis points, to give heightened significance to important events, to give an account of important missions accomplished, to display and rejoice in successes or just to give homage." (Lane, 1981, p. 210) Lenin's memory was to be revered, not questioned.

During most of the Soviet period, there was little public criticism of Lenin, even from dissidents. In fact, when some historians—emboldened by glasnost—began to question the Lenin myth, they were greeted with shock. Vasili Selyunin, one of the first historians who took a skeptical look at Lenin's life and work, observed that he found it difficult to question the Lenin myth. This was especially true because he found himself suggesting that Lenin had started the process that led to the forced labor camps of Stalin. "Understand," he said, "it's not a joy to write this. My jaws lock sometimes. But it is necessary. . . . We cannot repeat this." (*Washington Post,* June 7, 1988, p. A17)

A practical purpose is the fifth characteristic of myths. In the case of political myths, that purpose can be social control through the mechanism of persuasion. In other words, myths can be used to persuade people to hold certain political beliefs and attitudes—and, when necessary, to act on them. The myth of Lenin was very practical as a vehicle which could be put to persuasive use by the CPSU. In a country that until recently had had high levels of illiteracy, the use of concrete, nonverbal symbols and easily understood stories was politically important. Highly abstract and intellectual ideological formulations were beyond the comprehension of most of the Soviet people.

Lenin, however, was a real person who could be (and was) depicted in photographs, statues, paintings, books, movies, and plays. All of these media were used to convey some vital "truth" about him and the country he founded: He had been flesh and blood with all of the joys and sorrows associated with being human—he was someone people could relate to personally (children were taught to call him "Uncle Lenin"). At the same time, as a symbol, he embodied the values and norms of Marxism-Leninism and the Bolshevik Revolution. The combination of his very human image and a carefully selected set of interpretations of reality was intended to promote allegiance to the Soviet Union and the Communist Party. This allegiance, in turn, was linked to loyalty to the particular regime in power at the time.[2] During most of the Soviet period the heroic myth of Lenin seemed to succeed very well—at least on the surface. As Friedrich and Brzezinski (1965, p. 91) noted many years ago, myths "play a vital role in totalitarian dictatorships."

Even while the Soviet Union was disintegrating, many people found the destruction of the myth of Lenin far more threatening than negative revelations about any other Soviet person or event. As one highly placed supporter of Gorbachev's reform said: "Remember, the very limited democratic tradition we do have is in Lenin's NEP [New Economic Policy]. To begin assaulting that would lead to a terrific loss of confidence in peoples' souls. Millions of people still can't believe there was a cult of Stalin. So to take a tough look at Lenin too soon would not be wise." (*Washington Post,* November 1, 1988, p. A21) Thus, Gorbachev and his supporters utilized the Lenin myth (especially NEP) to mobilize support for reform while focusing the hard, cold light of historical reality on Stalin. (Smart, 1990)

It is important to remember that mythic thinking and scientific thinking are very different processes. In science, the ability to use objective, concrete observation and replicable experimentation to evaluate a proposition is central and definitive. Myths, however, are made up of symbols and stories, objects of belief. By definition, they are not amenable to disproof by any generally agreed-upon method. A myth becomes important when people *believe* it to be true and when they act on that belief. If a person behaves as if a myth is true, there is a sense in which—for all practical purposes—they have made it true. For example, there is no universally accepted, concrete archeological evidence that Jesus ever existed. Millions of people, however, have lived their lives believing that he did, and this choice has had a powerful effect on them and on the course of history.

Myths serve four general functions in people's lives. (Nimmo & Combs, 1980, pp. 20–24) First, because myths are easily understood, they make life's

---

2. Although the basic information conveyed remained substantially the same, each regime gave it a unique spin, to take into account developments in the Soviet Union and the rest of the world.

events easier to grasp and perhaps to accept. This function is particularly important when situations are unavoidable (as in natural disasters) or when a regime wants to impose hardships on its subjects. The victorious Bolsheviks inherited a land that was economically underdeveloped and educationally backward by European standards. In addition, it had been devastated by World War I and the civil war that followed the Bolshevik Revolution. To repair the human and material damage inflicted by warfare, as well as to catch up with the more developed European countries, the Communist regime needed to convince the people to work hard and to make tremendous personal sacrifices. The idea of building a utopian society for their children and their children's children was a powerful incentive. (Luke, 1985) And so, central to the mythology of the Soviet Union was the idea that its people were engaged in the building of communism and that this effort would result in a society more affluent and just than any society the world had ever known. The mythology asserted that deprivation should be endured in the present because the future payoff would be so great.

Second, myths give people roles in life by providing "a sense of self, wholeness, and importance that cold, scientific, technological thought simply cannot supply." (Nimmo & Combs, 1980, p. 23) A central myth of the Soviet Union was that communism was changing human nature, creating a new type of person: the builder of communism who was central to the goal of establishing the good society Soviet-style. (Vasilenko, 1985) People who measured up to the standard were considered to be assets to the society and to be of high moral worth. What was expected of a builder of Soviet communism was the following:

> devotion to the cause of communism, love for the socialist Motherland, for the socialist countries;
>
> conscientious labor for the good of society: who does not work does not eat;
>
> concern of each person for the conservation and increase of social property;
>
> a high consciousness of social duty, intolerance toward violations of social interests;
>
> collectivism and comradely mutual aid; one for all and all for one;
>
> humane relationships and reciprocal respect between peoples: person to person— friend, comrade and brother;
>
> honesty and truthfulness, moral purity, simplicity, and modesty in social and personal life;
>
> mutual respect in the family, concern for the upbringing of children;
>
> irreconcilability toward injustice, parasitism, dishonesty, careerism, greed;
>
> the friendship and brotherhood of all the peoples of the USSR, intolerance toward nationalistic and racial hostility;
>
> irreconcilability toward the enemies of communism, of the cause of peace, and of the freedom of nations;
>
> fraternal solidarity with the workers of all countries and with all peoples. (Bogdanova & Kalinina, 1984, pp. 10–11)

Taken from the Program of the CPSU, which was in effect from 1961 to 1986, this "Moral Code of the Builder of Communism" specified what each person could do in order to be part of the creation of a utopian future. It offered people identities designed to make them feel that they were important actors in the drama of transforming their country.

Third, because myths are shared, they forge bonds between people and create community. The idea of community, in the form of the collective, was the central organizing principle of the Soviet social order. The builder of communism did not work alone. He or she was a member of societal subgroups that coordinated the effort of individuals, uniting them in working toward common goals. Membership in collectives was not optional. Everyone who entered a school or took a job automatically became part of one. (Kiprianov & Kuznetsova, 1986) The collective connected individuals to the larger society: "By means of [the collective] two opposite streams of social activities meet—from society to the individual and from the individual to society. As the direct means by which a person carries out his life's work, the collective's functions draw him into the life of society." For adults, the collective was supposed to be "family," the place where they spent their "most active and fruitful time." (Vasilenko et al., 1985, p. 49) Thus, the collective was intended to create community—binding people together by strong social bonds.

The myth of the collective, in turn, was tied to the wider social myth, which was about the function that collectives supposedly played in the society. In reality, the collective was chiefly a means of social and political control over individuals. In the mythology, it was presented as groups of individuals banded together to realize the utopian goals of the Soviet Union. Article 8 of the Soviet Constitution adopted in 1977 stated that

> Labor collectives take part in discussing and deciding state and public affairs, in planning production and social development, in training and placing personnel, and in discussing matters pertaining to the management of enterprises and institutions, the improvement of working and living conditions, and the use of funds allocated for developing production and for social and cultural purposes and financial incentives. (as translated in Barry & Barner-Barry, 1991, p. 336)

This is not an accurate description of the actual role collectives played. They did not have the impact on public policy that Article 8 asserts. According to the myth about the building of communism, however, collectives were the organizing force that made things happen. This myth was supposed to make people feel that, through the decision-making function of their collectives, they were important actors in the shaping of a utopian future for the USSR.

Fourth, and perhaps most important from the point of view of the Soviet experience, myths can be manipulated to achieve goals. Clearly, an individual who identified as a builder of communism and strived to conform to the Moral Code became an effective tool in the hands of the CPSU. The work of people organized into collectives could be channeled and monitored to facilitate implementation of the policies of the Party leadership. When people accepted the mythic hero Lenin as a role model, they brought to the experience of "building communism" the ideas and values that the regime was associating with Lenin. This made it easier for them to identify themselves as participants engaged in a heroic task, following in the footsteps of the heroic Lenin. The CPSU, after all, was leading them, and it was the party of the mythic hero Lenin. (Ito, 1992, p. 279)

The mythology about Lenin and the building of communism did not exist in isolation. It was part of the master mythology of the Soviet state. Master myths are "broad, overarching myths that constitute the collective consciousness of an entire society." (Nimmo & Combs, 1980, p. 26) To control the beliefs of the Soviet people, the leadership attempted to create a set of master myths that would channel the emotions and efforts of Soviet citizens in desired directions. This effort was a clear example of the use of persuasion in the service of social control.

MASTER MYTHS OF THE SOVIET STATE

There are three types of master myth. (Nimmo and Combs, 1980, pp. 26–27) The foundation myth tells the story of a country's origin. The sustaining myth is "a core belief, a central motif, in which the ideal culture patterns are embedded." (Tucker, 1987, p. 22) The destiny myth is the story of a country's ultimate role in history.[3]

In the Soviet Union, the revolutionary experience and an extreme simplification of Marxist-Leninist ideology lay at the heart of the three master myths. Both were subject to modification and distortion to serve the purposes of those in power. Despite frequent changes in the details, the overall picture painted by the Soviet master myths remained stable. The role of the myths also remained the same: to control beliefs and behavior through persuasion.

The Foundation Myth

The Bolshevik Revolution in 1917 marked the symbolic founding of the Soviet Union, and the mythology that grew up around the revolutionary period became the foundation myth of the USSR. The mythic interpretation of the Bolshevik Revolution is summed up nicely at the beginning of a book by Vasili Kas'ianenko entitled *The Soviet Way of Life,* which was published 1985, the year Gorbachev came to power:

> The Great October Socialist Revolution marked a basic turning point in the historical fate of our Motherland, marking the beginning of the formation of socialist

---

3. Nimmo and Combs (1980) and Tudor (1972) refer to this as the eschatological myth. We use the term *destiny* because it has fewer religious overtones.

civilization. The Leninist concept of a proletarian revolution and the construction of socialism based on the teachings of Marx and Engels ideologically armed the Party and the working class in their struggle against the bourgeoisie for a new life which would bring good fortune to the workers. (Kas'ianenko, 1985, p. 9)

Several things about the Soviet foundation myth are evident from Kas'ianenko's summarized version. First, the Soviet Union is implicitly regarded as an extension of the Russian Empire. And, in truth, the country that initially emerged from the 1917 revolutions was nominally Russian; the Soviet Union did not officially come into being until 1922. Thus, both the focus of the Soviet foundation myth and the major Soviet founding father (Lenin) were Russian. The many other ethnic groups played bit parts, if they were given credit for participating at all. Their relegation to minor roles is particularly important, for the Soviet leadership later tried to persuade both the Russian and the non-Russian ethnic groups to internalize a common Soviet national identity. One reason this effort failed was that the Soviet foundation myth related almost exclusively to the Russians. It excluded a large portion of the Soviet population while feeding the belief of one ethnic group that it was naturally superior. It is interesting to note that by the time of Gorbachev, the Russians were about to become a minority (albeit a privileged minority) within the Soviet population.[4]

Second, the foundation myth claimed that the October Revolution established a new form of civilization—a "socialist civilization," Kas'ianenko says. The implication was that all previous forms of civilization were seriously lacking. This judgment in effect dismissed the historical and cultural heritages of the constituent peoples of the Soviet Union, even though some of them—like the Central Asians—could boast of a rich cultural heritage. Even the Russian tsarist heritage was dismissed as the heritage of the official revolutionary "enemy." By 1985, few people had personal memories of the days immediately after the Revolution, when a new world of possibilities seemed to have opened up and it was easy to be a "true believer." As a result, the Soviet foundation myth had little historical or emotional appeal for most citizens of the Soviet Union during the Gorbachev era.

Third, the Soviet foundation myth set forth a story about the desired social order—a Eurocentric social order. Under Stalin, the young Soviet state turned inward and isolated its people from the outside world in order to modernize as rapidly as possible. The model for transformation, however, was that of the industrialized West. The ancient civilizations of places like Georgia, Armenia, and the Muslim republics were ignored. In addition, the foundation myth lacked reference to the natural environment and to the human life cycle, both of which are classic mythological themes. (Lane, 1981, p. 192) Thus, the foundation myth was not based on anything that all of the Soviet people had in common. In fact,

---

4. According to the 1989 Soviet census, the Russians made up 50.8 percent of the Soviet population. (*Narodnoe khoziaistvo SSSR v 1990 g.*, 1991, p. 77)

with its emphasis on a Europeanized and Russianized utopia, it was based on much that had the potential to divide them.

Finally, the foundation myth asserted that the new "socialist civilization" was the creation of the working class and its vanguard, the CPSU, and that it would usher in a world of "good fortune" (Kas'ianenko's phrase) for the workers. The Bolshevik Revolution was hardly a creation of the working class. Although many workers and peasants participated in the fighting, it was first and foremost the creation of a small, tightly knit group of professional revolutionaries. The new "socialist civilization" that followed was largely the creation of the CPSU led by Stalin. Only by strictly limiting the availability of information about the world outside the Soviet Union could the CPSU leadership preserve the notion that this new life had brought "good fortune" to the workers.

Another important aspect of the foundation myth was its tie to an official ideology—Marxism-Leninism—and its interpretation of the basic nature and sources of that ideology. According to Christenson and his colleagues (1981, p. 4), "a political ideology is a system of beliefs that explains and justifies a preferred political order, either existing or proposed, and offers a strategy (institutions, processes, programs) for its attainment." Thus, ideologies are very much like myths. Unlike myths, however, reasonably well-developed ideologies like Marxism-Leninism are primarily appeals to rationality and logic rather than to emotion. They attempt to construct an intellectually viable, integrated belief system.

In the early works of Marx, "we find both a preoccupation with the problem of achieving a morally coherent world and a rudimentary vision of a future communist society . . . nothing that can be described as a mythical account." (Tudor, 1972, pp. 115–116) Only with the writing in 1845–46 of *The German Ideology* did Marx and Engels (1964) lend their ideological system to mythmaking. In that work, "for the first time, the destiny of the revolutionary proletariat [is] set forth as a dramatically coherent sequence of events." (Tudor, 1972, p. 116) Certainly, the ideology that dominated the Soviet political-economic system had a strong intellectual core derived from the writings of Marx and Engels, supplemented by the writings of Lenin.

Although some ideologies are clearly different from myths, others contain a certain amount of overlap. Like master myths, ideologies offer "an interpretation of the past, an explanation of the present, and a vision of the future." However, rather than being formulated in dramatic form, ideologies present "an ordered arrangement of logically related ideas offering an explanation and vision of human destiny." (Christenson *et al.*, 1981, pp. 4–5) In other words, whereas myths are primarily designed to appeal to our feelings and our taste for the dramatic, ideologies are primarily designed to appeal to our capacity for logic and intellectual thought.

What do they have in common? In the Soviet case, there were five important similarities. Both the mythology and the ideology were simplifications of complex political realities. Both were designed to be persuasive, to motivate the population—the ideology being aimed more at the well-educated, the mythology more at the poorly educated or uneducated. Each claimed both truth and universality. Both were millennial, looking toward a utopian future. Both had heroes, sacred texts, and rituals.

In the Soviet Union, there were also important differences between the ideology and the mythology. The formal Marxist-Leninist ideology was articulated, verbal, systematic, and explicit. People could pick up a book and read the writings of Marx, Engels, and Lenin—they were easy to find. The mythic formulation was evident in the ubiquitous symbols and slogans (the color red was everywhere), in most works of art (usually of dubious esthetic merit), in the agitation and propaganda system, and in all but the most advanced, scientific sectors of the educational system.

Another difference stemmed from the fact that Marxism arose in a period of societal stress in western Europe and continued to be elaborated during a period of growing crisis in Russia. The mythology played a part in the revolutionary period, but it became much more developed as the situation in the new Soviet Union stabilized. It was used to mobilize the people behind the goals of the Bolshevik regime.

Another difference was in the audience. Formal Marxist-Leninist ideology was most attractive to people who were relating to the Soviet political system in a mainly intellectual way (on the surface, at least). Its mythological variant was aimed at nonintellectuals, at people who were relating to the Soviet political system on a more emotional basis.

During the years after the Bolshevik Revolution, Marxist-Leninist ideology underwent many modifications as different Soviet leaders manipulated it for their own purposes. Nevertheless, the ideological core, which was tied to the mythology, tended to remain reasonably constant—even when it bore little or no resemblance to reality. The Soviet leadership tried to use Marxism-Leninism as a source of legitimacy and as a tool for persuasion. As a source of legitimacy ideology can be used "to justify an existing social system," lending authority to the decisions made by the current leadership. As a tool of persuasion it can be used to project a desirable future social order motivating the people to work hard to achieve that goal.

How did the foundation myth treat Marxist-Leninist ideology? Kas'ianenko has this to say:

Marx and Engels developed a genuinely scientific dialectical-materialistic interpretation of history, substantiating the global-historical mission of the working class, its role in the revolutionary renewal of society. . . . [They] demonstrated the objective necessity of a dictatorship of the proletariat for the accomplishment of the transition from capitalism to communism. . . . [They] were the first to attempt to describe the communist way of life and work.
    V. I. Lenin scientifically substantiated the path and method of eliminating the foundations of the past, the form of life and work of the people and the establishment of a socialist society. Lenin's plan for the building of socialism armed the party with a concrete program for the creation of a new way of life by the workers themselves. (Kas'ianenko, 1985, pp. 9–10)

Thus, the intellectual construct takes on a more dramatic form. This also warrants closer scrutiny.

Notice the use of "scientific" (*nauchnyi*) in connection with the theories of Marx and Engels. Not only are they scientific, they are "genuinely" (*podlinno*) scientific. The dictionary definition of the Russian word for science (*nauka*) is "A system of knowledge about the lawful [according to natural law] development of nature, society and thought, and also a single branch of such knowledge. *Social science. Natural science. ...* " (Ozhegov, 1988, p. 319, emphasis in the original) English dictionary definitions encompass this meaning, but in popular usage *science* tends to connote a particular, rigorous, experimental methodology and the theories that inform it. In the English-speaking world it is not customary to refer to bodies of philosophical thought, like Marxism, as scientific. (e.g., McLellan, 1979)

As a tool of persuasion, Marxism-Leninism was repeatedly characterized as scientific, implying a status that corresponded with the purely intellectual (and usually quantifiable) theories of the natural sciences. Doing so was easy because of the way in which the Russian word for science was commonly used. It had its mythic advantages as well. Associating Marxism-Leninism with science gave the weight of inevitability to any idea or prediction that bore the label "Marxism-Leninism." For example, the 1961 Program of the Communist Party of the Soviet Union stated that "socialism will inevitably succeed capitalism everywhere. Such is the objective law of social development. Imperialism is powerless to check the irresistible process of emancipation." (Kaiser, 1986–87, p. 237)

When Marx and Engels, in Kas'ianenko's words, "demonstrated the objective necessity of a dictatorship of the proletariat," they did not do it by scientific experimentation. They did it by arguing logically from a carefully chosen set of assumptions. Any philosophy is only as good as its assumptions, and Marxism-Leninism is no exception. But when Marxism-Leninism was being used mythically, the identification of its assumptions—let alone the questioning of them—never came up. Its validity was simply asserted, not proven. And the telling took on more and more the form of a story, rather than a philosophical or scientific discourse.

In fact, for Kas'ianenko to say in a book published in 1985 what he says about the goodness of the life led by the workers is absurd on anything but a mythic level, given the realities of life in the Soviet Union. That the state would wither away at any time in the foreseeable future was an untenable proposition. In fact, the Soviet government bureaucracy was enormous and growing. It showed no inclination to wither away. For the bureaucratically besieged Soviet citizen, of course, the notion that communism would bring with it a withering away of the state was attractive. Yes, it required a suspension of disbelief, but humans longing for a better life are often willing to suspend disbelief.

The presentation of ideas in mythic form encourages magical thinking. For example, the senior anchor of Soviet television described his feelings when, in 1961, Khrushchev promised that communism would be achieved within his lifetime: "As Khrushchev spoke those words, the sun came out—and the entire [CPSU] Congress seemed to light up. See, we told each other, even nature believes in our cause. That's when my wife and I decided to have our first daughter. We hoped that she would live under communism." (*Washington Post*, December 29, 1991, p. A26)

This mythological treatment tends to downplay Marx and Engels's writings about socialism and to give the impression that Lenin's "plan for the building of socialism" was an enhancement, rather than an action plan for the realization of their goals. This impression reinforces the heroic myth of Lenin as philosopher and as leader of the forces that triumphed in 1917. Note that Marx and Engels "substantiated" (*obosnovali*) the role of the working class in history, and Lenin "substantiated" Marx and Engels. Thus, the mythic hero, Lenin, is given a central role, and the philosophy becomes as much Leninist as Marxist.

Finally, note that the Party is empowered to act on behalf of the workers, to administer the program by which the workers themselves would create a new way of life. This arrangement might have made sense in 1925, but it made very little sense in 1985. By then, the workers were employees of an enormous bureaucratic state that was run by the CPSU (and, to a great extent, for the CPSU). The workers were cogs in the machine of the state. By 1985, more and more of them were coming to recognize their status, and it is hard to believe that Kas'ianenko did not recognize it too. The myth, however, was used to persuade the workers that things were not as they seemed—that the workers were more important than they perceived themselves to be.

To summarize, the foundation myth was designed to persuade the people of the transformational importance of the Bolshevik Revolution, to convince them that it meant the creation of a new and better world—a utopia based on scientific Marxism-Leninism. The myth presented the Bolshevik Revolution and the founding of the Soviet Union as events of epic proportion because they were *scientifically guaranteed* to lead to the utopian transformation of the old Russian Empire and then the entire world. The guarantee came from the "scientific" theories of Marx, Engels, and Lenin. The workers and peasants of the Soviet Union could make it all happen if they did their share in a great dramatic surge into the future. This idea was developed in the Soviet sustaining myth.

The Sustaining Myth

The sustaining myth[5] emerging from the revolutionary period was that the Soviet people were an essentially egalitarian collective of workers engaged in the (ultimately and inevitably successful) task of building socialism and then communism. (Tucker, 1987, p. 46) The myth was intended to keep everyone working hard to achieve the utopia for which the Bolshevik Revolution was fought. Each Soviet citizen was obliged to do his or her share. In the early years

---

5. Von Laue refers to this as the guiding myth. (Von Laue, 1993, p. 132)

after the Revolution the entire CPSU was so involved in this persuasive effort that it did not even bother to create a separate propaganda organization. (Von Laue, 1993, p. 132) Later, the Party created a complex agitation and propaganda network that reached into all corners of Soviet society with its persuasive messages. Socialist realism[6] in literature and the arts, as well as strict orthodoxy in education and scholarship, reinforced this persuasive effort.

In reality, the Soviet people were not well suited for transformation into unified, highly motivated, self-starting workers or citizens. They had little in common culturally, linguistically, religiously, or ethnically. Much divided them. For example, wide gaps separated city-dwellers and rural peasants (not to mention the tribal peoples of Asia and the Transcaucasian region). The intellectuals had little contact with the masses, and the CPSU elite became increasingly alienated from the people it was supposed to be serving. These divisions were intensified by the animosity of many ethnic groups toward those who occupied neighboring territories and who in many cases were their historical enemies. Moreover, almost everyone resented the imperialist Russians.

For most of the Soviet people, the centuries-old habit was to be passive subjects rather than active citizens. And this passivity carried over into the workplace. The Protestant work ethic, which energized the industrial development of Europe and America, was not part of the culture of the Russian Empire. Thus, those who were supposed to be the builders of communism were generally uneducated, unskilled, and unambitious.

Despite the factors that tended to undermine it, the sustaining myth was developed, maintained, and elaborated. It was soon bolstered by coercion—which, paradoxically, prevented much of the change in human behavior that the sustaining myth encouraged. As a 69-year-old Russian put it: "How could people like me believe in the ideals of [Soviet] society when so much force was used against us?" (*Washington Post,* September 8, 1993, p. A26)

To support the Soviet sustaining myth, the CPSU from the very start attempted to eliminate or at least limit all information that might contradict or raise questions about what the Soviet people were being asked to do. Information from the outside world was reduced to a minimum, and the Soviet people were told that they were living a life superior to the lives of the oppressed masses in the noncommunist world. For example, the 1923 Soviet Constitution declared:

There in the camp of capitalism we find national animosities and inequalities, colonial slavery and chauvinism, national oppression and pogroms, imperialist brutality and wars.

Here in the camp of socialism there is mutual confidence and peace, national freedom and equality, and the fraternal collaboration of nations peacefully dwelling side by side. (Von Laue, 1993, pp. 132–133)

---

6. Socialist realism dictated that writers, poets, composers, and other artists depict only people and events that supported the mythology.

The Soviet Union, in other words, was the most advanced country in the world, and its toiling masses were leading the way to a utopian future. This proposition was merely asserted, not proved. But there was no need for objective proof, for the Soviet people had little or no outside information that might cause them to question the sustaining myth.

Also, to support the sustaining myth, the CPSU subjected the people to an increasing barrage of persuasive messages constantly reinforcing the myth. Like the foundation myth, the sustaining myth invoked a Russified Marxism in the service of the goals of the CPSU. To return to *The Soviet Way of Life:*

> The cumulative result of the economic, socio-political and spiritual development of Soviet society demonstrates that, based on the steady growth of the national economy and increase of its scientific and technical potential, the country will continue perfecting the whole system of social relationships, all spheres of Soviet communal life. Together with the creative energy and initiative of the masses, the social policy of the CPSU and the Soviet government has guaranteed the steady movement of our society toward even higher levels of social progress. (Kas'ianenko, 1985, p. 207)

The ultimate goal, of course, was a communist utopia, and Kas'ianenko (p. 207) observes that as a result of the policies of the CPSU and the Soviet government, "the sprouts of a communist community are already appearing."

Again, several things are worth noting. First, sustaining myths have the basic function of "enhancing the maintenance of political relationships." (Nimmo & Combs, 1980, pp. 26–27) One relationship is between the Communist Party and the government. Notice that Kas'ianenko mentions the CPSU before the Soviet government. This is not an accident or an oversight. It is a clear indicator of both the close relationship between the two organizations and the fact that the CPSU was primary. The CPSU generated major policy initiatives; the principal role of the Soviet government was to implement them. In this way, the CPSU and the government combined to perform the functions that normally fall to the government alone in a contemporary Western political system.

The other basic political relationship that was enhanced and maintained by the sustaining myth was between the people and their Party-led government. According to the myth, the policies emanating from the CPSU leadership combined with the effort of the Soviet people to create an infallible coalition; success could be guaranteed.[7] In fact, Kas'ianenko asserted that little bits of evidence ("sprouts") of the inevitable triumph of communism were already appearing. The relationship that would make it all happen, of course, was the CPSU as leader, the government as intermediary, and the people as followers. Kas'ianenko's words "creative energy and initiative," however, imply that the masses were actively shaping their destinies rather than passively carrying out a destiny shaped for them by others. Such a myth has the very practical purpose

---

7. The Russian verb *obespechivat',* to secure or guarantee, is put in the past tense. The process is going to be carried out. It is a sure bet.

of sustaining the effort of the population without which the continued growth and strength of any state is impossible.

Finally, the mythic goal of all this effort was the triumph of communism, the supposed ultimate goal of the Bolshevik Revolution. The sustaining myth envisioned the creation of the first communist state in the Soviet Union. Thus, Soviet citizens were called the "builders of communism," and one of the goals of child-rearing was to create better builders of communism. (e.g., Bogdanova & Kalinina, 1984, pp. 148–149) From the start, the major emphasis was on economic development. Immediately after the Bolshevik Revolution Lenin emphasized that economic progress was vital to Soviet survival: "War is inexorable and puts the question with unsparing sharpness: either perish or catch up and overtake the advanced countries economically as well." (Von Laue, 1993, p. 86) This never changed. At the end, the impetus for and central focus of Gorbachev's reforms was economic. As Gorbachev urged his people to work hard for perestroika, his words were often eerily similar to those of past Soviet leaders.

A key indicator of the Party's vision of the ideal Soviet citizen and worker was "The Moral Code of the Builder of Communism."[8] Predictably, the first element in this code is "devotion to the cause of communism," which is followed closely by "conscientious labor for the good of society." The moral code ends with "Irreconcilability toward the enemies of communism, of the cause of peace, and of the freedom of nations." This leads to the third type of master myth, the destiny myth.

The Destiny Myth

The myth that we call a destiny myth is also known as an eschatological myth, signifying the end of the world. The destiny myth describes the destruction of the old and its replacement by something new. In the Soviet Union, the focus was on a complete change in the way life is lived, not on a religious concept of the end of the world itself. "The old order is abolished and the new order comes into being, but the world as such remains." (Tudor, 1972, p. 92) In the case of the Soviet Union, this new order was to be a utopian one. The utopia would be established by the Soviet people, and its benefits ultimately would spread to the rest of the world. In other words, the destiny of the Soviet Union was to create a utopian order that would transform social relationships throughout humanity.

The ultimate historical role of a nation is identified in its destiny myth. The Soviet mythology, then, was not designed just to maintain the revolutionary momentum of the people inside the Soviet Union (i.e., the sustaining myth). Ultimately, the destiny of the Soviet Union was to be the "turning of the revolutionary dynamism out upon the world," the "export of the revolution."

---

8. See page 117.

(Tucker, 1971, p. 15) This outward movement was, of course, in service to the goal of World Communism, which would bring to the rest of the world the utopia created in the Soviet Union. The capitalist world was to be destroyed, and a communist utopia was to take its place. "In the classic Bolshevik conception, the revolutionary constituency begins with the working classes of the revolutionary homeland and embraces the working classes of all countries, and the international bourgeoisie (or 'international imperialism') is the enemy." (Tucker, 1971, p. 15) The destiny of the Soviet Union, therefore, was to demonstrate the superiority of its political-economic system and, in doing so, to lead the entire world toward a utopian communist future.

This destiny myth was designed to be a source of pride and inspiration for the Soviet (or at least the Russian) people. It encouraged them to see themselves as leaders in a "global anti-Western revolt, proud of having been the first to leap forward into a new era of human history, sure of possessing the foundations for the most advanced social order in the world." (Von Laue, 1993, p. 94) When the Communist International was founded in 1919, the Soviet people were cast in the role of saviors of the human race: "Humanity, whose entire civilization lies in ruin, is threatened with complete annihilation. There is only one force that can save it, and that is the proletariat." (as quoted in Von Laue, 1993, p. 116)

MYTHS, RITUALS, AND PERSUASION

The master myths were designed to be employed by the Soviet leaders in their effort to use persuasion as a mechanism of social control. Persuasion is a form of communication that is intended to evoke a behavioral response. The most useful and durable behavioral responses are given by people who have internalized the beliefs and values that the persuaders are communicating. Mere compliance with what is demanded is a very fragile basis for the mobilization of a population to sacrifice and work toward ambitious goals—and the goals of the Soviet leaders were very ambitious. Internalization minimizes the need for supervision and virtually eliminates the need for force. Compliance, in contrast, is seldom based on anything but force or the threat of force—including the use of the stick and the withholding of the carrot. Thus, if the Soviet rulers were to gain authority through legitimacy and were to minimize the use of power as a social control mechanism, they had to persuade the population to internalize appropriate beliefs and values. The master myths were the centerpiece of that effort.

Internalization, however, is not accomplished overnight: It takes time, patience, and, in cases like the Soviet Union, a certain amount of generational change, plus the careful education of the new generation. Faced, however, with a country in ruins and a civil war, the Bolsheviks instituted War Communism, the hallmark of which was the use of force. Stalin based his programs of industrialization and collectivization on coercion, often in its most brutal forms. The purges were an extension of that brutality and were followed by the horrors of World War II and the Nazi invasion of the European Soviet Union. From the beginning, power was the modus operandi of the Soviet political system. Its leaders learned to resort to force at the slightest provocation. Moreover, the Soviet people came to expect and fear it. Most of them became accustomed to complying with what was expected of them, and many learned to play the system for their own ends in a cynical and self-aggrandizing way.

Given this context, slow internalization of the beliefs and values contained in the Soviet mythology was a luxury. The persuasive effort was remarkably successful in the early years of the Soviet Union but did not remain so in the long run. (Kaiser, 1986–87, pp. 242–243) The coercion used by the Soviet leadership offset the persuasiveness of its words. Some of the Soviet people, it is true, did seem to internalize most or all of the mythology, and everyone probably internalized at least some of it. (Bem, 1970; Milburn, 1991) But the rapid collapse of the Soviet Union suggests that by the 1980s most of the people most of the time had simply learned to go through the motions. (White, 1984) They complied with what was expected of them—until the threat of force was significantly reduced or removed.

Going through the motions suggests ritual. In this connection, it is interesting to note that as the years passed and the use of force became less pervasive and brutal, the Soviet leadership put increasing emphasis on ritual. Generally defined, ritual "is a stylized, repetitive social activity which, through the use of symbolism, expresses and defines social relations. Ritual activity occurs in a social context where there is ambiguity or conflict about social relations, and it is performed to resolve or disguise them." (Lane, 1981, p. 1)[9] In other words, ritual is a highly rule-bound form of persuasion.

A symbol, in this context, can be thought of as something tangible that evokes something that is intangible. Because beliefs, values, and social relationships are not objects, they must take on symbolic form to be perceived or communicated. Language is the most obvious symbolic system for use in such communication, but there are others, including clothes, colors, statues, and music. The Soviet leadership used virtually the entire range of possible symbols.[10] Whatever the vehicle, what is important is that people understand the symbolic content. Because most Soviet symbols were not very subtle, it is safe to assume that most Soviet citizens understood their message most of the time. Whether they bought the message is another matter.

The Soviet master myths were communicated to ordinary Soviet citizens primarily through symbols and rituals incorporating symbols. There was an inconsistency between the mythological (and ideological) portrayal of Soviet society and the everyday realities of life experienced by the Soviet people. Rituals were designed to smooth over or even deny those inconsistencies. They

---

9. We make extensive use of Lane's research in this section, and we acknowledge this use here in order to limit references to direct quotations.
10. For a listing and analysis of types of Soviet symbols, see Lane, 1981, Ch. 11.

were not supposed to be publicly acknowledged or discussed.[11] Anyone who called attention to them was quickly quieted—sometimes with harsh finality. Most people, of course, did not discuss them, and it is probably safe to assume that they, somewhat cynically, took the inconsistencies in stride. Also, many lacked the information that would have made some inconsistencies obvious. Given this context, it was logical for the leadership to use ritual as a means of maintaining the status quo through persuasion.

Leonard Doob (1983, p. 54) makes the point that "powers possess *guns and symbols*." (emphasis in the original) In the Soviet Union, as the use of guns decreased, the use of symbols increased. The turning point was the end of the regime of Nikita Khrushchev, in 1964. In his secret speech to the Twentieth Congress of the Communist Party in 1956, he began to disclose the brutalities of Stalinist rule and initiated the de-Stalinization of the Soviet mythological system. Stalin as hero and savior of his country was repudiated, and most of the overt symbols of Stalin as mythic hero were removed from public places.

De-Stalinization, however, presented the Soviet leaders with a problem. By indicating that they were less willing to use brute force than previous leaders had been, they risked lessening their ability to maintain social control. At the same time, the drabness and spiritual poverty of most of Soviet life were giving rise to popular demands for more celebrations to mark the major events of both private and social life. The obvious direction for the people to turn was toward religion, but the officially atheistic state wanted to avoid that.

From the lower echelons of organizations such as the Communist Youth Organization (Komsomol) and the Knowledge (Znanie) Society came the suggestion that the political leadership offer the people more publicly sanctioned ceremonies—a larger and more diverse system of rituals. The Khrushchev regime seized on this idea, which continued to be implemented under Brezhnev and Kosygin. Because power had been the overriding social control mechanism of all previous regimes, however, the people had no strong commitment to the ideas contained in the official mythology. Thus, with less ability and inclination to use raw power, the leadership had to intensify its use of persuasion to establish the legitimacy that undergirds true political authority.

Perhaps even more disquieting to the post-Stalin leaders was the failure of their predecessors to capture the minds and hearts of the first generations of truly Soviet people—men and women born after the revolutionary period. Most of these new Soviet people were not motivated by an internalized commitment to Soviet values. They were motivated by raw materialism. Trying to gain their support on material grounds alone (an exchange) would have made the leadership dangerously dependent on the performance of the Soviet economy. (Ito, 1992) The likelihood, however, that the command economy would be

---

11. What people—particularly those who were well educated and informed—said and did in private situations was an entirely different matter. Robert Tucker (1971, p. 140) paints a picture of the Russian as someone who has a "dual personality"—who has "a role and self-identity in official Russia, but also a hidden unofficial existence and identity."

able to produce the material abundance desired by this younger generation was small. Thus, the CPSU had little choice but to try to strengthen persuasion as a social control mechanism by means of ritual.

That effort would not have been necessary if Marxism-Leninism (in either its mythological or its ideological form) had been adequately internalized by a majority of the Soviet people. The leadership would have possessed more legitimacy, and social control would not have been a major problem. Yes, there still would have been the need to make life less drab, but rituals could have been designed to enhance the fulfillment of the spiritual needs of the people. Because of the ongoing problem of social control, the primary goal of ritual had to be the use of persuasion as a control mechanism. This led to a mentality in which joy and spiritual depth were often subordinated to shallow and simplified preaching and propaganda.

There were two types of rituals. One type had to do with natural processes—the life cycle and the seasons of the year. These rituals involved the marking of births, marriages, and deaths, as well as seasonal celebrations such as the festivity that took place annually during the white nights[12] in Leningrad (now St. Petersburg). The other type had to do with the Soviet mythology and included ceremonies for initiation into political or social collectives, work-related occasions, military-patriotic expressions, and the remembrance of important historical events. The symbols for the latter type of ritual were better developed than those for the former.

Overall, however, this ritual system was characterized by a confusion of sources and aims and an overly intellectual approach to a form (ritual) that is designed to touch the emotions and spirit. As a means of social control, the politically persuasive rituals were a failure. Very few of them survived the collapse of the USSR. During the Gorbachev reform period there was an explosive growth in traditional religion and in occult practices, which continued into the period of independence after 1991. In addition, there was a revival of nationalistic symbols and rituals. Thus, it is safe to assume that very little of either the Soviet mythology or its accompanying ritual survives and that where it does survive its adherents are likely to be older "true believers" in Soviet-style communism.

THE FAILURE OF SOVIET MYTHOLOGY

The reasons for this failure are complex. There is, however, a bottom line. The Soviet Union collapsed, and it collapsed very quickly. If the Soviet people had effectively internalized the beliefs and values embodied in the mythology, it seems likely that the Soviet system would not have been abandoned so rapidly. Its swift demise is a sign that the commitment of most of the Soviet people to

---

12. St. Petersburg is so far north that there is a period of time in June when the sun never completely sets. These nights are called white nights.

the beliefs and values of the Soviet mythological system was shallow and fragile. Let us examine a few of the more obvious reasons for this failure.

The first is time. The Soviet Union existed for less than seventy-five years. Inculcating a new mythology or religious system is not the work of a few decades. Most of the world's major mythologies have developed over centuries, not years or decades. "[B]oth Christian and Islamic ritual have had centuries to lodge themselves in the collective psyche and to develop appropriate ritual forms and symbolism." (Lane, 1981, p. 240) If the Soviet leaders were trying to create some sort of political religion, they did not have the time needed to establish it firmly in the consciousness of the Soviet people. The bulk of the ritual that they developed was less than thirty years old when the Soviet Union collapsed. The mythology was older, but still very young for a mythology.

In this connection, it is worth noting that the Soviet ritual-makers used some of the devices that early Christian leaders and missionaries used when they were trying to convert the pagans. Many pagan myths, deities, and rituals were Christianized and incorporated into Christian practice. In the same way, the Soviet ritual-makers tried to incorporate deeply ingrained forms and ideas from Orthodox Christianity and Slavic paganism. The tactic worked for the Christian church. It is tempting to speculate about whether it might have worked for the Soviet Union as well. The Christian church, however, had centuries; the Soviet leadership had only decades.

Another reason for the failure of the Soviet mythology was the fact that it was based almost exclusively on the cultural and religious heritages of western Europe (Marxism) and the Slavic nationalities. It incorporated virtually nothing from the rich heritages of the non-Slavic peoples of the Soviet Union. This omission had two major consequences. First, the mythology was so poorly designed that it could not be accepted and internalized by people who were neither Slavic nor focused on Europe. For the Muslims of Soviet Central Asia, it could not have been more alien; its official atheism was in sharp contrast to their Islamic heritage. Local efforts to rectify these problems by modifying some of the rituals did not make a significant difference. Second, when the mythology began to be translated more and more into rituals, particularly life-cycle rituals, many Soviet citizens were forced into behavior that was not only alien but repugnant. For example, the Soviet Solemn Registration of the New-Born Child ritual was supposed to take place within a month after birth. This requirement ignored the Islamic rule that the mother and child be completely secluded for the first forty days of the newborn's life. (Lane, 1981, p. 232)

Because the Soviet mythology was Marxist-Leninist and because Marxism-Leninism was officially atheistic, there was little to feed the spiritual needs of the people. The various ethnic groups of the former Soviet Union have deep and lasting spiritual heritages. For the most part, they took the form of religion in the pre-Soviet period. To say that one was Russian Orthodox was equivalent to saying that one was a citizen of tsarist Russia. (I. M. Dolgopolova, personal communication, 1962; White, 1979, p. 39) Correspondingly, the interconnection between Islam and the governments of the Muslim nations is still a widespread phenomenon. The imposition of a regime that not only was secular but also preached atheism and punished traditional religious worship created a deep spiritual void. The Soviet mythology had no compensating spiritual base. It gave the people little help in filling their need for a meaningful spiritual component in their lives.

This lack of spirituality had a great deal to do with the fact that people born after the revolutionary period were highly materialistic—dialectical *materialism* was at the center of their official credo. Because of government opposition, spirituality was not an attractive option. As a result, many of the satisfactions available were in the material realm. (Ito, 1992, p. 292) If the Soviet state had been able to "deliver the goods," if the Soviet leadership had been able to exchange material prosperity for loyalty, the outcome might have been different. But it was not, and social control became more and more important as the materialistic population invented ways to get what it needed in spite of the failings of the Soviet economic system. The black market and official corruption thrived.

This materialism was related to the fact that the mythic system was tied to certain predictions about the material future, both immediate and long-term. In the final analysis, this was the Achilles' heel of the whole persuasive system. The advent of glasnost only confirmed what many of the more perceptive already suspected: Instead of living in the most advanced society in the world, they were living in a second-rate country with superpower weaponry. In the face of this awful truth, the complex web of lies and half-truths that constituted the persuasive system collapsed. To return to our original definition of myth, the "widely accepted belief that [gave] meaning to events" ceased to fulfill its function because it was no longer believable.

Even deeper than this, and contributing greatly to the vulnerability of the Soviet system was the underlying assumption that utopias of any sort are achievable here on earth. If the Soviet people were being conditioned to work so that a utopia could be achieved, it was not unreasonable for them to expect to see progress toward that utopia. Instead, much of what they experienced in their daily lives seemed to indicate "progress" in the opposite direction. More to the point, no scientifically verifiable utopias have ever existed on this earth, and it is reasonable to assume that none ever will—at least in the near future. What the Soviet mythology promised simply was not achievable.

When Gorbachev came along with his much-heralded glasnost, the Soviet people saw the utopian myth shattered once and for all. Not only had they made little progress toward the materialistic utopia they had been promised, but they had been shockingly brutalized by those who had promised it to them. Long before glasnost, cynicism had been growing. (Lapidus, 1984, pp. 703–710; Stites, 1988) The revelations of glasnost, however, left the Soviet people with little to fall back on other than cynicism and—ominously—nationalism. The promises of a utopia of material abundance came up against the hard realities of the basic unworkability of the Soviet economic system.

REFERENCES

Barry, D. D., & Barner-Barry, C. (1991). *Contemporary Soviet politics: An introduction* (4th ed.). Englewood Cliffs, NJ: Prentice-Hall.

Bem, D. (1970). *Beliefs, attitudes, and human affairs*. Belmont, CA: Brooks/Cole.

Bogdanova, O. S., & Kalinina, O. D. (Eds). (1984). *Osnovy kommunisticheskoi morali*. Moscow: Prosveshchenie.

Christenson, R. M., Engel, A. S., Jacobs, D. N., Rejai, M., & Waltzer, H. (1981). *Ideologies and modern politics* (3rd ed.). New York: Harper & Row.

Doob, L. W. (1983). *Personality, power, and authority: A view from the behavioral sciences*. Westport, CT: Greenwood Press.

Edelman, M. (1977). *Political language: Words that succeed and policies that fail*. New York: Academic Press.

Friedrich, C. J., & Brzezinski, Z. K. (1965). *Totalitarian dictatorship and autocracy* (2nd ed.). Cambridge, MA: Harvard University Press.

Ito, T. (1992). Eastern Europe: Achieving legitimacy. In G. Rozman (Ed.), *Dismantling communism: Common causes and regional variations*. Washington, DC: Woodrow Wilson Center Press.

Kaiser, R. G. (1986–87). The Soviet pretense. *Foreign Affairs, 65*(2), 236–251.

Kas'ianenko, V. I. (1985). *Sovetskii obraz zhizni*. Moscow: Izdatel'stvo Politicheskoi Literatury.

Kelman, H. C. (1958). Compliance, identification, and internalization: Three processes of attitude change. *Journal of Conflict Resolution, 2*(1), 51–60.

Kiprianov, A. I., & Kuznetsova, L. S. (1986). *Trudovoi kollektiv i aktivnaia zhiznennaia positsiia lichnosti*. Leningrad: Izdatel'stvo Leningradskogo Universiteta.

Lane, C. (1981). *The rites of rulers: Ritual in industrial society—the Soviet case*. New York: Cambridge University Press.

Lapidus, G. W. (1984). Society under strain. In E. P. Hoffmann & R. F. Laird (Eds.), *The Soviet polity in the modern era*. New York: Aldine.

Luke, T. W. (1985). *Ideology and Soviet industrialization*. Westport, CT: Greenwood Press.

Marx, K., & Engels, F. (1964). *The German ideology*. Moscow: Progress Publishers (written during 1845–46, but first published in 1932).

McLellan, D. (1979). *Marxism after Marx*. Boston: Houghton Mifflin.

Mead, G. H. (1959). *The philosophy of the present*. Lasalle, IL: Open Court.

Milburn, M. A. (1991). *Persuasion and politics: The social psychology of public opinion*. Pacific Grove, CA: Brooks/Cole.

Narodnoe khoziaistvo SSSR v 1990 g.: Statisticheskii ezhegodnik. (1991). Moscow: Finansy i Statistika.

Nimmo, D., & Combs, J. E. (1980). *Subliminal politics: Myths and mythmakers in America*. Englewood Cliffs, NJ: Prentice-Hall.

Ozhegov, S. I. (1988). *Slovar' russkogo iazyka*. Moscow: Russkii Iazyk.

Parenti, M. (1994). *Land of idols: Political mythology in America*. New York: St. Martin's Press.

Smart, C. (1990). Gorbachev's Lenin: The myth in service to perestroika. *Studies in Comparative Communism, 23*(1), 5–21.

Stites, R. (1988). *Revolutionary dreams: Utopian vision and experimental life in the Russian Revolution*. New York: Oxford University Press.

Tucker, R. C. (1971). *The Soviet political mind: Stalinism and post-Stalin change*. New York: Norton.

———. (1987). *Political culture and leadership in Soviet Russia: From Lenin to Gorbachev*. New York: Norton.

Tudor, H. (1972). *Political myth*. New York: Praeger.

Tumarkin, N. (1983). *Lenin lives! The Lenin cult in Soviet Russia*. Cambridge, MA: Harvard University Press.

Vasilenko, V. L., and a collective of authors. (1985). *Nauchnye osnovy rukovodstva formirovaniem novogo cheloveka*. Kiev: Izdatel'stvo Politicheskoi Literatury Ukrainy.

Von Laue, T. H. (1993). *Why Lenin? Why Stalin? Why Gorbachev?* (3rd ed.). New York: HarperCollins.

White, S. (1979). *Political culture and Soviet politics*. New York: St. Martin's Press.

———. (1984). The effectiveness of political propaganda in the USSR. In E. P. Hoffmann & R. F. Laird (Eds.), *The Soviet polity in the modern era*. New York: Aldine.

Wolin, S. (1985). Postmodern politics and the absence of myth. *Social Research, 52*(2), 217–239.

· 6 ·

THE SOVIET COMMAND ECONOMY: HOW IT WORKED AND WHY IT FAILED

*Accounting and control—these are the principal things that are
necessary for the "setting up" and correct functioning of the first
phase of communist society. . . . All citizens become employees and
workers of a single national state "syndicate." All that is required is
that they should work equally—do their proper share of work—
and get paid equally. The accounting and control necessary for this
have been so utterly simplified by capitalism that they have become
the extraordinarily simple operations of checking, recording, and
issuing receipts, which anyone who can read and write and who
knows the first four rules of arithmetic can perform.*

V. I. LENIN, *The State and Revolution* (1917) (as
quoted in Christian, 1966, p. 348)

*In the Soviet Union, as in most countries, there are in fact two
economic systems: the system described in law and decree, which
represents the way Soviet leaders would have the economic system
operate (the formal system), and the system as it actually operates,
sometimes at complete variance with the existing laws and decrees
(the de facto system). . . . In general, the reason the formal and de
facto systems diverge is that the formal system, although feasible
in the abstract, is infeasible in reality.*

ED HEWETT (1988, pp. 99–100)

In the Marxist-Leninist scheme of things, the economy was paramount. The
utopia that was enshrined in the Soviet myth was a materialistic one. The promises made to the Soviet people were overwhelmingly promises of material prosperity. The idea of spiritual wealth was discarded in favor of atheism. Religious
worship not only was absent in the Soviet scheme of things but was actively
discouraged. The official Soviet view of the world had the effect of focusing the
people's aspirations on the creation of an earthly utopia rather than a utopia that
they would enjoy after death. Given this view, it was essential for the Soviet
Union to achieve economic prosperity rapidly enough to maintain the validity of

the sustaining myth. It failed. After some early successes, achieved at great human cost, the economic system did not create the material prosperity that the Soviet people had been conditioned to expect. The disparity between expectation and reality was a major reason for the rapid disintegration of the Soviet Union, and it became an intractable problem for the successor countries.

The Soviet economy was the embodiment of Stalin's model of economic development and the prototypical command economy for the rest of the communist world. Ironically, the factors that contributed to its initial success inevitably fostered the economic stagnation that precipitated the collapse of the Soviet political-economic system. In this chapter we examine the command economy of the Soviet Union and the reasons why it sank into stagnation.

In the first section, we identify and discuss features that distinguish command economies from market ones, and we examine a characteristic limitation of command economies: a general inability to spur innovation and technological development. Subsequently, we examine the aspects of Stalin's strategy for development that gave the Soviet economy its distinctive character.

Although the Stalinist political-economic system served as the model for most other communist command economies, in some important ways the Soviet economy was unique. Stalin's development strategy represented one leader's response to circumstances that were peculiar to the Soviet Union. Granted, this response was ultimately generalized (some might say watered down) to become the generic model for the command economy. As carried out in the Soviet Union, however, Stalin's response to the development imperative was indeed distinctive.

Much of the distinctiveness of this strategy stemmed from its excesses: (1) its extreme commitment to rapid industrialization, (2) the extraordinary levels of sacrifice such industrialization required of the Soviet people, and (3) the ongoing and pervasive reliance on coercion. It is with a recognition of these excesses that we begin to unravel the paradox of the Soviet economic system: The Soviet Union was a superpower with an economy that in some ways resembled that of a Third World country. The very factors that allowed the Soviet Union to rapidly achieve its military superpower status contributed to the relative underdevelopment of other sectors of its economy.

In effect, economic Stalinism sowed the seeds of its own destruction even as it enabled the Soviet people to reap tremendous initial success. The inherent pathologies of the Stalinist command economy defeated all efforts at reform attempted by Stalin's successors. Their efforts failed because the system itself was the problem. Adjustments at the margins could not alter that fact and thus could not prevent the inevitable onset of the stagnation that impelled Gorbachev to initiate perestroika—a policy that turned out to be the beginning of the end.

BASIC FEATURES OF A COMMAND ECONOMY

All economic systems can be distinguished from each other on the basis of their decision-making structures, information-gathering mechanisms, and incentive systems. (Hewett, 1988, p. 98) These three components are in turn closely linked to the nature of property and property rights in a given society. A society's determination of what constitutes property, who owns it, and what rights accrue to property-owners provides the foundation for the society's economic structure.

Property[1]

Property comes in many forms: objects, resources, knowledge,[2] and personal skills. This straightforward list, however, belies the complexity of the property concept.

The very idea of property implies ownership, and different cultures have different notions about what can and cannot be owned. Native Americans, for example, traditionally did not believe that land, a basic resource, could be owned. And the idea that individuals own their personal skills and talents and can exchange them for a wage in a labor market is relatively recent. Societies also differ about who can own property and what the rights of property-owners are. In capitalist societies, property is defined quite broadly, and virtually all property is privately owned. Private property includes any and all combinations of objects, resources, knowledge, and skills that can be used to generate other products and services. In fact, "private ownership of the means of production" is a frequently cited definition of capitalism. Private ownership was the basic evil of capitalism according to Soviet ideology and myth.

Capitalism is basically a system of property relations. Individuals can own property, and as owners they are entitled to certain rights: (1) the disposal of residual income (profit), (2) the transfer of property,[3] and (3) property use. Residual income is the income that remains after the financial obligations associated with maintaining and operating property are met. With regard to residual income, the key concern is the right of disposal. When full rights of disposal exist, property-owners can spend (dispose of) their profit as they choose—using all of it for personal consumption, for example. Full disposal rights, however, obligate the owner to assume responsibility for any and all debts incurred from the use of the property. The joint stock company—a form of property that is a fixture of modern capitalism—was invented precisely to limit any single owner's debt liability. Moreover, in capitalist societies where almost full rights of disposal are recognized, bankruptcy laws specify how the debt obligations associated with property ownership will be handled.

Rights concerning the transfer of property specify the conditions under which an owner can sell, give, bequeath, or rent property. Not all property can

1. We have drawn much of the material in this section from Kornai. (1992, esp. Ch. 5, pp. 62–90) To minimize citations, we reference only direct quotations from this work.
2. Intellectual property is in this category. Copyrights and patents are designed to protect a person's rights to intellectual property.
3. Kornai (1992) labels these "rights of alienation."

be transferred by all four methods. It may be permissible to rent an object or resource but not to sell it. Alternatively, selling but not renting may be permitted. In capitalist societies, there are relatively few restrictions on rights of transferability.

Rights concerning the use or control of property specify who determines how property is used. These rights encompass issues of decision-making, management, and supervision. For example, think of the proprietor of a small, privately owned company. The owner decides what the company will produce and who will be hired or fired, as well as what price to charge for the products made. There is no single right of control; instead, there are numerous specific rights of control. In modern capitalist societies, actors or sets of actors who are not owners routinely make numerous decisions having to do with property use or property control.

That is an important point to emphasize, because people in capitalist societies tend to think of property rights as absolute. Given the fact that under capitalism owners do enjoy a large array of property rights, this misconception is understandable. Nevertheless, property rights need to be seen as bundles of rights that can be defined and combined in various ways. Some property rights can be exercised by individuals who are not the owners of the property. Consider, for example, a small shareholder in a joint stock company. Owning shares entitles the shareholder to pocket the income (i.e., dividends) that his or her shares earn. The shareholder can also sell stock at the prevailing market price at any time. Stock ownership, however, does not entitle the shareholder to exercise managerial control of the company. Managerial control, or determining how the property will be utilized, is exercised by a board of directors, a chief executive officer, and a hierarchy of managers.

Capitalism as a system of property relations always operates in the context of a market economy. Does this mean that capitalism and markets are synonymous? Can there be a market economy without capitalism? The ability to enter into an exchange relationship and, by extension, the existence of property to exchange are the basis for the creation of a market. Markets and capitalism, however, are not synonymous. The difference between market economies and capitalism is frequently blurred. This is not surprising because market economies and capitalism developed in the same time historic period, and because capitalism and markets work well together. However, capitalism represents just one type of property system, so market economies could conceivably exist in its absence, as long as there were some accompanying arrangement of decentralized property rights. (Gilpin, 1987, pp. 15–24; Lindblom, 1977, pp. 330–343)

In market economies (which have historically been capitalist), owners normally exercise a wide range of property rights. In command economies, they do not. For example, in the Soviet Union all of the Soviet people theoretically owned each factory and state farm. Only an elite few, however, exercised the rights of property ownership. Thus, for purposes of differentiating command from market economies, it is important to distinguish between who in theory owns the means of production and who in practice exercises the associated property rights. Historically in command economies, there existed a particular

kind of socialist property relations; private property was practically nonexistent and *public* ownership of the means of production prevailed. Thus, in
theory, property ownership in command economies is diffused throughout the
society—everyone owns the means of production. But not everyone can exercise the property rights that we typically associate with ownership. Therefore,
to understand systems with command economies, it is necessary to look past
the nominal owners and concentrate on who is really exercising property rights
and what social structures are being used.

The gulf between nominal ownership and the exercise of property rights
becomes blatantly apparent when we consider the major property forms in
command economies. A property form is a particular configuration of property
and property rights. In command economies two property forms predominate:
the state-owned firm and the cooperative.[4] "The property form of the state-
owned firm occupies the 'commanding heights' of the socialist economy."
(Kornai, 1992, p. 71) It is from such "heights" (an expression coined by Lenin)
that the entire economy can be controlled. Thus, in energy production, manufacturing, transportation, wholesale trading, foreign trade, banking, and insurance, state-owned firms operate exclusively. They also can be present in other
sectors. In the Soviet Union, where no private property forms were permitted
(except personal property, like cars and clothing) until the Gorbachev-era reforms, the state-owned firm prevailed.[5]

In an economy based on state-owned firms, rights of transferability do not
exist. No one possesses the right to sell his or her interest in the public sector.
The public, moreover, enjoys no right of disposal and no right to determine
how "its" property will be used. In other words, the "people"—the nominal
owners of the means of production in command economies—do not exercise
any property rights. As we just said, rights to transfer property simply do not
exist. Rights of disposal and control, however, do exist in command economies
and are exercised by a highly centralized decision-making bureaucracy.

This said, we must acknowledge that what constitutes residual income in a
state-owned firm is a far cry from the profit earned by a privately owned firm.
In a command economy, residual income is difficult to identify because no real
distinction is made between "profits" and what people in capitalist societies
call "taxes": "The sum of all payments to the state budget constitutes the
centralized net income of the state sector." (Kornai, 1992, p. 71) Moreover,
because the central decision-makers determine for the state-owned firms their
selling prices, the wages they pay their workers, the prices of the inputs they
use, and the contribution they owe to the state budget, "residual income" is

---

4. Property forms common in capitalist societies with market economies include (1) the family-
owned and -operated undertaking, (2) the owner-managed private firm, and (3) the joint stock
company. See Kornai (1992, pp. 67–70).
5. Although the entire state-owned sector was in theory the property of the Soviet people, we use
the term *state-owned* rather than *people-owned* because it better reflects the realities of the Soviet
economic system.

really only an arbitrary designation. Furthermore, none of the "profit" from a state-owned firm passes automatically into the pockets of anyone in the twin hierarchies (Party and government) of the decision-making apparatus, and, conversely, no one in either hierarchy covers from his or her own pocket any part of the losses incurred by a state-owned firm.

What form does managerial control take in a command economy? The state-owned firm is at the bottom of a large bureaucracy. The bureaucrats exercising direct control over the firm are separated organizationally from the bureaucrats handling the state's financial affairs. In the Soviet case, only at the highest levels of the Communist Party and the government were these two branches of the bureaucracy under unified direction.

The cooperative is the other basic property form in command economies. Historically, it was used most in agriculture. In the Soviet Union prior to the Gorbachev era, cooperatives were almost exclusively collective farms (*kolkhoz*). In theory, the cooperative "is a voluntary association of its members, in which the means of production form the collective property of the cooperative, and the membership itself elects its leaders." (Kornai, 1992, p. 77) In reality, Soviet collective farmers did not voluntarily establish their collective farms, nor did they freely elect their leadership. They could not choose to leave the cooperative, nor could they choose to join one if they had never been a member. They also could not hire outside labor to assist them in their own agricultural undertakings. To work the land was to be either a nonvoluntary member of a collective farm or an employee of a state farm (*sovkhoz*), a kind of state-owned agricultural factory.

The director of a Soviet collective farm was chosen (and could be removed) by persons in the upper echelons of the agricultural bureaucracy and thus was dependent on them. For example, the director could not independently decide how to use the cooperative's income. Income use was restricted by "general regulations and by occasional, specific interventions from above." (Kornai, 1992, p. 77) Members of the collective farm exercised no rights with regard to residual income. Nor did they have any rights of transferability or control. Higher authorities made decisions about the transfer of particular means of production (e.g., tractors, combines) from one collective farm to another, and these same authorities decided if and when two collective farms were to merge. The director did not even have the freedom to choose how the means of production (e.g., the land, the farm tools, fertilizer) would be used. The collective farm—in theory a cooperative—was as subject to bureaucratic control as the state-owned firm was.

Collective farmers in the Soviet Union, however, were entitled to farm some personally controlled land. These private plots were assigned to individuals or families by the cooperative. The cooperative could take a private plot back at any time and assign another parcel in its stead. To work the private plots, the peasants could sometimes rent equipment from the collective or state farm. In effect, peasants enjoyed partial property rights with regard to their household plots. Most important, they were allowed the right to dispose of the products of their plots by personally consuming them or by selling them in collective-farm markets. Not surprisingly, this ability to earn residual income (or profit) helped make the·private plot the most productive component of Soviet agriculture. The low productivity of the collective farms and the high productivity of the private plots demonstrate the connection between property rights and the incentive structures that operate in an economic system. We will explore this connection shortly.

Decision-Making

All economic systems have structures and processes designed for decision-making. In this regard, the fundamental question is: How will the responsibility for and control over the distribution of resources be determined? In a market economy, decision making is decentralized. The society's productive assets are, for the most part, dispersed throughout the society according to established rules about property and property rights. Decisions are made by numerous individuals exercising their property rights. These decision-makers, guided by calculations of self-interest, determine the disposition of their (and, by extension, society's) assets. Command economies typically have centralized systems for such decision-making.

In the Soviet Union, two hierarchies controlled economic decision-making: the Communist Party and the government. The top leadership of the CPSU was responsible for the most important decisions affecting the economy—for example, decisions about the allocation of productive resources among consumer goods, investment, and defense. The Party apparat was responsible for lower-level decision-making within these broad outlines. Thus, its hierarchy paralleled the hierarchy of government agencies, including those controlling the various sectors of the Soviet economy. The government bureaucracy was mainly responsible for implementing policies generated within the Party. (Hewett, 1988, pp. 98, 102) The parallel Party bureaucracy closely supervised the implementation process.

Economic goals were articulated, specific plans (production targets) were set, and plan fulfillment was enforced through a hierarchical system. Five-year[6] and annual plans established economic goals for the Soviet economy. Though widely regarded as the hallmark of the Soviet planning process, the five-year plans functioned more as statements of economic policy goals than as operational tools. The annual plans were tied more closely to the individual plans that specific enterprises or organizations were to fulfill. The annual plans often were inconsistent with the five-year plan currently in force. Only with regard to investment policy, where a relatively long time horizon is required, did the five-year plans have a significant practical impact on how the investment process developed. (Kornai, 1992, p. 111)

---

6. Stalin initiated the First Five-Year Plan in the 1920s. The guidelines of the Twelfth (and last) Five-Year Plan were promulgated in November 1985.

The annual plans covered every aspect of economic activity. It would be tedious to recount in detail all of the features of an annual plan, but a summary of the most important aspects will shed light on decision-making within the Soviet command economy. The annual plan specified overall production targets for the entire national economy. It also indicated how the responsibility for meeting those targets would be distributed among the main sectors of the economy—heavy industry, consumer goods, agriculture, transportation, and so on. The plan designated specific production figures for critical commodities, such as military hardware. In the Soviet Union, these critical commodities usually numbered in the thousands. Specific production targets were set for each critical commodity. Wherever possible, the targets were stated in quantitative terms, such as individual units or kilograms.

Because the annual plans were mandatory, not mere guidelines, they inevitably focused on striking a balance between the resources needed to produce goods and the uses to which goods would be put. An example is coordination between the mining and smelting of iron and the needs of factories making automobile parts. In turn, the output of automobile parts would have to be coordinated with the targets for automobile production. This emphasis on coordination constituted another important aspect of planning in the Soviet Union.

Establishing a proper balance for critical commodities was the direct responsibility of Gosplan (the State Planning Committee). The various departments of Gosplan negotiated with the production ministries about supplies and with all the ministries about how commodities would be used. For each critical commodity, Gosplan specified a balance between source and use. When a deficit was projected, Gosplan had to increase the input or reduce the output in order to try to balance the account.

Gosplan was ultimately responsible for economic planning, but it was by no means the only actor involved. It would have been physically impossible for the central planning agency to designate targets directly for every one of the millions of products that made up the Soviet economy. Beyond the list of priority products whose targets were centrally determined, production targets in the form of individual plans for individual producers were set throughout the administrative hierarchy. This was the only practical way to proceed, given the enormity of the task.

Thus, planning took place at every level of the administrative hierarchy involved in the control of the Soviet economy. At the top of the administrative hierarchy of the government was the Council of Ministers and its chair (*predsedatel'*) who was often referred to in the West as the Prime Minister because of his role as the leader of the government administrative apparatus. The Council of Ministers was composed of the heads of one hundred or more ministries and state committees, of which seventy played a role in the economic system. Some of these were all-union ministries that existed only at the national level; others were union-republic ministries that had counterparts in the republics and were directly responsible to the union-level ministry. (Hewett, 1988, pp. 107–108)

The plans that were presented to each enterprise or farm director were never viewed as guidelines. Rather, they were compulsory targets. With regard to plan fulfillment, the factory or farm director answered to the ministry. Ultimately, each ministry was responsible for the performance of the enterprises or farms it supervised. The planning apparatus served another important function with regard to running the national economy. It provided Party leaders with information about the economic system.

It would be a mistake to conclude, however, that in the command economy of the Soviet Union, the Party simply proposed and the government disposed. The Party was very involved in the day-to-day operation of the economy. Virtually all of the important economic administrators in the government, from ministers to local managerial personnel, were Party members. In addition, the parallel Party bureaucracy not only supervised the government bureaucracy but also played an active role in economic management. Thus, Party influence permeated the command economy.

Until the Gorbachev-era reforms, about ten departments within the CPSU bureaucracy were responsible for substantive areas relating to the economy. (Barry & Barner-Barry, 1991, p. 177) The CPSU and the government hierarchies worked together to run the economy. Depending on the type of economic decision to be made, one hierarchy or the other bore the primary responsibility for decision-making. The Party, for example, decided on the general policy pertaining to the development of nuclear power in the USSR. The government supplied technical and economic information, implemented the CPSU's decisions, and tended to the practical task of coordinating nuclear energy and other sources of energy to meet the economy's needs. (Hewett, 1988, p. 102)

Party involvement in the economy extended to local (*gorkom* and *raikom*) and provincial (*obkom*) Party officials who were held responsible for the economic performance of their localities and provinces. These Party officials could exercise considerable influence through their control over key appointments. Although they were urged not to intervene directly in the operational decisions of the firms in their regions, the fact that they were held accountable for the economic performance of these firms led local Party officials to intervene routinely in day-to-day management. (Hewett, 1988, p. 165)

The design of the decision-making system in the Soviet Union—the dual hierarchies—was intended to ensure the center's control of economic activity. It also reflected optimistic assumptions about achieving coordinated outcomes, in spite of the fact that thousands of enterprises and cooperatives operated under the supervision of a host of ministries. A primary function of Gosplan and other related state committees was to coordinate the activities of this elaborate hierarchy of interrelated and interdependent organizations. These other state committees included Gossnab (State Committee for Material-Technical Supply), Goskomtsen (State Committee for Pricing), and *Goskomtrud* (State Committee for Labor and Social Questions). Their efforts notwithstanding, problems of coordination abounded. These problems were due in no small part to the information system.

Information System

The information system provides the data that is used in economic decision-making. The critical question is, How does the economic system generate the data on which decision-makers base their choices? In a market economy, relative prices provide such information. That is, prices change in response to demand and supply (thus, the designation "relative"), and those changes inform the choices of individual decision-makers. In a command economy, the government hierarchy (not prices) is the primary source of information used in economic decision-making. In the Soviet Union, data supplied by the bureaucracy was used for both the broad policy decisions made by Party leaders and the routine bureaucratic decisions that affected the day-to-day operation of the economy. (Hewett, 1988, p. 192) The Soviet information system was huge, slow, and unwieldy and could never provide sufficient and timely information for effective and efficient economic decision-making.

Problems of efficiency were not unique to the Soviet Union. Such problems are typical of command economies. In fact, the information system of a command economy virtually guarantees inefficiency. Specialized task assignments coordinated from above can yield efficient outcomes only if those assigning and coordinating the tasks are fully informed. Moreover, efficient outcomes require that information be continually updated to reflect changing conditions of demand and supply. In the absence of relative prices, such updating is impossible. Thus, the problem of information always cripples the operation of a command economy. The problem is particularly acute when it is necessary to coordinate the efforts of a variety of specialized producers that contribute jointly to some complex final product.

Even under the best of circumstances, therefore, a command economy is inevitably inefficient. In actual operation it never approaches its formal design. Although the same can surely be said of every economic system, the gap between theory and practice is particularly wide in command economies.

Incentive Structures

Bureaucracies are authority structures in which orders flow down from above and are (in theory, at least) carried out by specialized personnel. Efficient outcomes are supposed to result (assuming, of course, that the orders are based on accurate and complete information). In reality, efficiency results only when some fairly rigorous conditions are met.

One important condition is that the administrators in the bureaucracy discharge their functions in a relatively mechanical way. "In an ideal bureaucracy, no one is unique." (Lindblom, 1977, p. 27) In other words, bureaucracy works best when staffed by people without emotions and personal circumstances that demand their attention. Because there are no such people, efficient outcomes can be approached in a bureaucracy only if the bureaucracy is staffed by people who are sufficiently motivated to perform their tasks well despite their emotional baggage and life situations. This brings us to the subject of incentives.

With regard to incentives, the basic question is: What kind of inducements are used to motivate productive behavior, and how well do they work? Indeed, the notion of motivating behavior simply puts a positive spin on controlling behavior. All incentives—material, symbolic, coercive—derive from various combinations of the four fundamental mechanisms of social control that we introduced in Chapter 1: power, authority, persuasion, and exchange.

In market economies, exchange predominates. Exchange relationships form the basis of all market systems. This does not mean, however, that coercive and symbolic incentives have no place in market economies. In the hierarchy of the modern corporation—a major player in market economies—employees are exhorted to higher levels of performance by incentives that are coercive (e.g., the threat of being fired) and symbolic (e.g., company pride) as well as material (e.g., wages and bonuses). Nevertheless, the essential exchange basis of the market economy means that calculations of material self-interest permeate the system. Economic actors—be they individuals or corporations—are driven to make choices that further their own individual or corporate material self-interest. These self-interested choices stem from the decentralized property rights that owners enjoy in market systems. For example, a promotion or raise can translate into the ability to buy a boat or a trip to Hawaii. Where self-interested choices also promote society's welfare, material incentive structures are largely automatic. (Kornai, 1992, pp. 71–76)

In command economies, however, social control is exercised far more through power, authority, and persuasion than through exchange. Although the same kinds of material, coercive, and symbolic incentives may exist in both command and market economies, their relative impact and effectiveness are dramatically different in each type of system. Material incentives like wage increases and bonuses that have a generally high degree of impact and effectiveness in market economies are typically much less effective in command economies. But the coercive and symbolic incentives that are much more important in command economies are detached from personal calculations of material self-interest. Thus, what usually happens in command economies is that the incentive structures officially in place, however constituted, tend to conflict with the individual's automatic impulse to pursue material self-interest. (Lindblom, 1977, p. 74) And unsanctioned material incentives typically run counter to the officially sponsored incentive system.

The heart and soul of any modern economy are its productive facilities or enterprises. Indeed, given the fact that consumer preferences did not drive production decisions in the Soviet Union, enterprise directors and their workers (along with their counterparts in the agricultural sector) were arguably the most essential participants in the economy. Motivating their efforts was an array of primarily coercive and symbolic incentives.

Plant managers feared losing their positions if they failed to deliver on important production targets. Interestingly, the threat of being fired for inadequate job performance—a typical coercive incentive in a capitalist society—

was seldom applied to the average Soviet worker. Only the most outrageous behavior resulted in job loss. It must be added, however, that during certain periods, most notably the Stalin-era purges, workers and plant managers alike feared sanctions far worse than losing a job. Tatyana Zaslavskaya describes the role of power in the workplace during the immediate post–World War II period:

> A plan for an enterprise handed down from above had the force of law and non-fulfillment entailed political and criminal responsibility. Unprecedentedly harsh standards of discipline at work and with regard to production were the rule in enterprises and institutions. Being late for work, overstaying the lunch break, not to mention attempts to take home any of the scrap products from work, were punished by imprisonment, or exile to a corrective labor camp. (Zaslavskaya, 1990, p. 21)

These were only some of the economic crimes in force. Some, like counterfeiting, had parallels in the West. Most, however, were peculiar to a command economy.

"Antiparasite laws," which came into existence in the late 1950s, for example, required Soviet citizens to work unless they had a very good reason (i.e., disability) not to work. Such laws are far less necessary in market economies, where automatic incentives induce individuals to offer their labor in exchange for a wage. Because it was nearly impossible to get fired, laws also forbade and set punishments for worker absenteeism and tardiness and, of course, prohibited the pilfering of state property.

The dearth of property rights in the Soviet Union created lasting legacies. Rights to make a profit, for example, were severely restricted to activities such as selling produce in a collective-farm market. Here automatic incentives created a situation in which household plots accounted for a disproportionate share of agricultural output (see Tables 6-1 and 6-2). However, the prohibition of speculation[7] inhibited the widespread development of entrepreneurship. (Barry & Barner-Barry, 1991, pp. 155, 279–280) Criminal prosecutions and penalties for engaging in prohibited speculative activity were enforced with varying degrees of intensity. They were used often enough, however, to pose a real threat to those who wanted to exercise economic initiative. In addition, periodic ideological campaigns, reinforced by heavy doses of intimidation, aimed to root out "bourgeois influences" in the society. Thus, the sharing of information and the exercise of individual initiative—both important for encouraging innovation and efficiency—were effectively discouraged. (Zaslavskaya, 1990, pp. 25–26)

In the Soviet economy both symbolic and material incentives, by and large, proved ineffectual because they worked at cross-purposes. For example, a formal system of bonuses—a material incentive—was supposed to motivate

---

7. If the profits were large enough, speculation could be, and on occasion was, punished by death.

TABLE 6-1
Types of Soviet Farms

	Millions of Hectares[1]		
	1960	1970	1980
Total land under production	1,113.6	1,120.2	1,114.9
Collective and state farm land	1,043.6	1,041.0	1,043.2
Privately cultivated land[2]	70.3	79.15	71.69
Percentage of total land in private use	6.3	7.1	6.4

[1]One hectare equals 2.70 acres.
[2]Private land usage totals are compiled from the following categories found in *Narodnoe khoziaistvo:*
    a: Private plots used by collective farm workers (Priusadebnye uchastki v pol'zovanii kolkhoznikov)
    b: Land personally used by laborers and white-collar workers (excluding collective farm workers) (Zemli v lichnom pol'zovanii rabochikh i sluzhashchikh [krome uchastkov na kolkhoznykh zemliakh])
    c: Other land users (prochie zemlepol'zovateli)
    d: Kolkhoz land used personally by laborers and white-collar workers (zemli kolkhozov v lichnom pol'zovanii rabochikh i sluzhashchikh)
Sources: *Narodnoe khoziaistvo SSSR za 60 let.* Statisticheskii ezhegodnik (Moscow: Gosstatizdat 1961). p. 299; *Narodnoe khoziaistvo SSSR za 70 let.* Statisticheskii ezhegodnik (Moscow: Gosstatizdat 1971). p. 222; *Narodnoe khoziaistvo SSSR za 80 let.* Statisticheskii ezhegodnik (Moscow: Gosstatizdat 1981). p. 219.

and guide both managers and workers to meet or beat their production targets. The desired impact of such bonuses, however, was largely circumvented in practice by complex special arrangements between Gosplan and the ministries as well as between the ministries and the firms under their control. These arrangements were usually struck with two central considerations in mind— considerations rooted in Marxism-Leninism, the primary basis of symbolic incentives in Soviet society.

The first consideration was the idea that a firm should at least be able to cover the wages of its work force, as well as a minimum level of bonuses, regardless of performance. The second consideration was the idea that no firm should be so successful that it could offer bigger bonuses to its workers than were being offered to workers in other plants producing similar goods. For all practical purposes, enterprises were not allowed to go bankrupt and thus lacked a powerful incentive that in market economies stimulates labor productivity. The actual incentive structure with its floor (below which no enterprise would be allowed to sink) and its ceiling (above which no enterprise could aspire to rise) discouraged self-interested, motivated workers and managers from producing at increasing levels of efficiency. (Hewett, 1988, p. 208)

So far, we have described how in command economies the official incentive structure frequently runs counter to the self-interested calculations of individuals, how personal initiative is discouraged by legal prohibitions, and how symbolic incentives can undermine the impact of material incentives. It is

TABLE 6-2
Soviet Agricultural Production by Type, 1960–80[1]

Category	Socialized	Private	Total output
	Percentage	Percentage	Millions of tons
Meat			
1960	59	41	8.7
1970[2]	65	35	12.3
1980	69	31	15.1
Milk			
1960	53	47	61.7
1970	64	36	83.0
1980	70	30	90.9
Potatoes			
1960	37	63	84.4
1970	35	65	96.8
1980	36	64	67.0

[1]Socialized sector combines state farm (sovkhoz) and collective farm (kolkhoz) production.
[2]This change reflects the importation of US feed grain during the 1970s. This would not have increased meat production in the private sector.
Sources: Pockney, B. P. (1991). *Soviet statistics since 1950* (p. 228). New York: St. Martin's Press.
Directorate of Intelligence (1988). *Handbook of economic statistics* (pp. 67–8). Washington, DC: Central Intelligence Agency.

certainly fair to say that the problem of incentives is ubiquitous in command economies. In an environment where material and symbolic incentives are not particularly effective, coercion is an indispensable component of the incentive system.

The fact of the matter is that power and the social structures that promoted its exercise largely defined the political economy of communism. This point is made by Janos Kornai (1992, p. 33): "The key to an understanding of the socialist system is to examine the *structure of power* . . . [T]he characteristics of the power structure are precisely the source from which the chief regularities of the system can be deduced." (emphasis in the original) Thus, deprivation or the threat of deprivation is routinely used to compel productive behavior in command economies. Unfortunately, the reliance on power has unintended consequences—consequences that distort and undermine the long-term performance of a command economy.

Why is this the case? In Chapter 1 we examined power as a mechanism of social control. In that discussion, we identified coercion as the practical basis of power, and we identified the response to coercion as compliance. Whether the person being coerced thinks that what he or she is being pressured to do (or not do) is right or wrong is irrelevant. He or she is motivated to comply in order to avoid the physical or psychological pain that can result from either loss or deprivation. Someone dominated by power exercises only limited control over his or her own destiny. In other words, the person's response to power is a *subject's* response.

The psychological impact of long-term subject status can be profound. Stanley Renshon (1974, p. 1) writes of a basic need shared by all human beings "to gain control over [their] physical and psychological life-space." Of course, no one ever gains complete control over one's life. However, for people subject to the ongoing exercise of power for the purpose of *social* control, the sense of *personal* control can be seriously compromised. The other mechanisms of social control—authority, persuasion, and exchange—do not have the same impact. With authority and persuasion, people accept the necessity to surrender some personal control. Exchange allows the widest latitude for personal control because it establishes social control by structuring choices that induce self-interested responses from others. Only power wrests control from its subjects.

It is hardly surprising, therefore, that the exercise of power produces a host of negative feelings and emotions in those subjected to it. Primary among these emotions are anger, frustration, cynicism, and, sometimes, abject fear. How these emotions combine and how intensely they are felt varies from one individual to another. Moreover, the level and kind of coercion at work, as well as the length of time that coercion is used are also involved. In the extreme case of victimization through brute force and terror, survival dictates that these emotions be meticulously suppressed. In less extreme situations of long-term subjugation, anger and frustration are frequently expressed through passive-aggressive behavior and sometimes through violent acts of rebellion.

The negative feelings caused by the exercise of power poison efforts to transform power relationships into authority relationships. Authority elicits an internalized acceptance of control based on legitimacy. With authority, people respond positively to commands and directives because they see them as right and proper. This response contrasts sharply with the conforming response extracted through the use of power. Power arouses resentments instead of a positive emotional response. Thus, the pervasive reliance on coercive incentives in a command economy complicates and distorts efforts to operate the economy through the use of incentives derived from authority, persuasion, and exchange.

We can underscore this point by focusing on one set of actors who are the key to success in all command economies: enterprise directors. In the hierarchy of the command economy, enterprise directors are responsible for meeting the production targets that come from above, and they are the primary conduit of information on which production decisions are based.

When enterprise directors or plant managers are motivated to meet their production quotas because they fear reprisals, this fear colors all of their management decisions. They urge their workers implicitly or explicitly to meet the quantitative requirements specified in the plan, but they do not encourage workers to maintain quality standards. As a result, the goods produced are woefully inadequate.

Products made at one facility may be intermediate goods that are inputs for the productive endeavors at another facility. Shabby or insufficient inputs compromise and complicate the efforts of other enterprise directors as they strive to meet their own plan targets. Thus, they hoard the inputs required to produce their designated outputs, and they rely on unauthorized suppliers if they cannot obtain inputs through regular channels.

From the standpoint of the enterprise director, those measures are necessary accommodations to meet the imperative of production quotas—an imperative driven by fear. But they are also illegal accommodations that undermine the authority relationships on which the hierarchical decision structures of the command economy are based. In addition, they serve to channel misleading, incomplete, and grossly inaccurate information to those who set the production targets in the first place. In this way, the exercise of power further strains the already enfeebled information system of the command economy.

We confront, therefore, a basic contradiction inherent in command economies. The exercise of power is an integral part of the incentive system, but it subverts decision-making and information-gathering, other fundamental aspects of any economic system. It follows that the greater the reliance on power to compel desired behavior and outcomes, the greater will be the distorting effects on the economic system as a whole. As we underscore in our discussion of the legacy of Stalin's development strategy later in this chapter, the Soviet Union offers a good example of the damaging consequences of an excessive reliance on power. Nowhere are the limitations of a command economy more evident than in the areas of technology and innovation.

Technology and Innovation

Russia was the last of the Great Powers of nineteenth-century Europe to begin the process of industrialization. Although late industrialization had negative consequences, particularly for military capability, it also had positive consequences. One advantage of industrializing after the "first wave" is access to technology. Late industrializers are not usually placed in the position of having to reinvent the wheel.

Raymond Vernon (1966) devised a model of the product cycle to explain the technological dynamic of economic development. According to Vernon's model, technological innovations emerge from an advanced industrial economy. At first, the innovator enjoys a monopoly on the technology, markets the resulting products in its domestic market, and exports them to other developed economies. As the technology matures, producers in other developed economies duplicate the technology and begin to produce and export the products. The innovator no longer has a monopoly on the technology and may no longer even be the most efficient producer. Other economies have newer plants and equipment, and they may have improved the technology.

Eventually the mature technology becomes the standard technology. At this last stage, developing economies adopt the technology and produce the products associated with it. They become the world's biggest and most efficient producers of products using now-standard technology, in large part because of their relatively low standards of living and wage costs. They then can use the revenues generated to advance their own economic development.

According to Vernon's model, all technological innovations go through this cycle: from innovation, to mature technology, to standard technology. According to Vernon, the product cycle is the engine of economic growth and global economic development. Eventually, in his view, more and more countries will join the ranks of potential innovators as the level of economic development begins to equalize over time.

An important implication of Vernon's model is that all countries that industrialized after Great Britain in the late eighteenth century enjoyed the benefits of technology transfer. Russia and, later, the Soviet Union were no exceptions. The key to economic development, however, is moving from the status of technology importer to technology exporter. How can a country use technology to join the ranks of the innovators? This subject stirs considerable controversy in the literature on economic development. Raymond Vernon and other liberal economists believe that the product cycle and the international investment and trade resulting from it are benign processes that, if allowed to work, will produce global economic development. Dependency and modern world systems theorists argue that economic development from a position of dependence in the global capitalist economy is difficult, if not impossible.[8]

Import substitution is one strategy countries use to move from importing technology to developing their own technology. Stalin's economic development strategy represented an extreme variation of import substitution. At first, Stalin relied on some imports of capital equipment (such as the machines that make the machines that make other products), paying for them with agricultural exports. His preference, however, was to go it alone. The success of his policy hinged on the ability of the Soviet Union to use imported technology as a springboard to technological innovations and scientific breakthroughs. In some sectors, particularly those with military applications, the Soviet Union achieved this level of development. In many more, however, an inability to innovate blocked the technological development of the Soviet economy.

Innovation occurs in the competitive environment of a market economy because survival in the marketplace often depends on innovation. "Make it better, faster, and cheaper" is the motto of every successful entrepreneur. This survival incentive was not present in the Soviet economy. Inefficient enterprises seldom went out of business, and workers seldom feared losing their jobs. This "safety net" seriously dampened the incentive to innovate. Innovation was further discouraged by a system that refused to offer sufficient rewards for ingenuity and inventiveness. Moreover, innovators were likely to be resented or rejected, because the culture did not value people who "stood above the crowd" and made their fellow workers "look bad."

---

8. For a more complete discussion of economic development from dependency and modern world systems perspectives, see Evans (1979) and Wallerstein (1974).

The lack of a competitive economic environment complicated the process of innovation in yet another way. In a competitive market economy, identifying successful innovation is easy. Successful innovation sells, yielding great profits for the innovator. Profit, of course, is the basic measure of economic success in market economies. One of the major inadequacies of command economies is that there is no similar indicator of success.

Soviet economic history is rife with ludicrous examples of the consequences of trying to use measures other than profits or market share to quantify economic performance. A now-classic example has to do with the production of chandeliers. Nikita Khrushchev is reported to have complained, "It has become the tradition to produce not beautiful chandeliers to adorn homes, but the heaviest chandeliers possible. This is because the heavier the chandelier produced, the more a factory gets since its output is calculated in tons." (Kohler, 1968, p. 507) Product quality did not matter. Products embodying the latest technology did not matter. The only thing that mattered was meeting plan goals whether measured numerically or by weight.

Despite the inherent problems, however, some sectors of the Soviet economy did innovate and maintain a relatively high level of quality. The Soviet economic system could perform well when an undertaking received the focused attention of Party and government officials. Examples include the production of world-class turbines for hydroelectric stations, the development of long-distance, high-voltage transmission lines, and, of course, the development of a formidable military capability based primarily (though not entirely) on Soviet technology. Accounting for these successes, Ed Hewett (1988, p. 217) writes: "When the attention of the government and the party turns to an industry, product, or process, innovative activity quite naturally picks up." He adds that fleeting or sporadic attention proved insufficient to force innovation. Innovations occurred when the undertaking received long-term, continuous attention—and when the requirements for inter-ministry collaboration were modest.

The example of the nuclear power industry nicely illustrates the possibilities and limits of innovation in civilian sectors with a high priority. The top-level attention given that industry resulted in the development of an impressive array of technologies based almost entirely on Soviet research. Efforts at innovation, however, were significantly less successful when the goal was to create a manufacturing base to produce the equipment necessary to build the power plants. This uneven success is easily explained. Manufacturing the equipment and building the plants, unlike developing nuclear power technologies, required the coordinated involvement of numerous ministries. Where coordination was necessary, even for projects deemed highly important, the chances for successful innovation decreased. The net result for the Soviet nuclear power industry was Chernobyl and a large number of other plants in desperate need of either refurbishing or elimination. (Hewett, 1988, p. 217)

Soviet efforts at innovation were generally most successful in the defense-related sectors of the economy. Several factors account for this success. One is the setup of the command structures for civilian and defense-related activities. The formal setup looked about the same in each. Comparable ministerial systems were linked to parallel Party organizations. A Military Industrial Commission, however, supervised the activities of the nine defense machine-building ministries, and each defense plant had a senior military officer who served as quality control inspector. The quality control officers were on the military payroll and had no vested interest in whether the plant made its plan targets. Their commitment was to ensure the quality of the product. Also, on-site design bureaus were attached to defense plants, so experimental designs could be tested on the premises. In contrast, in the civilian sectors, applying technology was far more difficult. Research and development were often conducted at great distances from the production plants, and the implementation of the new technology was not as closely supervised by outside persons concerned only with quality. (Hewett, 1988, pp. 215–219)

Another factor favoring defense-related innovation was competition. One reason why innovation was lacking in the civilian sector is that there was no competition. This was not the case in the defense sector. Cold War competition between the United States and the Soviet Union and the perception that the United States posed a serious national security threat strongly encouraged research, development, and the deployment of new weapons systems.

The national security aspect of defense-related economic activities also guaranteed the high priority, close scrutiny, and coordinated effort necessary for successful innovation. In addition, the security element created an incentive that civilian production could not match. It tapped into the patriotism of the work force, as well as the age-old Russian cultural preoccupation with invasion threats from other countries. Both of these sparked initiative and productive labor.

When Mikhail Gorbachev assumed the top leadership position in 1985, he was justifiably concerned about the status of technology and innovation in the Soviet economy. His reforms, particularly perestroika, were intended to solve economic problems. The stagnant economy that he inherited, however, was not exclusively the product of problems inherent in the design of command economies. Soviet economic problems were as much a result of excesses peculiar to the Soviet Union as weaknesses endemic to command economies. The excesses were largely the legacy of Stalin's economic development strategy. Consequently, rectifying flaws in the formal command economy (which is exactly what Gorbachev's early reform attempts tried to do) simply could not work. To appreciate the magnitude of Gorbachev's task as he confronted the challenge of economic reform, an understanding of Stalin's legacy is required.

THE LEGACY OF STALIN'S ECONOMIC DEVELOPMENT STRATEGY

Stalin consolidated his control over the CPSU apparatus and used this base of support to become top Soviet leader in 1928. Under Stalin, a brutal reorganization of the political-economic system was carried out. It directly affected all segments of the society, and it resulted in the creation of the command economy. Through the collectivization of agriculture and the central planning system, Stalin was able to divert societal resources (both human and material) from the agricultural sector and amass the capital necessary to build heavy industry. The magnitude of this accomplishment should not be underestimated. Although an increase in heavy industry is a normal result of economic development, under Stalin the Soviet Union achieved unparalleled levels of industrial development in both size and speed. In an extraordinarily brief period of time, Stalin transformed the Soviet economy.

According to Gregory and Stuart (1994, p. 87), "between 1928 and 1937, heavy manufacturing's net product share of total manufacturing more than doubled, from 31 percent to 63 percent. . . ." The Soviet Union achieved in a decade the level of development in heavy industry that took other Western societies from fifty to seventy-five years. During this period, the increases in the rates of industrial investment, as well as the speed with which resources were shifted from agriculture to industry were also unprecedented. (Gregory & Stuart, 1990, p. 124)

The success of Stalin's command economy during the 1930s and again during the post–World War II reconstruction period is attributable to the leader's unrelenting drive to industrialize. From this one overwhelming priority, the command economy of the Soviet Union was erected. From it, moreover, the distinctive features and characteristics of the Soviet economy were derived. In other words, Stalin's commitment to industrialization was the root from which all other features of the Soviet economy sprang. These features secured for Stalin and his successors a heavy-industry base and formidable military might, but they proved insufficient and even damaging to long-run economic success. In effect, the very factors that spawned its initial success inevitably sank the Soviet economy into stagnation.

This industrialization imperative was the primary (but not the only) force that drove collectivization in the agricultural sector. Industrialization demanded enormous levels of sacrifice, which was unequally imposed on the Soviet population. Prolonged sacrifice, in turn, created its own distorting effects on the economy, as did the excessive use of coercion. Nowhere is the damaging impact of sacrifice and coercion more evident than in the agricultural sector. In the next sections, therefore, we analyze the impact of Stalin's industrialization drive. We consider the rationale for this imperative. Then, we examine the distinctive features of the Soviet economy which sprang from the overriding priority to industrialize (i.e., prolonged sacrifice and reliance on power). We also explore their synergistic and largely harmful effects on the Soviet economy.

One Overriding Priority: Rapid Industrialization

The ability to identify priorities and specify corresponding production targets is a central feature of a command economy. The ability to establish economic priorities—to rank economic goals for a society—may seem a definite advantage for a political-economic system. Indeed, for reasons peculiar to the Soviet system, establishing clear priorities initially contributed to its success. How-ever, the seeming logic of this process evaporates when viewed from an eco-nomic point of view.

In most circumstances, it makes no sense to rank one important and socially necessary service or product over another. For example, is medical care more socially valuable than housing? The question smacks of the absurd. Both are necessary. For society, the overwhelming concern is one of proportion: how much medical care versus how much housing. Determining the intrinsic value of products and services—that is, ranking them in order of importance—is usually irrelevant to practical decision-making.

Even though it may be irrelevant to rank housing as more important than medical care or vice versa, what is frequently crucial are decisions about ex-panding or reducing the production of certain goods and services relative to others. To make efficient decisions about expanding or reducing production in one area, decision-makers need information about the impact of each option on the production of other goods and services. In addition, conditions of demand and supply fluctuate constantly, and decisions about expanding or reducing production of goods and services must always be subject to change. Thus, the only priorities that make any economic sense at all are transitory priorities—priorities that change as conditions of demand and supply change.

In market economies, transitory priorities are arrived at by means of the mechanism of relative prices. Comparing prices gives would-be producers (and consumers) information to help them make their production (and consump-tion) choices. Equipped with such signals, they are constantly choosing produc-tion (and consumption) combinations. Their choices have relatively little to do with any particular product's intrinsic utility. Rather, these choices reflect mo-mentary preferences based on current conditions of demand and supply. For example, a person may decide to buy clothing rather than athletic shoes on a given day because clothing is on sale at that moment and athletic shoes are not. Correspondingly, if people are willing to pay more for athletic shoes than for dress shoes, a manufacturer may decide to devote more resources to the produc-tion of athletic shoes. These choices have nothing to do with the intrinsic value of athletic shoes relative to other kinds of apparel; they do, however, reflect transitory priorities in the form of relative prices. Without such naturally gener-ated information, production planners in command economies have difficulty in coordinating the mix of products.

Bureaucratic coordination is less efficient than market coordination. If effi-ciency through transitory priorities and relative prices were the only rationale for establishing an economic system, the command economy would never have been created. The argument against bureaucratic coordination and rank-ordered priorities becomes less compelling as factors other than efficient out-comes become more important to the decision-makers.

For a classical or neoclassical economist, efficiency is the best criterion for all production and consumption decisions. In a world of scarcity, it makes sense to find the allocation of resources that eliminates as much waste as possible. However, when security is the primary criterion, efficiency ceases to have much relevance. Historically, for most Russians, survival under harsh climatic conditions and under threat from foreign invaders was more important than efficiency in societal decision-making. Stalin translated this preoccupation with security into one overriding social priority: industrialization.

Stalin viewed industrialization as the key to Soviet survival. He understood that industrialization was the basis for a modern military, which was necessary for defending against foreign enemies. (Tucker, 1990, p. 45, 50) Survival was a very real concern. Failure to keep pace with the industrializing West (including Japan) contributed greatly to Russia's military defeat in the Crimean War (1854), the Russo-Japanese War (1905), and World War I (1914–17). Security threats from abroad continued to loom large. The British, French, and Americans sent troops to aid the counterrevolutionary efforts of the White Russians during the civil war that followed the 1917 Bolshevik Revolution. From a Bolshevik perspective, this action constituted a foreign invasion. When Stalin embarked on his policy of rapid industrialization, he justified it as a way of avoiding repetition of these mistakes of the past. He also pointed to the current "capitalist encirclement" of the Soviet Union as a reason why a future war was inevitable. Thus, rapid industrialization was Stalin's way of preparing the Soviet Union for the future task of repelling an invading army. (Daniels, 1985, p. 170; Tucker, 1990, pp. 57–58, 74–76)

The importance of rapid industrialization for Stalin and his associates extended beyond the necessity for military preparedness. Industrialization was deemed vital to the continued existence of the Soviet political-economic system: "Industrialization was seen as the panacea that would protect Russia (and the Communist regime) from outside attack and that would create the proletariat necessary to end the anomaly of a worker's government in a peasant country. . . . [T]he rapid expansion of industry also would by itself serve to furnish legitimacy for the Party leadership and thereby to strengthen its political support." (Hough, 1969, pp. 5–6) Thus, Stalin decided to industrialize with unprecedented rapidity.

This priority was logical from a security if not from an economic perspective. It presupposed the willingness of the people to sacrifice, as well as the ability of the government to impose sacrifice. In addition, it indicated willingness to absorb the inevitable resource waste as well as the efficiency losses that undoubtedly would follow. Rapid industrialization was initially successful, and it did greatly aid the Soviet Union's ability to repel the Nazi attack during World War II. However, it created economic distortions that did not go away and ultimately contributed to the system's failure.

Industrialization is never an easy or painless process. It requires the accumulation of tremendous financial, material, human, and technological resources for the building of an interdependent network of factories that produce everything from machine tools to finished goods. This resource requirement was particularly burdensome for the newly established Soviet Union. In the 1920s, the Soviet Union was still a relatively poor country with an overwhelmingly agricultural economy. (Gregory & Stuart, 1994, pp. 31–33; Nove, 1989, p. 1–16) Industrialization had begun in Russia during the late nineteenth century, but it had been seriously compromised by the devastation of war and the chaos of revolution. Most important, industrialization had been made more difficult in the Russian case by the low productivity of the agricultural sector—the dominant sector of the economy. (Nove, 1989, p. 15)

Productivity is a measure of output per worker. Increasing productivity is essential to economic growth, because it means the economy can produce more per worker and it frees up resources to be used elsewhere. Low productivity in agriculture—all else remaining equal—meant that Russia, and later the Soviet Union, had seriously limited resources to put into its industrialization effort. Imperial Russia had relied on large infusions of foreign capital to offset the impact of meager domestic savings caused by low agricultural productivity.[9] By contrast, the Soviet leadership, afraid of becoming indebted to and dependent on foreigners, adopted a go-it-alone posture. (Gregory & Stuart, 1990, p. 124)

Thus, the inadequacy of resources caused by low productivity in agriculture and no significant foreign investment were combined with the priority of security. The result was that the sacrifice required for rapid industrialization was enormous. The leaders of the Soviet Union needed to divert huge amounts of resources from the agricultural sector into the fledgling industrial sector. In addition, they needed to restrict consumption, compel savings, and vigorously channel investment into heavy industry. Forced collectivization in agriculture and the widespread use of terror were the means used to achieve this outcome.

Forced collectivization was initiated under Stalin during the First Five-Year Plan in order to establish cooperative agriculture. Collectivization provided a way to resolve the nagging ideological issue of landownership and property rights in a socialist society. (Conquest, 1986, pp. 13–24, 58–82; Tucker, 1990, pp. 58–60) Collectivization also provided a way to create economies of scale in agriculture. It was believed that fewer and larger agricultural units would be more efficient to operate and therefore more productive than large numbers of small farms. Collectivization was supposed to raise agricultural productivity. (Conquest, 1986, p. 108; Nove, 1989, p. 139)

Stalin was not the only one among his contemporaries who endorsed the idea of collectivization. During the 1920s, official opinions differed on the rate and methods that should be employed to achieve collectivization, but there was considerable support for the idea of collectivization. Nikolai Bukharin, for example, argued for collectivization, but only in the context of massive agricultural modernization.[10] According to Bukharin, there needed to be enough farm machinery and land to assure the peasants that they would not starve and to ensure that collectivization would indeed raise agricultural productivity. (Con-

---

9. During the period 1880–1913, Russia was a large debtor country. Russian efforts toward economic development were significantly boosted by the receipt of money from abroad to finance domestic capital formation. Foreign capital accounted for approximately 40 percent of industrial investment during the immediate pre–World War I period. For a discussion about the role of foreign investment in Russian industrial development, see Gregory and Stuart (1990, pp. 41–42), Gregory (1979, pp. 379–399), and Nove (1989, pp. 8–9).

10. Bukharin was influential in the early days of the Soviet Union. He is widely credited as one of the primary architects of the New Economic Policy briefly tried in the 1920s. Bukharin and his ideas were rehabilitated by Gorbachev as he sought to reform the Soviet economy.

quest, 1986, pp. 79–80) As implemented under Stalin, however, collectivization epitomized the use of arbitrary terror on the Soviet people.[11]

Stalin instituted the policy of forced collectivization in 1929. Kulaks—
prosperous peasants—were the designated enemies of the collectivization process. Because it was believed that they might sabotage the new collective farms,
kulaks were excluded from joining them. However, the definition of who was a
kulak was subject to continual change. Eventually, any person who resisted
forced collectivization was considered an "ideological" kulak and along with
"real" kulaks was subject to the brutal policies and tactics associated with
"dekulakization" (Conquest's term). As a result of "dekulakization," approximately 6.5 million people lost their lives. (Conquest, 1986, pp. 300–305)

Peasants of all economic levels resisted moving onto the collective farms.
Under this program, the state expropriated all of the peasants' property, including livestock. The peasants responded with a massive slaughter of livestock.
According to Robert Tucker (1990, p. 182), the extent of the slaughter was
enormous: 47 percent of all cattle, 65 percent of all sheep, and 47 percent of all
horses. The slaughter of horses was particularly critical, because at that time
the Soviet Union did not rely much on mechanical farm equipment. Collectivization directly led to the famine of 1932–34. It has been calculated that about
7 million people died during this famine.[12] (Conquest, 1986, p. 303) The 7
million who died of hunger plus the millions who died during forced collectivization and dekulakization underscore the extent to which sacrifice and terror
were used to accomplish Stalin's goals.

The combination of coercion and sacrifice proved successful—at first. During
the 1930s, the Soviet Union made significant progress toward modernization
and industrialization. It experienced an extremely rapid shift of resources from
agriculture into industry. In terms of resource diversion, Stalin achieved in just
over a decade (1928–40) what other industrializing societies took from thirty to
fifty years to accomplish (see Tables 6-3 and 6-4). Moreover, private consumption in the Soviet Union sharply declined. As a byproduct of industrialization,
such a decline is not unusual. Typically, over a 30-to-50-year period, countries
that go through the industrialization process experience a 10-to-20-percent drop
in private consumption as a percentage of gross national product (GNP).

What was unique in the Soviet experience was the size and speed of the
decline. "In 1928, private consumption accounted for 80 percent of Soviet
GNP. By 1940, this figure had dropped to 50 percent." (Gregory & Stuart,
1990, p. 125) What these figures mean is that the Soviet people experienced a
precipitous drop in their standard of living. Why did this decline occur? Most
of the meager resources (wages or farm products) the people had at their

---

11. For a detailed discussion of the theoretical and policy debates pertaining to agriculture as
well as the struggle for power that dominated Soviet politics in the 1920s, see Conquest (1986,
pp. 58–93).

12. Conquest (1986) estimates that 14.5 million people died as a result of forced collectivization,
dekulakization, and famine. To understand how he arrives at these estimates, see pp. 299–307.

Table 6-3
The Outcome of Stalin's Industrialization Plan, 1928–1940

Structural Shifts in Major Economic Sectors	1928	1940
Total GNP (billions of 1937 rubles)	141.1	261.9
Share in net national product[1] (percentages)		
Industry	28	45
Agriculture	49	29

Population Changes: Share of Workers in the Labor Force (number of workers in thousands)[2]		
Agriculture	1,735	2,976
Industry	3,773	10,967
Percentage of Labor Force		
Agriculture	71	51
Industry	18	29

[1]Calculated by the following formula: GNP − Adjustment for capital repairs − Depreciation = Net national product. [2]Not including workers employed in other categories.
Sources: Bergson & Kuznets, Gregory & Stuart, Joint Economic Committee of the United States Congress.

disposal were taken away by the state through taxes or ridiculously low purchase prices for agricultural products. And Stalin's emphasis on the development of heavy industry and on military preparedness meant that relatively few consumer goods were produced. Thus, even if someone had money, there was little to buy.

The Impact of Long-Term Sacrifice

Whether Stalin and his associates realized it or not, they took a big gamble when they imposed such sacrifice on the people. In effect, they wagered that the ends would ultimately justify the means—that the benefits of industrialization would legitimize the Communist regime despite the economic deprivation and the routine use of brute force and terror. These were not groundless calculations. People are often willing to sacrifice in the short run for the promise of future benefits.

The Russians and the other peoples of the Soviet Union were no strangers to hardship. Recall that in Chapter 2 we discussed how the struggle for survival made a profound impact on Russian attitudes and beliefs about the security of the group, individual freedoms, authority, power, and leadership. Their political culture predisposed the Russians, in particular, to value community welfare over the exercise of individual freedoms, as well as to expect and tolerate absolutist rule. Under the Soviet regime, this extraordinary tolerance was re-

Table 6-4

The Comparative Percentage of Change in Volume of Industrial Output in 1932 (Index 1928 = 100)[1]

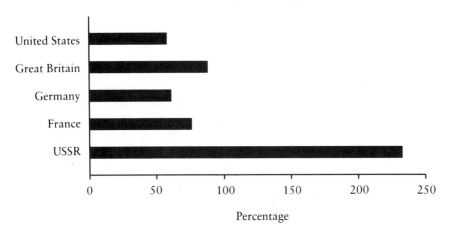

Percentage

[1]Large structural changes in index numbers tend to overstate growth rates. Figures for capitalist countries are from *Wochenbericht, Institut für Konjunkturforschung*, Berlin, no. 41, January 11, 1933, and *Bulletin Mensuel de Statistique*, no. 3, 1934.
Source: Marcel & Canter.

inforced by promises of future economic plenty in the sustaining myth of Marxism-Leninism (Luke, 1985), as well as by the ever-present threat of foreign invasion.

The key to utilizing sacrifice as part of a program of economic development is to make it a short-term phenomenon. In the Soviet experience, however, sacrifice became a way of life. The industrialization drive of the 1930s was followed by the agonizing destruction of World War II, which gave way to the demands of postwar reconstruction and the Cold War. Such sustained sacrifice ultimately breeds economic stagnation and political decay. It also breeds cynicism in the people being continuously asked to sacrifice for a prosperous future that never seems to arrive.

Sustained sacrifice aggravates an inherent problem of command economies, that of incentives. Political-economic systems aim to control human behavior in order to achieve socially desired outcomes. Take the example of Soviet industrial laborers. In an authority hierarchy, managers and supervisors make claims on their employees' time and labor, assigning them various tasks. The Soviet labor force was urged to work hard and be devoted to the socialist order. At the same time, they recognized the potentially painful consequences of overt resistance. These incentives, however, were at odds with their notions of material self-interest. They could choose to exhaust themselves working for others on a daily basis. For their efforts, they would receive meager compensation and find little that was attractive to buy with it. Alternatively, they could go through the motions of a day's work, making a minimum effort and saving their energies for private services they offered on the side. Often this moonlighting was done on a barter basis. For example, an industrial laborer might solve the plumbing problems of a store manager in exchange for some choice cuts of meat. In this way, many Soviet workers improved their family's living standard. From the standpoint of personal well-being, the rational choice is obvious. Incentives arising from personal calculations of material self-interest prevail. Given the abysmal productivity record of Soviet industry, it is clear that large numbers of Soviet workers understood the nature of their options and chose in favor of personal well-being.

Why give 100 percent in an environment where job security is essentially guaranteed and where such efforts will do little to improve personal living standards? Besides, how could an exhausted worker meet the hardships of everyday Soviet life, such as the endless lines for food? Of course, the artificial incentive structures of the command economy motivated some people to diligent and productive labor. They respected and responded positively to authority, strove for the banners and medals given to workers who were highly productive, and anticipated the promised future material utopia built by their sacrifices.[13] However, the continued viability of these incentives over time depended on the achievement of some significant progress. Perpetual demands for sacrifice, especially when the sacrifices were not borne equally, diluted the effectiveness of existing incentives and made material self-interest more attractive. Continued demands for sacrifice undermined the already weak incentive structure of the Soviet economy.

The intense focus on heavy industry and military preparedness severely crippled the production of consumer goods and services. People accumulated massive savings because during the early years of the regime there was relatively little to buy and in later years what was available in the government stores was of poor quality. With few desirable goods and services to purchase, wages were not a strong incentive to worker productivity. The observation "They pretend to pay us and we pretend to work" came to reflect the attitude of the average Soviet employee.

Coping with scarcity, especially in quality goods and services, became the Soviet way of life. For growing numbers of people, self-interest took precedence over long-term societal goals. Perpetual shortages created compelling incentives for individuals with access to scarce goods and services to exploit this access for personal gain. Employees routinely syphoned off resources from their places of work for private use. Not infrequently, these workers used propositions put forth by Marxism-Leninism to justify their self-interest-motivated actions—for example, the proposition that productive assets in a

---

13. Tatyana Zaslavskaya writes of Soviet willingness to sacrifice for economic reconstruction and development after World War II. "Constantly hungry, ill-clothed, ill-shod, we were prepared to put up with the disorder of our lives patiently and to postpone the satisfaction of our most basic personal needs until such time as the problems of the nation as a whole had been solved." (Zaslavskaya, 1990, p. 22)

socialist society belong to the "people." That which belongs to everyone, belongs to no one.

More troubling for would-be economic reformers like Gorbachev, endless shortages gave the bureaucrats (*apparatchiki*) who controlled the distribution of scarce goods and services a great deal of administrative power, which they exercised to enhance their personal status. (Simis, 1982) They could decide who got what, and often these decisions were made in their own self-interest rather than in the interest of society as a whole. Thus, shortages created potent personal incentives that corrupted even those who were charged with making decisions and administering the Soviet command economy. Eventually the decision-making hierarchy itself was undermined.

We introduced the concept of administrative power in Chapter 3, in our discussion of empire. Administrative power is the ability to control human activity by wielding instruments of coercion, whether those instruments are sticks or carrots. In the economic sphere, control over the distribution of commodities or services—such as scarce products or admission to prestigious universities—translates into a formidable ability to influence the actions of others.

In the Soviet Union, the bureaucracy's blatant exercise of administrative power for personal gain eventually became routine. Two consequences followed from this development. First, the bureaucracy obstructed all attempts at economic reform. That the bureaucrats would resist efforts to reform a system from which they derived tremendous personal benefit is hardly surprising.[14] Second, the regime's foundation of legitimacy and authority was undermined. An official who makes allocation decisions based on self-interest is not only thwarting authority but is also demonstrating to a wider audience the real basis of control in the society: power.

Power and Its Long-Term Impact on the Economy

In many respects, power is the flip side of sacrifice. Centuries of economic hardship and insecurity had predisposed the Soviet people to sacrifice, but neither historical nor cultural determinants alone can account for the depth of sacrifice they endured to achieve Stalin's economic miracle—and continued to endure in service to the perpetuation of the Stalinist system. The ability and willingness of the Communist Party of the Soviet Union to use instruments of power undoubtedly compelled sacrifice that would not otherwise have been forthcoming.

Power controls through fear. Fear is a potent motivator, and few leaders have exploited it so extensively and so brutally as Stalin. Brute force and

---

14. In this context, glasnost can be viewed as part of Gorbachev's strategy to wrest power from the entrenched bureaucracy so that his program of economic restructuring, perestroika, might have some chance of success.

coercion were integral features of Stalin's "revolution from above." The purges and the forced collectivization of the peasants during the 1930s were certainly the most obvious manifestations of the role of coercion under Stalin. They were, however, not the only ones. The exercise of power became ubiquitous throughout the society.

We have already examined the place of power in Russian political culture and power itself as a defining characteristic of empire. The issue we must now consider is the ramifications of power for the Soviet economy. Unquestionably, Stalin's reliance on power to promote rapid industrial development and forced collectivization was consistent with the Russian tradition of absolutism. The popular response and the economic results of its application in the Soviet era are also consistent with the strengths and weaknesses of power as a method of social control.

Among historians and economists there is considerable debate about the economic impact of Stalin's reliance on terror and brute force. The debate centers on the question of whether Stalin could have achieved his economic goal of rapid industrialization without heavy doses of coercion. This speculation, however, tends to miss the point, because Stalin did achieve considerable success (defined in terms of industrialization), and he did it by relying on power. It is hardly a stretch, therefore, to conclude that the exercise of power contributed to the early success of the Stalinist economic development model. But establishing power as the cornerstone of Soviet economic development had long-term negative consequences: It ultimately undermined the integrity of the system.

After the death of Stalin, the Soviet leadership grew less willing to resort routinely to overt coercion to achieve its economic aims, but the exercise of power in other forms continued. Thus, it would be a mistake to conclude that power as a method of social control in the Soviet political-economic system grew less relevant after Stalin. Granted, the roles and impact of power changed from Stalin to Gorbachev. Stalin used brute force to compel sacrifice and to eliminate foes of his development strategy. Stalin's successors, including Gorbachev, labored to dispel the enduring (and destructive) political and economic consequences that resulted from Stalin's use of power. Nevertheless, whether the focus is on the use of power or on the consequences of its use, the relevance of these methods of control for understanding the post-Stalinist economic system cannot be denied.

According to the basic design of a command economy, coordinating resource production and distribution is assured through "a continuous vertical chain of relations [which] stretches from top to bottom." (Kornai, 1992, p. 98) The success of this kind of bureaucratic coordination is supposed to come from accurate information flowing vertically, both up and down, between the ministries and their enterprises. In the political-economic system of the USSR, the dual hierarchies of Party and government complicated bureaucratic coordination and rendered it more difficult. The widespread fear of reprisals—the result of routine reliance on coercion—further compromised economic management. In practice, therefore, bureaucratic coordination among the various ministries and between firms within the same ministry proved unworkable.

The practical result of the routine use of coercion was that officials in both hierarchies, up and down the chain of command, did what they had to do to meet their plan targets and safeguard their personal positions and prerogatives. Ministries increasingly tended to organize themselves as self-contained economic units. The strategy of each ministry was to control everything that contributed to the production of the narrow range of final products for which it was responsible. Coordination among the ministries grew less and less relevant as the practice of ministerial autarky grew.

The pursuit of autarky is based on the proposition that independence is always preferable to dependence. Specialization and cooperation are risky because they imply dependence. It may be economically efficient to specialize, relying on others to provide critical inputs to the production process. But specialization requires cooperation and creates interdependence. If you were a Soviet factory manager producing screwdrivers, for example, and another factory produced the handles, you were dependent on the handle-producer to fulfill your plan. Dependence was a risky position for anyone who had reason to doubt the willingness or ability of others to cooperate.

Officials in the economic ministries had ample reason to question the system's ability to coordinate the efforts of the various ministries. After all, coordination is one of the inherent difficulties associated with the command economy. Officials also had reason to question one another's willingness to cooperate and coordinate their efforts. In an economic environment of chronic shortages where everyone fears reprisals if targets are unfulfilled, supplying inputs for others is inherently risky. It is far less risky to strive for economic independence or autarky. Although Soviet planners discouraged the practice, they could do little to stop it. (Hewett, 1988, p. 176)

In their ongoing struggle to meet plan targets, enterprise managers resorted to a wide range of tactics, many of which were illegal.[15] As we have already mentioned, one common tactic was the illegal hoarding of critical inputs. (Gregory & Stuart, 1990, p. 187) Enterprise managers also routinely relied on the "shadow economy" to obtain necessary resources. The shadow economy had no formal organization; it was entirely made up of individuals and transactions. Nevertheless, it became an integral, albeit illegal, feature of the economic system.

The shadow economy included "expediters" or "fixers" (*tolkachi*) who used bribes, engaged in black-market transactions, and arranged barter deals between enterprises on behalf of plant managers eager to obtain needed supplies. It also included "moonlighters" (*shabashniki*) who provided construction services for cash whenever enterprises wanted to undertake a project that the official system would not support. (Hewett, 1988, p. 177) Such exchanges were clearly outside the formal authority structure of the command economy.

---

15. In the Soviet Union, the rule of law (and hence authority) could always be dispensed with when officials faced more pressing needs or goals. The rule of law was subordinated to the rule of men in the economy as well as in the political system.

This kind of exchange developed not only because the formal system did not work but because those responsible for economic performance feared reprisals. The fear of punishment compelled enterprise managers, among others, to jury-rig the system, to make it *appear* to work. Meanwhile, those at the highest levels of the CPSU and the government usually looked the other way because they also needed the system to appear to work if they were to be sure of keeping their positions and perks.

Less tolerable from the perspective of the Soviet leadership was the black market (*chernyi rynok*), or second economy. It nevertheless evolved to supply consumers with the high-quality goods and services that they were determined to obtain. People generally had money with which they could purchase the goods and services they desired. But goods and services of high quality were difficult to find legally. Consequently, substantial profits were available to people willing to violate the laws prohibiting private economic activity in order to supply quality or trendy goods (like blue jeans from the West) and services (like auto repair). The second economy encompassed a number of different types of activities: skilled laborers operating without licenses, private work on the job (e.g., a mechanic repairing someone's car and pocketing the money), unreported production at an enterprise, pulling resources out of the formal system to produce goods privately, and brokering or selling information. (Hewett, 1988, p. 179)

There was considerable overlap between the shadow and second economies, but they served distinct purposes and were generated by different motivations. The shadow economy enabled state-owned firms to obtain the inputs they required to meet critical output targets; plant managers scrambling for resources were largely motivated by the fear of being punished if they did not meet plan goals. The second economy developed because consumer preferences were largely ignored in a system driven to industrialize and to ensure its security in a hostile international environment. Constant consumer demand provided enticing opportunities for anyone willing to risk punishment. Here again was a situation where material self-interest operated in direct opposition to symbolic and coercive incentives. Over time, symbolic incentives became increasingly weakened because fewer and fewer people believed in and respected a system that proclaimed equality and promised that sacrifice would be rewarded. The depressing reality revealed a system in which promises went unfulfilled and the burden of sacrifice was not equally shared. Members of the elite were mostly exempt from the kind of sacrifice demanded from ordinary people, and most ordinary people were aware of this disparity.

A major indicator of elite status was a nomenklatura position. The nomenklatura included important Party, government, military, and industry officials, plus high-level technocrats and scientists as well as other key members of Soviet society. Once one had a nomenklatura position, one had access to special shops stocked with goods not generally available to the public. This elite had special hospitals and clinics, chauffeur-driven limousines, and even designated lanes on major highways. (Goldman, 1992, pp. 98–99) Members of the nomenklatura also wielded tremendous power, which they could use to generate additional personal advantages through bribery or other questionable practices. Thus, nomenklatura positions were clearly worth protecting, and moving up through the nomenklatura was a desirable goal. It is important to add, however, that the nomenklatura not only wielded power to enhance their personal well-being; they themselves became victims of the coercion, for they were the ones who had the most to lose. It is also worth pondering the kind of pent-up resentments that were undoubtedly harbored by ordinary people whose well-being and security were affected by members of the nomenklatura who exploited their positions for personal gain.

Local Party officials who were held accountable for the economic performance of their provinces, regions, or cities also could not trust the formal system to supply critical inputs for their producers. Thus, they played a critical role in coordinating economic activity. This role extended well beyond their ability to make appointments, to control key Party posts in the local economy, and to influence higher policy-making officials. They inevitably became involved in the day-to-day operations of the economic units for which they were responsible.

In practice, economic coordination by local Party leaders meant that a small part of the resources of one enterprise or other type of economic unit could be used to meet the urgent needs of another. It also meant resolving disputes that arose between various departments or officials. (Hough, 1969, p. 235) Successful coordination of this kind, however, usually required that local Party officials compel or authorize enterprise directors and other administrators "to break the law or violate some directive or plan indicator." (Hough, 1969, pp. 235, 253) Economic coordination through local Party organs became a regular feature of the informal economic system. Jerry Hough, among others, credits it for a considerable number of the economic successes that were achieved. Like other aspects of this adulterated system, however, it also contributed to the stagnation that ultimately gripped the Soviet economy.

The CPSU was among the few organizations (along with the military and the KGB) in which authority based on legitimacy actually existed to some significant degree. It is ironic, therefore, that one of the few authority structures in the Soviet Empire actively undermined the development of other authority structures that were essential to long-term political stability. Moreover, coordinating local economic activity also compromised the fabric of authority relationships within the CPSU itself. This effect is related to one of the pathological symptoms of empire. Local Party elites increasingly become prey to divided loyalties: Should they work to enhance the aims of the center, or should they work to enhance their personal power and economic well-being?

By the Brezhnev era, the latter alternative increasingly took precedence over the former. Rampant corruption was common, tacitly encouraged by the Brezhnev regime's look-the-other-way policy. Widespread corruption aggravated the gross inefficiencies that plagued the Soviet economy; corruption ultimately led to chronic stagnation. From a political perspective, Brezhnev's look-the-other-way posture represented a makeshift strategy to stem the tide of imperial decay. Ultimately, however, it wound up subverting the system.

THE FAILURE OF PRE-GORBACHEV ECONOMIC
REFORM EFFORTS

The Khrushchev era (1954–64) ushered in what is sometimes called the Golden Age of the Soviet Union. It witnessed the diminished use of terror as a method of coercion, rapid economic growth (see Table 6-5), and serious attempts at economic reform. Khrushchev realized that Stalin's campaign of forced collectivization had effectively smothered incentives to productivity in the agricultural sector. Thus, many of his economic reforms were aimed at raising agricultural productivity by increasing local Party supervision and direction of on-farm affairs. (Breslauer, 1982, p. 123)

Within each zone of the rural districts, "instructor groups" were set up. Each instructor was assigned to mobilize resources on one or two collective farms. These groups of three or four individuals functioned as "zonal party secretariats." They were supposed to provide technical expertise on agricultural matters. Individuals in these groups were also expected to reside within the zone they supervised, in order to facilitate their effective intervention in the day-to-day operation of the collective farm. (Breslauer, 1982, p. 123)

During this period, moreover, many collective farms were combined and reorganized into even larger farms. Still others were converted into state-owned agricultural organizations modeled after factories (*sovkhoz*). This period also saw, for the first time, a major change in the reward system in agriculture. Peasants were to be paid at least partially in money on a more regular and frequent basis. Prior to Khrushchev, farm workers were compensated with money that was based on a percentage of the harvest less all debts owed to the farm. (Gregory & Stuart, 1990, pp. 141–142) During the Khrushchev reforms, these communal debts were written off. (Nove, 1989, p. 321) There were also major increases in chemical fertilizers and other agricultural inputs. Finally, Khrushchev attempted to equalize Stalin's uneven distribution of resources between the agricultural and the industrial sectors. (Gregory & Stuart, 1990, p. 142)

Beyond the reforms in agriculture, steps were taken to address deficiencies in the production and availability of consumer goods. Yet even under Khrushchev, foreign trade was not a source of consumer goods. Foreign trade grew rapidly during this period, but the Soviet Union continued to import primarily machinery and equipment and to export raw materials. (Gregory & Stuart, 1990, p. 145)

In addition, there was much discussion about defects in the economic system, and potentially significant changes were initiated. Most important of these were the Sovnarkhoz Reforms of 1957. These reforms aimed to improve the planning system on which Soviet production was based. They attempted to change the basis of the planning system from a ministerial to a more regional one through the creation of regional economic councils (*sovnarkhozy*). By decentralizing economic control, Khrushchev hoped among other things to thwart the ministries' practice of striving for autarky, which had resulted in

TABLE 6-5
Economic Performance During the Khrushchev
Period

Category	Percentage of Change		
	1951–55	1956–60	1961–65
GNP	5.8	6.0	4.9
Industry	10.6	9.8	6.6
Agriculture	4.1	4.1	2.4
Trade	10.4	8.5	4.7
Services[1]	2.3	2.2	4.5

[1]Includes military personnel costs.
Source: Joint Economic Committee of the United States Congress. (1979). *Soviet economy in a time of change* (p. 136). Washington, DC: U.S. Government Printing Office.

variable and generally high production costs. (Hewett, 1988, pp. 223–224) As it turned out, however, the problems of the newly created regional economic councils were similar to those of the ministries they replaced. In response to these problems, Khrushchev opted against fundamental economic change; he pursued instead more organizational shuffling, which ultimately proved ineffectual. (Gregory & Stuart, 1990, p. 146)

Because many of the Khrushchev reforms were attempts to decentralize control, they engendered hostility within the Moscow-based bureaucracy. Khrushchev's enemies called his reforms "hare-brained," but there was no denying that the early Khrushchev period marked a time of rapid economic growth. One reason for this accelerated growth was Khrushchev's permission of open discussion about the deficiencies of the Stalinist system and his search for ways to correct them. At the very least, this posture of openness worked to improve the flow of information relevant to economic decision-making. The Khrushchev reforms, however, did not significantly alter the intrinsic weaknesses of a command economy, and Khrushchev was ousted in 1964. Not surprisingly, his ouster coincided with a marked decline in economic growth (see Table 6-3).

Leonid Brezhnev and Alexei Kosygin replaced Khrushchev. It fell to Kosygin to chart the course of continued economic reform. Among other things, Kosygin's reforms included an attempt to use measures other than inventory or quantity to determine plan fulfillment. The shift was toward quality indicators—such as the usability of the product produced—and against production for production's sake. Other Kosygin reforms included a plan to give more decision-making responsibility to enterprise managers and a plan to create a system of bonuses for workers. (Gregory & Stuart, 1990, pp. 146–148)

The reforms had little real impact. Control returned to the central ministries, and the regional economic councils created under Khrushchev as part of his effort to decentralize decision-making were abandoned. In fact, there was a 60 percent expansion in the bureaucracy between 1966 and 1977. The net effect of this development was that the ministries controlled all allotments of re-

TABLE 6-6
Soviet Aggregate Performance: Average Annual Growth, 1961–1987

Category	Percentage of Change[1]					
	1961–65	1966–70	1971–75	1976–80	1981–85	1985–87
GNP	4.8	5.0	3.1	2.2	1.8	1.7
Agriculture[2]	3.6	3.7	−.6	.8	2.1	1.2
Industry	6.5	6.3	5.4	2.6	1.8	2.0
Trade	4.8	7.1	4.7	2.8	1.7	1.0
Services	4.4	4.3	3.4	2.7	2.2	2.5
Leaders	Khrushchev ⟶					
		Brezhnev ⟶				
						Gorbachev ⟶

[1]Calculated at factor costs in 1982 prices.
[2]Excludes intra-agricultural use of farm products but does not make an adjustment for purchases by agriculture from other sectors.
Source: Directorate of Intelligence *Handbook of Economic Statistics, 1988* (p. 60). Washington, DC: Central Intelligence Agency.

sources and equipment, as well as investment. They also set all of the incentive schedules used in the state-owned firms. By the 1970s, any attempt at real reform was abandoned in favor of the status quo. At best, the Kosygin reforms sought to refine Soviet economic planning and to make centralization work better. (Gregory & Stuart, 1990, pp. 148–151) The result of these efforts was a decline in economic performance. Table 6-6 offers a summary of economic performance from 1961 through 1987.

In the final analysis, this period marked a modified return to Stalinism. An expanding, centralized bureaucracy attempted to control all aspects of the economy. The use of terror and intimidation also returned, although terror was not used in all of the ways and to the extent it had been used under Stalin. By the time Kosygin died in 1980, his reforms had clearly failed. A period of stagnation had set in. After Brezhnev's death in 1982, the economic decline continued under the leadership of Yuri Andropov and Konstantin Chernenko.

Bureaucracies by their very nature resist change and risk. In the Soviet Union, the political culture reinforced this tendency. Bureaucratic power, combined with intransigence, opened up the potential for corruption. Increasingly, Brezhnev signaled the bureaucrats that he would look the other way, if they would continue to support him in the top leadership position. He in effect gave the green light to official corruption, but so did the increasingly unworkable command system.

Most of the economic plans could not be fulfilled unless those responsible acted in illegal or questionable ways. Thus, factory managers with plans to fulfill did whatever was needed to fulfill them, and the unofficial incentives that motivated government officials to pursue their narrow self-interest at society's expense came to be widely accepted as "the natural privileges of those in power." (Barry & Barner-Barry, 1991, p. 287) What remained was a system in which bureaucrats at all levels concerned themselves mainly with the day-to-day preservation of their power, privileges, and status. All of these factors created a system that was virtually impossible to reform.

Looking back on the Soviet era, analysts now date the onset of economic stagnation to about 1970. By the beginning of the 1970s, the Soviet economy was showing signs of decline. Factors that had spurred years of impressive growth rates had begun to reveal their negative side effects. Evidence of this was easy to spot:

1. Labor productivity (i.e., labor output per hour) growth rates were too low and declining.
2. A tremendous waste of material and capital continued despite efforts by planners to promote efficiency.
3. Suppliers showed little regard, if not outright disdain, for consumer demand.
4. Enterprises paid wages that were not related to work performance. The inevitable result was imbalances of supply and demand as producers made goods that were not wanted and consumers' requirements went unmet.
5. Would-be innovators struggled in an environment where self-interested bureaucrats called the shots, interbranch coordination was difficult, information was scarce and carefully guarded, and rewards were meager.

These problems resulted in an increasingly stagnant economy, but they were largely ignored under Brezhnev. His muddling through perpetuated stagnation, which in turn hastened imperial decay and did nothing to help the process of building and sustaining the legitimacy of the Soviet regime. In the words of one analyst, "without economic growth, the regime [was] unable to fulfill its part of the unofficial 'social contract' under whose terms the public renounced any say about public affairs in return for a slowly rising standard of living." (Mandelbaum, 1991–92, pp. 171–72)

As the 1970s drew to a close, the situation became more and more of a problem. The average Soviet consumer developed increasingly sophisticated demands. In 1981, moreover, the USSR confronted the security challenge posed by President Ronald Reagan. It was apparent to Andropov, Brezhnev's successor as General Secretary, that the domestic and international demands of the 1980s could not be met without sweeping reform of the economic system. Andropov tried to begin the process, but his own failing health interfered. Serious reform efforts were put on hold after his death, as the old and ailing Chernenko took the helm. Economic reform had to wait until Andropov's protégé, Mikhail Gorbachev, became General Secretary in March 1985.

REFERENCES

Barry, D. D., & Barner-Barry, C. (1991). *Contemporary Soviet politics* (4th ed.). Englewood Cliffs, NJ: Prentice-Hall.

Bergson, A., & Kuznets, S. (1963). *Economic trends in the Soviet Union* (p. 36). Cambridge, MA: Harvard University Press.

Breslauer, G. W. (1982). *Khrushchev and Brezhnev as leaders: Building authority in Soviet politics.* London: Allen & Unwin.

Christian, H. M. (Ed.). (1966). *Essential works of Lenin.* New York: Bantam.

Conquest, R. (1986). *The harvest of sorrow: Soviet collectivization and the terror-famine.* New York: Oxford University Press.

Daniels, R. V. (1985). *Russia: The roots of confrontation.* Cambridge, MA: Harvard University Press.

Evans, P. (1979). *Dependent development: The alliance of multinational, state and local capital in Brazil.* Princeton, NJ: Princeton University Press.

Gilpin, R. (1987). *The political economy of international relations.* Princeton, NJ: Princeton University Press.

Goldman, M. I. (1987). *Gorbachev's challenge.* New York: Norton.

———. (1992). *What went wrong with perestroika?* New York: Norton.

Gregory, P. R. (1979). The Russian balance of payments, the gold standard, and monetary policy. *Journal of Economic History, 39*(2), 379–399.

Gregory, P. R., & Stuart, R. C. (1990). *Soviet economic structure and performance* (4th ed.). New York: Harper & Row.

———. (1994) *Soviet and post-Soviet economic structure and performance* (5th ed.). New York: HarperCollins.

Hewett, E. (1988). *Reforming the Soviet economy: Equality versus efficiency.* Washington, DC: Brookings Institution.

Hough, J. F. (1969). *The Soviet prefects: The local party organs in industrial decision-making.* Cambridge, MA: Harvard University Press.

Joint Economic Committee of the United States Congress. (1962). Dimensions of Soviet economic power (pp. 659–660). Washington, DC: U.S. Government Printing Office.

Kohler, H. (1968). *Scarcity challenged.* New York: Holt, Rinehart and Winston.

Kornai, J. (1992). *The socialist system: The political-economy of communism.* Princeton, NJ: Princeton University Press.

Lindblom, C. (1977). *Politics and markets: The world's political-economic systems.* New York: Basic Books.

Luke, T. W. (1985). *Ideology and Soviet industrialization.* Westport, CT: Greenwood Press.

Mandelbaum, M. (1991–92). The end of the Soviet Union. *Foreign Affairs, 71*(1), 160–183.

Marcel, S., & Canter, H. J. (Eds.). (1934). *Summary of the fulfillment of the First Five-Year Plan for the development of the national economy of the U.S.S.R.* (2nd ed., p. 30.). Moscow: Iskra Revolutsii.

Nove, A. (1989). *An economic history of the USSR* (2nd ed.). New York: Penguin.

Renshon, S. A. (1974). *Psychological needs and political behavior.* New York: Free Press.

Simis, K. M. (1982). *USSR: The corrupt society: The secret world of Soviet capitalism.* New York: Simon & Schuster.

Tucker, R. C. (1990). *Stalin in power: The revolution from above, 1928–1941.* New York: Norton.

Vernon, R. (1966). International investment and international trade in the product cycle. *Quarterly Journal of Economics, 80,* 190–207.

Wallerstein, I. (1974). The rise and future demise of the world capitalist system: Concepts for comparative analysis. *Comparative Studies in Society and History, 16,* 387–415.

Zaslavskaya, T. (1990). *The second socialist revolution.* Bloomington: Indiana University Press.

· 7 ·

THE PERILOUS TRANSITION FROM A COMMAND TO A MARKET ECONOMY

You are in the process of transforming your entire economy while you develop a new constitutional democracy. . . . It boggles the mind, and you have my respect for the effort.
PRESIDENT BILL CLINTON (*Washington Post,*
January 14, 1994, p. A27)

They say we have to tighten our belts for the reforms. But I feel as though we are laboratory animals who have been torn apart by these belts.
TATYANA KUZMINA (*Washington Post,*
January 24, 1994, p. A1)

When Mikhail Gorbachev became general secretary of the CPSU, he assumed the leadership of a political-economic system in disrepair and decay. In Gorbachev's estimation, economic stagnation was the root cause of the problems plaguing the Soviet Union. He thought that if this condition were reversed, other problems would disappear—or at least become more manageable. What Gorbachev failed to realize was that economic stagnation was more a symptom than a cause. By attacking the symptom through his programs of perestroika and glasnost, he inadvertently worsened deterioration and hastened the collapse of the Soviet Union.

In this chapter we consider Gorbachev's futile efforts to reform what proved to be an essentially unreformable economic system. We explore the major structural and stabilization challenges confronting any leaders aiming to convert a command economy into a market economy. And we examine the political as well as the economic perils facing the successor countries as they attempt to transform the command economy of the former Soviet Union into market economies.

GORBACHEV'S ILL-FATED REFORMS

Gorbachev outlined the major themes of his economic reform agenda in a speech that he delivered on December 10, 1984, four months before he assumed leadership as general secretary. In this speech, he called for a program of intensification (*intensifikatsiia*), acceleration (*uskorenie*), openness (*glasnost'*), and restructuring (*perestroika*). (*Pravda*, December 12, 1984) It is clear that openness, intensification, and acceleration were the dominant themes of Gorbachev's early reforms (1985–86). Perestroika became the major focus only in 1987, when Gorbachev's efforts took a fundamentally different turn.

Each theme was subject to reinterpretation but none more so than glasnost. A professed goal throughout the Gorbachev period, glasnost took on a meaning and significance that few could have anticipated. In this section, we examine the evolution of the Gorbachev reforms from the early emphasis on "intensifying" the existing command structure (1985–86), to radical restructuring based on glasnost and democratization (1987–91).

The First Wave of Reform, 1985–1986

During his first two years as general secretary of the CPSU, Gorbachev seemed intent on making the Soviet economy work as well as the East German economy.[1] To this end, Gorbachev endorsed the creation of superministries that would make the decision-making structure of the USSR resemble that of East Germany. The strategy was to take groups of economically related ministries and cluster them under a single superministerial body. The objective was to improve strategic planning and coordination. The identification of clusters and the boundaries between them took place in 1985–86. Gorbachev announced the creation of the first superministry (for machine building) in October 1985.

A similar organizational structure was fashioned for agriculture. In November 1985, Gorbachev created Gosagroprom, a superministry that was to take charge of Soviet agriculture. It combined five ministries and one state committee, each of which had previously controlled some aspect of food-growing or food-processing.[2] Gorbachev's impulse toward increased centralization was also evident in the creation of the State Quality Acceptance Committee (Gospriemka). This agency was charged with bringing about a radical improvement in the quality of goods produced. By January 1987, Gospriemka agents were inspecting the outputs of almost all major industries in the Soviet Union. (Goldman, 1992, pp. 89–90; Hewett, 1988, pp. 335–337)

---

1. German reunification has revealed that the East German economy was riddled with the same kind of waste and inefficiency that plagued the Soviet Union. Nevertheless, in the mid-1980s East Germany was widely viewed as having the most successful command economy.

2. By the winter of 1986, seven superministries had been created, and there were plans for the creation of three more. (Hewett, 1988, p. 336)

His apparent commitment to increased centralization notwithstanding, during 1985 and 1986 Gorbachev experimented with decentralization. He believed that for the superministries to be effective, industrial enterprises would have to be responsible for day-to-day operational and financial decisions. In May 1985, the Soviet government began an experiment, announcing that three important factories[3] would be assigned considerable decision-making authority and would function as semi-autonomous financial entities. The plan was designed to allow the enterprises to keep a percentage of their ruble profits, as well as a percentage of their hard-currency earnings from exports. The experiment, however, was never fully implemented. A promised 40 percent enterprise share of hard-currency earnings was later reduced to 20 percent, and, as it turned out, Gosbank (the State Bank) was hard-pressed to let the enterprises keep even that much. Nevertheless, the idea of decentralization and enterprise autonomy remained important in Gorbachev's later reform proposals. (Goldman, 1992, pp. 92–93; Hewett, 1988, pp. 303–304)

Throughout 1985 and 1986, Gorbachev created a virtual flood of new policies, including those just discussed. Undoubtedly, Gorbachev felt under considerable political pressure to do something, even if there was a strong chance that the "something" would have to be reversed in the not-too-distant future. In retrospect, it is clear that during his first years as general secretary, Gorbachev did not fully appreciate the magnitude of difference between the economic goals he espoused and the economic reality he faced. His goals for the economy did little more than raise people's expectations. Between 1987 and 1990, Gorbachev would take bold steps to bridge the gap between rhetoric and reality. What few understood at the time, however, was that he was trying to reform an unreformable system. Ultimately, his efforts served only to undermine it.

Discipline and hard work were always considered integral to reform. Problems in this area were generally referred to as "the human factor" (*chelovecheskii faktor*). (Gorbachev, 1987; Tsipko, 1989; Zaslavskaia, 1986) Early on, Gorbachev realized the futility of trying to motivate ordinary people to greater effort and discipline in a political-economic environment rife with corruption and secrecy. Thus, one of his first official acts was to intensify the anticorruption drive begun by Yuri Andropov. He also launched a campaign against alcoholism, since drunkenness was a major factor lowering the productivity of the Soviet work force. The antidrunkenness effort was particularly difficult to sustain, however, because the sale of alcoholic beverages was a major source of government revenue. In fact, the first three years of this campaign cost the Soviet treasury 37 billion rubles. (Miroshnichenko, 1988, p. 21)

Like the economic reforms themselves, glasnost evolved both as a concept and as a process. At first, Gorbachev called for "openness," but what actually happened was a gradual process. Slowly during 1985 and 1986, Gorbachev

---

3. The number was later reduced to two: the Volga Automobile Plant and the Frunze Scientific Production Combine.

permitted more and more discussion of once-taboo subjects, including criticism of the regime as well as of the system itself. The events of 1986 demonstrate the erratic use of glasnost during Gorbachev's first years as general secretary. In February, at the Twenty-seventh Congress of the CPSU, he called for the open discussion of subjects previously considered forbidden. But in April, glasnost was forgotten in an ineffectual attempt to keep the Chernobyl disaster a secret from both the Soviet people and the outside world.

Despite this wavering and uncertainty about the limits of glasnost, Gorbachev continued to stress the need to expose incompetent and corrupt officials. He understood that as long as abuses went unchecked, workers would have no interest in striving to make economic reform a success:

> We have come to the conclusion that unless we activate the human factor, that is, unless we take into consideration the diverse interests of people, work collectives, public bodies, and various social groups, unless we rely on them, and draw them into active constructive endeavor, it will be impossible for us to accomplish any of the tasks set, or to change the situation in the country. (Gorbachev, 1987, p. 29)

At first, he hoped to persuade the regional press to support his policy of openness and thus to run interference for individuals courageous enough to come forward with information about official corruption. The constraint that all whistle-blowers face is the ability of powerful and well-connected officials to muzzle and punish those who expose waste and corruption. This problem can be reduced with adequate press coverage and the mobilization of mass support for whistle-blowers. Gorbachev quickly realized, however, that this approach was inadequate to the task at hand. More often than not, he failed to get the press coverage he wanted because local editors did not want to criticize local Party officials. What was needed, Gorbachev came to believe, were some institutionalized procedures that could involve the public and be used to hold bureaucrats accountable for their actions. Accordingly, he broadened and deepened the concept and process of glasnost to embrace "democratization." (Goldman, 1992, pp. 102–103) This reform emerged, along with his more radical economic reforms, in 1987.

The Second Wave of Reform, 1987–1988

In 1987, Gorbachev introduced reforms that broke with the command economy and steered the Soviet Union toward a market economy. Market economies have three basic components: (1) decentralized decision-making, (2) relative prices that provide necessary information to buyers and sellers, and (3) an incentive system based on competition. In varying degrees, the economic reforms introduced during this period contained these components.

As of May 1, 1987, the establishment of small private businesses was made legal. (*Pravda*, November 21, 1986) In an effort clearly designed to draw a wide range of black-market activities into the legal economy, the Law on

Individual Labor Activity permitted people to establish privately owned and operated businesses. As of July 1, 1988, a new law on cooperatives encouraged additional private economic initiatives. (*Pravda,* June 8, 1988) The majority of businesses set up during this period were in the service sector—tailor shops, beauty salons, cafes, restaurants, and so on. Private economic initiatives also expanded into other activities, including agriculture and small-scale manufacturing. At first, however, the laws governing these private ventures were quite restrictive. For example, small businesses were taxed at exorbitant rates, and the bureaucratic obstacles that entrepreneurs had to overcome to create a small business were discouraging. Not surprisingly, these forms of free enterprise were slow to catch on, especially in agriculture. They grew, but too sluggishly to provide a groundswell of popular support for Gorbachev and his reform program. (Goldman, 1992, pp. 112–113; Smith, 1992, p. 252)

In January 1987, legislation was passed permitting foreign firms to open joint ventures in the Soviet Union. (*Pravda,* January 27, 1987) Because of a long process of amendment, the legislation did not go into effect until December 1988; then bureaucratic obstacles made it impossible for this law to have any immediate impact on the Soviet economy. This outcome was unfortunate. The legislation was intended to provide a way of drawing capital and technology into the stagnant Soviet economy, and it was hoped that the infusion of capital and technology would encourage innovation.

The economic rationale for the joint venture legislation was clear, but many critics opposed it on ideological grounds. The laws permitting joint ventures and private businesses represented a radical departure from the policies, practices, and ideological justifications that had previously defined the command economy. Conservative critics were especially opposed to allowing foreign capitalist firms access to the Soviet economy. True to long-standing cultural predispositions, they objected to foreign access on security as well as ideological grounds. Gorbachev tried to defuse the criticism. To make these reforms more ideologically acceptable, he began to invoke the New Economic Policy of Lenin. To quell fears about security, he sought to put an end to the Cold War. This dual strategy was intended to appeal to Soviet citizens and to attract Western investment and relieve the Soviet economy of its huge military burden.

A highlight of the early reform period was a reexamination of Soviet history, including a more complete and accurate look at Stalin and his legacy. Nevertheless, well into his tenure in office, Gorbachev continued to believe in the viability of the Soviet form of socialism. In *Perestroika* (1987, p. 44) he wrote, "[S]ocialism as a social system has proved that it has immense potentialities for resolving the most complex problems of social progress. We are convinced of its capacity for self-perfection, for still greater revelation of its possibilities and for dealing with the present major problems of social progress which arise as we approach the twenty-first century." Gorbachev's desire to "perfect" socialism, however, needed historical and ideological grounding. Resurrecting Lenin's short-lived NEP served this purpose. NEP had the advantage of having been endorsed by the mythic hero and "founding father" of the Soviet Union, and it had such a brief role in Soviet economic history that it had never had the chance to be discredited.

Thus, during the period after Gorbachev moved away from efforts to refurbish the Stalinist economy and before the gravity of the economic situation became clear, Gorbachev saw in Lenin's "valuable ideas" (1987, p. 48) the salvation of socialism.

These ideas sanctioned the activities of small private merchants and farmers whose choices would be governed by market forces. They recommended against a development strategy premised on self-sufficiency and independence. Foreign sources of capital, properly channeled, could help Soviet development prospects. Importantly, however, Lenin's ideas as reflected in NEP and as interpreted by Gorbachev also endorsed continued state control of heavy indus- try, but with increased decentralization through "self-management, profit-and- loss accounting, and the linking of public and personal interests [which under the Stalinist economic model] failed to be applied and develop properly." (Gorbachev, 1987, p. 48) This aspect of NEP was most clearly evident in Gorbachev's State Enterprise Law, which came into effect on January 1, 1988. (*Pravda,* July 1, 1987)

The purpose of the Enterprise Law was to decentralize decision-making in the state-owned enterprises that dominated the Soviet economy. Central plan- ners were to turn their decision-making authority over to enterprise managers. Although the law encouraged enterprise directors to act on their own, it did not give them complete freedom of action. They would still have to fulfill produc- tion goals specified in state orders. However, the proportion of production devoted to filling these orders was to decrease substantially over time.

During the first year of the Enterprise Law's implementation, approximately 85 percent of production was designated to go to meeting state orders; the enterprise director was to decide the disposition of the remaining 15 percent. It was anticipated that the goods produced as part of this 15 percent (which would grow over time) could be sold at prices significantly higher than state- controlled prices. These higher prices, in conjunction with greater control over product choices and wages, could create potent profit-making incentives for enterprise managers. It was also hoped that this process would create profit- able enterprises that would no longer have to depend on subsidies from the state to remain solvent. (Goldman, 1992, p. 119)

Gorbachev and his team of reformers understood that if this new approach were to succeed, the workers would have to support it. By and large, Soviet workers had long been disenchanted with a system that benefited only those in positions of power. Gorbachev needed to convince the average employee in a state-owned firm that workers' interests were an essential part of reform. In a bid to gain their support, therefore, the State Enterprise Law provided for the con- tested election of enterprise directors, who previously had been selected by the CPSU as part of the nomenklatura. It seems clear that the reformers aimed to replicate key features of the political-economic model pioneered in Yugoslavia.

The Yugoslav model was premised on the idea of market socialism. All nonagricultural productive facilities employing more than five persons were socially rather than privately owned, but they were not centrally controlled. Rather, they had self-management; enterprises were placed in the custody of their employees, who made decisions for the firm through democratically elected workers' councils. (Lindblom, 1977, p. 335) The Yugoslav experiment was supposed to demonstrate that "socially owned" enterprises could just as easily compete in a market environment as privately owned ones. The experiment went awry, however, after the death of Marshal Tito and the rekindling of long-standing hostilities between and among the many ethnic groups making up Yugoslavia.

What Market Economies Need to Succeed

Gorbachev's 1987–88 reforms revealed just how difficult the transition to a market economy was going to be. Market socialism never got off the ground. The political-economic system was particularly ill suited to make the transition to a market economy. To understand why this was the case, it is important to recall the defining characteristics of a market economy: (1) decentralized decision-making (whatever the configuration of property rights), (2) relative prices to identify viable options for decision-makers, and (3) an incentive system based on competition that rewards success and—by extension—penalizes failure.

Decentralized decision-making does not mean rule-less decision-making. In an economy where decision-making is decentralized, there must exist clearly understood and widely respected rules of the game. These rules specify who is entitled to make decisions about the disposition of productive assets and why they are so entitled. The rule structure of decision-making in market economies inevitably entails rules of ownership—in other words, rules about property. In capitalism, virtually anything can be privately owned, and ownership entails nearly complete control over the disposition of that which is owned. But capitalism represents only one possible configuration of property rights. Decentralized decision-making does not have to mean capitalism. It can mean something similar to what Gorbachev was trying to achieve with his 1987–88 reforms: private ownership of small shops, farms, and restaurants, for example, but public ownership of large productive facilities. In this context, "public ownership" means self-management with substantial worker control over decision-making.[4]

Public ownership of this sort requires well-established authority relationships. All parties (workers, managers, shopkeepers, farmers, and government officials) must understand, respect, and obey the rules of ownership specified by law. Gorbachev and the other reformers were unable to establish such

---

4. The key to making self-management work in a market context is to offset the temptation for short-run gains (e.g., in the form of increased wages) in favor of long-run profitability. The driving force of competition in the marketplace is supposed to help decision-makers weigh short- versus long-term options. But competition can do this only if the real possibility of failure (i.e., bankruptcy) exists. This was not the case in the tentative Soviet experiment with market socialism.

authority relationships. For one thing, the existing command economy worked (to the extent that it worked at all) because people ignored, thwarted, or otherwise circumvented the law while the government looked the other way. This does not mean that there were no rules of the game. There were, but the rules that mattered were based not on authority but on power relationships. Attempts to supplant power and replace it with authority were resisted by those who benefited from the status quo: the economic bureaucracy in the CPSU and in the government. Indeed, officials in the economic ministries did their best to sabotage implementation of the State Enterprise Law.[5]

Prices were not relative; they were set by Goskomtsen.[6] Prices remained fixed for long periods of time, and when they were altered, the price changes reflected only supply-side considerations like production costs. Changes in consumer demand had no impact. Demand in excess of supply resulted in long lines, bartering, bribery, and black-market transactions, rather than an upward adjustment in price. Likewise, supply in excess of demand did not result in lower prices. The prices paid to producers remained the same. Thus, prices bore little relation to the actual conditions of supply and demand. They functioned as measures in an elaborate accounting system: "Far from being a carrier of market information, [a price was] more like a bookkeeping entry." (*The Economist,* October 20–26, 1990, p. 13)

The role of money in the Soviet economy was similarly attenuated. Money serves two purposes for market economies. It serves as a medium of exchange and as a store of value. The ruble, the Soviet national currency, was a medium of exchange. Prices were set in rubles. They facilitated the allocation of resources and the distribution of goods and services. In this way, the ruble functioned much like the US dollar or the Japanese yen. The ruble's role as a store of value, however, was severely limited. As a store of value, money is an asset that people are willing to accumulate in the expectation that it can be used to acquire other things of value (goods and services) at some point in the future. Because prices in the USSR were fixed without regard for the changing conditions of demand and supply, prices had little relevance as an indicator of value. By extension, therefore, the ruble could not function as a store of value. Why was this the case?

In a market economy, people who accumulate money as savings have a pretty clear sense of what those savings can buy. They understand that they can choose to use their savings to purchase stereo equipment, or they can continue to save until they have enough money to make a down payment on a car. Regardless of whether they choose a stereo next month or a car next year, they

---

5. The proportion of production going to fill state orders was supposed to decline to 40 percent by 1990. In fact, however, state orders continued to claim 90 percent of production. (*The Economist,* October 20–26, 1990, pp. 11–12)

6. Goskomtsen was an administrative structure made up of an all-union organization with offices in each republic. The offices in the republics were charged with setting the prices for products of regional importance. See Hewett (1988, pp. 190–192).

have confidence that the "value" stored in their savings will be reasonably stable.

Consumers in the Soviet Union had no such confidence. They knew the posted prices of most goods and services, but (more often than not) the most desirable products were only theoretically available. An example of a "theoretically available" product might be a can of peas that could be found in the stores. When opened, however, it would be of such poor quality as to be inedible. Also, many stores promised that they would soon have goods that never appeared on their shelves or were sold out within hours. The typical Soviet consumer had sizable savings but could not think of money in terms of what it would buy; consumers could not think of money as a store of value. No amount of savings could guarantee anyone the ability to buy any specific good or service. A product that is not offered for sale *cannot* be bought, and a low-quality product that does not meet consumers' needs *will not* be bought.

What are the implications for government policy in a political-economic system where prices are mere "bookkeeping entries" and where money does not function as a store of value? Government is not constrained by the usual fiscal and monetary concerns that limit government policy options in market economies. Thus, little, if any, attention is paid to the impact on the economy of deficit spending by the government. Although the practice was denied until 1988, the Soviet government had been running budget deficits since the early 1970s. According to estimates made by the US Central Intelligence Agency, between 1978 and 1985 these deficits ranged from 10 to 17 billion rubles per year. After 1986, deficit spending increased substantially as a result of Gorbachev's efforts to revitalize the command structure through the creation of superministries. Deficit spending put more and more rubles into the economy, because deficit financing amounted to little more than printing more money.

Thus, in a command economy where prices are fixed, inflationary pressures are hidden. In the Soviet case, the problem of too much money chasing too few goods merely aggravated the other problems in the system—chronic shortages, long lines, corruption. When Soviet reformers took their first steps toward the creation of a market economy, inflation emerged as a serious problem. One of the first indications of its seriousness came when owners of the private businesses formed under the 1987 Law on Individual Labor Activity discovered that the prices they were forced to charge were much higher than the artificially low state-controlled prices. Their potential customers, on the other hand, thought they were price-gouging—even though product quality was usually high. (Goldman, 1992, p. 115) Charging high prices does not make it easy to build a successful business.

Inflation "occurs when the general level of prices and costs is rising." (Samuelson & Nordhaus, 1985, p. 226) Moderate inflation does not destabilize a market economy. Excessively high levels of inflation, however, can be destructive; people find themselves paying more and more for less and less.[7] High inflation also impairs the information-carrier function of prices. Inflation makes it difficult for anyone to decide whether price increases indicate an increase in demand, a shortfall in supply, or a government that is using its money-generating ability for political gain. Thus, inflation compromises the usefulness of money for decision-making by producers and consumers.

Inflation also undermines money's function as a store of value. It makes consumers uncertain about how much their money will buy in the future. When inflation is seriously lowering the purchasing power of money, why save? Why not spend money today when it has a known value? Fear of inflation encourages people to spend, and that spending feeds the inflation, increasing its destructive impact on the economy. Because money is losing buying power rapidly, workers demand higher wages. Producers who grant wage increases pass those costs on to consumers. Thus, the cycle feeds on itself. Consumers worried about rising prices continue to spend their money, adding to the total amount of money in circulation and thus increasing inflation. As prices continue to rise and workers continue to demand higher wages, the cycle begins another round. Inflation thus discourages saving and investment—the very things that sustain healthy economic growth and create jobs—and it focuses everyone's attention on meeting short-term consumption needs.

Under extreme conditions, inflation can be politically as well as economically destabilizing. When inflation reaches the point where people have difficulty meeting even their basic needs, social unrest increases rapidly, and a fertile ground is created for extremist ideas. In Germany's Weimar Republic (1919–33), for example, hyperinflation created a political-economic environment that aided the rise of Hitler and the Nazis.

The budget deficits of the Soviet government, caused largely by economic stagnation and the Cold War arms race, created inflation. In a command economy inflation could be ignored, but it complicated efforts to transform the command economy into a market economy. Gorbachev and his reformers had hoped that the 1988 State Enterprise Law would inspire enterprise managers and their employees to seize the opportunity to become profitable and self-sufficient—no longer dependent on government subsidies to meet their payrolls and other financial obligations. They thought that if government subsidies to industry and military spending could be drastically decreased, it would be

---

7. What is an excessively high level of inflation? Economists identify three broad categories of inflation: moderate inflation, galloping inflation, and hyperinflation. Although these distinctions tend to blur at the margins, moderate inflation usually refers to price levels that are rising slowly (generally 10 percent or less per year), and galloping inflation "occurs when prices start rising at double- or triple-digit rates of 20, 100, or 200 percent a year." (Samuelson & Nordhaus, 1985, p. 229) Once entrenched, galloping inflation leads to economic problems, but it does not necessarily devastate a market economy: "The surprising fact . . . is that economies with 200 percent annual inflation manage to perform so well." (Samuelson & Nordhaus, 1985, pp. 230–231) Hyperinflation is an entirely different matter. When price increases exceed 1,000 percent per year, money becomes worthless—with devastating political and economic consequences.

possible to bring deficit spending under control and eliminate a major source of inflation.

The State Enterprise Law, as well as laws pertaining to small businesses and cooperatives, was intended to generate more goods and services with prices determined by demand and supply. Unfortunately, these laws did not produce their intended result. State orders continued to claim the lion's share of enterprise production. Legal restrictions coupled with bureaucratic obstacles limited the number of privately owned businesses and cooperatives. The laws, however, did impress on Soviet reformers the fact that budget deficits and inflation were now important.

Market economies produce efficient outcomes because of competition. Producers are motivated by the lure of profits and by the fear of financial ruin. Their goal is "to make it better, faster, and cheaper." Competition is what keeps a market economy going; it is the source of innovation. Competition produces this result because of the nature of the incentives it creates. These include personal gain, the potential for wealth, and the luxuries that wealth buys. Looming in the background is the fear of failure, the potential for job loss and bankruptcy. These positive and negative incentives combine to motivate individuals to work hard, calculate shrewdly, and take chances. Their impact, however, is reduced considerably when the target population is risk-averse. Most of the Soviet people came from a culture that encouraged them to avoid risk-taking—not just in economics but in all aspects of their lives.

Risk is something that people who live in market economies accept as natural. "Nothing ventured, nothing gained" and "you win some, you lose some" are popular sayings. Yet the risks of the marketplace are daunting—so daunting that political-economic systems institute policies and practices to limit risk. Unemployment insurance, laws governing incorporation, and bankruptcy are but a few examples of how political-economic systems lessen the risks of the market.

Life in most of the Soviet Union with its harsh geographical and climatic conditions was always risky enough; people learned to avoid additional risks. For all its limitations, the command economy shielded them from risk-taking and, in doing so, reinforced their cultural aversion to it. Most people could count on having jobs, food, and housing—however unsatisfactory they might have been. Conversion to a market economy offered them the chance for a higher standard of living, but it also exposed them to unemployment, inadequate food, and lost housing.

Gorbachev's 1987–88 reforms represented a first step toward introducing competition and risk-taking into economic life. On this score, the laws pertaining to small businesses and cooperatives achieved far greater success than did the State Enterprise Law. Though slow to take off, the drive to establish small shops and restaurants eventually gained momentum. Today in much of the former Soviet Union, the small-business sector is the most dynamic. The problem was and remains infusing competition into the large enterprises that dominate the economy. Competition means letting these large enterprises sink or swim. It means letting inefficient producers go bankrupt; it means accepting the resulting increase in unemployment. Contemporary political leaders have been slow to adopt this attitude, and their reluctance is understandable, given the historical and cultural heritage of the people. But supporting inefficient producers means continued government subsidies, chronic budget deficits, and more inflation, all of which in turn complicate efforts to introduce a useful system of prices.

The Final Attempt, 1989–1991

By 1989 it was clear that the reforms instituted during the previous two years were not having their intended effect. Instead of steering the economy toward revitalization, they seemed to be pushing it toward collapse. Gorbachev's response was to flirt with—and then to retreat from—a number of radical reform proposals.

As the economy faltered, however, he did move dramatically toward political reforms intended to give government institutions real authority. To this end, important amendments to the 1977 Soviet Constitution were adopted in 1988 and 1989. Also in 1989, a commission was created to draw up a completely new constitution. In 1990, there were more amendments to the 1977 Constitution, including the elimination of all reference to the leading role of the Communist Party (Article 6). These changes created a new legislative system, a partially competitive legislative electoral process, and an executive position of president. The president was intended to be popularly elected, but Gorbachev chose to be elected president by a vote of the legislature in 1990. Future presidents would have been popularly elected. In sum, these reforms marked tremendous strides toward democratization. (Barry & Barner-Barry, 1992, pp. 74–81, 88–93)

By 1989, the reform movement had taken on a momentum that Gorbachev had not foreseen and could not control. By this time, it was clear that his early optimism about economic reform was unjustified, and his popularity among the people had dropped sharply. His failure to deliver on his promises and his lack of a popular mandate robbed him of the authority he had had in the early days of the reform. He clearly hoped that his vigorous pursuit of change in the direction of democratization would shore up popular support for his leadership and thus buy him some time to reverse the economy's tailspin. He also hoped that democratization would remove officials who had abused and exploited their positions for personal gain, thus eliminating a major obstacle to his economic reform efforts.

A deepening economic crisis increased Gorbachev's uncertainty about economic policy and hastened his embrace of democracy. In retrospect, it is clear that a consistent thread bound together the seemingly contradictory items on his reform agenda. Gorbachev understood that one of his major problems was the abuse and exploitation of the system for personal gain by those in high-ranking positions. He believed that if abuse, exploitation, and corruption could be eliminated, the political-economic system could be restored to political stability and economic vitality.

Gorbachev wanted to eradicate the abuse of power so that he could create political and economic structures based on authority. All of the reforms put forth under the labels of perestroika and glasnost, whatever their particulars, shared this central theme, this overarching goal. What Gorbachev failed to understand (as did almost everyone else) was that power and power relationships were not simply corroding the political-economic system of the Soviet Union, they *were* the system. The authority structures of the command economy had never functioned as designed. The economic system operated on the basis of power and primarily extra-legal exchange. To base reform on the elimination of corruption and the eradication of the abuse of power was to attack the very foundation of the system.

The collapse of the Soviet Union did not magically dissolve the problems associated with economic transformation. In the next section we sort through the various challenges of economic transformation by focusing on alternative strategies for moving from a command to a market economy. We also evaluate the progress of and prospects for economic transformation in Russia and some of the other successor countries.

THE CHALLENGE OF ECONOMIC TRANSFORMATION

The economic challenges of transforming from a command to a market economy can be grouped into two categories: restructuring and stabilization. Restructuring involves the dismantling of the component elements of the command economy and replacing them with those of a market economy. For the Soviet economy, restructuring meant (1) replacing the system of centralized decision-making and creating a system of decentralized decision-making, which, of course, necessitates rethinking property rights; (2) eliminating the system of fixed prices and replacing it with a system of prices driven by supply and demand; and (3) creating an incentive system based on competition.

Stabilization means establishing and maintaining an economic environment conducive to market functioning. Markets do not work well under conditions of inflation. In practical terms, therefore, stabilization largely means getting and keeping inflation under control. It also means instituting a banking system that can facilitate exchange as well as saving and investment. An effective banking system guarantees that money works both as a medium of exchange and as a store of value.

Any strategy to transform a command into a market economy must delineate a sequence by which the challenges of restructuring and stabilization will be tackled and must identify a timetable for implementing the transformation sequence. In this section, we examine three approaches to confronting the imperatives of economic transformation. Each was endorsed by prominent policymakers in the Soviet Union and later Russia.

The Shatalin Plan

The Shatalin Plan[8] was a widely acclaimed but ultimately aborted reform plan that called for a nearly complete transformation in five hundred days. For reasons to be outlined shortly, the speed of its proposed economic transformation proved inappropriate to the Soviet context. Nevertheless, examining the Shatalin Plan is worthwhile because its fairly complete reform agenda for economic restructuring and stabilization is useful for contrasting and evaluating subsequent reform proposals.

The Shatalin Plan proposed a definite sequence by which the challenges of restructuring and stabilization should be tackled, and it proposed to complete the major tasks of basic restructuring and stabilization in five hundred days. During the first hundred days of the plan there would be a massive sale of state assets and holdings. The sale of state assets was at the top of the agenda for several reasons. It would help to stabilize the economy. The proceeds from the sale could be used to offset the government budget deficit, a major source of inflation in the economy.[9] And the sale would go a long way toward reducing the supply of rubles. Excess money was a major obstacle to meaningful price reform. The Shatalin Plan also proposed restructuring the banking system during the first hundred days. It called for the banking system to be decentralized and open to private participation.

The second phase was to be implemented over the next 150 days. With the money supply reduced, the government could phase out price controls on most nonessential consumer goods. Prices on these items would be determined by demand and supply. Wages would be adjusted to cushion the impact on workers of price increases. Also, steps would be taken toward making the ruble a strong enough currency to be exchanged in international markets.[10] A drive to privatize at least half of all the small shops and restaurants would be initiated. Also, some of the economic ministries would be consolidated or eliminated.

The third phase, covering the next 150 days, would see continued efforts to sell state property, especially state enterprises, including those in heavy industry and construction. The Shatalin Plan gave up all pretense of salvaging socialism and public ownership of the means of production. Decentralized decision-making would be achieved not through self-management and workers' councils but by converting state-owned enterprises into private property. In the agricultural sector, the state and collective farms would be kept, but peasants

---

8. This plan was named after Stanislav Shatalin, the Soviet economist who was primarily responsible for it.

9. The Shatalin Plan also proposed to curb government expenditures by reducing the state's outlay for foreign aid by 75 percent, its military expenditures by 10 percent, and the budget for the KGB by 20 percent. See Goldman (1992, p. 217).

10. The ruble had never been used as currency anywhere outside the Soviet Union or in international trade.

would be allowed to set up their own farms if they wished to do so and could acquire the resources.

In the third phase, fewer prices would be controlled. Price decontrol, however, was not yet to extend to food, oil, gas, and pharmaceuticals. Before this could occur, a social safety net had to be created to distribute income supplements to the poor and unemployed, as well as to provide for the rationing of basic goods. Clearly, such a safety net would be a drain on government resources and could increase budget deficits, at least in the short run. Without it, though, the government would be unable to curtail its subsidies to inefficient enterprises, a necessary part of a competitive economic environment.

During the final hundred days of the Shatalin Plan, an appropriate, responsible, and flexible program for fiscal (tax) and monetary (currency and banking) policy would be put into place. The privatization of state industry would continue, and the government would ease inflation by releasing its commodity reserves.

No one believed that this program would be fully implemented in five hundred days (*Izvestiia*, September 4, 1990, p. 1), but the plan did recommend a rapid program of privatization and market development. Gorbachev was ambivalent about the Shatalin Plan. During the two years before the breakup of the Soviet Union, Gorbachev's economic reform agenda continually changed. One day he seemed to endorse plans for radical transformation and then, seemingly overnight, he would withdraw his support. Boris Yeltsin, president of the Russian Republic, was far less equivocal in his support for radical economic change. He demonstrated his commitment to fundamental restructuring of the Russian economy when he endorsed the Shatalin Plan. Even after Gorbachev backed away from it in September 1990, Yeltsin presented the plan to the Supreme Soviet of the Russian Republic, which proceeded to adopt it. (Goldman, 1992, pp. 216–220)

In the unsettled political environment of 1990–91, however, Yeltsin (like Gorbachev before him) backed away from the Shatalin approach. Nevertheless, Yeltsin continued to demonstrate his commitment to economic transformation through his political maneuvering. For example, on November 11, 1991, he sought and obtained from the Russian parliament the authority to legislate by decree, and he chose strongly reform-oriented economic advisers—most specifically Yegor Gaidar.

The Gaidar Approach

Using the extraordinary power he gained immediately after the failed coup of 1991, Yeltsin pursued reform along lines recommended by Gaidar. Gaidar's approach to reform was controversial. He urged "shock therapy"—the immediate and simultaneous implementation of all reforms.

The argument in favor of shock therapy is straightforward: Economic transformation cannot be introduced piecemeal because reforms implemented at an earlier point in time will unravel when additional reforms are introduced later.

The government cannot move against inflation, for example, until it stops printing excess money. It cannot pull the plug on the printing presses, however, if the government budget is not balanced. Balancing the budget means cutting government spending, which in Russia would mean cutting subsidies on food and to industries. But higher prices on food would push many consumers into poverty, and increased industry bankruptcies would raise the unemployment rate. Because expenditures could never be cut enough to balance the budget, new taxes would have to be levied. Moreover, additional money would be needed to help industry change over to a competitive market environment. In other words, restructuring and stabilization involve interrelated activities. Because this is the case, advocates of shock therapy recommend attacking everything at once.

Gaidar's approach to shock therapy was price decontrol. On December 3, 1991, he announced that the prices for most goods in Russia would be subject to market forces as of December 16, 1991.[11] His rationale was simple. As long as prices were kept below the level at which supply matched demand, demand would exceed supply. Shortages, long lines, bribes, and privileges for those in positions of power would be the inevitable result. Allowing prices to be determined by supply and demand would have immediate beneficial effects (assuming, of course, that inflation was under control). Store shelves would no longer be empty, and lines would be shorter. And, most important, with the promise of a reasonable profit, manufacturers would increase the supply of goods. The opportunities for profit created by price decontrol would create a positive incentive for industry to learn to compete in a market environment. (Goldman, 1992, pp. 232–233)

That was more or less what had happened in Poland when shock therapy was applied in January 1990. The results of shock therapy in Russia, however, were far less than envisioned. It immediately reduced demand as expected, but it did not cause the anticipated reaction from suppliers. In Russia, few private farmers and manufacturers were ready to take advantage of the profit opportunities offered. Apparently, Yeltsin and Gaidar expected a response similar to the one anticipated by the architects of the 1988 State Enterprise Law. In both cases, reformers expected price decontrol to fuel competitive responses by would-be beneficiaries (enterprise managers and their workers). What these reformers did not seem to appreciate fully is that it takes owners to act like owners. Unless people believe that they have a real stake in the outcome (the profits or the losses), they are not likely to engage in the risk-taking behavior that competition requires.

It is easy to explain what happened with the Enterprise Law. It was sabotaged from above. Moreover, it was in effect far too briefly to demonstrate whether or not self-management and a new interpretation of public ownership

---

11. This announcement set off an immediate panic, not only in Russia but in other republics. Under growing pressure, Gaidar postponed price decontrol until January 2, 1992. Anticipating the price increases, store managers began raising prices almost immediately.

could induce competitive behavior. Explaining why Yeltsin and Gaidar delayed acting on the ownership issue is more difficult. During the fall and winter of 1991–92, Yeltsin signaled his support of privatization but gave no specific details and did nothing. The result was that when price decontrol came, there were few owners ready and able to take advantage of it.

An Alternative to Shatalin and Gaidar

The Shatalin Plan endorsed the phasing-in of both price decontrol and privatization. The initial Gaidar Plan for shock therapy emphasized immediate and nearly complete price decontrol. A third approach, suggested by Yevgeny Saburov, once an economics minister under Yeltsin, was not tried. Saburov's strategy was to focus on privatization along with the creation of a banking system and tax program before price controls were lifted. (*Wall Street Journal,* November 6, 1991, p. A15) Given Russia's political-economic heritage, this approach, which tackled the ownership issue first, had much to recommend it.

Authority has an important role in market economies. All participants must understand, respect, and obey the rules of ownership specified by law. The establishment of such authority relationships is the foundation on which a market economy is built. Entrepreneurs will not invest, manufacturers will not produce, and middlemen will not bring buyers and sellers together unless they believe that what they do is accepted, considered legitimate, and protected by laws that are widely respected. Authority elicits an internalized response; it cannot be established overnight.

In the Soviet command economy, private economic activity had been illegal. Buying and selling for profit—"speculation"—was against the law. The idea of owning assets or property and making decisions about the disposition of those assets for personal gain was alien to most Russians. "Public ownership" had been deemed a euphemism for state control, or it had served as a rationalization for the pilfering of state property for personal use. In the absence of new ideas about ownership and new rules about property, it was unrealistic to expect price decontrol to inspire profit-seeking behavior. It is hardly surprising that Gaidar's shock therapy did not work.

Moreover, saying that owning and profiting from property is now encouraged (after years of maintaining the opposite) does not make it happen. Thus, Yeltsin's somewhat belated decree of January 29, 1992, declaring that private citizens were to have the right to purchase, sell, and arrange for the sale of any good at any place, was unlikely to generate an enthusiastic response. People were undoubtedly concerned that a pronouncement made one day could be revoked the next. Subsequent attempts by city officials to restrict the locations where buying and selling could take place and their insistence that all vendors be licensed probably confirmed the suspicions of some that the decree was not worth the paper it was printed on.

After January 1992, Yeltsin moved more dramatically toward privatization. In the fall of 1992 the Russian government began to issue vouchers worth

10,000 rubles each to every Russian citizen. With these vouchers, people were able to buy shares in any of the 5,000 to 7,000 medium and large factories (about 60 to 70 percent of Russian industry) that would be reorganized as joint stock companies. One of the biggest hurdles to the success of this grandiose privatization plan was public ignorance and skepticism. The *New York Times* (October 1, 1992, p. A1) reported poll results indicating that 38 percent of the respondents thought the voucher program was "just a showpiece, and as such will not change anything." The *Times* also reported that few people on the street had a clue about what to do with their vouchers. One woman who was interviewed stated, "You tell me where I can invest my voucher. How can I find an enterprise that is not going bankrupt? If there were any non-bankrupt enterprises, I'd invest in one. But I don't see any."

In December, however, when a pilot program offered shares in a pastry factory for sale to the public, interest was high. Fifty-one percent of the shares in the factory were sold to its employees, and the remaining 49 percent were sold to voucher-bearing individuals who chose to exchange their vouchers for a stake in the factory. The government expressed the hope that this would serve as a model for nationwide privatization. (*New York Times,* December 14, 1992, p. A1)

For the skeptical or the ignorant, a steadfast commitment to privatization could go a long way toward changing expectations and building new patterns of thinking and behaving. Anecdotal evidence suggests that such behavioral changes are apparent among workers who are now co-owners of the small businesses in which they work. The once-sullen clerks in a cheese shop in Nizhniii Novgorod, for example, now bustle efficiently and politely in a shop that has been expanded twice since they became co-owners. Accounting for the shop's success and the behavioral transformation of its clerks, deputy manager Vera Pavlova explained, "Higher salaries compensate for the psychological pressure of having to be polite." (*Washington Post,* April 8, 1994, p. A1)

An effective program of privatization, however, requires more than initiating schemes to sell or to distribute state-owned assets to workers and citizens. It also requires the establishment of laws governing contracts, securities, and bankruptcy. Such laws, which help to create a system of property rights, were largely absent from Russia's 1992–93 privatization effort.[12] Consequently, "business remained at the mercy of arbitrary state intervention." (*Washington Post,* February 20, 1994, p. A1) Moreover, without well-developed laws that specify and guarantee property rights and a judicial system to interpret the laws, it is impossible to establish the authority relationships necessary for successful conversion to a market economy. (McFaul, 1994, pp. 78–79)

Nowhere is a steadfast commitment to redefining property and property

---

12. As of early 1994, Russia had adopted bankruptcy laws but had yet to appoint or train bankruptcy judges to administer them.

rights more necessary than in agriculture.[13] In December 1991, President Boris Yeltsin issued a decree ordering state and collective farms to restructure themselves in 1992. For the "chronically unprofitable" farms (estimated to be between 2,500 and 3,500), fundamental restructuring was demanded. The profitable state farms and collectives could decide whether to retain their existing status or reorganize. The options included a number of forms of collective organization: joint stock farms, agricultural cooperatives, and communal ownership with limited responsibility. Farm members could also vote to disband and create individual peasant farms or an association of peasant farms in which the individual farmers would work together. (Wegren, 1993, p. 44)

Each option essentially altered property relations in agriculture. As we discussed in Chapter 6, the agricultural collectives of the Soviet era granted only nominal ownership to their members; all property rights were exercised by Party and government officials. What Yeltsin now proposed was to restructure agriculture so that the nominal owners either would become real owners or could vote to retain the status quo.

By July 1, 1993, more than 90 percent of the state and collective farms had been reorganized. Of these, only 34 percent—generally the financially strongest farms—retained their previous status. In addition, most of the reorganized farms chose some form of "collective labor organization" (phraseology that refers to communal ownership and people working collectively). "Collective labor organizations" differ markedly from "private labor organizations," where individuals own the land and hire labor to work on their farms. Each kind of landownership, with its accompanying labor organization (collective or private), is now permitted under Russian law.

Russia's agricultural labor force has demonstrated a preference for collective ownership forms. (Wegren, 1993, pp. 42–43) For example, many state and collective farms have transformed themselves into "closed" joint stock companies. Farm property is divided up into shares that only the farm's workers and managers can own. People outside the farm cannot buy these shares, and shareholders cannot trade or cash in their shares without the approval of a general meeting of the farm's shareholders.

The key issue in evaluating the efforts to change property relations in agriculture is whether the efforts cause demonstrable change in who controls the agricultural sector. The fact of the matter is that in 1993 the state still exercised considerable control over agriculture. Reorganized farms still had to meet delivery obligations to local or federal food funds.[14] Farms continued to

---

13. This point is underscored by Marshall Goldman. He argues (1993, p. 321) that the chance for successful economic reform in the Soviet Union and later Russia would have been enhanced if agriculture had been tackled first: "[S]oviet authorities might have been able to use agriculture as a stimulus to ignite the rest of the economy. If the Russians had begun by turning over the land to the peasants, the outcome might well have been different."

14. In 1993, obligatory food deliveries to the state were officially suspended. However, they were replaced by federal and regional food funds, which were to supply the military and other categories of consumers as well as territories that do not produce adequate quantities of the

receive state subsidies and benefits (accounting for aproximately 30 percent of government spending in 1993). And farm workers continued to be classified as state sector (not private sector) employees. Thus, "many former collective and state farms that chose not to retain their previous status have, in legal terms, undergone a cosmetic rather than a real change." (Wegren, 1993, p. 46) Anyone can appreciate the complexities of transforming the agricultural sector, but such a disparity between nominal and real change does little to advance the process of building the foundation of authority relationships that market economies require.

Building a foundation of authority on which a market economy can thrive is never easy. For most of the fifteen former Soviet republics a number of serious obstacles loom large. One is that corruption is rampant. People who derived tremendous personal benefit from their positions in the power structure of the Soviet Union have used their privileged access to financial and other resources to syphon wealth out of the country and into foreign bank accounts: "From nickel to guns, from oil to cash, Russia has become a paradise for smugglers, con men, and business managers looking for ways to profit from its considerable natural wealth." Estimates of capital flight from Russia in 1992 ranged from $4 billion to $15 billion.[15] (*New York Times,* February 1, 1993, p. A1)

This kind of illegal activity threatens the newly independent countries. They cannot afford to see their national wealth—assets that could be used to rebuild their economies—drained away. And how can they hope to build a foundation of authority relationships that respect property and laws if the people who are the most successful in society flagrantly abuse both laws and property?

Another obstacle to the establishment of authority relationships in many of the successor countries challenges the creation of viable market economies. This obstacle stems from the economic uncertainty that results from the real or perceived ineptness of government policy-making. Two of the most important sources of such uncertainty—hyperinflation and widespread unemployment—call for contradictory policy responses from government. Some economists, most notably Jeffrey Sachs, have argued that hyperinflation poses the gravest threat to the successful transformation to a market economy. (*MacNeil/Lehrer NewsHour,* January 21, 1994) Sachs recommends an aggressive policy to limit inflation. Such a policy would entail measures to balance the government's budget and, in the Russian case, a cessation of the subsidies that have sustained inefficient industries.

Of course, reducing or eliminating government subsidies risks massive unemployment as inefficient factories go bankrupt. Under the Soviet command economy, ordinary individuals did not have much, but they did have a job.

---

designated farm products. The federal government and regional officials were to establish quantities. The funds clearly indicate that the state remains a pivotal actor in agricultural procurement. (Wegren, 1993, p. 47)

15. Because of the illegal nature of much of this capital exodus, there is no way to get an accurate figure.

With little or no experience in a labor market, the unemployed would have few (if any) job-seeking skills. To make matters worse, they would be looking for jobs in an economic environment where jobs would be anything but plentiful. Moreover, joblessness and the economic insecurity it engenders would undoubtedly create increased social unrest and undermine the establishment of authority.

The expectation that government must do something to make workers' lives secure is reflected in the comments of a textile factory worker in a provincial town 250 miles east of Moscow: "We've been raised in the spirit of socialism and are accustomed to it. The government must help us." (*Washington Post,* June 28, 1992, p. A1) Some recommend that before subsidies to industry are eliminated, the Russian government must have in place a social safety net that includes unemployment compensation. This suggestion is reasonable, but, of course, the creation of a safety net would increase government expenditures and inflationary pressures.[16]

Throughout 1992 and 1993, Yeltsin followed a moderate path in dealing with economic uncertainty. He moved in the direction of privatization at the same time as many large state-owned factories cut back production (because supplies were unavailable or too expensive) while keeping their work force on the payroll. Yeltsin's room to maneuver was significantly limited by the emergence of Civic Union. A political organization made up of enterprise managers and their supporters, Civic Union became a formidable advocate for protection of Russia's heavy industry.

With little substantive action taken to cut industry's government lifeline, inflation was substantial. In 1992–93, a number of measures were introduced to cope with a situation that had created an inflation rate of 2,000 percent in 1992. In January 1993, price controls were reimposed on certain basic food products such as bread, milk, baby formula, and vodka. (*Washington Post,* January 6, 1993, p. A1) In February, the government sharply increased prices for natural gas and telephone calls. Although in the short run it was feared that these price increases could cause even higher levels of inflation, it was hoped that they eventually would dampen inflation by easing the need for government credits and subsidies. (*New York Times,* February 4, 1993, pp. A1, A3)

Then, in July 1993, in a badly handled move, the Central Bank announced on a Saturday (July 24) that as of the following Monday (July 26) all rubles printed before 1993 would be worthless. People would have two weeks (quickly extended to a month) to exchange 35,000 old rubles (quickly increased to 100,000) for new rubles. The remaining reserves of old rubles would have to be placed in bank deposits, earning interest considerably below the rate of inflation, for a period of at least six months before they could be exchanged. (*New York Times,* July 26, 1993, p. A8; July 27, 1993, p. A3)

---

16. Some analysts have suggested that this is an area where the advanced industrial states of the West could make a real contribution to market transformation. Western assistance could be used to set up a fund to aid workers who find themselves unemployed as a result of plant closings.

From the time Boris Yeltsin assumed office as Russia's president, he demonstrated considerable skill at building and maintaining popular support for his policies. The 1993 ruble episode left many analysts wondering what had happened to that skill. The poorly coordinated move did nothing to enhance the government's credibility. Quite to the contrary, the incident showed Yeltsin hurrying back from vacation, the Finance Ministry issuing a formal protest, and the prime minister supporting the Central Bank's move. People could easily wonder who was in charge. Such events work to undermine authority.

Yeltsin's frustration with economic reform was most profoundly evident in his move to disband the Russian parliament in the fall of 1993. The president and parliament had been deadlocked over reform measures for a long time, and Yeltsin's patience finally ran out. In a referendum on December 12, 1993, the Russian people approved their first post-Soviet constitution. The new Russian Constitution provided for a strong presidential form of government. Theoretically, the division of authority could permit President Yeltsin to take a more aggressive approach to economic reform. As a practical matter, however, the election results showed that a large proportion of the people—and a significant portion of the military—had expressed their unhappiness with their economic plight by voting for antireform parties and candidates.

In the Duma, the lower house of the Russian Federal Assembly (parliament), antireform parties gained more seats than the reformers, a working plurality. Although the makeup of the upper house, the Federal Council, was more strongly reformist, its members were not popularly elected like representatives to the Duma. (*Nezavisimaia Gazeta,* November 24, 1993, p. 1) This difference was highlighted by the fact that the Federal Council elected a reformist Yeltsin aide as its head, while the Duma elected an antireform former Communist and current member of the conservative Agrarian Party. Thus, even though the Russian Constitution now gives considerably more power to President Yeltsin than to the parliament, the election results put pressure on the Yeltsin government to be cautious about reform measures that might make the standard of living even worse for large blocs of the electorate. The response of the Yeltsin government was to name a new cabinet that was considerably more conservative than the previous one. Radical reformists either resigned or were not offered posts they were willing to accept.

The new Russian Constitution also established an independent Central Bank and, in marked contrast to the Soviet-era Constitution, guaranteed private property rights. By the middle of 1994, statistical data revealed increasing levels of income and consumption in Russia indicating that its economic free-fall might be slowing. According to the Working Center for Economic Reforms (a government agency), real income in April 1994 was up 20 percent from the previous year. Consumption rates were up 11 percent. Edward Layard, an adviser to the Russian government from the London School of Economics, noted that with these increases the Russian standard of living approximated what it had been in 1985 (the year Gorbachev came to power). With regard to the general status of production in the Russian economy, Layard commented, "I can't say Russia has reached the bottom. But it may be the case that the overall collapse has stopped, that the fall in output is flattening out." (*Washington Post,* June 21, 1994, p. A1)

These hopeful signs notwithstanding, it remains to be seen whether the new Russian Constitution will lay the foundation for the stable authority relations on which a market economy can be built. It also remains to be seen whether the conservative vote by the Russian electorate in the December 1993 parliamentary election will cause Russia to modify its economic institution-building process to slow down or perhaps even stop movement toward a fully functioning market economy. But here too, there are some hopeful signs. In June 1994, for example, the conservative-dominated Duma passed a tight government budget. The parliament's action increased the possibility that the moderate inflation rate of between 8 and 10 percent per month achieved in late 1993 and early 1994 could be sustained in the future. (*Washington Post,* June 28, 1994, p. A19)

BEYOND RUSSIA: ECONOMIC CHALLENGES IN THE OTHER REPUBLICS

Two years after the breakup of the Soviet Union, none of its former republics had achieved positive economic growth. The drop in gross domestic product for 1992 (*EBRD Economic Review: Current Economic Issues,* July 1993) ranged from −50 percent in Armenia to −5 percent in Turkmenistan. In Armenia, Azerbaijan (−30 percent), Georgia (−30 percent), and Tajikistan (−31 percent), the poor economic performance was largely a result of ongoing violence. In other countries, notably Ukraine (−14 percent) and Lithuania (−35 percent), the poor economic performance is not nearly as simple to explain. The economy of Ukraine deteriorated badly after independence, and everyone was surprised. Ukraine had been expected to make the transition to a market economy with relative ease.

In this section, we examine the condition of the Ukrainian and Lithuanian economies, which were expected to be the success stories of economic transformation. We consider the legacy of command-style interdependencies, focusing on the energy dependence of the Baltics and Ukraine. This dependence at least partially accounts for the problems they have experienced. We also examine the efforts of the Central Asian republics to transcend the interdependence patterns of the old regime and replace them with more market-based integration. Finally, we discuss another legacy of the Soviet era, environmental degradation. We examine the scope of the problem and the reasons why the newly independent countries have failed to take effective measures to remedy it.

Would-Be Economic Success Stories: Ukraine and Lithuania

At the time of independence, Ukraine's economic prospects appeared rosy. Ukraine had a diversified economy with a sizable industrial and agricultural base. Not plagued by the ethnic strife that sabotaged economic progress in many of the other republics, it had a relatively homogeneous, literate, and skilled labor force. Most analysts expected that Ukraine could make a relatively painless transition to a prosperous market economy. Two years later, Ukraine was on the verge of economic catastrophe. The estimated inflation for 1992 was 2,500 percent, and by mid-1993 monthly inflation rates had exceeded 50 percent. The projected budget deficit for 1993 was a staggering 9 or 10 trillion karbovanets (the Ukrainian currency), a figure that was substantially higher than projected total revenues. (Mihalisko, 1993, p. 54) In addition, industrial production for the year 1993 declined significantly. By the fall of 1993 the karbovanets had depreciated so rapidly against both the US dollar and the Russian ruble (a rather remarkable achievement given Russia's economic problems) that Ukrainian president Leonid Kravchuk imposed strict currency controls. Open buying and selling of hard currency were suspended, thus eliminating the only market mechanism for determining a realistic exchange rate for the karbovanets. (*New York Times,* November 4, 1993, p. A6)

The economy of Lithuania deteriorated similarly. In a January 1993 address clearly designed to underscore the poor state of the economy, President Algirdas Brazauskas announced that the 1992 gross national product was only 39 percent of the 1991 level. He also reported a 1992 inflation rate of 1,163 percent as well as a precipitous drop in personal family incomes (down 73 percent from 1989 levels). (Girnius, 1993, p. 28) Although Brazauskas may have somewhat overstated the severity of the economic crisis as a way of criticizing his political predecessors, there can be no denying that the Lithuanian economy was in a state of deterioration. As in Ukraine, this was surprising. Lithuania had not been subjected to ethnic strife, it had a relatively developed industrial base, and it had enjoyed relative political stability.

After independence, both Ukraine and Lithuania moved rapidly to transform their command economies into market economies. They liberalized prices and economic activity in general. These reforms, however, did not have the desired effect, because neither country successfully moved to privatize its economy.[17] The state-owned sector continued to dominate both economies. Ongoing subsidization of the state-owned sector ran up budget deficits and frustrated stabilization efforts, thus contributing to soaring inflation rates.

Privatizing state-owned enterprises has been a daunting challenge for all the republics. Generally recognized as an imperative by those advocating economic transformation, "privatization of large-scale enterprises responsible for the bulk of the region's [i.e., former Communist bloc's] industrial (and frequently agricultural) production has proved to be impossible." (Slay, 1993, p. 38) Ukraine and Lithuania were not exceptions to this generalization. The absence of credible privatization programs has aggravated the efficiency problems of state enterprises by increasing managerial and worker uncertainty about the

---

17. Only in Poland, Hungary, and the Czech Republic has the transition from socialist to capitalist property relations and from a command to a market economy been thorough as well as rapid.

future. "Rather than undertaking restructuring programs to lower costs and improve commercial prospects, state enterprises have frequently reacted passively to market signals, waiting instead for ... central subsidies and directions." (Slay, 1993, p. 36) This passive resistance to market reforms undermines the economy as a whole.

Economic prospects for both Lithuania and Ukraine were further compromised by the Soviet-era interdependencies that linked the periphery to the decision-making center. There is no doubt that the deterioration of Lithuania's economy was in part due to Russia's economic woes. For example, Lithuania had difficulty obtaining payment for goods delivered to Russia and to other members of the Commonwealth of Independent States (CIS). (Girnius, 1993, p. 28) Another problem was the "energy shock" experienced by Lithuania and Ukraine, as well as by Estonia and Latvia, when they stopped benefiting from artificially cheap Soviet energy resources. In the next section, we explore the impact of energy dependence on these economies and consider the efforts of the Central Asian republics to forge new economic ties.

Prospects for Market-Based Integration: The Baltic States, Ukraine, and the Central Asian Republics

The Baltic states (Estonia, Latvia, and Lithuania) and Ukraine have long been dependent on Russian oil and natural gas exports to fuel their economies. During the Soviet era, oil and gas were supplied to them at heavily subsidized prices and paid for in soft (i.e., nonconvertible) rubles or in goods. After the breakup of the Soviet Union, Russia began to limit its oil exports to the other successor countries and to insist on higher prices. Russia threatened to demand payment in hard (i.e., convertible) currencies from the Baltics, Ukraine, and other countries that have economic and political policies at odds with Russian policies. Thus Russia used its energy resources to achieve economic gains, and its leaders demonstrated their willingness to use Russian resources as a political lever. (Kramer, 1993, p. 41)

The Baltics were among the countries most affected by the Russian-induced oil shock. After the breakup, Russia at first agreed to continue exporting oil to these states at 70 percent of their 1991 levels. The oil was to be bought at world market prices and paid for with rubles or by barter. Russia reneged on this agreement, however. As of February 1992, Estonia had yet to receive a first shipment for the year, and throughout 1992 Latvia and Estonia experienced serious shortfalls in their expected deliveries. These shortfalls created serious dislocations, including reduced industrial production and unemployment. Unreliable energy supplies also led Baltic leaders to impose draconian energy conservation measures. (Kramer, 1993, pp. 41–42)

A parallel saga unfolded in Ukraine. After the breakup, Russia reduced its shipments of oil and natural gas to Ukraine. Throughout 1993, the persistent inability of Ukrainian enterprises to make payments on these shipments raised the specter of further cuts. Ukraine's energy dependence reflects its overall economic dependence on Russia. Before the breakup of the Soviet Union, Ukraine spent 20 percent of its national income on imports from Russia and earned about the same percentage of its national income from exports to Russia. After independence, this seeming "balance" evaporated. In 1992, Ukraine ran a 295.3-billion-ruble deficit in trade covered by intergovernmental agreements with Russia; this represented 6.6 percent of Ukraine's gross domestic product. Although Ukraine ran a surplus with Russia in trade not covered by such agreements, there remained a significant overall deficit. (Whitlock, 1993, pp. 38–39)

Ukraine's major problem was its dependence on Russia for energy. Although Ukraine has energy resources, during the Soviet period central economic planners favored cheaper and more abundant sources of energy from Russia, Turkmenistan, and Azerbaijan. Consequently, Ukrainian production of natural gas and oil dwindled sharply in the 1970s and 1980s. Ironically, as its fuel production was being drastically curtailed, Ukraine experienced considerable growth in its energy-intensive heavy-industry sector. Thus, by 1993, Ukraine's energy requirements far outstripped its previous production levels, and virtually all of its oil imports and 70 percent of its natural gas imports came from Russia. (Whitlock, 1993, p. 39) The resulting deficit, in and of itself, would not have been so troubling if Ukraine were running trade surpluses with other countries or if it were experiencing significant foreign investment. But by 1993, neither of these had happened; Ukraine's export sector remained weak, and there was little foreign investment. Throughout 1993, therefore, Ukraine accumulated debt obligations to Russia—obligations that it increasingly could not meet. (Whitlock, 1993, p. 39)

What are the implications of continued Ukrainian dependence on Russia? The answer to this question depends on Russian motivations and intentions. Already there are indications that Russia intends to use Ukraine's ever-worsening balance-of-payments problem to Russia's political advantage. Witness the deal Yeltsin struck with Kravchuk to buy back from Ukraine its half of the former Soviet Black Sea fleet. Almost immediately, Kravchuk backpedaled on the deal, but the writing was clearly on the wall. Russia was willing to use its position of relative economic strength to secure political objectives. The interesting question is, What exactly are Russia's intentions and motivations vis-à-vis Ukraine? Some have suggested that if Ukraine's economic difficulties are not eased relatively quickly, they will drive Ukraine to forsake its independence and seek to reunite with Russia. This may be precisely what Russian leaders hope will happen. Or, Russian leaders may not want to shoulder the economic burdens of Ukraine.

Of all the republics of the former Soviet Union, the Central Asian republics were the least interested in complete political and economic independence. Having achieved such independence, however, Kazakhstan, Kyrgyzstan, Tajikistan, Turkmenistan, and Uzbekistan have endeavored to replace their Soviet-era links to Moscow and to each other with greater market-based integration.

This represents a considerable challenge. The interdependence created by the Soviet command economy makes their transition to market economies difficult and the transition to market-based integration even more difficult. This problem is aggravated by violence in Tajikistan, by the diverse political structures that have emerged in these countries, and by regional interethnic hostilities.

Under the Soviet command system, management of the economy was structured vertically, and horizontal links between ministries and between enterprises were discouraged. Thus, as the top layers of the decision-making hierarchy were eliminated, reduced, or divested of their power by Gorbachev's reform efforts, the economy was left with few legal mechanisms for distributing goods and services among the various branches, sectors, and enterprises at the local or regional level. After the breakup, the newly independent countries were left with serious internal and international distribution problems. It is hardly surprising, therefore, that trade between the Central Asian republics dropped significantly between 1988 and 1992. Given the nature of specialization in the command structure, Central Asia had been transformed into a supplier of raw materials, especially raw cotton. (Marnie & Whitlock, 1993, p. 55) Therefore, trade among the new Central Asian countries is likely to be limited by the fact that they cannot obtain from one another the finished goods they need.

If market integration among the newly independent countries is to be achieved, the legacy of Soviet-era interdependence must be overcome through the creation of new economic relations. After gaining independence, the Central Asian leaders began to explore various ways to establish new economic relations among themselves, with other members of the CIS, and with Western firms. This exploration began with a series of summit meetings of Central Asian leaders. The result, however, was much rhetoric and little in the way of concrete measures increasing economic cooperation and integration. Efforts in this direction were complicated by the military conflict in Tajikistan and by the very different economic strategies pursued by the Central Asian governments. Kazakhstan and Kyrgyzstan forged ahead with liberal reforms, but Uzbekistan and Turkmenistan seemed determined to maintain considerable central control over their economies. (Marnie & Whitlock, 1993, pp. 39–40)

The establishment of new economic relations may be more easily achieved through the CIS. Aware of the advantages in both the short and the long run of increased economic cooperation and integration, all of the Central Asian republics have forged economic ties through the CIS. These have taken the form of bilateral trade agreements. Although such barter arrangements assure continued delivery of important commodities, they have been criticized as reminiscent of the old Soviet distribution system. Nevertheless, "they have become the foundation of continued CIS trade links amid general disintegration." (Marnie & Whitlock, 1993, p. 38) Moreover, most of the CIS members (including four of the five Central Asian countries) have agreed to form a customs union of sorts, in which they keep tariff barriers among themselves low or nonexistent and maintain uniform tariffs against non-CIS members.

Economic integration could also take place in a regional setting that extends beyond the countries of the former Soviet Union. In 1985, an Economic Cooperation Organization (ECO) was founded by Iran, Pakistan, and Turkey. In

November 1992, the Central Asian states, Azerbaijan, and Afghanistan joined. The long-term aim of the ECO is to eliminate tariff and other barriers to trade among its members. Thus far, however, little progress has been made in getting rid of trade barriers. The organization has functioned more as a forum for bilateral negotiations.

Turkey demonstrated considerable interest in creating economic and other links to the Central Asian countries. Turkey's leaders viewed their country as "the bridge for Western investment and economic cooperation with the Central Asian states." (Marnie & Whitlock, 1993, p. 41) In 1992, Turkey granted a total of $1 billion in aid and trade credits to Central Asia. Most of the aid and credits were arranged through bilateral agreements. (*The Economist,* December 26–January 8, 1993, p. 46) Iran also worked to create closer economic and political ties with Central Asia. The Iranian government promised economic assistance for Turkmenistan, especially assistance in developing the Turkmen oil and gas industry.

The ECO was also interested in developing a transportation and communications infrastructure—linking roads with railway networks and establishing an airline. Such an infrastructure would reduce the need for the landlocked Central Asian countries to go through Russia to get to the rest of the world. This would be a long-term project, however, with little immediate payoff for Central Asia. Moreover, at present, none of the non–Central Asian members of the ECO—Afghanistan, Iran, Pakistan, and Turkey—has the economic resources to boost appreciably the economies of the Central Asian countries.

Thus, despite potentially advantageous ties of economic cooperation within the CIS and with other regional partners, the Central Asian countries have sought economic cooperation with the West as their primary strategy for meeting their short- and medium-term economic goals. They have been especially interested in attracting foreign investment to help them develop processing and refining facilities for their raw materials. Uzbekistan, for example, has targeted mining, the oil and gas industry, gold, ferrous metals, chemical fibers, and plastics for development and expansion. Uzbek leaders want not only to achieve self-sufficiency in these sectors but to become exporters as well. They are also anxious to reduce their dependence on the export of raw cotton. They envision a future in which Uzbekistan will export finished cotton textiles, instead of raw cotton. The Uzbek program for economic development, like the programs of the other Central Asian countries, requires the development of joint ventures with Western partners.

Environmental Degradation

A tragic byproduct of the Soviet era is environmental deterioration. (Feshbach & Friendly, 1992) The extreme emphasis on industrialization during the Soviet period largely explains the blatant disregard for the environment. Because of the generally low quality of the manufactured goods produced in the Soviet Union and the Soviet bloc, these countries relied on exports of raw materials to earn hard currency, and they extracted raw materials with little (if any) regard for the environment. Because of aging equipment and outdated technology, Soviet production was very inefficient. This productive inefficiency also had important consequences for the environment: "Less metal was extracted from ore mined in the USSR at a far higher energy cost, more material was wasted in production (the machine building industry lost more than 20% in metal shavings alone); and low production quality required the maintenance of excessive spare parts." (Golitsyn, 1993, p. 33)

This indictment of the Soviet command economy does not imply that market economies have better environmental records. The drive to make products better, faster, and cheaper has led to flagrant abuse of the environment everywhere and, in turn, has led many to view a habitable and healthy environment as a kind of collective good. Everyone enjoys the benefits a healthy environment affords, such as clean air and unpolluted water. Because no one can be denied enjoyment of healthy air, however, no one can derive a profit from producing or safeguarding it—so no one does. Thus, the government in market economies typically has to step in and regulate households and industries to protect the environment. Also, like the United States, the newly independent countries of the former Soviet Union have the challenge of cleaning up the battlefields of the Cold War—the nuclear weapons production facilities.

One major difference distinguished the Soviet Union from the United States and other Western states with regard to despoliation of the environment. In the Soviet Union, little concrete information about the condition of the environment was made available to the public. The ability to control information and the inherently coercive nature of the Soviet political system gave Soviet leaders greater latitude to despoil the environment for political or economic purposes. The toll on the environment of Soviet-era policies is enormous. Air and water pollution is extensive.

The main airborne pollutants include carbon monoxide, sulfur dioxide, and nitrogen oxides (which combine with water in the atmosphere to form acid rain). Levels of soot and heavy metals in the air are also high. Figures for the period 1981–89 that the USSR Ministry of Natural Resources and Environmental Protection supplied to the United Nations Conference on Economic Development show that total emissions of airborne pollutants in the Soviet Union reached a peak of 108 million tons in 1983. By 1989, the levels had dropped to 95.5 million tons—which is still very high. (Golitsyn, 1993, p. 34)

The Soviet Union had abundant but unevenly distributed supplies of fresh water. Thus, water pollution problems are greatest in the successor countries with the scarcest supply of water, most notably in Central Asia. Water pollution there is the result of years of improper agricultural practices, including the overuse of fertilizers, pesticides, and defoliants. Practically all of the water from the Amu Darya and Syr Darya rivers has been diverted for irrigation. Those rivers flow into the Aral Sea, which has been shrinking dangerously. This shrinkage has resulted in the destruction of regional ecosystems that depended on the sea and its tributaries. The combination of water shortages and contaminated drinking water has led to outbreaks of disease and a sharp increase in infant mortality. (Golitsyn, 1993, p. 36) The Soviet agricultural, industrial, and mining practices that flagrantly wasted natural resources and polluted the air and water also created serious problems of soil deterioration, desert creation, and deforestation.

Moreover, the heirs to the Soviet Union have to contend with the legacy of nuclear waste and nuclear disasters from weapons production and from power plants. According to Alexei Yablokov, adviser to Boris Yeltsin on the environment: "Radioactive contamination is the number one environmental problem in this country. . . . The way we have dealt with the whole issue of nuclear power, and particularly the problem of nuclear waste, was irresponsible and immoral." (*Washington Post,* September 7, 1993, p. A1) The scale of nuclear contamination in the former USSR has become evident only over the last few years. In the aftermath of the 1986 Chernobyl disaster, the Soviet people learned about other catastrophes, including a series of accidents between 1948 and 1967 at a plutonium-producing plant near the city of Chelyabinsk in the southern Urals. They also learned about the haphazard dumping of nuclear waste at various sites that has already created significant maritime nuclear pollution.

Cleaning up the environment presents formidable challenges to the newly independent countries. One challenge is changing production practices in agriculture and industry so that existing problems are not made worse. Another challenge is cleaning up the mess that already exists. The severe economic recession that plagued all the successor countries when they became independent resulted in short-term relief for the environment. Declining production reduced the stress on natural ecosystems. This reprieve, however, cannot last. Anxious to restore economic activity and improve living standards, post-Soviet leaders are unlikely to divert scarce resources to environmental protection and cleanup. Ecologically sound economic growth is likely to be regarded as a luxury they cannot afford.

Ecologically sound growth requires "minimizing the use of nonrenewable resources, controlling waste, recycling processed materials, and reorganizing production so that the waste products of one production cycle become inputs for another." (Golitsyn, 1993, p. 42) Achieving these goals in production will require people who have lived their whole lives under the Soviet system to fundamentally transform the way they think about the economy and the environment. It will also require a massive infusion of investment capital to redesign and reconstruct existing production facilities and to introduce new technologies. Capital is in short supply, so for the foreseeable future, producers are likely to use existing facilities and existing production practices at the expense of the environment.

The shortage of capital also will compromise efforts to clean up the environmental mess. Technologies exist for treating sewage and industrial waste, but without the capital, sewage treatment facilities will not be built. Nor will other technologies that could help ease environmental problems, such as installing catalytic converters for limiting harmful automobile emissions.

Some environmental problems, of course, transcend existing technologies. Nuclear cleanup is a particularly vexing problem for which there currently is no good technological solution. The best that can be done is to prevent existing waste from further degrading air, water, and soil. Containing nuclear waste, however, is itself a technologically challenging and very expensive endeavor. At present, most of the problems associated with nuclear waste containment are being ignored, and nuclear power plants of questionable safety continue to operate. In Ukraine, for example, with its energy dependence and balance-of-payments difficulties, nuclear power remains an important source of energy.

For the foreseeable future, environmental problems will likely go unaddressed. These problems, however, are of such magnitude that they transcend national borders. As the Chernobyl disaster demonstrated, the international community has a vested interest in the environmental status of the former Soviet Union. In 1993–94, the international community demonstrated some willingness to commit resources for the environmental cleanup of the former Soviet Union. The United Nations and the World Bank backed a plan in late 1993 to coordinate efforts to save the Black Sea from ecological collapse. Only modestly funded ($25 million for three years), the Environmental Management and Protection Program of the Black Sea faces a monumental clean-up challenge. (*Washington Post,* June 20, 1994, pp. A1, A10) Also, in July 1994, the Group of Seven approved a $1.8 billion program to close the Chernobyl nuclear power plant and to upgrade safety standards at three other nuclear plants under construction in Ukraine. (*Washington Post,* July 9, 1994, p. A16) How the international community, most particularly the advanced industrial countries, will respond over the long term to the environmental challenge created by the Soviet Union remains to be seen.

To summarize, the transformation of the Soviet-era command system to market-oriented economic systems is a formidable undertaking. Since the breakup, Russia and the other newly independent countries have confronted a host of factors that have complicated their efforts to restructure and stabilize their economies. Not the least of these complicating factors has been the challenge of rebuilding the political foundations of their societies. Without a solid base of authority, neither political stability nor economic prosperity can be assured. In the next two chapters, we explore the likelihood of the various successor countries' achieving the legitimacy that democracy can confer.

REFERENCES

Feshbach, M., & Friendly, A. Jr. (1992) *Ecocide in the USSR*. New York. Basic Books.

Girnius, S. (1993). The Lithuanian economy in 1992. *RFE/RL Research Report, 2*(16), 28–32.

Goldman, M. I. (1992). *What went wrong with perestroika?* New York: Norton.

———. (1993). The Chinese model: The solution to Russia's economic ills? *Current History, 92*(576), 320–324.

Golitsyn, G. (1993). Ecological problems in the CIS during the transitional period. *RFE/RL Research Report, 2*(2), 33–42.

Gorbachev, M. (1987). *Perestroika: New thinking for our country and the world.* New York: Harper & Row.

Gregory, P. R., and Stuart, R. C. (1990). *Soviet economic structure and performance* (4th ed.). New York: Harper & Row.

Hewett, E. (1988). *Reforming the Soviet economy: Equality versus efficiency.* Washington, DC: Brookings Institution.

Kramer, J. M. (1993). "Energy shock" from Russia jolts Baltic states. *RFE/RL Research Report, 2*(17), 41–49.

Lindblom, C. (1977). *Politics and markets: The world's political-economic systems.* New York: Basic Books.

Marnie, S., & Whitlock, E. (1993). Central Asia and economic integration. *RFE/RL Research Report, 2*(14), 34–44.

McFaul, M. (1994). The dynamics of revolutionary change in Russia and the former Soviet Union. In M. T. Klare & D. C. Thomas (Eds.), *World security: Challenges for a new century* (2nd ed., pp. 63–84). New York: St. Martin's Press.

Mihalisko, K. (1993). Ukrainians and their leaders at a time of crisis. *RFE/RL Research Report, 2*(31), 54–62.

Miroshnichenko, L. (1988). Vo schto obkhoditsia tresvost'? *Ogonek,* no. 39, pp. 20–23.

Samuelson, P. A., & Nordhaus, W. D. (1985). *Economics* (12th ed.). New York: McGraw-Hill.

Slay, B. (1993). The postcommunist economic transition: Barriers and progress. *RFE/RL Research Report, 2*(39), 35–44.

Smith, G. (1992). *Soviet politics: struggling with change* (2nd ed.). New York: St. Martin's Press.

Tsipko, A. C. (1989). Chelovek ne mozhet izmenit svoei prirode. *Politicheskoe Obrazovanie,* no. 4, pp. 68–78.

Wegren, S. (1993). Trends in Russian agrarian reform. *RFE/RL Research Report, 2*(13), 46–57.

Whitlock, E. (1993). Ukrainian-Russian trade: The economics of dependency. *RFE/RL Research Report, 2*(43), 38–42.

Zaslavskaia, T. (1986). Chelovecheskii faktor razvitiia ekonomiki i sotsial'naia spravedlivost'. *Kommunist,* no. 13, pp. 62–73.
Zaslavskaya, T. (1990). *The second socialist revolution.* Bloomington: Indiana University Press.

· 8 ·

THE BREAKUP OF THE SOVIET UNION AND THE SEARCH FOR DEMOCRACY

The overall balance sheet of Soviet nationalities policy, now in its seventh decade, is certainly positive, because the Soviet system endures. It does seem, however, that the difficulty of holding together is increasing. . . . Should there be a vacuum of authority, . . . the USSR would disintegrate as rapidly as did the old empire of the tsars.

ALAIN BESANÇON (1986, p. 9)

[N]ever before in history has an empire vanished from the map in just a few days.

ZHORES MEDVEDEV (*Washington Post,* January 12, 1992, p. C1)

If the breakup of the Soviet Union seemed abrupt in 1991, the basic nationalistic impulses that led to it had been building for a while. During the Gorbachev period, "the ethnic variable . . . emerged as the key social and political reference point in the Soviet Union." (Rakowska-Harmstone, 1986, p. 259)

In this chapter, we discuss Mikhail Gorbachev's effort to renegotiate the relationship between and among the various political subunits of the Soviet Union. This effort failed as growing numbers of them began to demand more sovereignty or outright independence. In the context of this political debate, secession—always a theoretical possibility—became a real issue. Before any of these problems could be solved, however, the 1991 coup attempt dealt a death blow to the USSR. The Soviet Union disintegrated, leaving fifteen successor countries. None was ethnically homogeneous, though several came close. In some, the titular nationality represented only a slight majority or less than a majority of the total population. Most claimed to want democracy, though several saw it as a long-run rather than a short-run goal.

To assess the potential for the establishment of stable democratic governments in the successor countries, we examine eight conditions necessary for stable democracy. Because it would be unwieldy to examine all fifteen countries with reference to all eight conditions, we focus on a few former Soviet republics as examples—usually choosing two or three successor countries to illustrate each particular point. In Chapter 9, we continue this discussion by examining the democratic potential of the countries in each region of the former Soviet Union, drawing on all eight conditions as needed. First, however, we set the stage by discussing the legal structure of the USSR, as well as the efforts of the republics increased self-rule or independence during the last years of the Soviet Union.

A NEW UNION TREATY?

The Treaty on the Formation of the USSR (Union Treaty), adopted December 30, 1922, was the basis for the founding of the Soviet Union. It was signed by representatives of the four original republics: (1) the Russian Soviet Federated Socialist Republic (RSFSR, now the Russian Federation); (2) Ukraine; (3) Byelorussia (now Belarus); and (4) the Transcaucasian Republic (now Armenia, Azerbaijan, and Georgia). Although a declaration that was signed at the same time stated that the union was voluntary, the non-Russian territories had already been brought under Moscow's rule by the Red Army and thus had no real choice. In fact, at first there was discussion of simply making those territories part of the RSFSR. This option was opposed by those (including Lenin) who preferred a structure that had at least the appearance of federalism. They were concerned about the impression it would make on the internationalist movement if theoretically independent republics were formally abolished. (Sheehy, 1990b)

The Union Treaty was incorporated into the Soviet Constitution of 1924. Although it was dropped from the constitutions of 1936 and 1977, "almost all its provisions were in fact reproduced in those constitutions." (Goble, 1990b) Most notable is the fact that the treaty and all three constitutions "retained the notion of the sovereignty of the republics and the provision that a Union republic [had] the right to secede." (Sheehy, 1990b, p. 20) During the Gorbachev period, the republics used these constitutional principles as the basis for their declarations of sovereignty and demands for independence.

During the 1920s, however, "the republics rapidly lost any real powers they still had, and the Soviet Union became essentially a unitary state." (Sheehy, 1990a, p. 15) The main vehicle for the imposition of unitary rule was the CPSU, which was the effective policymaker for the Soviet government at all levels. The CPSU "did not even formally recognize the federal principle in its internal organization." (Szporluk, 1992, p. 86) Regional subdivisions of the Party corresponded to the boundaries of the republics, but these subdivisions were treated as regional branches of a single party. For example, when the Lithuanian Communist Party voted to split with the CPSU in 1989, Gorbachev asserted that "no part of the CPSU has the right to decide the question of its independent existence on the basis of its own program and rules, without taking into account the position of the CPSU as a whole." (Girnius, 1990a, p. 8)

With the advent of glasnost and democratization, the various ethnic groups became much more openly restive under the power-based, centralized rule of the Communist Party. They began to demand more real control over their own destinies; 1990 was a pivotal year. As an Uzbek nationalist observed: "Whether Gorbachev likes it or not, there is not a republic in the country that did not experience in 1990 a rebirth of national consciousness, a sense that independence is superior to dependence and that Moscow can no longer dictate our destinies." (*Washington Post,* December 31, 1990, p. A1) In fact, by 1990, not just republics but minority groups within republics were asking for sovereignty or independence.

Some of the republics merely wanted more self-rule; others invoked their constitutional right to secede from the union. By the end of 1990, ten of the union republics had made formal declarations of sovereignty, and another five had declared independence. In addition, numerous subrepublican units of government had declared themselves sovereign. One of Gorbachev's economic advisers rather wryly observed: "It's getting to the point where sooner or later someone is going to declare his apartment an independent state." (*Washington Post,* December 31, 1990, p. A10)

The five republics declaring independence were the three Baltic republics, Georgia, and Armenia. The Baltic republics invoked the Nazi-Soviet Pact of 1939 and its secret protocols to support their claim that they had been annexed illegally. The Lithuanians also cited a treaty signed in 1920 between Lithuania and Soviet Russia in which the latter renounced all claims to Lithuanian territory. (Vardys, 1992, p. 472) Estonia and Latvia based their claims to independence on similar 1920 treaties. (Clemens, 1991, pp. 40–44) Georgia denounced the treaty that was signed in 1921 between Georgia and the RSFSR, as well as the 1922 Union Treaty, asking the USSR government to begin talks leading to the independence of Georgia. Armenia was the first to initiate the process of secession, asserting what it claimed was its constitutional right.

Before 1990, Gorbachev had seen no need for a new union treaty and had resisted proposals that one be negotiated. But, as nationalism grew and as many of the nationalities (including the Russians) began to make serious demands for more self-rule, he reluctantly concluded that a new treaty was needed to redefine the relationship between the national government and the subnational governments. Clearly, he failed to respond in an appropriate and timely manner to the growing seriousness of the nationalities problem. By 1990 the job of holding the Soviet Union together was much more difficult than it would have been if he had responded earlier.

Gorbachev initiated the process of writing a new union treaty. Negotiating a treaty that would meet the nationalistic and other concerns being expressed in the union republics proved to be a formidable task. The patience of the nationalists had grown short and their grievances more strongly felt. The effort to negotiate a treaty that a majority (if not all) of the union republics would be willing to sign was to continue up until the final months of the USSR. In fact, the attempted coup on August 19, 1991, was timed to disrupt the official signing ceremony for a new union treaty on August 20. After the coup, the whole notion of a union treaty was abandoned as the various republics rapidly declared their independence from the Soviet Union.

SOVEREIGNTY, INDEPENDENCE, AND SECESSION

Internal sovereignty is the ability of a state to exercise control over its territory, free from external interference. The republics declaring sovereignty were primarily concerned with gaining more control over their own internal affairs by reducing interference from Moscow. They were not asking for the complete control usually implied by the term "sovereignty." Although there was considerable variation in the contents of the republics' declarations of sovereignty, at the heart of most of them was the assertion that republican laws had supremacy over all-union laws—an assertion that gave republican legislatures the power to nullify all-union laws with which they disagreed. These declarations of sovereignty were primarily motivated by the desire of the republics to gain effective control over their economic and natural resources. The USSR Supreme Soviet responded to these demands for sovereignty by passing a law reaffirming the supremacy of all-union law until a new union treaty was signed.

Most of the republics declaring sovereignty were content to let Moscow handle defense and foreign affairs. For them, a renegotiated union treaty might have been adequate. But republics declaring independence wanted complete control over their own affairs—the supreme internal and external control usually implied by sovereignty. Although the Soviet Constitution of 1977 (like the constitutions that preceded it) provided for the right of the union republics to secede (Article 72), there was no law on the mechanics of secession. In other words, a republic could in theory secede, but nothing specified the steps it had to take to accomplish this goal. Until the 1980s there had been no need for such a law; the right to secede had been meaningless.

Pressed by nationalist claims and increasing interethnic violence, Gorbachev promised that he would create a law on the procedure for secession. He made this promise during a visit to Lithuania on January 11–13, 1990. In the Baltic republics, Gorbachev's promise was seen as a ploy to trick them into tacitly accepting the idea that they were legally part of the USSR. A Lithuanian journalist summed up their reaction: "You cannot get a divorce unless you are married. We were never married, we were raped." (Girnius, 1990b, p. 6) On April 3, 1990, the USSR Supreme Soviet passed a law "On the Procedure for Resolving Questions Associated with the Secession of a Union Republic from the USSR."[1] As noted by an American expert on the Soviet nationalities prob-

---

1. O poriadke resheniia voprosov, sviasannikh s vykhodom soiyznoi respubliki iz SSSR, *Vedomosti S*̃*ezda Narodnykh Deputatov SSSR i Verkhovnogo Soveta SSSR*, no. 15, April 11, 1990. An English translation of the law appears in *Current Digest of the Soviet Press*, 42(15), pp. 20–21, 32.

lem, the law was "intended not to facilitate independence, but to make it impossible." (Goble, 1990a, p. 1) No political leader wants to preside over a loss of territory, and Gorbachev was no exception. He was, however, saddled with Article 72 of the Soviet Constitution giving union republics the right to secede. His solution was to make secession so difficult, expensive, and time-consuming that no republic would be able to complete the process.

Briefly, the secession process began with a referendum in the union republic seeking independence. The decision to hold the referendum could be made by the republican legislature acting on its own initiative or in reaction to a petition from one-tenth of the population of the republic. All permanent residents eligible to vote in Soviet elections were permitted to vote. At least two-thirds of the population had to approve the decision to secede. If they did not, the republic would have to wait at least ten years before holding another referendum. If secession won the necessary votes, there would be a transition period of not more than five years. During this period, the republic was required to come to some agreement with the Soviet Union on matters such as the disposal of USSR-owned facilities; the resolution of financial, credit, and contractual matters; and the determination of the citizenship of the people residing in the republic.

According to the provisions of the secession law, the USSR could insist that a seceding republic compensate the USSR for Soviet capital investment and non-fulfillment of contractual obligations. Given the fact that the Soviet Union owned all the large enterprises and transportation facilities and that the command economy made the republics highly interdependent, meeting this requirement would involve a prohibitively large amount of money. For example, Gorbachev let it be known that Moscow would be asking Lithuania for 17 billion rubles for capital investment and 4 billion rubles for undelivered production. At the official exchange rate then in force, 21 billion rubles were worth approximately $33 billion. (*New York Times,* March 8, 1990, p. A14) Also, the seceding republic had to pay for the resettlement of Soviet citizens who chose to leave the republic. Clearly, secession would not be cheap.

Seceding republics also faced the possibility of losing territory. Concentrated groups of ethnic minorities would have the right to vote to remain part of the USSR. Under this process Azerbaijan would almost certainly have lost Nagorno-Karabakh. Virtually all of the republics had some significant ethnic enclaves that they could have lost in the secession process. In addition, the seceding republic would have to negotiate the status of any lands that it acquired after joining the Soviet Union. For example, a small piece of land on which Vilnius, the capital of Lithuania, is located had been part of the Byelorussian Republic (Belarus). The law would have permitted Byelorussia to, in effect, demand possession of the territory, thus depriving a seceding Lithuania of its capital city. Gorbachev did give Lithuania notice that he intended to ask for surrender of the Lithuanian Baltic port city of Klaipeda. (*New York Times,* March 8, 1990, p. A14)

Finally, during the fifth year, one-tenth of the population could demand another referendum. If fewer than two-thirds of Soviet voters currently living in the republic voted to confirm the secession decision, the process would come to a halt and the republic would remain in the union. Although it is not certain, presumably another referendum could not be held for ten years, for a vote of less than two-thirds in the initial referendum would clearly have had this result.

We will, however, never know. The Law on Secession was—with one minor exception—never used. On September 21, 1991, the Armenians held a referendum on secession, and 99.31 percent of the voters opted to secede from the Soviet Union. (Fuller, 1991) By then, however, the vote was largely meaningless. A month earlier, the failed coup had taken place in Russia, radically changing the political situation. As its first official act, the postcoup government of the Soviet Union had recognized the independence of all three Baltic republics. And, more important, a stampede to leave the Soviet Union had begun. On the second day of the coup, August 20, Estonia became the first union republic to declare independence. By the end of August, eleven more republics had followed suit. The RSFSR (Russia), Kazakhstan, and Turkmenistan soon completed the breakup. Diplomatic recognition followed more slowly.

The Soviet Union had fallen apart. President Boris Yeltsin of Russia moved quickly and decisively to declare the Communist Party of the Soviet Union illegal and to seize control of the property of both the Party and the government. By the time Gorbachev resigned on December 25, 1991, there was—for all practical purposes—no Soviet Union. What remained were fifteen fledgling countries facing a long struggle to reinvent themselves.

CONDITIONS NECESSARY FOR STABLE DEMOCRACY

Democratic government was the initial stated goal of most of the new countries. Very few of the Soviet nationalities, however, had any significant historical experience that would prepare them for participatory democracy. And those that did, such as Lithuania and Estonia, had experiences that were very limited. In general, the Soviet people were used to being subjects, not active participants in the governing of their countries. They were also accustomed to governments that had unlimited power over their subjects. Given this history, we might wonder whether democracy has any chance of taking root and thriving in the Soviet successor countries.

Democracy is, in its essence, majority rule. However, a significant number of the citizens of a democratic country need to create certain conditions in order for their democracy to be stable. For purposes of analysis, we regard these conditions as the political culture of democracy. It is based on eight assumptions:

1. Internal political disputes should be solved peacefully.
2. Government should be limited, and those who govern should be subject to the same rules as those they govern.
3. Those who are active in politics should be able and willing to compromise—to settle for less than everything they want.

4. The political-economic system should maintain a relatively high level of economic development.
5. There should be widespread control over politically important resources.
6. Adult citizens should have the right and the duty to take part in their own government.
7. Different racial, religious, or ethnic groups should live together in peace and a spirit of mutual trust.
8. Minorities should be able to vie for control over the government without fear of reprisal.

Let us consider each condition individually.

Domestic Peace

Political cultures differ widely in the extent to which violence is considered an acceptable way to solve political rivalries and disputes. On the one hand are people who are willing to use violence on the slightest pretext. On the other are people who regard violence as an undesirable last resort. Democracy tends to thrive when the people and their leaders assume that violence will not be used unless the existence of democracy is threatened.[2] Why is this condition important? Violence creates fear, hostility, and distrust among competing political groups and interests. Democracies, however, are built on trust. (Bellah et al., 1991, p. 3) For example, the minority has to trust that if it participates in an election, its candidates will not be imprisoned or murdered by their opponents.

When we look at the histories of the Russian Empire and the Soviet Union, we see that violence was a commonplace of political life. Military conquest built the Russian Empire, and military strength sustained it. The Soviet Union was established by a violent revolution in the midst of World War I and at the cost of a bloody civil war. History indicates that "it has proved nearly impossible to establish a stable, long-lived constitutional democracy after widespread violent turmoil has brought down or followed the collapse of an autocratic regime." (Willhoite, 1988, p. 113) Despite assertions to the contrary,[3] the Soviet Union was never a democracy; it was an absolutist regime and an empire based on power. Within this context, it is interesting to consider how the lessening of violence after Stalin's death and the relatively violence-free regime of Gorbachev affected this situation. Certainly, the members of the old guard who led the 1991 failed coup were operating by the old rules. The threat of violence in the form of military power was their chief strategy. But, with minor exceptions, violence was not used during the coup attempt, and a major reason for this avoidance of violence was the refusal of significant segments of the military forces to attack.

---

2. This assumption excludes the use of violence to combat crime.
3. The preamble to the 1977 Soviet Constitution asserted that "genuine democracy for the working masses" had been "established." (Smith, 1992, p. 348)

During the 1993 insurrection stemming from the clash between President Yeltsin and the parliamentary leadership (including Vice President Alexander Rutskoi), the armed forces attacked, but they were very uncomfortable about the role they were forced to play. According to Alexei Arbatov, a military analyst at the Russian Academy of Sciences, "They followed orders, but they feel there is nothing to be proud of. They feel disgusted." (*Washington Post,* October 22, 1993, p. A26) Particularly notable was the fact that Yeltsin waited to use force until there seemed to be no other alternative. Instead he tried exchange, negotiating through the patriarch of the Russian Orthodox Church. He also opened an employment center within walking distance of the parliament building. The center offered legislators a year's salary and a job if they would sign away their membership in the parliament. Repeatedly, Yeltsin called for a peaceful resolution of the dispute. But when the mobs supporting the legislative leadership became violent, attacking the Ostankino radio and television center, city government offices, and the cordon of soldiers around the parliament building, Yeltsin brought in the tanks and ordered them to fire.

Aside from the relatively small mobs that fought on behalf of the parliamentary leaders during the insurrection, however, the Russian people did not become politically violent. Through the early years of independence they maintained a commitment to peaceful change that is extraordinary, considering the hardships most of them endured. It is impossible to be certain about much at this early point in the history of the Russian Federation, but there is evidence that this element of Russian political culture may be beginning to change. Shortly after being chosen prime minister in 1993, Viktor Chernomyrdin stated that the use of coercive measures was no longer effective in trying to solve the problems of the economy. (*Washington Post,* January 29, 1993, p. A20) Thus, the people and most of the leaders of Russia seem to be learning the restraint necessary for stable democracy. This does not mean that there will be no lapses; it simply means that in Russia things are generally headed in the right direction.

The situation has been different in some other parts of the former Soviet Union. An obvious case in point is Georgia. Georgia's passionate drive toward complete independence from the Soviet Union was precipitated by an act of Soviet military violence. In 1989 in the capital, Tbilisi, Soviet soldiers turned a peaceful protest into "Bloody Sunday" by killing more than twenty demonstrators and wounding many others. This assault radicalized the Georgians and changed their desire for increased sovereignty into an uncompromising demand for independence. Georgia's movement toward independence, however, was accompanied by considerable interethnic hostility.[4] During the Gorbachev period, the people of Georgia had become heavily armed, and violence between political and ethnic groups had became common. In October 1990, Georgia took its first decisive step toward establishing a democratic form of govern-

---

4. Georgia has four major ethnic groups: Georgians, Ossetians, Abkhazians, and Azerbaijanis.

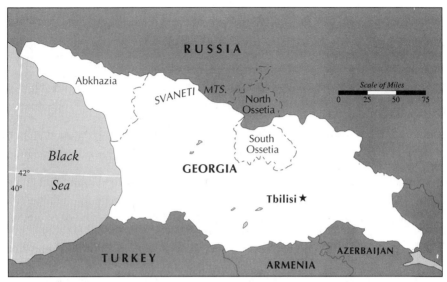

MAP 8-1 Georgia

ment by holding parliamentary elections. The winning coalition was headed by Zviad Gamsakhurdia.

Georgia's formal declaration of independence came on April 9, 1991 (the second anniversary of Bloody Sunday). Subsequently, Gamsakhurdia was elected president, receiving 86.5 percent of the vote. (*Washington Post,* May 28, 1991, p. A16) Very quickly, however, he began losing support because he started acting like an autocrat. He jailed political opponents and censored the press. In addition, he tried to take away from the non-Georgian ethnic groups the limited autonomy they had possessed under Soviet rule. Opposition to him grew rapidly and culminated in an attack on his headquarters in the Georgian parliament building. Eventually he fled from the country.[5] His presidency had lasted about two hundred days. The Military Council that took over the government suspended the Constitution and declared a state of emergency. A short time later, Gamsakhurdia's supporters in western Georgia began to wage a guerrilla campaign against the Military Council. In an attempt to establish its authority, the Council even considered restoring the Georgian monarchy.

Finally, in March 1992 Eduard Shevardnadze agreed to take charge of the Georgian government. He was the former CPSU leader in Georgia and the former Soviet foreign minister under Gorbachev. Meanwhile, the fighting continued—most notably in South Ossetia and Abkhazia (see Map 8-1). In addition, terrorist activities spread throughout the country and into Tbilisi

---

5. Soon, however, he returned to the western part of Georgia to lead his followers in fighting his successors. On December 31, 1993, the Georgian military surrounded the band of rebels he was leading, and he committed suicide.

itself. Despite the violence, elections for a new parliament were held in October 1992, and the largest number of seats (though not a majority) was won by the Communist-dominated Democratic Union Party. Shevardnadze ran for parliamentary chair (a post to be held by someone not allied with any political party) and won with 96 percent of the vote. (Fuller, 1993, p. 20) Immediately after these elections, however, actions were taken that were chillingly similar to Soviet rule, such as the suppression of all dissent. Shevardnadze soon found himself fighting three civil wars—with the Abkhazians, the Ossetians, and the followers of Gamsakhurdia. By the autumn of 1993, he had lost Abkhazia and was trying to fend off Gamsakhurdia's supporters, who were advancing into the territory east of Abkhazia. Finally, he was forced to call for Russian military help and, as a quid pro quo, promised to join the Commonwealth of Independent States, which was dominated by Russia.

Georgia clearly has a long way to go before establishing the kind of domestic peace that is the foundation for most of the other conditions necessary for stable democracy. When violence is widespread—as it was during the initial years of Georgian independence—the basic trust needed for the operation of democratic institutions cannot be established. Moreover, the use of violence to settle political rivalries and disputes is a habit that dies hard. Violence is self-perpetuating in that each victim, in turn, feels justified in using violence to avenge the violence he or she has experienced. Where political violence is rampant, stable democracy is impossible.

Limited Government

The most common form of democratic government in the world today is constitutional democracy. In such a system, a constitution serves to establish the basic institutions of the government and to specify what they can and cannot do. Limited government is related to the issue of violence, because (as the legendary sociologist Max Weber reminds us) "a state is a human community that (successfully) claims the *monopoly of the legitimate use of physical force* within a given territory." (Gerth & Mills, 1958, p. 78, emphasis in the original) Constitutions and laws usually place strict limitations on the circumstances under which government officials may legitimately use physical force, such as in response to crime or foreign invasion.

A written constitution and a set of laws do not automatically limit what government officials can do. For most of Soviet history there was a written constitution.[6] But it could not be enforced in any meaningful way because no government organ or official was given the power or authority to enforce it. Thus, the Soviet leadership could—and did—ignore it with impunity.

---

6. There were three successive USSR constitutions, passed in 1924, 1936, and 1977. The first constitution after the Bolshevik Revolution was the Russian Soviet Federated Socialist Republic Constitution of 1918.

Not all constitutions are in written form. The United States has a written constitution, but the British have an unwritten constitution that is a set of traditions and laws which are respected and followed and thus place real limits on the British government. An effective constitution, whether written or unwritten, forms the basic law of the land for all, including government officials and ordinary citizens—it creates "a government of laws, not of men."

During its final years, the Soviet Union began to move toward limited government. In December 1989 the USSR parliament created the Committee for Constitutional Supervision. The first real test for the committee came in April 1990 when Gorbachev issued a decree that gave the USSR Council of Ministers the right to control all demonstrations and public events in downtown Moscow. This function had formerly been the prerogative of the city government. The committee ruled that Gorbachev's decree was in violation of the USSR Constitution, and the Gorbachev regime accepted its decision. Ruling by ruling, the Committee for Constitutional Supervision began to establish the principle that the Soviet leadership could no longer consider itself above the law. (Teague, 1990; Thorson, 1992)

In October 1991 the newly established Russian Federation created a Russian Constitutional Court. The judges were elected by the Russian legislature and given the power to determine the constitutionality of laws and official acts. Within a few months the Court had overturned a presidential merger of the KGB and the MVD and had declared Tatarstan's referendum on sovereignty unconstitutional. The rulings of the Constitutional Court could overturn legislation and official acts, and its decisions were final. Its first important decision came in 1992, when it was asked to rule on a decree issued by Yeltsin banning the CPSU and confiscating its property.[7] Thirty-seven pro-Communist legislators challenged the constitutionality of this decree, and the Court agreed to hear the case. After months of hearings and deliberations, the Court issued a ruling that upheld most of Yeltsin's decree. It did, however, permit a reformed Communist Party to compete on an equal basis with other political parties in elections, and it restored some of its confiscated property. The ruling stood, and the Russian Federation had taken an important step toward limited government.

This development was compromised, however, by the fact that the Court chose to take a political role in the dispute between President Yeltsin and the leadership of the Russian legislature. Its chair took an active and public position in favor of the legislature. After the 1993 insurrection, Yeltsin suspended the Constitutional Court, saying that it had played a part in pushing the country toward civil war. Thus, the first attempt to establish the principle of having an apolitical interpreter of the Russian Constitution proved, ultimately, to be a failure—after a promising start. The post-Soviet Russian Constitution that was approved in December 1993 retained the Constitutional Court. The Court kept its authority to rule on the constitutionality of federal laws and

---

7. An English translation of the decree appears in *Current Digest of the Soviet Press, 43*(45), p. 4.

decrees (Article 125). One task of this body will be to establish its legitimacy as interpreter of the Constitution. Unfortunately, however, its jurisdiction in matters of constitutional interpretation is much narrower than was the jurisdiction of the previous Constitutional Court. (Tolz, 1994, pp. 5–6)

In general, it is difficult (if not impossible) for most Russians to think of government in terms of institutions rather than in terms of the people who occupy positions within institutions. Their political culture has always centered on the idea of rule by a strong central figure. Limited government, however, is government in which institutions, not people, are the central factor. Limited constitutional government is based on the assumption that the occupants of positions in government institutions change and that those who currently occupy positions are bound by the law. It will be difficult for the Russians to shake off the conviction that "it is sufficient to find the right leaders in order to create a proper political system in Russia." This notion, combined with a "traditional disrespect for the law," will work against the establishment of limited government in the near future. (Tolz, 1993, p. 9)

Notable for its early success in establishing limited government is Lithuania. It was one of the first of the successor countries to draft and ratify a post-Soviet constitution. The popular vote to ratify the new Lithuanian Constitution was held at the same time as parliamentary elections. In these elections Vytautas Landsbergis and his nationalist followers, who had led Lithuania in its successful fight for independence, were voted out of office. They won only 52 of the 141 parliamentary seats. The big winner was the Lithuanian Democratic Labor Party (LDLP), which won 73 seats. Subsequently, Algirdas Brazauskas was elected chairman of the legislature and acting president. Two things were remarkable about this election. The LDLP was the former Lithuanian Communist Party, and Brazauskas had been the CPSU "party boss" in Lithuania when the Lithuanian Communist Party officially voted itself out of the CPSU.

Landsbergis and his followers accepted their loss gracefully, assuming the role of loyal opposition with an eye to the first popular presidential election in 1993. In that election, however, the LDLP again won. Brazauskas got a clear mandate, winning 60 percent of the popular vote. Brazauskas made the following comment: "Now we can say that Lithuania is a democratic country with a democratic system." (*Washington Post,* February 16, 1993, p. A23) Thus, Lithuania has a post-Soviet constitution and the experience of a peaceful turnover of government authority. Limited government seems to have a good chance in Lithuania.

Compromise

In stable democratic systems, supporters of policy alternatives seldom get exactly what they want. Because of the necessity to build majority coalitions for any policy, they must compromise to arrive at a policy position that can command majority support. Such bargaining "is one of the most continuous and characteristic modes of behavior in [stable democratic] political life." (Barner-

Barry & Rosenwein, 1985, p. 169) What this means, however, is that the participants have to be willing to settle for the proverbial half a loaf. To people accustomed to absolutism, this is an alien frame of mind. They must learn how to resolve conflict by using offers and counteroffers to reach a mutually acceptable compromise. Such bargaining is very different from the use of threats and counterthreats characteristic of political systems based on power. In a democracy, political bargaining is based on the authority the democratic system gives the participants and on the idea of exchange.

Bargaining is not an easy technique to master. Even in stable democracies, some participants are better than others at successfully orchestrating a compromise. James MacGregor Burns (1978) divides leaders into two categories: transformational[8] and transactional. Transactional leadership is not unlike the relationship between buyers and sellers in a marketplace. (Burns, 1978, p. 258) In a transactional political relationship, the participants approach one another "with an eye to exchanging one thing for another: jobs for votes, or subsidies for campaign contributions. Such transactions comprise the bulk of the relationships among [participants], especially in groups, legislatures, and parties." (Burns, 1978, p. 4) For a stable democracy, it is particularly important that activists in interest groups, parties, legislatures, and executive agencies are able to reach satisfactory compromises regarding important issues.

It must be emphasized, however, that compromise requires a psychological stance of willingness to settle for less than everything wanted. Also, the achievement of a compromise requires the participants to have bargaining skills and experience. Neither of these was highly developed in the Soviet political system—except perhaps in small leadership groups within the CPSU, such as the Politburo. (Arbatov, 1993) If compromise decisions were reached, neither the fact that they were compromises nor the process by which they were reached was given much (if any) publicity. The official Soviet policy of democratic centralism was far more centralist than democratic and thus tended to project the impression of monolithic unity. Within a political system characterized by paternalism, this impression fostered the illusion that political policies were being made by persons who knew what was best for the "people" (*narod*). Questioning these policies or presenting alternatives was always clearly discouraged—sometimes violently.

One former Soviet republic that began its independent existence by making a concerted effort to institutionalize compromise was Moldova. After an early flirtation with the idea of uniting with Romania during the perestroika era, the Moldovans (who are ethnically Romanian) settled on a policy of defining themselves as one of two independent Romanian countries. The primary goals of the newly independent Moldova were statehood and the preservation of its

---

8. A transformational leader is one who "raises the level of human conduct and ethical aspiration of both leader and led, and thus . . . has a transforming effect on both." Burns cites Gandhi as "the best modern example" of a transforming leader. (Burns, 1978, p. 20)

territorial integrity. To this end, its leadership spent much of 1992 creating what they called a government of national consensus.

The government of national consensus was intended to represent as faithfully as possible the ethnic and political makeup of Moldova. This approach to building a government coalition was carried out by extensive bargaining between the government leaders and respresentatives of ethnic groups, political associations (which were not well enough developed to be called parties), and socioeconomic interests. The government of national consensus that emerged reflected the major ethnic and political interests in Moldova. (Socor, 1992) There were, however, two major omissions. There was no representation of the Moldovan Popular Front, which was weakening but still campaigning for unification with Romania. And there was no representation of the Russians who were carrying out a violent battle for secession in the eastern part of Moldova (the so-called Dniester Republic) and who were supported by nationalist groups in Russia and by the Russian military.

The Russians east of the Dniester River (see Map 4-2, p. 108) posed by far the most serious threat facing the new government. Although they represented a minority (25.5 percent) within that territory, their military control of the area enabled them to cut the other eastern Moldovans off from participation in Moldovan institution-building. Much of their power came from their support in Russia, where they were able to whip up nationalistic fervor and garner political support by accusing Moldova of violating Russian rights. Although neutral observers found no such violations (Socor, 1994, pp. 17–18), the rebelling Russians were able to use the Russian mass media and political process to pressure the Russian government to take a stand against Moldova. Nevertheless, the new government of national consensus repeatedly tried to encourage the Russians to rejoin Moldova by offering them posts in the government and urging their legislators to stop boycotting legislative sessions.

In February 1994, the Moldovan electorate supported major compromises regarding citizenship, language, and autonomy for the Dniester east-bank residents and the Gagauz territories. The Gagauz (an ethnic group comprising 3.5 percent of the population) were willing to compromise. The separatist Communists east of the Dniester were not. Instead, the Russian minority used military force to consolidate its control over the Moldovan east bank. And Russian Federation ultranationalists continued to show strong support for the east-bank Russians who were supporters of a "Soviet-style socialism and the restoration of Moscow's control over the region." (Socor, 1994b, p. 20)

While the west-bank Moldovans were carefully building coalitions through bargaining and compromise, the Russian Federation government was being paralyzed by a bitter fight between President Yeltsin and the parliament. The fine art of bargaining and compromise lost out to crude posturing, threats, and obstructionism. The main antagonists were President Yeltsin and the Russian parliamentary chair Ruslan Khasbulatov. Their primary concern was the division of power between the president and the legislature. The underlying issue was control over the nature and pacing of economic reform. For more than two years after the August 1991 attempted coup, the Russian government was increasingly deadlocked by this struggle.

Prior to and during the attempted coup, Khasbulatov had been a supporter of Yeltsin. Shortly afterward, however, he became Yeltsin's most bitter foe for reasons that are not entirely clear—although "he was said to be angry because Yeltsin had not included him in his inner circle after taking over the reins of power from . . . Gorbachev." (Rahr, 1993, p. 13) Whatever the reason, during October 1991 he began attacking Yeltsin. For almost a year and a half, until Yeltsin won a referendum on April 25, 1993, Khasbulatov was implacable in his effort to shift as much power as possible away from the president and to the parliament. A major characteristic of this period was the parliament's refusal to compromise with Yeltsin—or, if it did compromise, its unwillingness to keep its part of the bargain. Just before the referendum, the parliament tried to impeach Yeltsin, but the motion was narrowly defeated. It seemed "that at times Khasbulatov regarded the executive and the legislature as institutions competing for supreme power in the country rather than as part of a single democratic system." (Rahr, 1993, p. 16) Thus, during the crucial years after independence, the Russian parliament largely neglected its legislative duties. Discussions about policy were stalemated, and political decision-making was at a virtual standstill. This period ended in violence.

During September 1993 Yeltsin tried to dissolve the parliament, an act clearly in violation of the much-amended Soviet-era constitution then in force. (Tolz, 1994, p. 3) The parliamentary leadership, joined by Vice President Rutskoi and supported by the chair of the Constitutional Court, responded by declaring the parliament supreme. They asserted that Yeltsin was no longer president and officially replaced him with Vice President Rutskoi. After about two weeks of standoff, armed clashes began between the military forces supporting Yeltsin and crowds of the parliament's supporters (or, at least, the enemies of Yeltsin). Yeltsin kept repeating that he would not use force to end the dispute, but when the pro-parliament forces became violent, he sent in the armed forces, repelling an attack on the headquarters of Moscow radio and television, on the Moscow mayor's office building, and on the forces surrounding the parliament. In the end, the armed forces attacked the parliament building. The parliamentary leadership was defeated, and the building was left a fire-scarred hulk. Yeltsin ruled alone until the December 1993 parliamentary election.

This reluctance to compromise reflects both the political heritage of the people involved and a basic misconception about democratic institutions. Lack of compromise had the effect of pushing the Yeltsin government in an authoritarian direction and causing it to resort to force. More important, it complicated and postponed the most vital task of all: the adoption of a post-Soviet constitution. The achievement of stable democracy in Russia will depend on a basic shift in Russian thinking about compromise. Throughout Russian history "the negative attitude to compromise has affected the general attitude to political opposition in Russia." The traditional attitude is "that a political opponent should be crushed rather than listened to and accommodated." (Tolz, 1993, p. 9)

Economic Development

Successful democracies are usually found in countries that have attained a relatively high level of economic development. Economic resources are critical in democratic political competition. The more economic resources are available, the more they are accessible to potential competitors in the political arena. If resources are plentiful, one party's acquisition of additional resources does not necessarily mean that another party has lost them. As a matter of fact, in democratic systems such as that of the United States, possession of economic resources, especially large amounts of money, is a key to political success in both elections and policy-making.

A stagnant or shrinking economy makes necessary the acquisition of additional economic resources at the expense of others. In turn, this increases the likelihood that political-economic conflicts will turn violent, because the stakes are much higher. Thus, as a general rule, the more wealthy and productive a country is, the more stable is its democratic system and the less likely competitors are to resort to violence—violence that can lead to the destruction of the democratic system. It is also important to note that stable democratic governments create many of the conditions necessary for economic growth and prosperity, such as the legal and societal circumstances for reasonably secure savings and investment.

Stable democracies have historically been countries with relatively high levels of economic well-being. Here the prospects of the successor countries range from dismal to guardedly hopeful. None of the former Soviet republics has thrived economically during the immediate post-Soviet period. One of the saddest stories is that of Armenia.

Under Soviet rule, Armenia was a relatively prosperous union republic. But glasnost led the Armenians to demand the annexation of Nagorno-Karabakh, the Armenian-dominated enclave within Azerbaijan. Having ruled over Nagorno-Karabakh for many decades, Azerbaijan was understandably reluctant to give away a significant part of its territory. This dispute escalated into a vicious war. As if the war were not enough, the Armenians suffered a massive earthquake in 1988. This natural disaster destroyed approximately half of Armenia's industrial base and a large proportion of its housing stock. Moreover, before the war, oil-rich Azerbaijan had supplied most of Armenia's energy. A blockade that ended the flow of oil and lasted for years further crippled Armenia's economy. Armenia's recourse to its other neighboring countries was limited by the fact that it is a Christian country surrounded by Muslim countries toward which it has historical animosities. Armenia's only source of supplies was Christian Georgia—itself convulsed by civil war and terrorism. When the single gas pipeline that ran through Georgia was blown up, Armenia was left dark and cold.

Armenia's former prosperity rested primarily on the skills and hard work of its people—on what it could offer to the rest of the Soviet Union. As its economic situation worsened, it became increasingly unable to offer subsistence to its own people, let alone produce anything significant to sell abroad. By 1993, basic civilization was breaking down as communications, transport, medical facilities, and even running water became scarce. A Western resident observed: "Welcome to hell. Everything is reduced to primal needs. No one is talking or thinking about anything else." (*Washington Post*, January 30, 1993, p. A1) The conversation took place as the reporter and the commentator watched a pack of hungry dogs attack a man crossing a street in Armenia's capital.

To say that Armenia is not ready for the introduction of stable democracy is a gross understatement. The Armenians have been reduced to a level at which mere physical survival demands all of the energy most people have. Although Armenia was one of the early republics demanding independence from the Soviet Union, that independence has not (to put it mildly) lived up to its promise. By 1993, people were starting to look longingly toward the past. One Armenian remarked: "There has never been a good period in Armenian history. But under Soviet power it was better. A year ago, when we voted for independence, people didn't feel that way. Now they do." (*Washington Post*, January 30, 1993, p. A16)

Although Armenia represents an extreme case, it is impossible to find a successor country that might be pointed to as an example of significant economic prosperity. All of them have struggling economies. In fact, most of their major political disputes revolve around what to do about their economies. At this point, however, a stagnant rather than a shrinking economy is the best most can hope for. In either case, there is not much to go around. One person's gain is another's loss. Such conditions do not provide a solid base for stable democratic systems.

Distribution of Resources

Societies differ greatly in the extent to which control over valued resources is distributed. On the one hand, control of societal resources can be highly centralized. On the other, control over resources can be broadly dispersed. For both individuals and groups, control of the aspects of the social environment that affect their personal and group interests is a basic need. For an individual, political activity can serve as a means to fill this need—at least in part. (Renshon, 1974) For a politician or an interest group, control of resources can furnish a political base for the gaining of political office or policy objectives. In the contemporary US political-economic system, for example, the amount of money a politician or interest group controls has a powerful effect on the individual's or group's success or failure in political competition.

The widespread distribution of politically important resources facilitates broad participation in the political process. It also encourages the peaceful acceptance of losing, because the losers can always hope to acquire a winning combination of resources in the future. The concentration of control over politically important resources in the hands of a relatively small number of people discourages competition because losing seems inevitable to the "have-nots." Without adequate competition, democracy withers.

Many resources are needed for success in the competitive political world of democracy. At the very least, those wishing to challenge incumbents need organizational and economic bases. Organizing and directing resources toward political ends is not a skill that is widely shared among the people of the former Soviet Union. Like their forebears for hundreds of years, they grew up in a highly centralized state where all political and economic power flowed to and from the center. People who have grown up in Western democracies tend to regard the gathering and organization of resources for political competition as second nature. This was never the case for the Soviet people or for the people of the Russian Empire before them. Building and funding groups to compete for government office or to gain policy goals is alien to them. Post-Soviet political activists are faced with two major problems: (1) breaking the old CPSU monopoly on resources and (2) moving from one-party systems to true party competition.

Turkmenistan is a prime example of a successor country in which independence and the adoption of a new constitution did little to affect the extreme centralization of control over resources that prevailed in Soviet times. Turkmenistan's leader, Saparamurad Niyazov, the former leader of the Turkmenistan Communist Party who had been elected president under Soviet rule in October 1990, was elected president of post-Soviet Turkmenistan in June 1992. An unchallenged candidate, he got 99.5 percent of the vote—a result reminiscent of elections in the pre-Gorbachev Soviet Union. His policy was to avoid political and economic instability by using political repression to create a stable environment for foreign investment. As in Soviet times, he ruled through the old Turkmen Communist Party (renamed the People's Democratic Party) and kept tight personal control over the entire government and political apparatus. Some Western-influenced intellectuals tried to form opposition parties, but they were denied the resources—such as media access—to do so. (Brown, 1992b)

In the Russian Federation the situation initially seemed more hopeful, for a multitude of political movements, coalitions, and parties sprang up both before and after independence. There were, however, two catches: (1) This more widespread distribution of resources was largely limited to the urbanized areas, and (2) many of the fledgling centers of political influence were not stable enough to effectively amass and utilize the political resources available to them. Also, control over resources was heavily concentrated in the hands of former CPSU officials, who—seeing the handwriting on the wall—had transferred Party assets to themselves and were using them as the resource base for a second career.

Out in the Russian countryside, things remained much as they had been under Soviet rule. The people who controlled resources were the same. True, they might be heading the local governing council, rather than the local CPSU committee, but their faces were the same and so for the most part were their methods of governing. In the words of Mikhail Shishov, mayor of Morshansk, a town of five thousand, "At lower levels, the reactionary forces and the old elite are just too strong. This is the defeat of the democrats. The communists still control the levers." (*Washington Post,* January 27, 1991, p. A15) Moreover, the battle this local elite waged was over the pace of change and the control of existing wealth. The old elite exerted considerable effort to slow down change and to keep resources out of the hands of young businessmen, new private farmers, and others. (Richards, 1990)

By mid-1994, there were four major groups of politicians and parties in Russia: the liberal reformers, the liberal centrists, the centrists, and the nationalist-communist coalition. Each had an edge with regard to some political resources. The liberal reformers and the nationalist-communist coalition had the clearest political agenda. The liberal reformers and the liberal centrists had the most influence over the mass media. The centrists had the best financial support—mainly from oil producers and the military-industrial complex. The Communists were the best organized, while the nationalists had the most charismatic leaders and the most dramatic and easily understood messages. (Rahr, 1994, p. 6)

While the distribution of resources in Russia is far from ideal, it is clearly superior to that in Turkmenistan. There is some reason to be guardedly optimistic that this trend will continue. By mid-1994, Russia had entered a period of relative political and economic stability. There was some evidence that the privatization program was creating the foundation for stable and gradual change. The political arena was characterized by a myriad of competing parties and other political groups. Finally, "national politics [had] evolved in large measure into a competition among lobbies—the oil and gas industry, the agrarian sector and the military-industrial complex." (*Washington Post,* July 7, 1994, p. A13) If the economy continues to stabilize and the right-wing groups continue to have limited appeal, the distribution of resources should widen, providing a firmer basis for pluralist politics.

Participation and Citizenship

Because democratic government is based on popular participation and majority rule, the assumptions people make about their relationship to the government—what they should or should not do—are critical. Ideally, citizens in a democracy are able to assume that they all have the same rights and duties and that they are equal before the law. They also can assume that every citizen has both the right and the duty to participate actively in government, whether as a political activist or as an ordinary member of the electorate. Citizens in a democracy can assume that the government is "us" and that "we" are responsible for what it does and does not do.

Democracy does not flourish when the electorate—or a significant part thereof—sees the government as "them." In this situation, people tend to see themselves as subjects with duties but without the right to be involved in the choice of government leaders or in policy-making. On an extreme level, a person who is alienated from the government may see the government as foreign or fundamentally separated from its subjects. (Kaplan, 1976, pp. 117–118) In this extreme (but not rare) case, government is assumed to be just another misfortune to be avoided or endured. A participating citizenry is at the heart of the democratic idea. Without it, genuine and stable democracy cannot exist or, at best, can exist in form only.

This is especially important in the countries of the former Soviet Union where most of the people have regarded themselves as subjects for hundreds of years. Democratic citizenship implies that the individual has both rights and duties with regard to the government; it calls for a participatory stance. This does not mean that the entire adult population is involved in politics. In fact, in the United States, which has a democracy that many in the former Soviet Union regard as a model, voter turnout in presidential elections is seldom above 60 percent of those eligible to vote. In the former Soviet Union, in contrast, voter turnout was normally around 99 percent (at least according to official Soviet reports).

Voting was a required act. Local Communist Party activists exerted enormous energy to get all of the voters to the polls. The problem was that there was only one name on the ballot. A candidate who received less than 50 percent of the vote could be defeated, but this outcome was rare. Now that many of the people in the former Soviet Union can vote in contested elections, voter turnout has dropped to percentages that are far closer to American turnout figures.

In the Baltic states (Estonia, Latvia, and Lithuania), the people began the post-Soviet period with a strong sense of themselves as active citizens. After independence, the question of who could participate was a major political issue. The debate took the form of a preoccupation with citizenship laws. The most divisive issues centered on ethnicity. There was a general agreement that people who could claim Estonian, Latvian, or Lithuanian ethnicity would automatically become citizens—even if they had resided in another country during World War II or at the time of the Soviet takeover. Eligibility for citizenship also extended to the descendants of those who had lived outside the Baltic states. The problem was what to do about people who had become residents of the Baltic republics after the Soviet takeover.

The Lithuanians constituted over 80 percent of their country's population and were relatively unthreatened by non-Lithuanian political participation. They made the acquisition of citizenship relatively easy for persons of all ethnic backgrounds who were residing in Lithuania at the time it became independent. The vast majority of the population opted for citizenship regardless of ethnicity. For those who had to be naturalized, reading knowledge of Lithuanian and knowledge of the basic principles of the Lithuanian Constitution were required, along with a ten-year period of permanent residence and a secure source of income. Certain categories of persons, such as convicted criminals and drug abusers, were ineligible for naturalization.

At the time of the 1989 census, the Estonians constituted about 62 percent of the population of Estonia. The other major ethnic group was the Russians,

with about 30 percent. Estonia adopted citizenship laws that granted immediate citizenship to all who were citizens on June 16, 1941, and to their descendants regardless of ethnicity. All others had to apply for naturalization. Application could be made only after a two-year period of residency starting on or
after March 30, 1990, and after demonstration of minimal proficiency in
Estonian. Finally, there was a one-year waiting period for processing applications. These requirements were seen by Estonians as promoting the integration
of people who had moved to Estonia during Soviet rule. The Russians, both
inside and outside Estonia, had a different point of view. (Bungs, Girnius, &
Kionka, 1992, p. 38; Kionka, 1993, p. 90)

Since the overwhelming majority of non-Estonians residing in Estonia were
Russians who lived primarily in Russian-speaking enclaves, the language requirement was seen as particularly discriminatory. Consequently, after the
laws were passed, relatively few noncitizens applied for citizenship. Noncitizens could vote in local and municipal elections, so lack of citizenship kept
them from voting only in national elections. The citizenship laws, however,
were not the only laws restricting the political participation of non-Estonians.
For example, membership in political parties was limited to citizens, as was
employment in fields such as the civil service and law enforcement. A 1993
law officially designated all noncitizens as aliens and specified their rights and
duties. That law and the others were, in large part, directed at the resident
Russian population and were an outgrowth of animosities that preceded Estonian independence.

The Russian government complained to the United Nations and to other
international organizations that Russians in Estonia were being denied their
human rights. This complaint did not evoke much sympathy. The Council of
Europe and the Conference on Security and Cooperation in Europe judged
Estonia's citizenship laws to be among Europe's most liberal. A European
Union commission also approved the law on aliens. (Kionka, 1993; Sheehy,
1993, p. 7)

The Latvians, unlike the Estonians, had difficulty adopting a permanent law
on citizenship. Their difficulty stemmed from the ethnic composition of Latvia.
As of the 1989 census, Latvians comprised only 52 percent of the population.
The other major group was the Russians, with 34 percent. (Bungs, 1992, p. 65)
Many Latvians were afraid to allow Russians and Russian-speakers to participate in the political process. Their concerns were not groundless. After independence "many of the leaders of the estimated 40,000 veterans who lived in
Latvia" were speaking "openly about restoring Soviet rule." (Krickus, 1993, p.
34) Perhaps because many Latvians considered such people to be a potential
threat to Latvian independence, the government found it difficult to pass citizenship and naturalization laws.

The failure to pass citizenship laws in a timely fashion retarded the development of the new Latvian political-economic system. Relatively soon after independence, Lithuania and Estonia were able to adopt post-Soviet constitutions,
but the Latvians were forced to continue to operate under an amended Soviet-
era constitution. It was a matter of chicken and egg. The Soviet-era legislature,

which had been elected in 1990, was not deemed suitable to enact a new citizenship law, but without a new citizenship law issues of who could or could not vote in a legislative election were difficult to resolve.

The eventual solution to their problem was to hold a parliamentary election in June 1993 despite the lack of a post-Soviet citizenship law. About 25 percent of the population—mostly Russians—were not allowed to vote. Many showed their dissatisfaction by holding a peaceful demonstration at the foot of the Statue of Liberty in Riga. (Bungs, 1993, p. 5) The Russian government charged Latvia with human rights violations involving the Russian and Russian-speaking minorities. Its complaints to international organizations included criticism of a draft citizenship law that Moscow judged to be discriminatory. As was the case with regard to Estonia, these claims were deemed to be without merit. (Krickus, 1993)

In 1994, the Latvian legislature passed a citizenship law that gave preference to persons having at least one Latvian parent. Preferential treatment was also given to persons who were living in Latvia on June 17, 1940, persons who had been married to Latvians for at least ten years, ethnic Estonians, and ethnic Lithuanians. Everyone was required to know Latvian. Excluded were persons "whom a court [had] recognized as having propagated the ideas of chauvinism, nationalism, and fascism as well as working against Latvian independence." (*RFE/RL News Briefs*, 6–10 June 1994, p. 20) Soviet military retirees were also excluded unless they were Latvian or spouses of Latvians. Clearly, this law reflected the problems the Latvians had writing a citizenship law. It also seemed designed to discourage ethnic Russians from seeking citizenship.

The ease with which Lithuania, Estonia, and Latvia have been able to move toward a post-Soviet civil society has been a function of the size of the majority held by the titular nationality in each country and the relative size of the Russian minority. These factors have affected their ability not only to carry out the nation-building process but to create nation-states free of the remnants of their Soviet past. By contrast, in some of the Central Asian countries there has been little change from the situation that prevailed during Soviet rule.

In Uzbekistan, issues of citizenship and democratic participation did not even arise. All power resided in the hands of President Islam Karimov and the Communist Party, which had changed its name (to People's Democratic Party) but little else in its structure or functioning. In 1992, Karimov was elected president with 86 percent of the vote and a 95 percent turnout. Although he was opposed, the power structure of the People's Democratic Party got out the vote and prevented the political opposition from having much effect. The two main sources of political opposition, the Muslims and the intellectuals, were neutralized. After his victory Karimov got the parliament to pass a law allowing him to appoint local government leaders who were personally under his command.

Thus, while giving lip service to the idea of pluralist democracy, Karimov put into place a ruling structure that effectively prevented any real popular participation in the governing of Uzbekistan. Although there was considerable unrest, particularly among students, and although Karimov's neocommunism seemed to be provoking strong and increasingly united opposition, observers were of the opinion that it was "unlikely that there will be an effective democratic opposition to Karimov in the near future." (Brown, 1992a, p. 25) The preoccupation with the nature and extent of popular participation that is evident in the Baltics is absent from Uzbek politics. For most Uzbeks the government is still "them"; for a growing number of Balts it is "us."

Tolerance

Homogeneity in the cultural, ethnic, religious, and linguistic characteristics of a population fosters the good communication and basic trust that are crucial to the success of participation in democratic systems. Many democracies, however, are heterogeneous. When heterogeneity is the case, there must be a norm of respect and toleration for differences, as well as generally agreed-upon values that give rise to a satisfactory level of political equality. Diversity is most likely to become a problem when it is combined with the geographical clustering of ethnic groups and historical animosities. Canada, for example, is one of the more stable contemporary democracies, yet it has experienced considerable turmoil over the status of its French-speaking minority. This situation is worsened by the heavy concentration of French-speaking Canadians in one province, Quebec.

Again, trust becomes an issue. In a democracy, every group must be prepared to entrust its traditions, religion, and language to political leaders who do not share them. A history of intergroup violence or hostility puts trust in short supply. In Canada, English-speakers so greatly outnumber French-speakers that a French-speaking government at the national level is currently a practical impossibility. Thus, the continuation of stable democracy in Canada depends on the willingness of the French-speaking minority to trust the English-speaking majority to safeguard their interests. In any democratic system it is important for minorities to understand that they possess certain protections against discrimination by the ruling majority.

What constitutes adequate protection becomes more of a problem as the diversity of the population increases. Lithuania is an example of a country with a relatively homogeneous population. It has benefited from this homogeneity and has policies, such as the citizenship law discussed above, aimed at accommodating its minority population. Georgia presents a different picture. Georgians make up 69 percent of the population and have no serious contenders for ethnic dominance. The other major ethnic groups are Armenians (9 percent), Russians (7 percent), and Azeris (5 percent).

As far back as the Gorbachev era, Georgia has had major problems involving ethnic minorities. Armenians, Russians, and Azeris have always had the option of moving to Armenia, Russia, or Azerbaijan. That choice was not available to smaller minority groups with traditional homelands in Georgia: the Abkhazians (1.5 percent) and the South Ossetians (1.2 percent). (*Narodnoe khosiaistvo SSSR v 1990 g.*, 1991, p. 67) During the Gorbachev period, interethnic violence erupted between the Georgians and the Azeris, the South Ossetians, and the Abkhazians. Georgian-Azeri tensions caused a movement of Azeris to Azerbaijan. Tensions with South Ossetia and Abkhazia led to war.

At the root of the conflict was a mutual antagonism dating back to the entry of Georgia into the Soviet Union and to the creation of the South Ossetian Autonomous Region and the Abkhazian Autonomous Republic. Aggravating the situation were two factors: (1) the "Georgia for the Georgians" policy voiced by Zviad Gamsakhurdia, and (2) a law passed by Georgia's legislature in 1990 preventing the Abkhazian and South Ossetian nationalist parties from participating in elections.

The South Ossetians desired reunification with the North Ossetians, who had the status of a republic within the Russian Federation. (See Map 8-1, p. 215.) When the South Ossetians were stopped from participating in elections, their legislature declared independence from Georgia. The response of the Georgian legislature was to abolish South Ossetia as an autonomous region and declare it an undifferentiated part of Georgia. After that, violence between the Georgians and South Ossetians escalated into a vicious civil war.

The Abkhazian situation was somewhat different. Unlike the Ossetians, the Abkhazians were a distinct minority (18 percent) within Abkhazia (see Map 8-1, p. 215), greatly outnumbered by the Georgians (45.7 percent). (Fuller, 1992, p. 3)[9] There have always been tensions between the Abkhazians and Georgians, but they came to the surface in 1978 when the Abkhazians began a campaign to secede from Georgia and become part of the Russian Republic. While Moscow did not permit this, it did make certain concessions to Abkhazia. As a result, Abkhazian-Georgian antagonism increased. In August 1990, having been prevented from participating in legislative elections (like South Ossetia), the Abkhazian legislature declared independence. The declaration was possible because Georgian lawmakers had boycotted the session. As it had done when South Ossetia declared independence, the Georgian legislature immediately annulled the Abkhazian declaration. Then the Georgian government and the Abkhazian government vied for power in Abkhazia. By the time of the breakup of the USSR, Georgia and Abkhazia were engaged in civil war. It continued into the post-Soviet period and eventually forced the Georgians into a rapprochement with Russia and membership in the Commonwealth of Independent States.

Pluralism

Minority status does not necessarily stem from cultural, ethnic, religious, or linguistic differences. Minority status can reflect policy differences that cut

---

9. This situation changed radically when the Georgian military lost control of Abkhazia in 1993. Fearing violence at the hands of the victorious Abkhazians, hundreds of thousands of non-Abkhazians fled.

across ethnic, religious, and other lines. In a stable democracy, citizens who have policy goals that differ from the goals of the current leadership are confident that their right to dissent is protected. The first ten amendments to the US Constitution—the Bill of Rights—contain some fairly explicit provisions ensuring that American citizens can exercise their basic rights without interference by the majority, even if the majority finds what they say or do unacceptable. If policy differences can be used as an excuse for the persecution or elimination of individuals and groups, there can be no adequate discussion of policy alternatives, and the electorate is deprived of the ability to make informed choices among competing candidates and policies.

The proliferation of political movements and fledgling parties in the last years of Soviet rule seemed to be a good sign. The Soviet people, however, have had little experience with anything but monolithic single-party rule. They are not familiar with the give-and-take of pluralist systems. Democratic political groups in the successor countries find it difficult to form workable coalitions and tend to be torn apart by internal strife. In addition, they lack experience in conducting democratic elections and effective political campaigns. Thus, not surprisingly, politics in the first years after the fall of the Soviet Union tended to be shaped more by charismatic or powerful individuals than by institutionalized parties. In the long run, this type of rule does not sustain democratic insitutions.

The newly independent countries can be divided into two groups: those that are making some effort to move toward pluralism and those that are overtly preserving single-party rule. Despite its ethnic diversity, Moldova seemed to make relatively good progress toward building a multiparty system. Uzbekistan, in contrast, continued to be governed by Communist conservatives much as it was during the Soviet period.

As we discussed previously, the Moldovans showed their ability to compromise by putting together a government of national consensus. Then on February 27, 1994, Moldova held its first post-Soviet national election. Twenty-six parties and movements took part. They represented the diversity of the political spectrum in Moldova and were based "variously on socio-economic, ethnic, and ideological criteria, on patron-client relationships and on external allegiances." (Socor, 1994a, p. 8) During the campaign, four political blocs emerged. One bloc supported an independent Moldova, distinct from Romania. It was centered on the Agrarian Democratic Party. A pro-Romanian bloc made up of the Popular Front and related groups called for close relations and eventual unification with Romania. A liberal bloc, centered on the Liberal Convention and the Reform Party, campaigned for less regulation and taxation of business as well as for laissez-faire capitalism. A left-wing bloc consisting of the Socialist Party and Edinstvo (the Internationalist Movement for Unity) campaigned for a reversal of economic reforms and for more power to be given to Russian-speakers, as well as full membership in the Commonwealth of Independent States and closer ties to Russia.

Eventually, the bloc in favor of an independent Moldova emerged triumphant with the victory of the Agrarian Democratic Party. What is more important, however, is that the election campaign firmly established the principle of multiparty elections. The four blocs that emerged spoke for well-defined constituencies that are likely to persist and form political alliances in the future. Thus, the election seems to indicate that Moldova is well on its way to establishing a healthy pluralist political system—not including, however, the Russians on the east bank of the Dniester River, where a Soviet-type system persisted.

By contrast, Islam Karimov, elected president of Uzbekistan in late 1991, established a government determined to stifle pluralistic opposition. Through refusal to allow participation by any significant political parties or movements and by physical attacks, Karimov's government forced all serious opposition underground. A major issue was fear of the rise of Islamic fundamentalism. For example, the 1991 Law on Public Organizations makes the Islamic Renaissance Party illegal. Birlik (Unity), a mass political movement, took the position that all religions—as well as atheism—should be respected, but it also supported a central place in public life for Islam. The Uzbek government charged that Birlik supported Islamic fundamentalism. This accusation impeded Birlik's ability to gain support among the sizable Russian minority. (Cavanaugh, 1992)

Beginning in November 1991, Birlik repeatedly tried to register as a political party, but the Ministry of Justice repeatedly refused permission. On November 25, the minister of justice explained to Birlik representatives why Birlik could not be registered: "The People's Democratic Party of Uzbekistan [Karimov's party] is the governing party. We are its representatives, and we carry out its decisions. And when you come to power, you can do as you like." (Cavanaugh, 1992, p. 21) He neglected to mention that only political parties (not political movements) were allowed to field political candidates in presidential elections. The sole party that was registered was small and weak. It was permitted to run a candidate against Karimov, but he got only 12 percent of the vote. Birlik, despite its mass support, was not a registered political party and thus was unable to participate in the election and challenge Karimov for the presidency.

Also, the Uzbek leadership took measures reminiscent of empire. After his election as president, Karimov reorganized much of the government. One measure created prefects (hakim) appointed by the president and answerable to him. They presided over the regions and in effect "institutionalized the impotence of the regional parliaments and the all-encompassing power of the president." (Cavanaugh, 1992, p. 22) Newspapers that did not completely agree with the government were suppressed in various ways, ranging from being closed down to being censored and denied access to paper. Birlik's leaders were attacked, and many were arrested; the organization was thrown out of its headquarters. Intersoiuz, an organization of non-Uzbeks, was harassed until it ceased to exist. (Critchlow, 1992a, p. 9)

In an attempt to seem democratic, Karimov's government created some puppet political parties. They were intended to give the appearance of pluralism and contested elections. The reality was that genuine political parties that might pose an electoral threat to the regime could not participate because they were not allowed to register. Karimov's position was that only this approach to rule would prevent anarchy and promote the economic growth of Uzbekistan.

He stated: "If maintaining discipline and order in society is called dictatorship, then I am a dictator." (Cavanaugh, 1992, p. 24) In May 1992, a Birlik leader warned that "representatives of [the] ruling powers will start shooting without hesitation. . . . The present government is ready to shed any amount of blood in order to hold on to power." (Cavanaugh, 1992, p. 22) A Russian political activist described Uzbek politics as "a combination of Stalinism and Khomeinism." (Critchlow, 1992a, p. 10)

THE PROBLEM OF CHANGE

Changing from the absolutist rule of the Russian and Soviet empires to modern nation-states poses an enormous challenge for the newly independent countries. Installing democratic forms of government makes the challenge even greater. Democracy is a difficult form of government because it makes so many demands on the people as well as on politicians and government officials. Given the political culture that the successor countries inherited from centuries of absolutist and imperial rule, they are not particularly good candidates for stable democracy—at least in the near future. Their effort to make the transition from a command economy to a market economy only complicates the situation.

As we look at the current status of the former Soviet republics, what is striking is the fact that many of these new countries really are trying to learn how to make democratic political systems and market economic systems work. Effort does not always lead to success, but success is impossible without it. Right now, these countries need three things they do not currently possess: (1) adequate economic resources and experience with market economics, (2) adequate political resources and experience with democracy, and (3) time. Time is the most crucial—it is the key to the acquiring of the other two. For now, there is a race between the forces of construction and the forces of collapse, and no one now knows what the outcome will be.

In the next two chapters, we attempt to assess the future of post-Soviet Eurasia. Our focus is on clusters of countries that formed regions within the former Soviet Union and that might become regions or parts of larger regions in the post-Soviet world. In Chapter 9, we consider the internal political and economic situations within the constituent countries of these regions. In Chapter 10, we consider intergovernmental ties and conflicts among the countries of the former Soviet Union.

REFERENCES

Arbatov, G. (1993). *The system: An insider's life in Soviet politics.* New York: New York Times Books.

Barner-Barry, C., & Rosenwein, R. (1985). *Psychological perspectives on politics.* Englewood Cliffs, NJ: Prentice-Hall.

Bellah, R. N., Madsen, R., Sullivan, W. M., Swidler, A., & Tipton, S. M. (1991). *The good society.* New York: Vintage Books.

Besançon, A. (1986). Nationalism and Bolshevism in the USSR. In R. Conquest (Ed.), *The last empire: Nationality and the Soviet future* (pp. 1–13). Stanford, CA: Hoover Institution Press.

Brown, B. (1992a). The presidential election in Uzbekistan. *RFE/RL Research Report, 1*(4), 23–25.

———. (1992b). Turkmenistan asserts itself. *RFE/RL Research Report, 1*(43), 27–31.

Bungs, D. (1992). Latvia. *RFE/RL Research Report, 1*(27), 62–66.

———. (1993). Moderates win parliamentary elections in Latvia. *RFE/RL Research Report, 2*(28), 1–6.

Bungs, D., Girnius, S., & Kionka, R. (1992). Citizenship legislation in the Baltic states. *RFE/RL Research Report, 1*(50), 38–40.

Burns, J. M. (1978). *Leadership.* New York: Harper & Row.

Cavanaugh, C. (1992). Crackdown on the opposition in Uzbekistan. *RFE/RL Research Report, 1*(31), 20–24.

Clemens, W. C. (1991). *Baltic independence and Russian empire.* New York: St. Martin's Press.

Critchlow, J. (1992a). Uzbekistan: Underlying instabilities. *RFE/RL Research Report, 1*(6), 8–10.

Fuller, E. (1991). Armenia votes overwhelmingly for secession. *Report on the USSR, 3*(39), 18–20.

———. (1992). Abkhazia on the brink of civil war? *RFE/RL Research Report, 1*(35), 1–5.

———. (1993). Eduard Shevardnadze's Via Dolorosa. *RFE/RL Research Report, 2*(43) 17–23.

Gerth, H. H., & Mills, C. W. (1958). *From Max Weber: Essays in sociology.* New York: Oxford University Press.

Girnius, S. (1990a). The Lithuanian Communist Party versus Moscow. *Report on the USSR, 2*(1), 6–8.

———. (1990b). Gorbachev's visit to Lithuania. *Report on the USSR, 2*(4), 4–7.

Goble, P. (1990a). Gorbachev, secession and the fate of reform. *Report on the USSR, 2*(17), 1–5.

———. (1990b). Gorbachev's new federalism won't work. *Report on the USSR, 2*(27), 13–14.

Kaplan, M. A. (1976). *Alienation and identification*. New York: Free Press.

Kionka, R. (1993). Estonia: A difficult transition. *RFE/RL Research Report, 2*(1), 89–91.

Krickus, R. J. (1993). Latvia's "Russian question." *RFE/RL Research Report, 2*(18), 29–34.

Narodnoe khoziaistvo SSSR v 1990 g.: Statisticheskii ezhegodnik. (1991). Moscow: Financy i Statistika.

Rahr, A. (1993). The rise and fall of Ruslan Khasbulatov. *RFE/RL Research Report, 2*(24), 12–16.

———. (1994). Who will succeed Yeltsin? *RFE/RL Research Report, 3*(24) 6–7.

Rakowska-Harmstone, T. (1986). Minority nationalism today: An overview. In R. Conquest (Ed.), *The last empire: Nationality and the Soviet future* (pp. 235–264). Stanford, CA: Hoover Institution Press.

Renshon, S. A. (1974). *Psychological needs and political behavior: A theory of personality and political efficacy.* New York: Free Press.

Richards, S. (1990). *Epics of everyday life: Encounters in a changing Russia.* New York: Penguin.

Sheehy, A. (1990a). Moves to draw up new union treaty. *Report on the USSR, 2*(27), 14–17.

———. (1990b). Sidelights on the Union Treaty of 1922. *Report on the USSR, 2*(39), 17–20.

———. (1993). The Estonian law on aliens. *RFE/RL Research Report, 2*(38), 7–11.

Smith, G. B. (1992). *Soviet politics: Struggling with change.* New York: St. Martin's Press.

Socor, V. (1992). Moldova's new "government of national consensus." *RFE/RL Research Report, 1*(47), 5–10.

———. (1994a). Moldova's political landscape: Profiles of the parties. *RFE/RL Research Report, 3*(10), 6–14.

———. (1994b). Moldova. *RFE/RL Research Report, 3*(16), 17–22.

Szporluk, R. (1992). The national question. In T. J. Colton & R. Legvold (Eds.), *After the Soviet Union: From empire to nations* (pp. 84–112). New York: Norton.

Teague, E. (1990). Constitutional watchdog suspends presidential decree. *Report on the USSR, 2*(42), 9–11.

Thorson, C. (1993). Russia's draft constitution. *RFE/RL Research Report, 2*(48), 9–15.

Tolz, V. (1993). The Moscow crisis and the future of democracy in Russia. *RFE/RL Research Report, 2*(42), 1–9.

———. (1994). Problems in building democratic institutions in Russia. *RFE/RL Research Report, 3*(9), 1–7.

Vardys, V. S. (1992). Lithuanian national politics. In R. Denber (Ed.), *The Soviet nationality reader: The disintegration in context* (pp. 441–483). Boulder, CO: Westview Press.

Willhoite, F. H. (1988). *Power and governments: An introduction to politics.* Pacific Grove, CA: Brooks/Cole.

· 9 ·

THE UNCERTAIN TRANSITION FROM ABSOLUTISM TO . . . WHAT?

> *Getting a fix on post-Soviet politics . . . is about as easy as judging*
> *a symphony by its opening bars. The ear picks out isolated notes*
> *and chords; melody and rhythm elude it. Worse, we risk being*
> *misled by false echoes of some half-remembered music.*
>
> TIMOTHY J. COLTON (1992, p. 17)

What might the future hold for the fifteen countries that emerged from the fall of the Soviet Union? No one really knows, but one thing is certain. Eurasia will never be the same. Some of these countries might build the democracies that they say they want. Others almost certainly will not—at least in the foreseeable future. Even those that do build stable democracies will not have political-economic systems that are carbon copies of the United States. Although several have tried to imitate US institutions and principles, they are finding that their unique cultures and histories incline them toward their own versions of democracy. All the developed democracies can or should do is to support these efforts as best they can and give these fledgling nation-states the benefit of their experience, if asked.

So, at this point in history, what can be said about the shape of things to come? Very little in the way of specifics. At best, we can try to assess how the successor countries began their period of independence and where they may be heading. More often than not, such an assessment becomes a litany of obstacles. On a more positive note, it is also possible to recognize their strengths—the characteristics that may aid them in building the institutions that modern nation-states need. Finally, because interdependence was a major feature of the Soviet political-economic system, we must view each successor country within the context of the others.

Of particular importance are the clusters of countries that have been the historical regions in that part of the world. Because most of the former Soviet republics are traditionally thought of as members of regional groups and because these regional groups have cultural, historical, and, usually, linguistic

236

factors in common, this chapter is organized on a regional basis. Each country that is part of a historical regional grouping is discussed in the context of that region. An exception is Moldova. It is not part of any traditional region of the former Soviet Union and is discussed within the context of its relationship to neighboring Romania. Account is also taken of the fact that Russia not only is part of a historical East Slavic region but, beyond the Ural Mountains, may constitute a separate entity—northern Asia.

All fifteen Soviet successor states are engaged in institution-building. To a greater or lesser extent, they are trying to fashion the structures and identify the functions of their post-Soviet political-economic systems. That is, they are trying to find their preferred mix of power, authority, persuasion, and exchange and give it shape in new political and economic institutions. At present, all have an abundance of conflicts but lack sufficient rules for resolving or containing them. When such rules are explicit, they are embodied in constitutions, laws, executive decrees, and administrative regulations. When they are implicit, they are expressed as traditions or habitual ways of getting things done.

For the former Soviet republics, the most important step in the process of building viable nation-states is the ratification of post-Soviet constitutions. Several have taken this step. Others are still operating under constitutions written when they were republics of the Soviet Union. In countries still using Soviet-era constitutions, a confusing mix of constitutional amendments, statutes, executive decrees, and administrative regulations leaves everyone uncertain about what the law is and whether it should be obeyed. In 1993, for example, the Russian legislature got rid of Russia's residency law, but the mayor of Moscow announced that he did not approve of the change and would ignore the legislative action.[1] (*Washington Post,* September 18, 1993, p. A16)

During the early years of the post-Soviet period, the successor countries, for the most part, were operating under rule systems that tended toward the rule-less end of the spectrum. Very few were immediately able to create institutions that were more than partially rule-bound. In these circumstances, both public officials and private citizens tended to fall back on the rules that had operated during the Soviet period. In times of crisis, people tend to revert to the patterns of behavior that are most familiar, regardless of whether they are desirable or undesirable.

Some successor countries were virtually rule-less because violence and corruption had undermined whatever constitutions or other sources of law they possessed. The region in which institution-building was most impeded and rules were most ignored was Transcaucasia. In this area, comprising Armenia, Azerbaijan, and Georgia, attempts to build post-Soviet institutional frame-

---

1. Under Soviet law, people who wanted to move to Moscow had to obtain special permission and fulfill certain requirements. One could obtain permanent resident status in Moscow by marrying a person already living there. Permanent residents would marry nonresidents to enable them to gain residency permits. These so-called paper marriages were usually not consummated and were dissolved when the nonresident obtained permanent resident status.

works were largely unsuccessful because all three nations tried to create new political and economic institutions in the midst of interethnic and political violence.

TRANSCAUCASIA: ARMENIA, AZERBAIJAN, AND GEORGIA

Transcaucasia entered the Soviet Union as a single political entity. Only later was it divided into the union republics of Armenia, Azerbaijan, and Georgia. In this region, ethnic and religious hostilities have been the most devastating. The people of Transcaucasia have been too busy fighting one another to spare much energy for the more mundane process of building the institutional base for a nation-state. Most of the fighting has been over the issue of which territories should make up which nation-states. During the Gorbachev era, Armenia and Azerbaijan began a war over Nagorno-Karabakh. In Georgia, animosities between and among the rival indigenous ethnic groups and political factions kept the country in constant turmoil during the last years of the Soviet Union and afterward.

From the start of the post-Soviet era, the basic problem in Transcaucasia was the clash between two principles: self-determination and territorial inviolability. Both Armenia and the Armenian majority living in Nagorno-Karabakh invoked the principle of self-determination. They demanded that Nagorno-Karabakh be taken out of Azerbaijan and made part of Armenia or that it be given its independence. Azerbaijan countered by invoking the principle of territorial inviolability, asserting that Nagorno-Karabakh was part of Azerbaijan and should remain there. Similarly, the Abkhazians and the South Ossetians invoked the principle of self-determination, asking to be separated from Georgia. The Abkhazians wanted to be independent. The South Ossetians wanted to join North Ossetia in order to create a united Ossetia within the Russian Federation. Georgia's position, based on the principle of territorial inviolability, was that Ossetia and Abkhazia should remain part of Georgia.

The claims being made in all of these cases were grounded in well-established principles of international law. The problem was that in the real world of Transcaucasia, the principles clashed and there was no generally accepted set of rules for reconciling them. (Barkin & Cronin, 1994) The parties thus attempted to resolve their conflict by means of power in the form of military action. All of the parties seemed to see themselves as players in a zero-sum game: The side that won would win everything, and the losers would lose everything. During the early post-Soviet years, when the primary focus should have been on institution-building, efforts at compromise (often using outside mediators) were repeatedly unsuccessful.

The situation was aggravated by the fact that armaments were plentiful. For example, Georgia's only luxury hotel posted a sign asking guests to check their armaments at the door. (*Washington Post,* May 21, 1994, p. A15) A diplomat on the scene estimated that the Transcaucasus region had enough weaponry to continue fighting for twenty years. (*Washington Post,* September 12, 1993, p.

A36) Thus, the peoples of Transcaucasia could, if they chose, engage in armed conflict far into the post-Soviet period. This kind of violence and lack of tolerance are usually incompatible with the establishment of any form of stable democracy or market economy.

Not surprisingly, this situation has had a negative effect on the internal institution-building efforts of all three states. During the first years of independence, all three experienced serious problems due to the political strife, lawlessness, and economic collapse—problems that were fed by interethnic violence. As we noted previously, Zviad Gamsakhurdia, Georgia's first freely elected chief executive, was forced out of office in a violent confrontation on the streets of Tbilisi. In Azerbaijan, "supreme power changed hands three times within a period of as many months." (Fuller, 1993a, p. 17) Armenia maintained some semblance of political stability, but the economic effects of war reduced life to the level of subsistence or less, and the government had difficulty withstanding constant pressure from opposition forces. Nagorno-Karabakh became a permanent battlefield.

Armenia was the only Transcaucasian country in which there was reasonable stability in political leadership in the early years of independence. Also, a meaningful opposition was permitted to exist. One of the chief problems was the sheer weariness of the population. Armenians were drained economically and psychologically by their constant support for the fighters in Nagorno-Karabakh, economic blockades, the inability to be economically self-sufficient, and the effects of the 1988 earthquake.[2] Only 17 percent of the Armenian population voted in the October 1992 parliamentary elections. (Fuller, 1993a, p. 20) Clearly, Armenia's primary need was for an end to the violence over Nagorno-Karabakh.

By mid-1994, the efforts of several mediators had not resulted in a long-term settlement of the Nagorno-Karabakh dispute. Mediation efforts by Russian Defense Minister Pavel Grachev and the Conference on Security and Cooperation in Europe (CSCE) were ineffective because of a lack of close cooperation among the mediators. (Fuller, 1994c) At the same time, the Armenian political leadership was becoming more embattled.

Drafting and ratifying a post-Soviet constitution was not easy. The government favored a strong presidential system while the opposition favored a parliamentary system. The debate over the constitution mirrored the differences between the Armenian leaders and their rivals "on virtually every crucial issue currently facing the country, to the extent that the debate [became] a surrogate vote of no confidence." (Fuller, 1994b, p. 6) Meanwhile, the second strongest political party, the Armenian Revolutionary Federation, which had a majority in the parliament of Nagorno-Karabakh, was threatening to overthrow the Armenian government and take power.

---

2. As of the beginning of 1993, "plans to rebuild the towns in northern Armenia devastated by the earthquake . . . [had been] abandoned for lack of funds; up to half a million people remained homeless." (Fuller, 1993a, p. 20)

It is virtually impossible for a country to be deeply involved in a war while building a stable democracy and making an effective transition to a market economy. If the problem posed by the war were to be solved, the relative homogeneity of Armenia (93 percent Armenian), its natural resources, and the high level of skills and education of the population might give reason for optimism about its long-term prospects for stable democracy and a viable market economy. As long as the political violence—or the threat of political violence—continues, however, the Armenians are in danger of slipping into extremist politics and internal turmoil.

The population of Azerbaijan is also quite homogeneous. Azeris constitute 83 percent of the population. (Fuller, 1994a, p. 53) Oil-producing and oil-related industries could form the basis for a thriving market economy. Like Armenia, however, Azerbaijan has been handicapped by the drain on its resources caused by the fighting over Nagorno-Karabakh. Its first two post-Soviet presidents were forced to relinquish office because of popular anger over serious military setbacks. When the parliament voted to reinstate the first president, there was serious civil unrest. Several days of negotiation among the opposing groups resulted in the creation of a coalition government that ruled until June 7, 1992, when elections took place. Abulfaz Elchibey, candidate of the Azerbaijani Popular Front, received almost 60 percent of the vote.

Both the compromise that led to the creation of a coalition government and the popular election of a new president would have boded well for the democratic potential of Azerbaijan, if the new government had been able to rule effectively. Its first actions, however, showed little sense of what democracy is all about. For example, the government issued a decree that "empowered the police to arrest and detain people for up to thirty days and to search private homes." (Fuller, 1993a, p. 21) The rationale, of course, was the war. Also, by the end of 1992, inflation was at an annual rate of 800 percent, and the war was costing an estimated 25 to 30 million rubles per day. Finally, the fact that the war was being chiefly waged on Azerbaijani territory caused a serious drop in agricultural production. And, again, a government fell.

Approximately one year after Elchibey was elected, military defeats, economic decline, and alleged corruption among his supporters cost him most of his legitimacy. Threatened by a rebel warlord and his own loss of support among the people, Elchibey fled the capital. The reins of government were then assumed by Geidar Aliev, former member of the USSR Politburo, former Communist Party first secretary, and former USSR deputy chair of the Council of Ministers. The Azerbaijani parliament voted to strip Elchibey of all his power except the direction of foreign policy and the right to sign or veto legislation. The rebel warlord was put in charge of the Ministries of Defense, National Security, and Internal Affairs. Aliev was elected chair of the Azerbaijan legislature. In August 1993, a popular referendum officially ousted President Elchibey, leaving Aliev (who called the election) the full powers of the presidency. Subsequently, Aliev was elected president, winning a suspiciously Soviet-like 98.8 percent of the vote. (Fuller, 1994a, p. 54)

Azerbaijan has attempted to adopt some of the trappings of democracy. But the demands put on its political and economic systems by the fighting over Nagorno-Karabakh have seriously compromised its efforts. Drawing any conclusions about Azerbaijan's potential to establish a stable democratic system is difficult. The pluses are Azerbaijan's economic potential and its homogeneity. But the minuses greatly outnumber the pluses. The most obvious is the non-democratic actions of both the Elchibey and the Aliev governments. It is difficult to ascertain whether either government might have acted less autocratically if Azerbaijan had been at peace. Certainly, both Elchibey and Aliev had to be aware of the role that war played in forcing Elchibey's two immediate predecessors out of the presidency.

Until the Nagorno-Karabakh situation is resolved, assessment of Azerbaijan's potential for stable democracy is impossible. As one resident of the capital said: "There is no security, no stability, no law, no food, and no money. What do I need freedom for: If we have a choice only between anarchy and dictatorship, I choose dictatorship. Let a strong leader restore order." (Fuller, 1993b, p. 28)

Georgia too began its independent existence torn by violence. Here, however, the violence was more clearly a civil war, rather than a partially international conflict like the one being fought in and around Nagorno-Karabakh. If Georgia insisted on retaining its Soviet-era boundaries—and this was the policy of all early Georgian leaders—there was no clearly satisfactory solution to the grievances of either the South Ossetians or the Abkhazians. The Georgians constituted only 69 percent of the population, but no other ethnic group commanded more than 9 percent. In fact, within the former Abkhazian Autonomous Republic, which demanded independence from Georgia, the Abkhazians made up only 18 percent of the population.[3] The situation in Abkhazia, however, was complicated by the fact that the Georgians were in effect fighting two enemies: (1) the independence-minded Abkhazians and (2) the supporters of ousted President Gamsakhurdia.

As we discussed in Chapter 8, Georgia's first popularly elected president, Zviad Gamsakhurdia, had acted in an authoritarian manner and was eventually forced from office. Many were optimistic when former Soviet Foreign Minister Eduard Shevardnadze agreed to return to Georgia and try to lead the country out of its political and economic chaos. Shevardnadze formed a State Council that ruled the country until parliamentary elections were held in October 1992. Prior to this election, the law was amended to mandate the election of a parliamentary chair who would not be a member of any political party. Shevardnadze ran unopposed and got 96 percent of the votes cast. (Fuller, 1993a, p. 23)

Given the skill and commitment with which Shevardnadze had carried out his duties as foreign minister in the Gorbachev regime, many thought that his election as chief executive would herald a more peaceful and democratic era. The new regime, however, moved quickly to carry out a "witch-hunt that targeted

---

3. These figures represent the situation prior to the fall of Sukhumi, the capital of Abkhazia. After that, there was a large-scale movement out of the region by non-Abkhazians.

not only known supporters of Gamsakhurdia but also anyone unwise enough to express even the most innocuous criticism of" Shevardnadze. (Fuller, 1993a, p. 23) Finally, Shevardnadze forced a reluctant parliament to give him emergency powers—in effect a three-month dictatorship—by threatening to step down from office. Democratic institution-building bowed to the demands of war and of an economy that was barely functioning. (*Washington Post*, September 15, 1993, pp. A21, A22) Shevardnadze also presided over the military loss of Abkhazia and the continued battle with the forces loyal to Gamsakhurdia. In desperation, Shevardnadze did what the Georgians had previously refused to do: He asked for help from the Russian military and agreed to join the Commonwealth of Independent States.

If the Transcaucasian countries are considered with reference to the conditions for stable democracy, the lack of domestic peace and any workable rule system for resolving conflict emerge as major obstacles. Moreover, this situation is an impediment to stable government of any form, as well as to economic viability. Until the people of this region learn to live together in peace and mutual respect, their chances for building successful nation-states are slim. At present, then, the prognosis for these countries is not good. In contrast, one of the regions in the former Soviet Union where domestic peace seems firmly established is the Baltic states. Given the fact that they have been able to avoid any serious violence, what are their chances for building stable democracy?

THE BALTIC STATES: ESTONIA, LATVIA, AND LITHUANIA

Estonia, Latvia, and Lithuania became part of the Soviet Union after World War II, as a result of secret protocols to the Treaty of Non-Aggression of 1939 signed by Hitler's Germany and Stalin's Soviet Union. These protocols created a Soviet sphere of influence that encompassed all three. Between World War I and World War II, these countries had been independent; they were forcibly annexed to the Soviet Union in 1940. Thus, unlike the other former union republics, the Baltic states had some recent experience with independence. Their experience with democracy, however, was limited. All had tried to establish democratic forms of government in the 1920s, but by the middle of the 1930s all had become authoritarian—Lithuania in 1926 and Estonia and Latvia in 1934. (Clemens, 1991, p. 7; Raun, 1987)

During the Gorbachev years, the Baltic republics were at the forefront of union republic demands for independence. But they managed to avoid violence. The only violence that occurred during the pre-independence period was a few brief, armed clashes between the Balts and the Soviet military. Thus, unlike the Transcaucasian countries, the Baltic states have enjoyed domestic peace. Also, they have all taken significant steps toward establishing limited democratic governments and pluralist political systems.

The efforts of Lithuania, Latvia, and Estonia to rebuild their shattered economies have been weakened by their dependence on Russia for energy and other essentials. Because they are small and not economically developed enough to be self-sufficient, they must find ways to integrate themselves into the world economy and bring about rapid economic development. These are some of the things that they have in common. They are not, however, identical with regard to many of the factors that affect their futures. As we discussed in Chapter 8, they vary considerably in their relations with minority ethnic groups and their willingness to extend citizenship and participatory rights to nonindigenous people. Thus, each needs to be considered separately.

Estonia began to write a post-Soviet constitution while the August 1991 attempted coup was still in progress. On August 20, 1991 (the second day of the coup), Estonia declared its complete and immediate independence, creating an ad hoc Constituent Assembly. This governing body was charged with preparing a new constitution to be submitted to the Estonian people for approval by referendum. After considerable debate, particularly on the issue of a strong presidential system versus a strong parliamentary system, the final constitution provided for a strong, unicameral parliament and a weak president. The draft constitution "was not an elegant, rigorous document, but it was serviceable." On June 28, 1992, 67 percent of Estonia's eligible voters went to the polls and approved this constitution by 91 percent. (Kionka, 1992b, pp. 58, 77)

Approval cleared the way for the election of a parliament and president. It was also a test of Estonia's grasp of the importance of compromise, distribution of resources, tolerance, and pluralism. On September 20, 1992, Estonians voted for their first post-Soviet president and parliament. The result was inconclusive. No presidential candidate or parliamentary party gained a clear majority.

This outcome tested the Estonians' ability to compromise. What emerged was a parliamentary coalition composed of five free market–oriented parties, the Estonian National Independence Party, and the Moderates. Although much divided them, they were able to coalesce around their common support for the acceleration of market reforms. In the presidential election, no candidate achieved a clear majority. The winner of the popular vote was Arnold Ruutel with 47 percent; he was followed by Lennart Meri with 29 percent. This outcome threw the election into the new parliament. There was considerable opposition to Ruutel, formerly a member of the Estonian Communist Party Central Committee. As a result, the parliament elected Meri, an author, diplomat, and filmmaker, by a vote of 59 to 31. (Kionka, 1992c, p. 9) The election was peaceful, and the electorate accepted its result, giving the winners the ability to act from a position of authority rather than power.

This political campaign marked a step toward the establishment of a pluralist political system. Sixteen parties or electoral coalitions, plus some independent candidates, took part. There were four dominant political groups, and each of them fielded presidential candidates. Aside from the poor condition of Estonia's economy (which the new government was given a clear mandate to remedy), the main concern related to democracy in Estonia is ethnic diversity and Estonians' willingness to let all ethnic groups participate equally. Recall from Chapter 8 that non-Estonians—especially Russians—found it difficult to gain citizenship. Thus, few Russians were able to vote. The Russians claimed that the citizenship law prevented 40 percent of the population of Estonia from voting. (Kionka, 1992c, pp. 6–7)

In its search for a stable democratic political system, Estonia needed to solve two major problems. First, it had to get its economy moving. In 1992, the first full year after independence, production decreased by 40 percent compared to 1991 (the final year of Soviet rule). Also, prices rose by 400 percent. (Kionka, 1993, p. 91) Meanwhile, the Estonian government instituted "tough monetary, budgetary, economic stabilization, and free market policies." (Kand, 1994, p. 92) These policies arrested the economic decline. In 1993, the annual inflation rate dropped to 30 percent, a considerable improvement over 1992. The problems that remained included low industrial output, outdated technology, the loss of traditional markets, and slow expansion of the private sector due, in part, to a lack of capital. Also, the agricultural sector suffered from the loss of Russian markets and a sharp increase in the cost of fuel and machinery. Even with these problems, Estonia ranked as one of the strongest economies among the former Soviet republics. And, it was gradually becoming more integrated into the European market, with Finland replacing Russia as its major trading partner.

The second problem facing the Estonian government was the need to establish cordial relations with its Russian and Russian-speaking minorities. The ill will that characterized the political debate over the citizenship laws—as well as the laws themselves—impaired Estonia's ability to achieve the tolerance and inclusive pluralism that support stable democracy. Ethnic problems were particularly severe in Narva, which is on the border with Russia and has a population that is 90 percent non-Estonian. The residents of Narva held a referendum on territorial autonomy on July 17, 1993. The pro-autonomy side won by just over 59 percent, but the Estonian Supreme Court declared the referendum unconstitutional. Thus, Estonia was left with a disgruntled minority—particularly the Russians with just over 30 percent of the population. (Kand, 1994)

On the whole, however, Estonia moved toward democracy and a market economy much more successfully than did most of the other former Soviet republics. Its economic and ethnic problems, though serious, did not seem as insurmountable as the problems of the Trancaucasian countries. With time and patience on all sides (including Russia), Estonia is quite likely to emerge from the breakup of the Soviet Union as a viable democratic state with a workable market economy.

Unlike Estonia, Latvia did not immediately choose to draft a post-Soviet constitution. This decision reflected a basic division within Latvia on the issue of whether to reconstitute itself as the Republic of Latvia, which had been established in 1918, or to define itself as a completely new state. In the short run, the government chose the former course of action, and Latvia reinstated its 1922 constitution. This constitution, however, did not really function as the fundamental law of Latvia. A few of its provisions were followed and the rest ignored. Thus, it can be argued that post-Soviet Latvia began its political life without a constitution and without a clear intent to create one. Instead, it engaged in a prolonged debate over what the rules of conflict should be and where authority should reside. This situation delayed the adoption of basic laws, including a law on citizenship. It also led to the adoption of a revised Law on the Cabinet of Ministers (the original law dated back to April 1, 1925), which defined the organizational basis of the Latvian government—a job usually accomplished by a constitution.

Despite the lack of a viable constitution and a law on citizenship, Latvia held parliamentary elections in June 1993. Pluralism thrived as 23 political parties and groups fielded 874 candidates for the 100 seats in the parliament. This pluralism, however, extended mostly to the Latvians, because only citizens were allowed to vote and 79 percent of the citizenry was Latvian. By comparison, the Latvian share of the total population was 52 percent. Thus, a large number of non-Latvians were excluded from the electorate.

Of the twenty-three groups participating in the campaign, only eight managed to win seats. Notable was the fact that the People's Front, which led Latvia in its struggle for independence, lost badly; its list was chosen by only 2.6 percent of the voters. As a result, some of the important leaders of the independence movement did not gain seats in the first post-Soviet Latvian parliament. This defeat was largely due to a splintering of the Popular Front after independence. (Bungs, 1993b)

The largest number of newly elected members of the parliament belonged to Latvia's Way, which won thirty-six seats. This outcome meant that Latvian parliamentarians, like their Estonian counterparts, had to compromise and build coalitions in order to govern. But unlike the Estonians, they were not able to build a single coalition that could command a majority. On the positive side, they were able to elect Anatolijs Gorbunovs, former head of state and a member of Latvia's Way, as their chair. On the negative side, the smaller political parties and groups resisted compromise. This hindered the ability of the parliament to act, even to elect a president. After three rounds of voting, Guntis Ulmanis, a virtual political unknown and the grandnephew of the last president of the interwar Republic of Latvia, was finally elected.

With no clear majority and with a relatively inexperienced president, the parliament had difficulty passing the laws that Latvia needed to have an effective government as well as political and economic stability. No one group clearly had the authority. In addition, there are major economic, ethnic, and political problems that Latvia will have to solve.

Like the other former Soviet republics, Latvia faced a difficult economic situation. Its gross national product in 1992 was 44 percent less than its 1991 GNP. Industrial production dropped in 1992 by 33 percent. (Bungs, 1993a) Despite some positive signs in 1993, the standard of living for the average resident of Latvia continued to drop. By the end of 1993, 70 percent of the population was at or below the poverty level. (Bungs, 1994) On a more positive note, however, the Latvian currency (the lats) was one of the strongest currencies in the region. Also, the Bank of Latvia pursued a strong anti-inflationary policy, helping to make its banking system "one of the soundest in the region." (Paeglis, 1994)

Latvia did not make any significant attempt to include minorities in its initial institution-building process. Thus, many of the Russians and Russian-speaking people in Latvia were not represented. Their exclusion caused considerable dissatisfaction, which could create serious problems in the future if they choose not to accept the authority of the Latvian government. The exclusion of Russians and Russian-speakers also produced tensions with the neighboring Russian Federation, which saw Russians as being discriminated against in Latvia.

Finally, there was some question about whether the new legislators were well equipped to engage in the bargaining needed for parliamentary compromise and coalition-building. According to the director of the Latvian Institute of History, Latvia's politicians "from across the political spectrum are the products of a political culture that thrives on confrontation, not compromise." (Krickus, 1993, p. 34) This opinion seems to be supported by the fact that such a small country generated so many political groups and candidates for a mere one hundred parliamentary seats and by parliament's difficulty in electing a president.

Like Estonia, Lithuania gave a high priority to replacing its Soviet republican constitution with a post-Soviet constitution. Also, as in Estonia, there was conflict between those supporting a strong presidential system and those supporting a strong parliamentary system. These two groups were forced to compromise, however, when voters on May 25, 1992, rejected a constitution that favored a strong presidency. The result was a compromise constitution approved on October 25, 1992, by 58 percent of those eligible to vote. (Girnius, 1992, p. 9) At the same time, the Lithuanians held parliamentary elections.

As in Latvia, there was a high level of organized participation in Lithuania. Twenty-five parties and movements fielded candidates. They could be divided into three groups: (1) those who backed Vytautas Landsbergis, the musicologist who had led the Lithuanian movement for independence; (2) those who backed Algirdas Brazauskas, the former leader of the Lithuanian Communist Party and current leader of its successor organization, the Lithuanian Democratic Labor Party (LDLP); and (3) several centralist parties that backed neither Landsbergis nor Brazauskas. The only party that "could claim more than 10,000 members or functioned like a normal party in the Western sense of the word" was the LDLP. (Girnius, 1992, pp. 6–7) The LDLP scored a resounding victory, gaining a clear parliamentary majority of 73 of the 141 deputies. Thus, unlike the situations in Estonia and Latvia, coalition-building was not as vital an issue. Sajudis, Landsbergis's party, came in a poor second, with only 30 seats.[4]

The outcome of the parliamentary elections in Lithuania was shocking to many because in effect the former Lithuanian Communist Party was returned to office. Moreover, the LDLP had campaigned on a platform that "called for a slowdown in the pace of economic reform and an improvement in relations

---

4. In 1993, Sajudis became the Homeland Union (Conservatives of Lithuania) led by Landsbergis.

with Russia." Brazauskas's interpretation of the election results was that the "people had given their support to the forces of realism and moderation." (*Washington Post,* October 27, 1992, p. A21)

Because Lithuania's economy was far from healthy, the choice of the Brazauskas government to effect change slowly was fraught with pitfalls. But, then, so was an alternative policy of shock therapy. As in most of the other former Soviet republics that were seriously trying to establish democracy and a market economy at the same time, in Lithuania there were no painless choices. Trying to minimize the pain in the short run was likely to worsen it in the long run. Too much pain in the present, however, could cut short the careers of those making the decisions that the general public perceived as the sources of the pain.

Many commentators attributed Sajudis's defeat to its own internal divisions. Also, there was the fact that the people blamed it for a 50 percent decline in the average standard of living that had occurred since the beginning of 1991. A former Sajudis supporter observed: "People are scared. . . . They remember how the Communist Party took care of everything—even if not very well." (*Washington Post,* December 23, 1992, p. A20) After the parliamentary election, Brazauskas asked all groups to join in a coalition to help solve Lithuania's problems, but Landsbergis and his supporters refused, choosing the role of loyal opposition.

The victory of the LDLP was complete when, on February 14, 1993, Brazauskas won the popular election for the presidency with 60 percent of the vote. Landsbergis had decided not to run, so Brazauskas's only opponent was Stasys Lozoraitis, Lithuania's ambassador to the United States. While Brazauskas was well known and popular, Lozoraitis was a virtual unknown. He had been born into a diplomatic family and had lived most of his life outside Lithuania. Along with the dismal state of the economy, Lozoraitis's lack of knowledge about Lithuanian affairs became a major campaign issue.

Unlike Estonia and Latvia, Lithuania chose to be governed by one party— which could be blamed if life got worse and supported if it got better. And, as noted above, the state of the economy was not good. During 1992, the GDP had declined 35 percent, industrial production had declined 48 percent, and inflation had risen to 1,163 percent. (Girnius, 1993a, p. 29) Industrial production continued to drop in 1993, as did the standard of living. In addition, inflation remained a serious problem. (Girnius, 1994, pp. 101–102)

From the point of view of democracy, the peaceful transition from Sajudis to the LDLP was promising. The elections were held freely and honestly; the losers accepted the result and the role of loyal opposition. The Lithuanians seemed to be off to a good start with a government that could claim the authority that stems from a clear popular mandate. As in the other former union republics, however, the economy was a formidable challenge, and the LDLP seemed to have no comprehensive plan for dealing with it. "From the start, the [LDLP] seemed confused and even paralyzed, avoiding action on important matters and focusing on minor but politically divisive issues." (Girnius, 1993b, p. 17) In addition, the fact that the LDLP was the former

Lithuanian Communist Party was a potential problem. LDLP's placement of "party members in dominant positions at all levels of government . . . led to accusations that the LDLP [was] planning to reinstitute one-party rule." (Girnius, 1993c, p. 17) On the whole, however, in comparison with the other Soviet successor countries, Lithuania seems to have a good chance of establishing a stable democratic system in the relatively near future. Its potential for establishing a viable market economy and achieving a reasonable degree of economic self-sufficiency is less promising.

To summarize, in spite of serious problems, the Baltic states seem to have positioned themselves better than most other successor countries with reference to the institution-building necessary for stable democracy. Lithuania seems to be the most successful, and Latvia seems to have the most problems, but all three have done quite well, given their situations at the time of independence and immediately afterward. Thus, if there is cause for optimism about any region of the former Soviet Union, that region is the Baltic region.

MOLDOVA

Moldova became the Moldavian Soviet Socialist Republic by annexation during World War II. It is composed of three historical parts, Bessarabia, North Bukovina, and the eastern bank of the Dniester River, and is situated between Romania and Ukraine. Of all the former Soviet republics, Moldova is the only one with a titular nationality that has its own state outside the former USSR. The Moldovans and Romanians constitute the same ethnic group. Thus, present-day Moldova consists of most of the eastern half of the historical principality of Moldova; the western half is in Romania.

Like the Baltic states, Moldova began to make significant strides in democratic institution-building quite early. When Moldova became independent after the failed 1991 coup, a constitutional drafting commission was already at work. During the Gorbachev era, the Popular Front had sought annexation to Romania. That goal was subsequently abandoned, and the Moldovans decided to create their own country, independent of Romania. In this effort, they faced problems that were more serious than those faced by the Baltic states. Like all of the Soviet successor countries, Moldova inherited an economy that needed a major overhaul, and this meant inevitable economic deprivation for the Moldovan people. But, unlike the Baltic states, Moldova faced the problem of political violence (especially on the east bank of the Dniester), pressure to become part of Romania, and serious border issues with Ukraine.

The original goal of reunification with Romania was abandoned for many reasons. Foremost was the fact that the overwhelming majority of the people living in Moldova did not support reunification. This fact was even acknowledged by those who were in favor of reunification; their position, though, was that the public should be educated about the desirability of reunification. Was reunification really desirable? There seemed to be several good arguments against it.

First, Bessarabia had been part of Greater Romania in the past (1918–40 and 1941–44). While there had been some benefits for Bessarabia in that arrangement, such as improved education and increased upward mobility for the Bessarabians, there was a significant downside. Opponents of reunification evoked memories of Romanian overcentralization and insensitivity to the problems of Bessarabia. Also remembered were overtaxation, a stagnant economy, and dishonest officials sent to Bessarabia from Bucharest.

Second, Romania was in a state of chronic economic crisis during the initial years of Moldovan (and Romanian) independence. Having sufficient economic problems of their own, the Moldovans were not eager to be involved in Romania's. Also, remaining closely aligned with the former Soviet republics promised significant economic advantages. Because of the way the Soviet economic system had been managed, the Moldovan economy was highly interdependent with much of the former Soviet Union, in both production and markets. In short, "Moldova [saw] no economic incentive to political reunification with Romania . . . ; but the disincentives and risks [were] readily apparent." (Socor, 1992, p. 28)

Third, the fact that the Moldovans had been cut off from Romania since World War II (or longer in some areas) caused them to develop somewhat differently linguistically and culturally. These differences were especially apparent in technology. The predominantly agricultural Moldovans lagged behind their relatively advanced Romanian neighbors. Concern about this disparity was summed up by a member of the Moldovan parliament: "Suppose we unite. . . . What do we do if after a day or two, they begin treating us like second-class citizens . . . ? There is concern all around that if we unite, we will be marginalized and discriminated against." (Socor, 1992, p. 29)

Finally, Moldova's ethnic minorities feared reunification. Constituting 35 percent of the population, these groups were mainly Bulgarians, Gagauz, Russians, and Ukranians. They posed a threat of secession or, at least, civil unrest if Moldova decided to become part of Romania.

After weighing the pros and cons of reunification, the Moldovan leadership came to the early conclusion that interethnic harmony and nation-building could best be achieved by the creation of an independent Moldovan nation-state in which the nonindigenous ethnic communities would feel secure and able to participate in Moldova's political and social development. Thus, the Moldovans embraced the twin goals of independent statehood and preservation of Moldova's territorial integrity. In order to accomplish these goals, the Moldovan leaders created the government of national consensus, discussed in Chapter 8. This decision was reinforced by the results of the parliamentary election in 1994, when the Agrarian Democratic Party won. Agrarian Democrats were the center of a political movement for a Moldovan state distinct from Romania. (Socor, 1994)

The main barrier to the building of a stable democratic system in Moldova was an insurgency on the east bank of the Dniester River. It was both an internal and an international problem. The violence began soon after the 1991 coup attempt and during 1992 grew into outright warfare with Russian military participation. The goal of the insurgents was to secede from Moldova and become part of some future "Greater Russia." The Russians involved in the insurgency were only 30 percent of Moldova's Russian population. In fact, they were only 25 percent of the east bank population. But because of their military strength and support from Russian nationalists, they were able to isolate the east bank from participation in Moldovan society.

Although the leaders of the insurgency tried to stir up trouble in other parts of Moldova, long-term violence tended to be limited to the east bank. Elsewhere, there was considerable progress toward national consensus. The Russian Federation, however, refused to withdraw its military forces, citing a need to defend the local Russians against discrimination and "Romanianization" and asserting that the area "is historically and ethnically 'Russian land'." (Socor, 1993, p. 42) Thus, although Moldova made steady progress toward the establishment of a stable democracy, this goal cannot be achieved until the problem of the insurgency (and Russia's involvement in it) is solved. .

CENTRAL ASIA: KAZAKHSTAN, KYRGYZSTAN, TAJIKISTAN, TURKMENISTAN, AND UZBEKISTAN

Most of the land that now comprises the five successor countries of Soviet Central Asia only became part of the Russian Empire during the nineteenth century. Previously their history was one of little centralized rule, and their society was mostly tribal and nomadic. Central Asia gained political unity when the Russian Empire established a Turkestan Government-General to administer the territory. After the Bolshevik Revolution, these lands became the Turkestan Autonomous Soviet Socialist Republic. The division of Turkestan into five separate republics came about in 1925, and, at the same time, the inhabitants of these republics had an official "nationality" entered in their internal passports. Thus, "although each republic was named for a local nationality, none was a 'national homeland.' The Kirghiz, Uzbeks, and Tajiks all have border claims on one another—and large irredentist populations on which to base them—as do the Uzbeks, Turkmen and Kazakhs." (Olcott, 1992b, p. 112)

Early in the post-Soviet period, there was talk about reuniting the Central Asian countries to form a political entity resembling the former Turkestan. The idea of Turkestan can be traced back to the third century, and "to Central Asians the name is evocative of the former might and affluence of their region." (Critchlow, 1992a, p. 47) Nevertheless, the creation of a unified Turkestan seems unlikely for several reasons:

1. Violent clashes have occurred between the region's nationalities.
2. Regional leaders are not eager to give up their privileged positions and be subordinated to a larger political-economic system.
3. There is the fear that the leaders of one or more of the Central Asian states will dominate the rest; Uzbekistan is often mentioned.

4. Many of these same leaders fear the spread and potential strength of Islamic fundamentalism.
5. As artificial as these countries might originally have been, they now are a focus of loyalty for their titular nationalities.
6. The non-Turkic minorities in Central Asia do not support the idea of unification and might move to try to ally themselves with neighboring countries. Most threatening in this sense are the Russians who live in Kazakhstan along the Kazakh-Russian border and the Tajiks, who have strong ties with the Tajiks in Afghanistan.

Thus, it is likely that these countries will remain politically independent. (Critchlow, 1992a; Rupert, 1992)

Another potentially unifying force in the region is Islamic fundamentalism. The strength of this movement varies from country to country, but it is possible to make some generalizations. According to at least one observer (Rupert, 1992, p. 180), "the revival does not seek state power; most people at newly crowded mosques and Islamic bookstalls say they seek Islamic influence in government by electing 'good Muslims' rather than by installing a theocracy." But the power of Islam should not be underestimated. In all of the Central Asian countries, the Islamic fundamentalists have grassroots organizations that could grow into a formidable political force, if there is sufficient dissatisfaction with secular government policies or deeds. As of mid-1994, however, Islamic fundamentalism did not seem to be a serious threat. (Brown, 1994b)

Finally, it is important to remember that the collapse of the Soviet Union was primarily "a European event." (Rupert, 1992, p. 182) The Central Asians were far from enthusiastic about the idea of complete independence from the Soviet Union. In fact, it has been noted that they are examples of a rare breed: people forced to become independent. (Olcott, 1992b, p. 108) What little enthusiasm there was for independence came from small groups of intellectuals who were not able to appeal effectively to the common people. Thus, there has been a strong tendency for the members of the former CPSU elite to remain in power and for nationalists to demand more autonomy without cutting their economic ties with Russia. However, all of the Central Asian countries quickly began trying to build economic relationships with states outside the former Soviet Union.

The Central Asian countries have economies that are closely integrated with the rest of the former Soviet Union, as well as serious social and economic problems. (Marnie & Whitlock, 1993) Two of the most critical problems that they all—to a greater or lesser extent—have to solve are a high population growth rate and a disastrous environmental legacy. A close third is undereducation and a lack of technical skills among their indigenous populations. In the past, this deficiency was balanced by the presence of educated and skilled Slavs. Many of them, however, have been leaving because of rising ethnic tensions.

Of the five Central Asian republics, Kazakhstan and Kyrgyzstan made the most rapid initial progress toward establishing the basis for stable democracies. Kazakhstan was one of the more reluctant of the Central Asian countries to declare its independence. It attracted the most outside attention because it was the only Central Asian country to possess nuclear weapons. Moreover, it was the most Western oriented. (Brown, 1993a, p. 29) Kazakhstan was also distinguished by the fact that it was the least Islamic of the group, because the Kazakh "nomads preserved traditional animism and ancestor worship almost intact until about 200 years ago." (Rupert, 1992, p. 188) Thus, although Kazakhstan is Muslim, Islam there is diluted by an earlier religious culture and value system.

Kazakhstan is divided along ethnic lines. The north is primarily ethnic Russian, the south primarily ethnic Kazakh. This division made it difficult for the Kazakhs to adopt a post-Soviet constitution. When a draft constitution was first discussed in late 1992, the Russians staged demonstrations. They wanted both Russian and Kazakh to be the official state languages. They also wanted dual citizenship and local control over language, culture, and natural resources. (Brown, 1993a, p. 30)

The Kazakhs are not without rudimentary democratic traditions. They were nomadic tribes throughout most of their history. As such, they were governed by "a certain practical, grass-roots democracy." This means that "it was necessary for a tribal chieftain to gain popularity among his followers; otherwise, given the living conditions on the steppe, members of the tribe would merely wander off." (Critchlow, 1992b, p. 12) Critchlow sees this history as forming a basis on which the Kazakhs could begin the business of trying to establish stable democracy. However, it is also the basis for rule by strong, popular leaders, like the first post-Soviet president, Nursultan Nazarbayev. Immediately after independence, Kazakhstan seemed to make significant progress in establishing opposition political parties and in permitting them to act freely. In addition, an independent trade union confederation was allowed to lobby without interference, and an independent press was allowed to criticize the government.

Nazarbayev, who led his country into independence, moved cautiously. The first presidential election in an independent Kazakhstan was carried out in such a way as to eliminate any meaningful opposition. Nazarbayev also expressed some ambivalence about the relative priority that political and economic reform should have. Complicating any choices he might make was the fact that the Kazakhs were a minority in their own republic; as recently as the 1979 Soviet census, the Russians outnumbered them. (Brown, 1990, p. 19) By 1994 they had increased to 42 percent of the population—better, but still a minority. The Russians came in second with 38 percent. (Brown, 1994b, p. 16)

After independence the Kazakhs seemed to be trying to find a way of peaceably coexisting. Their minority status during most of the Soviet period led to a generally muted nationalist stance. The only party that was denied registration immediately after independence was a fanatical Kazakh nationalist party with a platform that supported "priority rights for the Kazakh . . . nation and Islam." (Critchlow, 1992b, p. 14) President Nazarbayev stated that one would need "a heart of ice and a mind of concrete" to curtail freedom to small doses when his people have not had their freedom for over seven decades. (Critchlow, 1992b, p. 13)

Within the limits of his cautious approach, Nazarbayev and his government seemed to be moving toward a type of pluralism that would permit the citizens of Kazakhstan to share power and feel secure about their status. In addition to the measures already mentioned, his government quickly took an important symbolic step to allay any fears the people of Kazakhstan might have about organizing around their political interests. Shortly after independence, the Kazakh legislature adopted a citizenship law that gave priority to guaranteeing the equality of citizens, forbidding not only ethnic and religious discrimination but also discrimination on the basis of political convictions. (*RFE/RL Research Report,* January 10, 1992, p. 61)

The initial period of independence, however, turned out to be a "honeymoon period." As Kazakhstan went about the business of establishing itself as an independent state, two threats to its stability loomed large. One was the daunting ecological problems that greatly complicated economic reform. Kazakhstan had been a center for Soviet research and testing activities that had generated major radioactive pollution.

Also, both the Kazakhs and the Russians saw themselves as victims of centuries of colonialism. This perception affected every aspect of political life. Russian Federation nationalists actively encouraged separatist sentiment among the Russians living in northern Kazakhstan near the border with Russia. As a result, Kazakhs questioned the loyalty of the resident Russians. Also, after decades of Russification, many Kazakhs were committed to the principle that Kazakhstan should be a Kazakh nation. A moderate Kazakh political leader expressed the sentiment of a large number of Kazakhs when he observed: "Kazakhstan should be built on Kazakh foundations. Let the Russians work next to us, study next to us, live with us. But one thing is no longer permissible: for them to be our masters." (*Washington Post,* February 14, 1994, p. A18)

During the first few years of independence, Kazakhs increasingly dominated the government, and the Russians felt threatened. Criticism of Nazarbayev was strongly discouraged, and no well-organized opposition movement was permitted to develop. In March 1994 the people of Kazakhstan chose their first post-Soviet parliament. The way the election was organized strongly favored ethnic Kazakhs and supporters of Nazarbayev whatever their ethnic identity. Many potential candidates were not permitted to run, including people who had criticized Nazarbayev, journalists, independent trade union leaders, and Russian nationalists. The outcome of the election was that Kazakhs won a 56 percent majority (significantly larger than their share of the population) and Russians took 27 percent (significantly less than their share of the population). Foreign observers, including a delegation from the Conference on Security and Cooperation in Europe, asserted that the election unfairly favored Nazarbayev supporters. According to one diplomat, "Nazarbayev's allies won at least two-thirds of parliament, and his opponents . . . less than 15 percent." (*Washington Post*, March 11, 1994, p. A19) The campaign and election both reflected ethnic tensions and indicated that true multiparty competition was a long way off.

Thus, although Kazakhstan's political leaders seemed to go through the motions of establishing a pluralist political system, when it came to practice they reverted to the habits acquired under Soviet rule. As the Chair of the Electoral Commission stated in defense of the electoral process: "It's impossible to change the psychology of people in a two-month campaign after 70 years of communism." (*Washington Post*, March 11, 1994, p. A19) What he did not add was that this observation applied to the leadership as well as to the people. Some observers attributed many of the problems with the election to "widespread unfamiliarity with domestic election procedures." (*RFE/RL News Briefs*, March 7–11, 1994, p. 8)

Like all of the other successor countries, Kazakhstan experienced considerable economic decline after 1991, as its economic relationships with the rest of the former Soviet Union were disrupted. Also, the ecological damage of the Soviet period became more apparent. After trying unsuccessfully to create some sort of central structure for economic cooperation among the successor countries, Nazarbayev began to explore the possibility of establishing relationships with corporations outside the former USSR in order to get help in exploiting Kazakhstan's considerable natural resources, which include oil as well as rare and nonferrous metals. Within Kazakhstan he began an aggressive drive toward privatization and a market economy while putting into place a social safety net to limit the effects of the transition on the people. In spite of this effort, "total output fell by a quarter in the two years after independence." (Brown, 1994a, p. 60)

The preservation of stability may be the key to the future of Kazakhstan. If the Russians become seriously dissatisfied, violence may occur. For the moment, however, the relative tranquillity of Kazakhstan has made residence there an appealing choice for most of its Russian population. If Kazakhstan can control the forces of Kazakh nationalism and give its Russian minority a meaningful role in the political-economic system, it can probably be regarded as one of the Central Asian countries most likely to achieve some form of stable democracy. Given Nazarbayev's apparent manipulation of the 1994 election, as well as the resulting underrepresentation of the Russian population, however, this future may be a long time in coming.

Like the Kazakhs, the nomadic Kyrgyz adopted Islam rather late in their history, and the influence of Islam on contemporary Kyrgyzstan has been limited. (Rupert, 1992, p. 189) The Kyrgyz constitute a majority (52 percent) of the population. The next largest group is the Russians, with 22 percent. (Olcott, 1992a, p. 257) Thus, Kyrgyzstan does not have the potential for ethnic divisiveness that challenges Kazakhstan.

Unlike Kazakh president Nazarbayev, Kyrgyz president Askar Akaev enthusiastically embraced democracy from the start. He had more freedom of action than the other Central Asian leaders, because he had never served as a Communist Party official. In fact, he banned the Communist Party immediately after the failed August 1991 coup and went "further than any other Central Asian leader in attacking the power of old elites, reforming local government bodies and even ordering the government to cede control over the press." (Rupert, 1992, p. 190) Akaev also tried to include minorities by attempting to balance his government appointments among regional, ethnic, and political groups. One commentator has concluded that "Kyrgyzstan is the nearest thing to a Western-style democracy to have developed in Central Asia." (Brown, 1992, p. 23) Akaev's policies were approved by the people in a referendum during January 1994. Ninety-five percent of the voters participated and gave Akaev a 96 percent vote of confidence. (*Washington Post,* February 1, 1994, p. A16)

Kyrgyzstan's major problem, however, is its economy, which "had been more closely tied to that of the rest of the USSR than the economies of the other Central Asian states and accordingly suffered more from the disruption of its previous sources of supplies." (Brown, 1993a, p. 34) During 1992, the output of industrial products fell by 20 percent and agricultural products by 40 percent. Also, like Armenia, Kyrgyzstan suffered from natural disasters, the most notable being a major earthquake in August 1992. The Akaev government tried to deal with these problems in several ways. It actively sought foreign investors to exploit Kyrgyzstan's raw materials, develop its agriculture, and create new light industry. At home there was a major push for privatization. Unfortunately, the people, accustomed to taking orders from the government rather than running their own farms and factories, showed little interest in privatization. (*Washington Post,* April 4, 1992, p. A18) Kyrgyzstan was also threatened by a civil war in neighboring Tajikistan—a war that could spill across their common border.

Like Transcaucasia, independent Tajikistan has been plagued with civil unrest and outright warfare from the beginning—and that beginning was not auspicious. Rakhmon Nabiev had been elected president by 66 percent of the voters in November 1991. Nabiev, a protégé of former Soviet leader Leonid Brezhnev and head of the Tajik Communist Party from 1982 to 1985, interpreted this election victory as a mandate to continue Communist rule. Thus, Tajikistan began its independence as the only former Soviet republic ruled by a party explicitly identifying itself as Communist. (Brown, 1993a, p. 35) This situation, however, led to the formation of an opposition coalition consisting of Muslim activists and democrats. The Communists and the opposition coalition were soon fighting each other in the south. The coalition was supported by Afghanistan, and the Communist government received help from Russia.

In September 1992, the opposition coalition forced Nabiev to resign from the presidency.[5] The country was them ruled by a motley combination of Communists and coalition members. Subsequently, the parliament got rid of the office of president and made its chair the head of state. The job was given to Imomali Rakhmonov, a former collective-farm director, who tried to build a

---

5. Rakhmon Nabiev died from a heart attack on April 10, 1993.

government representative of all regions of Tajikistan—with only modest success. The "anti-Islamic forces made it clear that they regarded consolidation of what they believed to be their victory over the democratic-Islamic coalition as more important than national reconciliation." (Brown, 1993b, p. 11) Thus, an important chance to build government authority was lost, and power became the political currency of Tajikistan. The armed insurgency continued.

Fearing reprisals from the neo-Communist government, thousands of Tajiks began to flee to neighboring Afghanistan. By August 1993, some estimates put the number of refugees living in Afghanistan at a hundred thousand. For the same period, the estimate of the dead was over twenty thousand. (*Washington Post,* August 22, 1993, p. C1) This refugee problem will not go away until there is peace in Tajikistan. The Tajiks have a fierce attachment to their ancestral homes, so it is safe to assume that they will continue to try to return—by force, if necessary. It is also evident that they will be supported by the Afghan *mujahedin,* who have the experience gained from almost a decade of fighting the Russians.

The refugees' fears were not groundless. Independent observers reported that the neo-Communist government was crushing its opposition brutally. A Russian officer reported that the progovernment troops were shooting Muslim forces even after they had surrendered. And "virtually all prominent opposition leaders [were] forced to flee Dushanbe [the capital] which [had] been turned into a government armed camp." (*Washington Post,* February 5, 1993, p. A31) Other opposition activists were charged with the crime of having incited civil war or disappeared and were presumed dead. "In mid-1993 all opposition groups were officially banned." (Brown, 1994b, p. 15)

Thus, on both sides of the Tajik-Afghan border there were "combatants instilled with implacable hatred and thirst for revenge. On the Afghan side, . . . a new generation of the *mujahedin,* many of them ethnic Tajiks, [was] taking over." On the Tajik side, "many, if not most, of the mid-level officers [were] veterans of the Afghan war. They saw some of their friends killed in battle and recovered the mutilated bodies of others, tortured to death after being taken prisoner." (*Washington Post,* August 22, 1993, p. C4) In July 1993, the Russians became officially involved in the war, notifying the United Nations Security Council that they intended to help the Tajiks defend themselves against aggression from Afghanistan. Thus, the war in Tajikistan represented "an armed conflict of incredible complexity where ideology, religion, clan rivalry and ethnicity [came] together." (*Washington Post,* August 22, 1993, p. C4)

Under Soviet rule, Tajikistan was the poorest of the republics. After independence, it had "the lowest per capita income, 70% unemployment in rural areas, . . . 5% annual growth in population, the lowest levels of educational attainment and the highest incidence of infant mortality." (*Far Eastern Economic Review,* September 24, 1992, p. 22) The technical and managerial elite, mostly Russians, chose to flee when civil unrest escalated and war broke out. Thus, in Tajikistan, within two years of independence, there was an all-out war involving the Russians and Afghans as well as the Tajiks. Domestically, the economy was on the point of total collapse, and the neo-Communist regime had moved to outlaw all opposition.

Stable democracy is unlikely to emerge in Tajikistan in the foreseeable future. None of the prerequisites that we discussed in Chapter 8 are present to any significant degree. The best that can be hoped for is a cessation of the violence. Of all the Central Asian countries, Tajikistan is definitely in the worst shape. It is not, however, the only one ruled by neo-Communists.

Both Uzbekistan and Turkmenistan had regimes that were throwbacks to the Soviet past. Also, Uzbekistan was concerned that the fighting in neighboring Tajikistan might spill over into Uzbekistan. Thus, it actively aided the Tajik Communists in their efforts to suppress their opposition. (*Washington Post,* February 5, 1993, p. A31)

Unlike Tajikistan's neo-Communist leaders, Turkmenistan's Communist government managed to keep the country "bathed in a deep, Soviet-style calm." (*Washington Post,* March 23, 1993, p. A10) After independence, Turkmenistan's political system remained much the same as it had been under Soviet rule. The Communist Party of Turkmenistan, renamed the Democratic Party, retained control of the Turkmen political-economic system.

In May 1992, Turkmenistan was the first Central Asian country to adopt a post-Soviet constitution. It instituted strong presidential rule. In a presidential election in June, Saparamurad Niyazov, the current president and previous head of the Turkmen Communist Party, ran unopposed, getting 99.5 percent of the vote in a Soviet-style election. "Niyazov told visitors that he feared political activities by competing groups would undermine the political stability that was one of the country's most important selling points for foreign investors." (Brown, 1993a, p. 35)

The Turkmen leadership set out to exploit the country's considerable natural resources, seeking economic ties with foreign countries and corporations. By the beginning of 1992, Western economists judged Turkmenistan to have the best chance of economic success of all the Central Asian countries. (Brown, 1993a, p. 34) Its only competitor was Kazakhstan, which was both larger and richer. Turkmenistan, known as "the Kuwait of [natural] gas," earned over a billion dollars in 1992. Its chief problem was that its gas pipeline ran through Kazakhstan, Russia, and Ukraine, and there was a dispute about how much those countries would pay for Turkmen gas. This caused Turkmenistan to seek foreign investors for a new pipeline to be built through Iran and Turkey. The aim of the Niyazov government was to create economic plenty in order to forestall the development of the chaos that had engulfed other successor countries. Movement toward real democracy was postponed into the indefinite future.

President Niyazov's policies had the support of a large proportion of his people. An ethnic Belarusian, retired and living in Turkmenistan, remarked, "We don't need this democracy. Let them keep it over there." (*Washington Post,* March 23, 1993, p. A16) In view of the economic hardships experienced by most of the people of the former Soviet Union, that is not an unreasonable position. Turkmenistan has peace, and it has the promise of economic security, perhaps even prosperity. What it does not have is the promise of democracy.

Uzbekistan, like Turkmenistan, continued to be ruled much as it had been during the Soviet period, even though it promptly adopted a post-Soviet constitution. The Communist Party was still in charge, but its name was changed to the People's Democratic Party. The president, Islam Karimov, was the former head of the Uzbekistan Communist Party, and the CPSU elite still monopolized important government posts.

With its central location and almost 20 million people, Uzbekistan can be regarded as "the key to the region's stability," but this stability is brittle. Uzbek politics emerged from the Soviet period as "a contest among five regions—Fergana, Khorezm, Samarkand/Bukhara, Surkhandarya/Kashkadarya, and Tashkent—with Fergana and Tashkent the most powerful." (Rupert, 1992, p. 187) As we noted in Chapter 8, any serious political opposition to President Karimov's rule was repressed. At first, he permitted a small, nonthreatening group of intellectuals to be registered as a legitimate political party—giving the appearance (but not the reality) of a pluralistic political system. In 1993, he dispensed with the facade, demanding that all parties and movements reregister. None was able to meet the reregistration deadline. Thus, the major opposition groups were no longer able to function legally, and their members were subjected to harassment. The rationale for this repressive policy was the need for stability in order to attract foreign investment. (Tokgozoglu, 1993)

President Karimov frequently said that in the long run Uzbekistan would become a pluralistic democracy. He did not believe, however, that pluralistic democracy was appropriate in the short run. He cited potential civil unrest as a major reason for his position. The first major outbreak of violence in Central Asia came in the same year (1990) Karimov first became president. It took place in the Fergana Valley, which continued to be restless after independence. Shortly after he was elected the first president of independent Uzbekistan in 1991, civil war broke out in neighboring Tajikistan. He interpreted this event as an example of the violence that could result from political liberalization and a reduction in the use of force. Another factor he used to justify his repressive policy was the fear of the spread of Islamic fundamentalism. This fear led to the passage of a law (and later a constitutional provision) banning political parties or movements from accepting financial support from religious organizations. (Brown, 1993c)

As the most populous Central Asian country, Uzbekistan considers itself a natural leader. This attitude has alienated the other Central Asian countries and interfered with early attempts at regional cooperation. (Brown, 1993a, p. 31) Because of its desire to keep the lid on any serious opposition, Uzbekistan caused friction with Russia by refusing, on occasion, to import liberal Russian publications. Uzbekistan and Russia also clashed over the post-Soviet price of cotton. After a brief flurry of hope when an oil field was discovered in the Fergana Valley in early 1992, Uzbekistan continued to base its economy on cotton—despite the problems of cotton monoculture and the environmental damage already caused by it.

Market reform made little progress after the Karimov government decided to make stability its overriding goal. Thus, Uzbekistan's best hope of improving its sluggish economy is by encouraging foreign investment in order to exploit Uzbekistan's substantial deposits of natural gas, coal, petroleum, uranium, gold, and other rare metals. (Cavanaugh, 1992; Tokgozoglu, 1993)

The prospects for stable democracy in Uzbekistan seem, at best, remote. President Karimov's decision to justify political repression in the name of stability, as well as the fact that the entire government was controlled by former Communists, meant that independence brought little or no real progress toward a less repressive government. The Karimov government's emphasis on power and stability and the stagnation of the Uzbek economy could invite, rather than discourage, political violence. According to one observer, "the repression of the democratic Uzbek nationalists may prove to have removed an important moderating force from the political scene, and the country may find its conservative communist leadership facing an Afghan-supported Islamic insurgency that would finish off hopes for rapid integration into the outside world." (Brown, 1993c, p. 6)

THE SLAVIC COUNTRIES: BELARUS, UKRAINE, AND RUSSIA

Belarus, Ukraine, and Russia have been closely intertwined over the centuries. The Eastern Slavs are defined linguistically. Far back in history, they were distinguished by the version of Slavic that they spoke. Subsequently, three distinct languages developed from this original language: Belorussian (White Russian), Ukrainian, and Russian. (Riasanovsky, 1984, pp. 17, 29)

Politically, they can trace their roots to Kievan Rus, ruled from the current capital of Ukraine, Kiev. Looking back at this history, Alexander Solzhenitsyn, the Russian novelist, spoke out in 1990, calling for the breakup of the Soviet Union and the creation of a Great Russian State made up of these three republics. (*Washington Post,* September 19, 1990, p. A1) The Soviet Union did dissolve, but a Great Russian State did not emerge. Rather, the three countries declared their independence. Russian nationalists in particular, however, believe that Belarus and Ukraine are properly part of Russia and should be incorporated into the Russian Federation. This conviction has caused much friction, particularly between Russia and Ukraine. Reunification was nevertheless attractive to some Ukrainians and Belarusians, who looked at the economic consequences of independence and decided that it was a mistake. (e.g., *New York Times,* September 8, 1993, p. A8)

Like several of the other former Soviet republics, Belarus began its independent existence ruled by conservatives and former members of the Communist elite. The first years of independence were characterized by the unsuccessful attempts of its democratic opposition to wrest control of the government from the Communist leaders and by an effort to shore up Belarus's faltering economy. The fact that the country's leaders were former Communists who still thought and acted much as they had under Soviet rule prevented any significant progress toward a truly post-Soviet political-economic system. The chair of the Belarusian legislature summarized the attitude of the government: "[V]ery competent Western politicians have a poor understanding of our structures. And in many cases, they hold up to us their own, nicely worked-out model. That model can't take root in our soil, not for the time being, at any rate. We have to find other methods." (*RFE/RL Research Report*, January 15, 1993, p. 12) The problem was that the government had no clear alternate program to pursue, so it tended to fall back on the familiar Soviet way of doing things.

The Belarusians retained a Soviet-era legislature that had been elected in 1990. Three-fourths of the members were Communist Party and government officials. This legislature was supposed to serve a five-year term. During the first half of 1992, however, the Belarusian Popular Front and some other political groups mounted a successful petition drive for a referendum on the following question: "Do you consider necessary the holding of elections in the autumn of 1992 to the highest organ of state power [i.e., the legislature] of the Republic of Belarus on the basis of the Law on Elections of People's Deputies of Belarus, the draft of which has been submitted by the [Belarusian] Popular Front opposition in the Supreme Soviet and, in that connection the early disbanding of the present Supreme Soviet?" (*RFE/RL Research Report*, January 15, 1993, p. 9) Enough signatures were collected and validated. But the members of the legislature accused the organizers of violating the law, and they voted to reject the referendum. The chair of the legislature later stated that he saw no violations of the law but voted against the referendum because it was a threat to Belarusian stability.

Meanwhile, Belarus continued to regard the 1990 Declaration of State Sovereignty as a de facto constitution. Although an effort to draw up a new constitution began in July 1990, the drafts were so controversial that the 1990 declaration continued to serve as a constitution during the first years of independence. A post-Soviet election law proved equally difficult to adopt.

There were several reasons for Belarus's post-Soviet political drift. One was the polarization of its politics; its politicians were unable or unwilling to compromise. This led to a situation in which there were fourteen registered parties and almost a hundred different political movements and organizations. Also, until July 1994, there was no leader whose authority had been legitimized by popular election. On July 10, 1994, the Belarusian electorate gave 80 percent of its vote to presidential candidate Alexander Lukashenko. Like previous post-Soviet Belarusian leaders, Lukashenko had no clear or comprehensive set of policy proposals. A Western analyst described him as "economically illiterate, suspicious of foreigners, simplistic in his views." (*Washington Post*, July 13, 1994, p. A20) Thus, the Belarus leadership seemed likely to continue to react to events, rather than to shape them.

One thing was clear, however. Lukashenko favored closer ties with Russia and no major break with the Soviet past. In this, he reflected the views of a majority of Belarusians. Although ethnically diverse, Belarus had no significant problem with nationalism—Belarusian or minority. In fact, a 1993 citizenship law simply conferred citizenship on anyone residing in Belarus. Correspondingly, language was not a problem for most residents. Many, including the prime minister, preferred to speak Russian, and parliamentary debates were in Russian. In fact, the attitude of most of the Belarusian people was one of apathy.

There was, however, one thing the Belarusians did want: a more prosperous economy. By mid-1994, the Belarusian economy was in dire straits, with prices doubling every six to twelve weeks. Even before independence, Belarus had declared its intention to move toward a market economy. But the cautious nature of its political leadership ruled out any immediate, dramatic progress. Rather, Belarusian leaders pursued a policy of strong government control over the economic reform process. As a result, both privatization and land reform were limited—both in the law and in its implementation. When impatience with the government's cautious approach grew and the economy continued to deteriorate, the government justified its position by saying that it needed to study the experience of the former socialist countries of eastern Europe. Lukashenko's campaign platform promised little in the way of more vigorous reform effort and some reversals, particularly in the privatization of industry.

The one area in which the government of Belarus did move decisively was in encouraging foreign investment. During this process, however, it tried to maintain a good relationship with Russia. Belarus depended on Russia for raw materials and as a market for its industrial and agricultural products.

Given the entrenched conservative leadership of Belarus, the chances for rapid movement toward either a stable democracy or a market economy are slight. As in Turkmenistan, the post-Soviet rulers of Belarus are essentially the same as the Soviet rulers. And, as in Turkmenistan, they have adopted the position that stability is to be the primary goal. Stability, however, can lead to stagnation.

During the first years of Belarusian independence neither the political system nor the economy moved very rapidly toward a viable post-Soviet political-economic system. It should also be noted, however, that brutal repression of the opposition did not occur in Belarus as it did in many other former Soviet republics. Thus, the possibility remains that, at the end of the term of the Soviet-era legislature in 1995, a new and more adventuresome leadership might come forward to lead Belarus out of its lethargy.

Both Ukraine and the Russian Federation started out making a much more vigorous attempt to move toward democracy than did Belarus. In both cases, however, most of the people involved in the attempt were products of the Soviet political system, and many were former Communist leaders. Thus, the central political issue in the first years of both Ukrainian and Russian independence was the struggle for political advantage between the executive and the legislature. This was not the ordinary competition for control over decision-making that characterizes all democratic systems. Rather, the struggle was over the basic issue of where more government authority should lie—with the legislature (particularly its leadership) or with the executive.

At the core of the problem is the fact that the Soviet people were used to a government of men, rather than a government of laws. The principle of limited constitutional government was alien to them. Thus, for example, they were likely to think in terms of the person serving as president, rather than in terms of the institution of the presidency. Their politicians and government officials (as well as many outside observers) had the same problem. This mentality tended to lead to decisions made with reference to the particular people occupying government positions, rather than with reference to the long-term effects the decisions might have on the institution being created.

In Ukraine, the focus of conflict was on control over economic decision-making. The crisis came to a head in April 1993, when President Leonid Kravchuk asked the parliament to give him the powers of the prime minister. Because the parliament was dominated by conservative former Communists and Kravchuk, the former CPSU ideological secretary in Ukraine, was proposing to slow down reform, many thought he would succeed. The current prime minister, however, immediately threatened to resign, and the parliament voted overwhelmingly to reject his resignation. In effect, it turned down Kravchuk's request in favor of a less conservative approach to economic reform.

Russia was a decisive player in this conflict. It had traditionally provided Ukraine with oil and gas at subsidized rates. Just before the crucial vote, Russia informed Ukraine that it would insist on world prices, retroactive to April 1.[6] With a budget deficit equal to Ukraine's entire economic output, the conservative parliament had little choice but to support reformists, like the current prime minister Leonid Kuchma. But the parliament continued to vote down Kuchma's more potentially painful economic reform proposals. (*Washington Post*, April 22, 1993, pp. A14, A17) At about the same time, Ukraine went into hyperinflation—with a government that had no comprehensive plan for slowing the rate of inflation. (Johnson & Ustenko, 1993)

In June, the situation worsened when the coal miners of the Donbas region went out on strike. They called for a nationwide popular vote of confidence in the president and members of the parliament, as well as for significant wage and income tax concessions. One of the miners said: "We voted for independence and for Kravchuk because we thought our Ukrainian black earth would make us richer. Instead we have become poorer and poorer, poorer even than our Russian neighbors." One banner read: "President Kravchuk, stop leading your people back to 1933."[7] (*Washington Post*, June 6, 1993, p. A29) The miners got everything they wanted: higher wages, a lower tax rate, and a referendum.

The referendum, scheduled for September 26, 1993, would have posed two questions: (1) Do you have confidence in the president of Ukraine? (2) Do you have confidence in the Supreme Council [the legislature] of Ukraine? (Mihalisko, 1993, p. 54) It was never held, however, because the Ukrainian parliament agreed to new elections two days before the referendum was to be held. Meanwhile, Kuchma, the reformist prime minister, had resigned, and

---

6. Russia later postponed the increase in the price of gas and oil.
7. The year 1933 was the height of the famine in the Ukraine caused by Stalin's collectivization and industrialization policies.

the post was given to an advocate of slow economic reform. Many of the reforms that had taken place were reversed. The former breadbasket of the Soviet Union became, in the words of the *Washington Post* (November 8, 1993, p. A1), a basket case. It was moving back toward a full-fledged Soviet-type command economy. By the end of 1993, Ukraine had the highest monthly inflation rate of all of the successor states, and its leadership had ruled out sweeping economic changes.

Ukraine was on the verge of total economic collapse. An economic crisis of this magnitude was surprising. In the early post-Soviet period, Ukraine had been judged the republic most likely to succeed economically. The situation was troublesome because this growing re-Sovietization and economic decline were taking place in a country with nuclear weapons. Ukraine had initially declared that it wanted to be a non-nuclear country, but all efforts to achieve that goal failed as the political leaders tried to use their nuclear weapons as a bargaining chip for foreign economic aid.

In 1994, the Ukrainian electorate went to the polls twice—to elect a new parliament and to elect a new president. The 1994 parliament was conservative, dominated by Communists who favored closer ties with Russia. The new president was the former reformist prime minister Leonid Kuchma. He agreed with the Communists in emphasizing the importance of closer economic ties with Russia. On the other hand, he campaigned for "harsh measures" to make the Ukrainian economy competitive in the world market, particularly emphasizing more rapid privatization. (*Washington Post,* July 12, 1994, p. A14)

The results of these two elections created the potential for two serious political problems. The fact that both President Kuchma and the parliament wanted closer ties with Russia caused fear among the ethnic Ukrainians who are concentrated in western Ukraine. In some of the heavily Ukrainian districts, Kuchma got less than 4 percent of the vote, whereas in some of the heavily ethnic Russian areas of eastern Ukraine he got almost 90 percent. This voting pattern raises the possibility of serious future ethnic divisions over the issue of Ukraine's relationship with Russia. On the other hand, the election also raises the possibility of strong economic policy differences between the conservative parliament and the more reform-minded Kuchma. This could further damage the already weak Ukrainian economy, which at the time of the election was experiencing a 40 percent decline in production and an estimated 44 percent real unemployment rate. (*Washington Post,* July 12, 1994, p. A14)

In short, Ukraine's chances of establishing either a viable market economy or a stable democracy in the near future seem slight, given the choices made by its leaders and electorate in the immediate post-Soviet period. Ukraine is not likely to begin moving decisively toward those goals until it gains a more unified and reform-minded leadership—probably drawn from a generation younger than its immediate post-Soviet leadership.

Like the rest of the former Soviet republics, Russia had a host of serious problems to overcome before it could move toward stable democracy. The core problem around which the others clustered was the economic problem facing all the newly independent countries: how to create a viable market economy out of the chaos left by the Soviet command economy. Given this central issue, the structure of the lawmaking and implementing institutions was of prime importance. Russia had to decide whether it would be governed by a system that featured a strong president or a strong parliament. This issue gave rise to deadlock while President Yeltsin and the leaders of the Soviet-era parliament argued over the distribution of authority. The first step toward resolving these difficulties was the ratification of a post-Soviet constitution.

As we discussed in Chapter 8, one of the major problems that the Russian government had to overcome in its early years of independence was the inability of its top leadership to master the twin democratic arts of bargaining and compromise. This failure eventually lead to the use of force by President Yeltsin against the Russian parliament. Yeltsin won because the military and security forces supported him. His victory, however, was bought at the price of fighting in the streets of Moscow and the shelling of the parliament building—a building which the Russians called the White House and which had been a symbol of the desire for democracy during the abortive coup of August 1991. Moreover, this victory left Yeltsin deeply indebted to the military.

The parliament was disbanded, its top leadership in jail.[8] This outcome left Russia to be led by a strong executive. President Yeltsin scheduled parliamentary elections and a referendum on a new constitution for December 12, 1993. The constitution presented to the people was one that featured strong presidential rule. (Slater, 1994a) Confusion was created by President Yeltsin's ambivalence about whether to serve out his five-year term or to hold a presidential election in June 1994—two years before the end of the term to which he had been elected during the Soviet period. Yeltsin finally decided to serve out his original term, so only a parliamentary election and constitutional referendum were held.

The Russian electorate approved the constitution, and it elected a new parliament dominated by conservatives and nationalists. The fact that the new constitution gave so much authority to the president seemed to have a leavening effect on the newly elected parliament—especially the lower house (Duma), where the nationalist and conservative forces were strongest. The Duma was so fragmented that the president's veto power was a serious threat to its ability to get anything done. Overcoming a Yeltsin veto by the two-thirds majority constitutionally required would be difficult without a high degree of cooperation among the various factions. (Tolz, 1994)

The Russian parliament began to function in a way that indicated that its leadership had learned something from the deadlock between Yeltsin and the previous parliament. The parliamentary leadership put a premium on cooperation among opposing groups and emphasized that parliamentary effectiveness depended on the members' ability to compromise and present a reasonably united front to the president. (Slater, 1994b) An American who had spent time

8. The lower house of the newly restructured parliament elected in December 1993 (Duma) granted amnesty to the imprisoned parliamentary leaders and the leaders of the 1991 coup.

with Ivan Rybkin, the new speaker of the Duma, characterized him as a person with a real commitment to compromise, adding: "Negotiating, building consensus, hammering out a bipartisan agreement—that's really [foreign to many Russians]. He has a greater than usual ability to step into other people's shoes." (*Washington Post*, March 4, 1994, p. A25)

The future of the institution-building process in Russia will depend—to a large extent—on its ability to resolve at least the most serious of the economic problems that we discussed in Chapter 7. It will also depend on the extent to which the president and the first post-Soviet parliament are able to cooperate and compromise to solve the country's problems. Many factors might disrupt that effort. Two, however, are crucial. One is the possibility that the strong presidency established by the new constitution could open the way to a reversion to autocratic rule. The tradition of rule by a powerful leader is very strong, and a country suffering hardships is prone to fall back on familiar ways of doing things. Thus, the future of real democracy (as opposed to the mere appearance of democracy) could hinge on whether Yeltsin and future Russian presidents permit themselves to be limited by constitutional government.

The other factor that could thwart cooperation between the president and parliament is the growth of nationalism in Russia. Nationalism could lead Russia into unwise adventures abroad and repressive policies toward non-Russian minorities at home. Many commentators thought that the strong showing of the nationalists in the 1993 election was a protest vote against economic hardship, but the growth of nationalist fervor cannot be discounted. It is thus important to take a closer look at regionalism in the former Soviet Union. In particular, it is vital to assess the influence that its disproportionate size and strength will give Russia, as well as Russia's relationship with the non-Russian people of the region—both outside and inside the Russian Federation.

At this point in history, one thing seems clear: No successor country lacks serious obstacles to the creation of stable democracy. Some countries like Estonia give cause for optimism. Others, like Georgia and Turkmenistan, seem virtually hopeless—at least in the foreseeable future. Democracy is not an easy form of government to institute. It requires an appropriate political culture, a reasonably healthy economy, and political skills that are largely absent among the people of the former Soviet Union. The fact that the West is placing so much emphasis on the rapid movement toward democracy may, in many cases, be self-defeating.

What is needed is a policy of aid, both monetary and nonmonetary, that takes into account the difficulties of establishing stable democracy and the fact that most of these countries are ill prepared to meet that challenge. The European democracies and the United States seem to have forgotten that their democratic systems did not appear overnight. Rather, they were the product of long, sometimes tortuous, processes extending over many years. Building a modern democratic nation-state, as well as a modern political-economic system to support it, takes time. To expect the newly independent countries to accomplish so many difficult institution-building tasks successfully in a very short period of time is simply unrealistic.

REFERENCES

Barkin, J. S. & Cronin, B. (1994). The state and the nation: Changing norms and the rules of sovereignty in international relations. *International Organization* 48, 107–30.

Brown, B. (1990). Kazakhs now largest national group in Kazakhstan. *Report on the USSR, 2*(18), 18–19.

———. (1992). Central Asia. *RFE/RL Research Report, 1*(39), 22–25.

———. (1993a). Central Asia: The first year of unexpected statehood. *RFE/RL Research Report, 2*(1), 25–36.

———. (1993b). Tajikistan: The conservatives triumph. *RFE/RL Research Report, 2*(7), 9–12.

———. (1993c). Tajik civil war prompts crackdown in Uzbekistan. *RFE/RL Research Report, 2*(11), 1–6.

———. (1994a). Central Asia: The economic crisis deepens. *RFE/RL Research Report, 3*(1), 59–69.

———. (1994b). Central Asia. *RFE/RL Research Report, 3*(16) 14–16.

Bungs, D. (1993a). The Lats return to Latvia. *RFE/RL Research Report, 2*(16), 33–38.

———. (1993b). The new Latvian government. *RFE/RL Research Report, 2*(33), 14–17.

———. (1994). Latvia: Transition to independence completed. *RFE/RL Research Report, 3*(1), 96–98.

Cavanaugh, C. (1992). Uzbekistan's long road to the market. *RFE/RL Research Report, 1*(29), 33–38.

Clemens, W. C. (1991). *Baltic independence and Russian empire.* New York: St. Martin's Press.

Colton, T. J. (1992). Politics. In T. J. Colton & R. Legvold (Eds.), *After the Soviet Union: From empire to nations* (pp. 17–48). New York: Norton.

Critchlow, J. (1992a). Will there be a Turkestan? *RFE/RL Research Report, 1*(28), 47–50.

———. (1992b). Democratization in Kazakhstan. *RFE/RL Research Report, 1*(30), 12–14.

Fuller, E. (1993a). Transcaucasia: Ethnic strife threatens democratization. *RFE/RL Research Report, 2*(1), 17–24.

———. (1993b). Azerbaijan's June revolution. *RFE/RL Research Report, 2*(32), 24–29.

———. (1994a). The Transcaucasus: War, turmoil, economic collapse. *RFE/RL Research Report, 3*(1), 51–58.

———. (1994b). Armenia's constitutional debate. *RFE/RL Research Report, 3*(21) 6–9.

———. (1994c). The Karabakh mediation process: Grachev versus the *CSCE? RFE/RL Research Report, 3*(23), 13–17.

Girnius, S. (1992). The parliamentary elections in Lithuania. *RFE/RL Research Report, 1*(48), 6–12.

———. (1993a). The Lithuanian economy in 1992. *RFE/RL Research Report, 2*(16), 28–32.

————. (1993b). Lithuanian Democratic Labor Party in trouble. *RFE/RL Research Report,* 2(24), 17–20.

————. (1993c). Lithuanian politics seven months after the elections. *RFE/RL Research Report,* 2(27), 16–21.

————. (1994). Lithuania: Former Communists fail to solve problems. *RFE/RL Research Report,* 3(1), 99–102.

Johnson, S., & Ustenko, O. (1993). Ukraine slips into hyperinflation. *RFE/RL Research Report,* 2(26), 24–32.

Kand, V. (1994). Estonia: A year of challenges. *RFE/RL Research Report,* 3(1), 92–95.

Kionka, R. (1992a). Food shortages and political metaphors in Estonia. *RFE/RL Research Report,* 1(13), 31–33.

————. (1992b). Estonia. *RFE/RL Research Report,* 1(27), 57–61.

————. (1992c). Free-market coalition assumes power in Estonia. *RFE/RL Research Report,* 1(46), 6–11.

————. (1993). Estonia: A difficult transition. *RFE/RL Research Report,* 2(1), 89–91.

Krickus, R. J. (1993). Latvia's "Russian question." *RFE/RL Research Report,* 2(18), 29–34.

Marnie, S., & Whitlock, E. (1993). Central Asia and economic integration. *RFE/RL Research Report,* 2(14), 34–44.

Mihalisko, K. (1993). Ukrainians and their leaders at a time of crisis. *RFE/RL Research Report,* 2(31), 54–62.

Olcott, M. B. (1992a). Central Asia's post-empire politics. *Orbis, 36,* 253–268.

————. (1992b). Central Asia's catapult to independence. *Foreign Affairs, 71,* 108–130.

Paeglis, I. (1994). The financial sector and monetary reform in Latvia. *RFE/RL Research Report,* 3(22), 40–47.

Raun, T. U. (1987). *Estonia and the Estonians.* Stanford, CA: Hoover Institution Press.

Riasanovsky, N. V. (1984). *A history of Russia* (4th ed.). New York: Oxford University Press.

Rupert, J. (1992). Dateline Tashkent: Post-Soviet Central Asia. *Foreign Policy, 87,* 175–195.

Slater, W. (1994a). Russia's plebiscite on a new constitution. *RFE/RL Research Report,* 3(3), 1–7.

————. (1994b). Russian Duma sidelines extremist politicians. *RFE/RL Research Report,* 3(7), 5–9.

Socor, V. (1992). Why Moldova does not seek reunification with Romania. *RFE/RL Research Report,* 1(5), 27–33.

————. (1993). Russia's army in Moldova: There to stay? *RFE/RL Research Report,* 2(25), 42–48.

————. (1994). Moldova's political landscape: Profiles of the parties. *RFE/RL Research Report,* 3(10), 6–14.

Tokgozoglu, Y. (1993). Uzbek government continues to stifle dissent. *RFE/RL Research Report,* 2(39), 10–15.

Tolz, V. (1994). Russia's new parliament and Yeltsin: Cooperation prospects. *RFE/RL Research Report,* 3(5), 1–6.

· 10 ·

HEIRS TO EMPIRE: REGIONAL POLITICS
IN EURASIA

*If Russian nationalism were to rise like a wave and sweep over us,
it would be another huge tragedy. It would lead to enormous
bloodshed.*

SERGEI KOVALEV
(*Washington Post*, October 29, 1991, p. A19)

*I'm afraid that in place of the big empire of the Soviet Union, we
may be seeing the creation of a new, albeit smaller Russian empire.*

TATARSTAN PRESIDENT MINTIMER SHAIMIEV
(*Washington Post*, November 22, 1993, p. A14)

These two quotations capture the major issue facing the newly independent
countries of the former Soviet Union. What role will Russia and Russian nationalism play in Eurasia? The Russian Federation is so much larger and more
powerful than any other country in the Eurasian region (excluding China) that
its dominance is virtually inevitable. Russia itself, however, is not a unified,
stable nation-state. It is still very much engaged in institution-building and
nation-building. It has neither the homogeneity nor the compactness that is
usual for nation-states. During the Soviet period, Russification was one of the
main vehicles for building a Soviet nation. Now that Russia exists independent
of the Soviet Empire, there has been a rise in the overt expression of Russian
nationalism. Where will it lead?

The regions of the former Soviet Union were eclipsed under Communist
rule. With independence they took on new importance. A core question for the
future is: Will new patterns of regional relations replace the traditional imperial patterns, or will the traditional patterns resurface? In this chapter, we
examine various aspects of this question. Will, for example, the Commonwealth of Independent States (CIS) survive as a regional organization? If the
CIS survives, is it likely to develop into an organization that facilitates political
and economic cooperation in the region, or will it simply promote Russian

domination of the "near abroad"? How will the legacy of empire shape regional relations? Will the former Soviet republics that surround Russia forge closer ties with new regional partners?

The major source of stability in the region could be the Commonwealth of Independent States—the focus of the first section of this chapter. It was born as the Soviet Union was dying. Its future, particularly its ability to promote regional cooperation and mutual respect between countries, will determine the shape of regional politics in the immediate future.

Occupying a lion's share of the territory of the Soviet Union and containing over a hundred of its ethnic groups, the Russian Federation poses problems that are qualitatively different from those of the other successor countries. Will it remain a political federation, content to influence its neighbors from afar—only occasionally and selectively making its presence felt on non-Russian soil? Or will it evolve into another empire—possibly expanding its borders as its power grows?

Russia, of course, has serious internal problems that raise questions about its own future territorial integrity. While it has been adopting a more assertive stance toward its neighbors, several of its political subdivisions have been trying to gain more sovereignty.

The future of regional relations may hinge on the status of the military and on the nature of civilian-military relations within Russia. Part two of this chapter, therefore, examines the Russian military. Finally, in part three, we take up the complex issues surrounding the future of the Russian Federation.

THE COMMONWEALTH OF INDEPENDENT STATES AND REGIONAL COOPERATION

After the failed coup of August 1991, the CPSU was disbanded, and Mikhail Gorbachev retained little real influence over events in the Soviet Union. Nevertheless, he continued to insist that the center had to survive and to push for a new union treaty. (*New York Times,* December 22, 1991, p. A13) At the same time, however, Russia's leaders moved to appropriate the ministries and properties of the central government, as well as the property of the CPSU. By November, the Ukrainian leadership had made it clear that Ukraine would not participate in anything that even remotely resembled the old order. The Soviet Union was dead, but some effective means had to be found to make Gorbachev (and, by extension, the rest of the world) understand this. Thus, a primary reason for the creation of the CIS by the Slavic republics (which together accounted for roughly three-fourths of Soviet land and wealth) was to mark the end of the USSR.

The founding of the CIS dates from December 8, 1991, when the leaders of Russia, Ukraine, and Belarus signed a formal agreement in Minsk.[1] On De-

---

1. For a translation of this document, see Sheehy (1992a, pp. 4–5).

cember 21, a protocol to the original agreement made eight other former republics founding members. Only Georgia and the three Baltic republics declined to join. Although the presidents of Azerbaijan and Moldova signed the original agreement, their parliaments did not ratify it, leaving their status ambiguous. Finally, on September 19, 1993, Azerbaijan's parliament ratified its membership. (*New York Times,* September 20, 1993, p. A7) At about the same time, Russia began to put considerable economic pressure on Moldova to join. Moldova's parliament, however, still could not muster enough votes for ratification. Moldova, however, did sign the Treaty of the CIS Economic Union and joined the CIS Committee of Foreign Ministers, as well as a convention on human rights and a convention on the free movement of labor. In addition, Moldova joined and contributed capital to the CIS Interstate Bank. As a result, Russia lifted some of its punitive economic measures but continued others. (Socor, 1994, p. 48) After its defeat by the Abkhazian rebels in the autumn of 1993, Georgia sought military assistance from Russia and promised to join the CIS. After obtaining pledges to vote for ratification from a majority of the members of the Georgian parliament, Parliamentary Chair Eduard Shevardnadze finalized Georgia's membership in December 1993. (Fuller, 1994, p. 57) On March 1, 1994, the Georgian parliament ratified Georgia's membership. When Moldova officially ratifies its CIS membership, the CIS will then include all of the former republics of the Soviet Union except the three Baltic republics.

At the time the leaders of eleven Soviet republics met in 1991 to sign the protocol extending the membership of the CIS, they accepted the resignation of Gorbachev—even though the Soviet president had not yet offered to resign. This action served to emphasize "their resolve to move beyond the Kremlin" while it gently but firmly forced Gorbachev's hand. (*New York Times,* December 22, 1991, p. A1) Boris Yeltsin, for one, realized how important voluntary resignation was to the legitimacy of the new order: "We do not want to carry on the tradition since 1917 of burying our heads of state and having to rebury them later or having to pronounce them criminals. A civilized state should end this practice." (*New York Times,* December 22, 1991, p. A1) Gorbachev finally resigned on December 25, 1991, and the Soviet Union was officially dead.

The creation of the CIS, however, had less to do with a desire to formally disband the Soviet Union and more to do with trying to control the centrifugal forces unleashed by the August coup attempt. This point was not lost on contemporary analysts. One saw a "crude logic" in the decision of the leaders of the three Slavic republics "to unilaterally declare a new course": "Multilateral negotiations were fruitless, the center was discredited, something had to be done fast and only the Slavic republics could do it." (*New York Times,* December 22, 1991, p. A13) This conclusion was premised on the idea that the Slavic republics were in the best position to redefine regional relations for the new era. Another analyst explained the action of the Slavic states along similar—though more pragmatic—lines. He saw Yeltsin as primarily "desperate to keep Ukraine from spinning away" and only secondarily interested in seizing an opportunity to oust Gorbachev. (*Far East Economic Review,* January 9, 1992, p. 13)

The leaders of the Central Asian republics had generally supported Gorbachev's call for a strong center. Kazakh president Nursultan Nazarbayev advocated keeping the military and the nuclear arsenal, as well as the currency and economic reform, under strong central control. Nazarbayev's call for a strong center was supported by the leaders of the other Central Asian republics, with the exception of President Askar Akaev of Kyrgyzstan, who was among the first to support the idea of a loose commonwealth. Not surprisingly, the Central Asian leaders were angered when the December 8 agreement among Russia, Ukraine, and Belarus effectively destroyed all hope of retaining a strong center. They demanded that they be given the right to join the Commonwealth as cofounders. Under pressure from the West (anxious to preserve some semblance of the old union), the Slavic republics acquiesced. Thus, on December 21 the protocol expanding the CIS was signed. (*Far Eastern Economic Review,* January 9, 1992, p. 13)

The CIS agreement recognized the independence of the eleven founders, as well as their existing borders. The eleven concurred that Russia would assume the Soviet seat on the United Nations Security Council. Russia, Ukraine, and Belarus already had seats in the United Nations General Assembly.[2] They agreed to push for the extension of membership to all the other newly independent countries. The top governing body of the CIS was a council of heads of state. The CIS Council was to be assisted by committees in key areas like foreign affairs, defense, and economics. Although a temporary arrangement for military command was accepted, the agreement left unsettled important questions about a common military policy and nuclear weapons control. Thus, the CIS was created to be "a transitional body whose main purpose was to provide a forum in which issues left unresolved by the collapse of the USSR . . . could be dealt with in an orderly way." (Teague, 1994a, p. 9)

Although the long-term outlook for the CIS as a political and economic organization remains unclear, there can be little doubt that the CIS eased the dismemberment of the Soviet Empire. This point was not lost on Belarusian leader Stanislau Shushkevich, who made the following observation: "[T]he question of division, of separation, has been dealt with in a civilized way, on the basis of talks between governments and parliamentary ratification of agreements . . . and that can be considered an achievement." (Mihalisko, 1993, p. 8) Nevertheless, it is useful to consider the possible future of the Commonwealth. Could the CIS affect the course of events with regard to important regional issues like economic development, environmental restoration, armed conflict, and the nuclear issue? The answer to this question

---

2. To secure Soviet agreement on the creation of the United Nations, the Allies had acquiesced to the Soviet demand that each Slavic republic be given its own seat in the General Assembly. Although the three had independent seats, they did not have independent voices.

depends on whether the CIS continues to exist and, if it does, on the kind of organization it becomes. Thus, in the rest of this section we discuss the Commonwealth's potential as an international organization or more specifically as an international governmental organization (IGO).

Before proceeding, however, we must consider what the term "international governmental organization" means. In 1984, Harold Jacobson (p. 8) offered what has become a generally accepted definition:

> An international governmental organization is an institutional structure created by agreement among two or more sovereign states for the conduct of regular political interactions. IGOs are distinguished from the facilities of traditional diplomacy by their structure and permanence. International governmental organizations have meetings of representatives of the member states at relatively regular intervals, specified procedures for making decisions, and a permanent secretariat or headquarters staff. In some ways, IGOs resemble governments, but they are not governments, for the capacity for action continues to rest predominantly with the constituent units, the member states. IGOs can be viewed as permanent networks linking states.

IGOs are particularly well situated to facilitate cooperation among member states. Increased cooperation among members, however, is not absolutely necessary. Thus, the universe of IGOs is a varied one. It encompasses, on the one hand, loosely constituted, multiple-purpose organizations like the Organization of American States (OAS), which serves more as an outlet for discussion and consultation than as a vehicle for joint decision-making. On the other hand, IGOs can be highly structured, single-purpose organizations like the North Atlantic Treaty Organization (NATO), in which joint decision-making is a regular feature. Then, of course, there is the European Union, formerly the European Economic Community (EEC). It has taken joint decision-making among sovereign states to a new plane, becoming the first IGO to transcend national sovereignty in limited but important ways. It is the first truly supranational organization.

Given the wide range of possibilities, how might the CIS evolve? Could it develop into an organization for joint decision-making by its countries? If it does, what range of issues might be within its jurisdiction? Alternatively, could the CIS become only a forum for discussion and consultation among its members? More ominously, could the CIS ultimately serve as a vehicle for Russia to reassert imperial control in the region? The prospects of the CIS can be assessed, first, by exploring the role of international organizations in establishing cooperative relations among states in the international domain. The experiences of three regional IGOs—the Organization of American States, the North Atlantic Treaty Organization, and the European Economic Community—can be used for purposes of comparison. Also relevant are the Warsaw Pact and COMECON (Council for Mutual Economic Assistance).

The OAS, NATO, and the EEC were created under the auspices of American hegemony during the Cold War. The Warsaw Pact and COMECON were similarly established by the Soviet Union. Cold War politics strongly influenced American and Soviet policy preferences, but they figured differently in the two situations. Thus, these regional organizations are quite distinct from one another. All are relevant to this discussion, however, because they offer insights about the possible roles of IGOs when great disparities of power exist among the states involved. There were tremendous differences between the IGOs of the Western alliance and those of the Soviet bloc. The Western organizations were based on relations among truly sovereign states. The Warsaw Pact and COMECON, though officially made up of sovereign states, actually promoted Soviet imperial control over the "outer empire"—the Soviet satellites of eastern Europe. The Warsaw Pact and COMECON cannot tell us anything about building cooperative relations among states, but they can demonstrate how IGOs can be used to try to impose imperial control.

International Governmental Organizations and Regional Cooperation

The first modern example of an international governmental organization was the Central Commission for the Navigation of the Rhine, established in 1815 by the Congress of Vienna. During the course of the nineteenth century the number of international organizations, both governmental and nongovernmental, grew steadily. This growth was in response to the expansion of international commerce, spurred by the Industrial Revolution and the technological advances that resulted from it. (Kegley & Wittkopf, 1993, p. 155) By World War I, there were roughly fifty IGOs. In 1940, there were about eighty and by the early 1960s, the number had exploded to approximately three hundred. (Wallace & Singer, 1970, p. 272; *Yearbook of International Organizations, 1991/92*, 1991, vol. 2, p. 1667)

An expansion of commerce causes the development of an increasingly complex division of labor and thus promotes interdependence within and among sovereign states. Commerce requires recognized, uniform rules of exchange. Within nation-states, under the auspices of government, a structure of uniform rules is accomplished by laws. The rules of exchange are accepted because they are promulgated by the authority and grounded in the legitimacy of the government. In the international domain, where such authority does not exist, rules are nevertheless necessary if commerce or other forms of cooperative relations are to develop. In the international political-economic system, the rules that guide behavior—commercial or otherwise—are not laws because there is no government that can enforce them. Actors in the international domain can *choose* to cooperate and can *agree* to behave according to mutually understood, though not necessarily explicit, rules.[3] International organizations, both

---

3. Consistent with our discussion in Chapter 1 of mechanisms of social control and the extent to which they are intertwined and "rule-bound," we continue to use the generic label "rule" to

governmental and nongovernmental, can facilitate such cooperation and can promote rule-bound behavior.

Of course, this assertion begs an obvious question. If authority in IGOs derives almost completely from their member states and if power continues to prevail in international relations, how can international governmental organizations foster cooperation? The international system is one of self-help. And self-help generally means making and implementing decisions independently. In a self-help environment, cooperation is difficult to achieve.

Cooperation means working together toward mutually desired goals and joint decision-making to determine who can or will do what and when. It requires rule-bound behavior. Partners in a cooperative relationship trust that each partner will honor its obligations to the others. In a self-help environment, actors determine whether it is in their interest to follow the rules on which the cooperative venture is based. At any time, they can defect from the rules and leave their partners in the lurch.

Thus, in the absence of an overarching government that can enforce rules, it is difficult to overcome what can sometimes be rather potent incentives to defect from cooperation. At the very least, actors have to overcome the impulse "to do unto others, before they do unto you"—a defensive incentive to be the first to defect from cooperation. Beyond that, a party to the cooperative agreement may determine that its self-interest is best served by taking advantage of the cooperative posture of its partners and then defecting. In such situations the offensive incentive to defect compounds the defensive incentives to avoid cooperation in the first place.[4]

Given this primary self-help orientation of states, how can IGOs facilitate cooperation among them? How do IGOs help to moderate the impulse of state actors to defect, and how do they promote the rule-bound behavior that cooperation requires? Basically, an IGO provides a forum for attitude change by the individuals who participate in it. Regularized interpersonal contacts in small group settings tend to engender positive attitudes among group members (Angell, 1969; McCormick, 1989; Riggs, 1977) and can lead to the internalization of organizational norms. These norms, in turn, encourage members "to regulate themselves in conflict bargaining situations." (Coplin, 1971, p. 300) Attitude changes thus create conditions conducive to accommodation and thus to cooperation.

So, at a minimum, international organizations create an environment condu-

---

describe what is actually a range of standards that mandate or guide human behavior. This range extends from laws that operate under the formal sanction of government to informal norms—that is, societal rights and obligations that are rooted in tradition and clearly understood by a society's members. When necessary for precision or clarity, we will specify the kind of rule to which we are referring.

4. Scholars have relied on game theory to describe and explain the difficulties of cooperation in international relations. Games have been used to depict situations where there are defensive reasons only ("Stag Hunt") and situations where both defensive and offensive reasons ("Prisoners' Dilemma") impede cooperation (see, e.g., Axelrod, 1984).

cive to cooperation, but they do not always produce it. When they do, international organizations are also *international regimes*. International regimes exist when states choose to establish regularized patterns of cooperative relations and "when the patterned behavior of states results from joint rather than independent decision-making." (Stein, 1990, p. 29) Regularized patterns of cooperative relations and joint decision-making yield sets of rules that inform the actions of states in a given issue area. An international regime, therefore, exists where implicit or explicit rules guide the otherwise independent decisions of state actors. In the context of such a regime, actor behavior becomes more rule-bound, cooperation increases, and conflicts become more manageable.

Although international regimes are frequently international organizations, they do not have to be. (Stein 1990, p. 46) As we consider the prospects for the CIS, this distinction is an important one. If some or all of the CIS members determine that independent decision-making best serves their national interests, the CIS may endure as an IGO, but it will not produce the cooperative behavior necessary for an international regime. Thus, depending on the choices of its member-states, the CIS could develop (or not) in a number of different ways. It could (1) disband; (2) remain a loosely organized forum for discussion and consultation; (3) become intergovernmental in name only as Russia uses it to reassert imperial ambitions; or (4) develop into an international regime (or set of regimes). To appreciate the various possibilities, we need to understand the conditions under which sovereign states will forgo independent decision-making and seek to regularize the patterns of their interactions with other states through joint decision-making.

Conditions under Which States Will Cooperate

States tend to give up independent decision-making when the results of their decisions are undesirable. Independent decision-makers acting simultaneously may create unintended and harmful consequences. For example, when independent decision-makers seek the same thing at the same time, there is a good chance that no one will get it.[5] Such dilemmas can be resolved only when actors agree to cooperate. Each actor is required to give up the most-desired (but unobtainable) option in pursuit of the best *obtainable* outcome. In so doing, the cooperating actors avoid a situation in which they get something considerably less desirable. The risk, of course, is that any actor may cheat and take advantage of the cooperative stance of others by defecting and acting to obtain his or her most-preferred option.

States come together to form international regimes because such regimes increase the rule-bound behavior among their members. They create rules that specify what constitutes cooperation and what constitutes cheating. Under conditions of high risk, actors who choose to give up independent decision-

---

5. In game-theory terms, this situation is the "prisoners' dilemma."

making and enter a regime must be assured of their own ability to identify the cheating of others. Therefore, in situations where there is a relatively high probability that other states will cheat, international regimes require more formality, or rule-bound behavior, than is necessary when cheating is less likely.[6] (Stein, 1990, pp. 39–40)

The highly formalized and intricate process that was required to establish and maintain a security regime through the various arms control and arms reduction treaties negotiated between the USSR and the United States offers the best example of cooperation under conditions of high risk. The stakes are not as high in the realm of economic cooperation, but there are still risks. After World War II, the United States and other market economies established trade and monetary regimes. Formalized in international economic organizations, they included the General Agreement on Tariffs and Trade (GATT), the International Monetary Fund (IMF), and the International Bank of Reconstruction and Development (the World Bank). These regimes were formed primarily to prevent the competitive cheating of the "beggar thy neighbor" policies practiced during the Great Depression. Such policies had resulted in ever-increasing tariff barriers (which restricted access to overseas markets) and in a destabilizing series of competitive devaluations of national currencies.

Another issue area fraught with the dilemma of common interests is the environment. Everyone wants to avoid the devastating consequences of escalating global warming. No one, however, wants to incur the considerable costs associated with altering or abandoning practices that contribute to global warming. Everyone's preferred option would be to behave without any reference to the consequences for the planet's atmosphere. But if all actions were based on the preferred options of individuals, the world would be affected by the devastating consequences of independent decision-making. The leaders of the states that dominate the international political-economic system are only beginning to consider the possibility of cooperation on environmental issues.

In summary, cooperation among state actors in the international system will occur when these actors determine that their interests are best served through joint decision-making and through a rule-bound pattern of state interaction. Although this prerequisite for cooperation can be straightforwardly asserted, the assertion in no way captures the complexity of identifying state priorities and assessing how best to achieve them. Part of the complexity derives from the fact that these are not unrelated processes. The criteria used to set priorities will inevitably have an impact on any assessment of means to the end. For example, if decision-makers identify their policy preferences according to short-term criteria, they will focus on how best to get quick results. Under circumstances where decision-makers focus on short-term goals and short-term

---

6. States come together to cooperate not only under circumstances of common interest, but also under circumstances of common aversion. According to Arthur Stein (1990, pp. 36–40), the risks associated with cooperating under situations of common aversion are considerably less than under circumstances of common interest.

means, the long-term benefits of cooperation (as well as the long-term costs of not cooperating) will be discounted in favor of quick results.

In addition, the mutual benefits of cooperation are more likely to be rejected if decision-makers use *relative* gains rather than *absolute* gains as a decision criterion. If decision-makers choose to gauge their priorities in terms of absolute gains, they ask: "How much do we stand to gain?" If they choose to use relative gains as a measure, they ask: "How will our gains compare with theirs?" In the power-driven domain of international relations, concerns about relative gains abound: "Even if we both could gain from cooperation, they may gain more. They might use their greater gains against us, so we are better off not cooperating at all." This argument can be carried further. Cooperation in the power-dominated environment of international relations can be rejected even when the parties determine they will gain equally from their mutual efforts. Because neither party can control what the other does with the gains derived from cooperation, the parties may choose not to cooperate at all. Under what circumstances, therefore, are international actors likely to adopt absolute instead of relative gains as the criterion for identifying and pursuing their preferences?

Contemporary history offers one example of such a circumstance. In the years immediately following World War II, the United States enjoyed a tremendous military and economic advantage over the other actors in the international system. Thus, choosing absolute over relative gains and pursuing economic cooperation with western Europe and Japan did not compromise its relative power status—at least in the short run.[7] Of course, another important reason for choosing absolute gains and cooperation with these countries was that the United States increased the relative power position of the Western alliance vis-à-vis the Soviet bloc.

American Hegemony and the Formation of Regional IGOs

Let us dwell a little further on the United States and its various global and regional preferences during the post–World War II period. As a military and economic superpower, it spearheaded the formation of many IGOs. Some of them developed as vehicles for cooperation; others did not. Whether or not an IGO created an international regime depended on the preferences of the United States. Russia, relative to its regional neighbors, is now in a position similar to that of the United States during the post–World War II period. An understanding of US preferences, how they were acted upon, and their consequences for international cooperation can shed light on possible avenues of development for the CIS. After all, Russia's preferences and how it chooses to pursue them will have a major impact on the future of the CIS.

---

7. Stein (1984) refers to this as the "hegemon's dilemma." Over the long run, by pursuing absolute gains through cooperation, the hegemon compromises its relative power position.

To demonstrate this point, we focus on three regional IGOs established after World War II: the Organization of American States, the North Atlantic Treaty Organization, and the European Economic Community. Each developed as it did largely because of US policy preferences. Each thus serves as an example of how a regional IGO can develop where great disparities in economic and military power exist among the associated states.

Chartered on April 30, 1948, the Organization of American States was created as an anti-Communist organization; and, in many respects, it represented an attempt to formalize the Monroe Doctrine.[8] In effect, the OAS created obligations for other states without restricting the rights of the United States to take immediate action when necessary to defend its security interests. In 1962 during the Cuban missile crisis, the United States blockaded the coast of Cuba, and the OAS endorsed its actions. Likewise in 1965, when the United States landed troops in the Dominican Republic, the OAS endorsed its actions. Subsequently in the Dominican Republic, the OAS played a central role in peacekeeping until elections were held a year later. Thus, the United States decided independently what constituted its security interests in the Western Hemisphere and then acted to get what it wanted without the prior assent of its OAS partners.

American leaders may have consulted with representatives from the other members of the OAS, but these consultations had relatively little impact on American policy choices. The other members of the OAS generally endorsed American decisions. This choice was preferable to having the consequences of US actions imposed on them, because it projected the image that OAS members were equals—even if the truth was that the United States was more equal than the others. The weaker OAS members believed that endorsing US decisions put them in a more favorable position than actively opposing US decisions would have done (Allman, 1984, pp. 218–219). The Cuban missile crisis and the invasion of the Dominican Republic reveal a pattern of interaction between the United States and the other members of the OAS that falls short of cooperation and joint decision-making. The organization served—and mostly continues to serve—as a forum for discussion and consultation, but it is not an international regime.

The North Atlantic Treaty Organization also emerged as a byproduct of the Cold War. This collective security pact promulgated in 1949 declared that an act of aggression perpetrated against one member would be considered an attack against all. The alliance spawned a formal structure for joint decision-making among its members. Although the United States has occupied a position of leadership and, as leader, has exercised considerable influence, it would be difficult to claim that NATO functions merely as a rubber stamp for US decisions and actions. NATO's role as a vehicle for joint decision-making has

---

8. In 1823, President James Monroe declared that the era of colonization of the Western Hemisphere was over and that the United States would not tolerate any renewed efforts by Europe to establish colonies in that hemisphere.

become increasingly obvious in recent years, even as NATO members have had to reconsider the organization's purpose now that the "Soviet threat" no longer exists.

Why did NATO but not the OAS develop as an international regime? Western Europe was on the geographical front lines of the Cold War. NATO members uniformly perceived the Soviet Union as a threat to their security. They shared a common interest in containing the Soviet Union, and they decided this goal required a collaborative response. NATO members, including the United States, understood that independent decision-making and action would leave them less secure than joint decision-making and action.[9] The same cannot be said of OAS members. They did not occupy the geographical front lines of the Cold War. For members other than the United States, this lack of geographic proximity reduced the perception of threat from the Soviet Union.

NATO included mutually recognized "great powers" in the international community as well as two long-time allies—the United States and the United Kingdom. These two states had already established a cooperative relationship with regard to security and military matters; they had successfully collaborated to defeat Germany in World War II. They could build on this relationship as they confronted the new security threat. There was no equivalent record of partnership among the states of the Western Hemisphere. The United States had a long history of dominating regional politics and saw little need to cultivate cooperative relations. It got what it wanted without them.

The Treaty of Rome (1957) created the European Economic Community. The original six members came together to form a customs union. They agreed to remove tariff barriers among members and adopt a common external tariff vis-à-vis the rest of the world. The breadth and depth of the regime and its accompanying organization have increased over the years. The EEC organization has become the European Union and now has sixteen members, with other states seeking entry. Despite some setbacks, it is moving toward forging its members' economies into one. The creation of the EEC and the interim steps that led up to it would never have happened when they did without the effort of the United States.

"Many of the cooperative arrangements between Western European states immediately following the Second World War can be said to reflect the way, through carrot and stick, the United States structured the choices and preferences of these states." (Stein, 1990, p. 48) Decision-makers in the US viewed economic cooperation in Europe as an important component of their Cold War strategy. They considered solid economic growth on the European continent as the best antidote to communism and, to this end, pushed for the formation of a common market in Europe. The point to underscore is that "great powers can

---

9. The obvious exception to this assessment was France. France preferred an independent stance vis-à-vis the Soviet Union. It left NATO for a number of years beginning in 1966. Some might argue that France got a "free ride" on the security that NATO provided. For more information on collective security and the free-rider problem, see Olson and Zeckhauser (1966).

often structure the choices and preferences of minor powers and thus shape regional outcomes." (Stein, 1990, p. 48)

From this brief examination of regional IGOs three points can be made about the circumstances that give rise to cooperation among states. First, states will choose not to give up independent decision-making in favor of cooperation through joint decision-making, if they get what they want without cooperating. Second, state actors will choose joint over independent decision-making, if they determine that independent action will leave them worse off than cooperation. Factored into this calculation will be considerations of short- and long-term costs versus short- and long-term benefits, as well as the importance of the IGO's purpose to their national interest. Third, great powers can shape the choices and preferences of lesser powers and thereby increase or decrease the likelihood of their cooperation.

Sometimes great powers do not simply aim to shape the choices of lesser states; they seek to control them outright. Under such circumstances, the sovereignty of the controlled states is effectively denied. This is what happened to the Soviet satellite states during the Cold War. The Warsaw Pact, a Soviet-sponsored regional IGO, functioned as a vehicle of imperial control.

The Soviet Empire and Regional IGOs[10]

The formation of the Warsaw Pact was formally announced at a November 1954 Moscow conference. The creation of a defensive alliance of the European Communist states, a reaction against NATO and the rearmament of West Germany, had a negligible impact on the policies of the United States and the Western alliance. Treaty or no treaty, the military establishments of the satellites were already at the disposal of the Soviet Union. Thus, from a Western standpoint, the establishment of a joint command structure hardly made a difference. Soviet troops stationed in eastern Europe after 1955 by virtue of the Warsaw Pact alliance did, however, provide a measure of internal security for the Communist regimes of these countries. This was particularly important in the face of nationalist forces.

Prior to Stalin's death in 1953, local Party officials following directives from Moscow struggled against the remaining bastions of autonomy, like the Catholic Church. They also endeavored to speed up collectivization. Their efforts, however, were only partially successful. The presence of Soviet troops helped these Party officials establish and sustain control. Ironically, the Warsaw Pact, which aimed to legitimize the continued presence of Soviet troops in eastern Europe, led to the strengthening of the satellite states' armies, which sometimes proved difficult to control.

Although the satellite armies were staffed by former Soviet officers and

---

10. In writing this section, we have drawn heavily on Ulam (1988). We cite this work only to acknowledge direct quotations.

closely supervised by security and Party organs, their allegiance could never be taken for granted. As the 1956 uprisings in Poland and Hungary demonstrated, the satellite armies posed a considerable danger to imperial control, and "the possibility of a clash with Soviet troops could not be excluded." (Ulam, 1988, p. 577) In Poland, for example, when events in October 1956 took an alarming turn from Moscow's standpoint and several Soviet military units began to move toward Warsaw, the Polish army was on the verge of counteraction. This was the case even though the Polish army was technically under the command of a Soviet marshal. In the Soviet Union, the problem of maintaining the allegiance of the armed forces in the face of potential nationalist sentiment was handled by stationing troops outside their own national homelands. This was not an option as the USSR endeavored to control the "outer empire." The eastern European satellite countries retained their national armies even though the officers were sometimes from the Soviet Union.

Thus, although the Warsaw Pact was supposed to be an alliance like NATO, it was as much a vehicle for imperial control as it was an organization for collective security. Unlike NATO members, who all recognized a common external threat and willingly suspended independent for joint decision-making, members of the Warsaw Pact were forced to give up decision-making altogether. The United States, as military hegemon of the Western alliance, exercised considerable influence in NATO and used its power to shape the policy preferences of its allies.[11] The United States, however, did not impose its decisions on them, nor did it exercise effective sovereignty over them. The same could not be said of the USSR and the Warsaw Pact countries.

COMECON, established in 1949, was another Soviet-sponsored regional IGO. Its establishment was the Soviet response to the Marshall Plan, a massive economic aid program that the United States launched after World War II to reconstruct the war-torn European economies. The Soviet leadership viewed the US economic program as part of an overall strategy "not only to salvage Western Europe, but through an infusion of American aid to enable Great Britain and France to resume their places as Great Powers and restore the pre-1939 world system." (Ulam, 1988, p. 436) Soviet leaders also worried that an economically vigorous western Europe would exert enormous counterpressure in response to Moscow's efforts to consolidate control over the eastern European satellites. They feared that prosperity in the West would work like a magnet, attracting the countries of eastern Europe. In fact, the USSR had to exert pressure to prevent Poland and Czechoslovakia from joining the Marshall Plan countries.

Adam Ulam characterizes the formation of COMECON as a Soviet propa-

---

11. G. John Ikenberry (1989) argues that in the immediate post–World War II period, US leaders were reluctant to exert influence and to expend resources for rebuilding and defending western Europe. The western European allies had to continually urge the United States to greater levels of influence and involvement in the region. Ikenberry uses the notion of "empire by invitation" to describe the situation.

ganda ploy. The Soviet leadership was slow to recognize the utility of economic aid in the conduct of modern diplomacy. During the early postwar period, the Soviet Union demonstrated a preference for exploitation over aid. The postwar trade agreements that the Soviet Union imposed on the countries of eastern Europe are a case in point. Through these agreements, the Soviet Union practiced "unabashed exploitation ... by means ranging from terms of trade weighted heavily in favor of Russia to the even more blatant device of joint stock companies." (Ulam, 1988, p. 436) Although COMECON was established as a counterpart to the Marshall Plan, it was initially used as a mechanism to facilitate the exploitative practices already in place. Not until the Khrushchev era did the organization begin to reflect the purpose articulated in its charter: to coordinate the economies of its members—presumably for their mutual benefit.

Using COMECON, the Soviet leadership aimed to integrate the command economies of eastern Europe with the economy of the USSR through specialization of trade and production. The idea was to forge economic links between the eastern European satellites and the imperial center. These links would be much like those between Moscow and the republics of the Soviet periphery. COMECON failed to achieve this end. One reason for this failure was that, despite economic and political pressure, the satellite countries resisted economic integration and the specialization that it implied. Each wanted a broad industrial base; not one wanted to become a specialized producer and risk sacrificing its long-term economic independence.[12] COMECON, like every other economic IGO except the European Union, did not possess supranational authority over its members. Each member had veto power and opposed all efforts to give the organization supranational authority.

Another reason for COMECON's failure to closely link the economies of the satellites and the USSR was that integrated planning arrangements among the members of COMECON never developed. Some economic coordination took place, but only preliminary steps were taken to generate common prices, cost schedules, and a convertible COMECON trading currency. (Gregory & Stuart, 1994, p. 214) Thus, when COMECON was dissolved on January 1, 1992, it had largely failed to serve the imperial designs of the Soviet Union. Because of its members' interest in maintaining national economic independence, COMECON's ability to function as a vehicle for joint decision-making on economic matters had been limited.

Our examination of two sets of regional IGOs established under the auspices of their respective superpowers has given us some idea about the range of possibilities open to the Commonwealth of Independent States. The CIS, too, is a regional IGO characterized by great disparities of power among its members—specifically between Russia and the other members. In the next section we

---

12. This tension between efficient specialization and economic independence also exists among states with market economies.

speculate about the CIS and its prospects as a regional IGO. Relations among CIS members in the foreseeable future are likely to be defined by three broad but pivotal and interrelated issue areas: security, economics, and the environment.

The CIS and Prospects for Regional Cooperation

In the domain of international relations, issues of security—"the measures states take to protect their territory"—are of paramount concern. (Art & Jervis, 1992, p. 2) The condition of mutual dependence pervades the international domain, but nowhere does it affect relations among states more ominously than with regard to security. This is the case because "the security of one state is contingent upon the behavior of other states." (Art & Jervis, 1992, p. 2) What one state does to safeguard its security is substantially dependent on what other states do. What states do to protect their security is also contingent on how their leaders define their security needs, and this is very subjective. What constitutes national security, therefore, is not "the absence of threat to acquired values," an objective definition of security, but rather, "the absence of fear that such values will be attacked." (Wolfers, 1962, p. 150) The fear of threat, in turn, stems from historical experience that has become ingrained in the political culture of a society.

We have referred many times to Russia's historical preoccupation with security. This preoccupation is not unwarranted. Over the centuries, Russia has been invaded numerous times. This fact of history cultivated a response that ultimately came to typify Russian and Soviet foreign policy: the creation of buffer zones. By controlling adjacent territories and the peoples who inhabited them, the Russians tried to discourage the invasion of the Russian heartland. More important, buffer zones gave the Russian and Soviet military advance points from which to fend off an attack from territories outside the empire. Security concerns, therefore, do much to explain the territorial expansion of the Russian Empire and the creation of the "outer empire" of eastern European satellites. Now that the Soviet Empire has collapsed, what security concerns does Russia have?

The Cold War is over, and the high-stakes political and military conflict between the Western alliance and the Soviet bloc is a thing of the past. Russia has inherited most of the Soviet strategic nuclear arsenal and can deter any number of would-be aggressors. Thus, Russia is unlikely to have to contend with a serious challenge to its territorial integrity from any of its former rivals: the United States, Europe (especially Germany), Japan, and China. Russia's political and territorial integrity may be at greater risk from nationalist ferment within the former Soviet republics. These conflicts could incite nationalist sentiments among ethnic groups within the Russian Federation and threaten the integrity of Russia itself. Russia may actually face a more significant threat to its security from the "near abroad" than from its traditional international rivals.

This assessment, it must be noted, does not address the subjective dimension of security. Political cultures do not change overnight, and it would be optimistic to expect the Russian people's culturally ingrained insecurities to evaporate.[13]

In early 1994, for example, moderates were the architects of Russian foreign policy. Their interpretation of Russian security interests in the region can be inferred from their words and actions. First, the moderates opposed the expansion of NATO. Lieutenant General Dmitri Kharchenko, writing in *Red Star* (*Krasnaia Zvezda*), the official Russian Defense Ministry newspaper, warned that the expansion of NATO "could lead to xenophobia and increase the popularity of radical nationalist parties and organizations." He added that it would "require rethinking our defense conceptions [and] redeployment of army forces." (*Washington Post*, January 6, 1994, p. A16)

Second, the moderates insisted that Russia be accorded a special protective relationship with the former Soviet republics. On this point, Russian Foreign Minister Andrei Kozyrev stated, "This is simple reality." (*Washington Post*, January 22, 1994, p. A10) Speaking generally about Russia and its relations with the "near abroad," President Boris Yeltsin said in a speech that marked the opening of the new parliament, "It is Russia's mission to be first among equals." (*Washington Post*, January 12, 1994, p. A13) In fact, "the reassertion of its hegemony over the former Soviet Union and, to a lesser extent, East Central Europe"[14] is clearly becoming "the centerpiece of Moscow's foreign policy strategy." (Crow, 1993, p. 1)

Third, the moderates opposed Ukraine's expressions of desire for, or intent to, establish independent control over a portion of the nuclear arsenal inherited from the USSR. They aimed to use political and economic pressure to force Ukraine into giving up its nuclear arsenal. Ukraine's deteriorating economy and the confluence of Russian and American interests on this issue gave a considerable boost to their efforts. Economic hardship gave Russian and American leaders considerable leverage over Ukraine on the nuclear issue. It made Ukrainian leaders more susceptible to the carrots and sticks that both the United States and Russia wielded (for example, the promise of increased aid and the threat of decreased access to and increased prices for critical imports).

How does or could the Commonwealth of Independent States serve Russian security interests? In the short run at least, it is unlikely to develop into a collective security alliance along the lines of NATO. A joint military command was tried—actually, it was just held over from the days of the union. Not surprisingly, the effort collapsed within eighteen months. The dissolution of the joint military command, announced in Moscow on June 15, 1993, marked in many respects the demise of "the last surviving 'all-union' institution of the former USSR." (Foye, 1993b, p. 45)

---

13. For this reason many analysts, including George Kennan, argue that it would be imprudent for NATO to expand its membership to include the states of eastern Europe and the Baltic region. (*McNeil/Lehrer NewsHour*, December 16, 1993)

14. East Central Europe is composed of Poland, Hungary, the Czech Republic, Slovakia, Romania, Bulgaria, and the countries of the former Yugoslavia.

Disagreements about the disposition of the Soviet military legacy had plagued the CIS from the start. Several CIS members, most notably Ukraine, grew increasingly concerned that the joint military command "would continue to represent the interests of Moscow rather than those of the CIS community as a whole." (Foye, 1993b, p. 45) Russian leaders discovered that their security interests were not being advanced either. Russia was not willing to finance a truly multilateral defense organization, and Russian determination to gain control over the nuclear weapons outside of Russia made the other CIS members suspicious. They feared that gaining control of these weapons was Russia's sole motivation for wanting a joint command. Moscow discovered that it could pursue its security interests "on the basis of bilateral agreements with other former Soviet states, minus the fiction of CIS involvement." (Foye, 1993b, p. 45)

At the same time, however, Russian leaders did not find the CIS entirely useless in security matters. Although Russia did not need to resort to joint decision-making to safeguard its security interests in the region, it continued to find the CIS useful. For example, in October 1993, Georgia's leader Eduard Shevardnadze requested Russia's military support in his struggle with the Abkhazians. In return, Russia asked for a promise that Georgia would join the CIS—something Georgia had resisted doing for almost two years. Russian leaders obviously believe that the CIS lends some sort of legitimacy to Russia's ongoing military presence and active interventions in the former republics. In CIS member Tajikistan, twenty-five thousand Russian troops propped up the neo-Communist Tajik government. Moreover, Tajikistan ceded nearly complete control over its economy to Moscow, "adopting Russia's ruble as its currency and letting Russia dictate the state budget." (*Washington Post,* January 8, 1994, p. A20) In Azerbaijan, the parliament ratified the CIS treaty only when it was made clear that Russia's aid could prove useful in Azerbaijan's armed conflict with Armenia.

Russian leaders have indicated that they are going to do what they think is necessary to prevent the creation of "security vacuums" along their country's perimeter. They prefer to take these actions under the auspices of the CIS, but they have certainly not ruled out the possibility of unilateral action. Their attitude seems very much like the US leaders' attitude toward the OAS. Although the OAS charter forbids unilateral military interventions in the Western Hemisphere, the United States has ignored this provision when its security interests were at risk. American leaders, however, have demonstrated a preference for acting under OAS auspices when possible and convenient. The same may be true for Russia and the CIS. (Lynch, 1994, p. 13)

Consistent with this position, Russia is actively promoting the idea that the United Nations and the Conference on Security and Cooperation in Europe (CSCE) should recognize the CIS as both a regional and an international organization. Russia's efforts are "closely connected with Moscow's reassertion of its influence in the former USSR, a trend that has come clearly into focus. . . ." (Crow, 1994, p. 33) Particularly important to Russia is international recognition of the CIS's and, by extension, Russia's role as regional peacekeeper.

"Peacekeeping . . . is a key element in Russia's general policy of recapturing and preserving its influence in this region." (Crow, 1994, p. 37) Peacekeeping provides a rationale for maintaining military bases in places where the presence of Russian troops would otherwise be deemed undesirable. Broadly interpreted, it also allows Russia a vehicle for opposing "aggressive nationalism" and for intervening to protect the rights of ethnic Russians living in the "near abroad." From Russia's perspective, moreover, international acceptance of the CIS serves an important defensive function. It is likely to prevent the deployment of other international forces for peacekeeping in what Russia considers "its exclusive sphere of vital interests." (Crow, 1994, p. 37)

Why would the other countries of the region choose affiliation with an organization that seems only to serve Russia's interests? The Baltic states, which refused to join the CIS, have found that opposing Moscow is difficult and potentially dangerous. Moscow removed its troops from Lithuania fairly rapidly but was far slower to withdraw troops from Estonia and Latvia. The Balts protested, but they could do little to force Russia to remove its military units. (Bungs, 1993; Kionka, 1992) Moreover, all three of the Baltic countries have felt the pinch of "energy shocks" resulting from the fact that Moscow has chosen hard-line energy export policies toward Soviet successor countries that have tried to go their own way in foreign policy. (Kramer, 1993) Countries in turmoil, like Georgia and Azerbaijan, have been driven to CIS membership because it has been a stipulated condition for Russian assistance. Thus, the CIS is unlikely to develop as an international regime for collective security. However, Russia's efforts to strengthen the CIS and obtain international recognition for it do indicate that the CIS could develop as an organization that advances Russia's security interests.

Will the CIS be more likely to promote true cooperation among its members on economic issues? The challenge in the economic sphere is to replace the imperial pattern of dominance by the center over the periphery with new patterns of market interdependencies. It would not be surprising, however, to find the Soviet successor countries avoiding even market-generated interdependencies. This is exactly what happened after the breakup of the Austro-Hungarian Empire in 1918. The newly created states disrupted long-standing commercial relationships when they established their own tariff barriers. They did this to obtain customs revenue to fund their fledgling governments, but they also wanted to create a measure of national economic independence.

In March 1992, all of the CIS members except Turkmenistan signed an agreement on principles of customs policy. They agreed to "try to secure the free movement of goods across signatories' boundaries and a common customs policy with third countries." (Marnie & Whitlock, 1993, p. 58) This agreement would seem to indicate a desire for a significant measure of cooperation among CIS members. But trade among the CIS countries markedly declined after they became independent. Instead of trading with former Soviet republics, CIS members increasingly formed trading relationships with countries outside the CIS. The World Bank has estimated that trade among the newly independent countries dropped by 50 percent in 1991 and 1992. For example, the proportion of Kazakhstan's exports that went to the former republics dropped from 91 percent in 1990 to 80 percent in 1992. Trade among CIS members continued to decline in 1993. (Whitlock, 1994, p. 15)

The possibility for economic cooperation has been severely limited, at least in the short run, by (1) the poor economic performance of all CIS members, (2) divergent economic policy choices, and (3) persistent trade imbalances that proved particularly detrimental to certain CIS members. In 1992, for example, economic coordination among CIS members was seriously compromised by the members' divisive monetary policies and efforts to increase sovereignty. These created particularly serious problems for Russia, so Russia responded with a number of unilateral monetary and trade policies that placed it in a more advantageous position. These included restricting the use of ruble credits by the other former republics. (Whitlock, 1994, p. 14)

This move raised the issue of the extent to which Russia would permit the other newly independent countries to continue to use the ruble as their primary currency. It also raised the issue of whether the CIS members would choose to continue to use the ruble or to establish their own currencies. At first, only one CIS member, Ukraine, chose to establish its own currency. Less than a year later, Kyrgyzstan made the same decision. The others decided to continue to use the ruble and thus became part of what came to be known as the ruble zone. Some elected to use the ruble as their sole currency (the Central Asian countries); others used the ruble along with their own national currencies (Belarus, Moldova, Armenia, and Azerbaijan). (Whitlock, 1993b, p. 36)

From the beginning, maintaining the ruble zone strained economic relations among the CIS members. The independent central banks of the members generated ruble credits that enabled them to run trade deficits and thus draw finished goods and resources from other CIS members—most notably Russia. This practice involved the transfer of scarce and valuable national products from the country with the trade surplus (usually Russia) to the country or countries with the trade deficit. (Whitlock, 1993a, p. 48) In effect, a bizarre "beggar thy neighbor" situation was created, largely at Russia's expense. In the summer of 1993, Russia called back all of its rubles and issued a new ruble. This action put the currency more fully under the control of Russian monetary authorities, and it forced the other CIS members "either to negotiate a coordinated monetary policy with Russia or to abandon the ruble altogether." (Whitlock, 1993b, p. 34) Thus, Russia gained control over both the use of ruble credits and the use of cash.

These moves hastened the end of the ruble zone. Outside of Russia, these actions were seen as an ultimatum: "Either stay in the ruble zone under Russian terms (that is, subordinate [your] monetary policies to the Russian Central Bank) or leave the zone and introduce [your] own national currencies." (Whitlock, 1994, p. 15) Turkmenistan and Moldova were the first to respond. They decided to leave the ruble zone. Belarus, Armenia, Kazakhstan, Uzbekistan, and Tajikistan signed preliminary agreements with Russia about the establishment of a new ruble zone. When it came to issuing the new rubles, however, Russia laid down such strict rules that Armenia, Kazakhstan, and Uzbekistan decided to stop using rubles and introduce their own national currencies. Belarus and Tajikistan decided to continue using rubles. At least in part, their decisions stemmed from the fact that conservatives took over the Belarusian government in early 1994, and civil violence gave Russia effective control of the Tajik economy.

Thus, as of 1994, the CIS seemed unlikely to evolve anytime soon into a vehicle for economic cooperation and coordination among its members. Most of its members had opted to introduce their own currencies, thereby enhancing their economic sovereignty. Trade between CIS members was declining significantly, and the members were looking as much toward the establishment of trade relations with countries outside the CIS as with their fellow members. These events, coupled with members' divergent strategies for economic development, left little basis for the creation of increased economic cooperation through the CIS.

For the foreseeable future, however, economic autonomy for the member countries will be limited by their continued interdependence with reference to some commodities, the dominant position of the Russian economy, and "relatively porous borders." (Whitlock, 1994, p. 17) As if in recognition of this reality, three of the Central Asian countries—Kazakhstan, Uzbekistan, and Kyrgyzstan—announced on February 1, 1994, the formation of a "common economic space." (Brown, 1994, p. 33) The main purpose of this agreement was to eliminate trade barriers. To this end, it sanctioned the removal of customs posts on their common borders. The agreement was in no way meant to inhibit bilateral economic relations between any of these three countries and other countries, nor was it seen as conflicting with the economic policies and programs of the CIS. (Brown, 1994, p. 33)

Thus, contradictory trends abound within the CIS on the matter of future economic relations. Some promote increased economic independence while others encourage greater cooperation. Because of these trends and because policymakers in the CIS have continued to assert the desirability of some form of integrated economic union, we cannot dismiss the possibility that eventually the CIS could become a vehicle for economic cooperation.

Cooperation by CIS members on environmental issues, however, is highly unlikely—at least in the immediate future. For example, the Aral Sea is rapidly drying up because of Soviet decisions about irrigation and agriculture along the rivers flowing into it. This has had a harmful effect on the regional climate and on the health of many of the Central Asian people. The Central Asian countries could choose to work cooperatively to prevent additional environmental damage. But they would have to weigh the long-term benefits of safeguarding and restoring this valuable resource against the short-term costs of changing the practices that have created the problem. The main short-term cost is an economic one. To stop taking water for irrigation from the rivers feeding the Aral Sea would eliminate valuable agricultural land.

The affected countries need this agricultural land. Thus, they would have a major economic incentive to defect from cooperation—or, to refuse to cooperate in the first place. There would also be an incentive to cheat—to use restricted water for irrigation. Conceivably, the CIS could play a supervisory role to discourage cheating. But given the current state of the economies of the affected countries, it is unlikely that they will be willing or able anytime soon to absorb the costs associated with eliminating or significantly reducing the irrigation that has so damaged the Aral Sea.

Thus, in three crucial areas—security, economics, and the environment—the CIS is not now playing a major role in regional cooperation. Moreover, the dominance of Russia raises the issue of whether the CIS will be able to establish a truly cooperative regime anytime in the near future. Currently, Russia seems to be using the CIS to advance Russian interests in the region rather than to build an international cooperative regime. Particularly important in this connection is the presence of Russian military units stationed in a large number of the former Soviet republics. These armed forces, combined with Russia's claim to a special status within the region, give Russia a means to assert its control over many of its neighbors.

THE RUSSIAN MILITARY

At the time of the breakup of the Soviet Union, the Soviet military had more than 4 million men-at-arms. Over half of them were conscripts serving two-year tours of duty. The largest branch was the army, with just under 1.5 million troops. The navy and the air defense troops numbered about a half-million troops each, followed by the air force with 460,000 and the Strategic Rocket Forces with 260,000. Nearly a half-million additional soldiers were assigned to work in railroad and construction units. The Soviet Union, in short, had the largest military in the world. The enlisted men and conscripts reflected the ethnic diversity of the Soviet Union, but the officer corps was overwhelmingly Slavic. (*Washington Post*, November 18, 1990, p. A28)

The withdrawal of military units from the satellite states of eastern Europe created a major problem for the Soviet military. Housing, always in short supply in the Soviet Union, was not available to accommodate the influx of servicemen and officers. Many of these troops were accustomed to a standard of living in the satellite states relatively higher than the living standards of their counterparts in the Soviet Union. What they came back to was a standard of living much inferior to the norm for the Soviet Union. As early as 1990, more than 160,000 military families lacked housing altogether, and another 74,000 were living in substandard conditions. (Foye, 1990, p. 5) By 1992, 195,000 officers were without housing, forced to live in makeshift shelters or with friends and relatives. (*Washington Post*, June 21, 1992, p. C4) The severe morale problems caused by such accommodations were aggravated by the "loss of face" resulting from the withdrawal from the eastern European satellites. (Foye, 1990)

In addition to the troops stationed in eastern Europe, the Soviet Union had military installations throughout the Soviet Empire. When the empire broke up, most of these troops stayed where they were while retaining allegiance to

Moscow. One exception was Ukraine, which laid claim to many of the troops stationed on its soil, including the Black Sea fleet. Ukraine demanded that the soldiers stationed there choose between Russia and Ukraine. (Foye, 1992; *Washington Post,* April 11, 1993, p. A24) The Ukrainian situation notwithstanding, most of the former Soviet career military eventually became part of the Russian armed forces, which numbered approximately 2.1 million in 1993. (Lepingwell, 1993b, p. 19) Given the already difficult housing situation created by the troops returning from eastern Europe, Russia did not attempt to bring home most of the servicemen stationed in the republics of the former Soviet Union. Thus, by the end of 1993, it was estimated that almost two hundred thousand Russian troops were stationed in the "near abroad." (*New York Times,* November 30, 1993, p. A1)

Russia's military is significantly weaker than the military of the Soviet Union and is facing a severe manpower shortage and low morale among the troops. (Foye, 1993c; Lepingwell, 1993a) As weak and demoralized as the Russian army is, however, many of the other former republics have virtually no military at all and are thus vulnerable to Russian threats to their sovereignty.

During 1993, it became clear that Russia was developing a military strategy that would allow it to reassert its hegemony over the other newly independent countries. This policy was couched in terms of peacekeeping. Beginning with a speech by Yeltsin on February 28, 1993, Russia made a series of proposals that amounted to the articulation of a special responsibility that Russia would assume for settling conflicts in the Eurasian region. Yeltsin's initial statement was: "I believe that the time has come for authoritative international organizations, including the United Nations, to grant Russia special powers as guarantor of peace and stability in this region." (Crow, 1993, p. 2) The military posture appropriate to such a regional strategy is one of rapidly deployable airborne troops instead of the huge tank armies that typified the Soviet posture during the Cold War. Having such units would permit Russia to withdraw the vast majority of its troops from the "near abroad." It would leave only "a presence along some of the troubled borders, like that between Tajikistan and Afghanistan." (*New York Times,* November 29, 1993, pp. A1, A10)

Given the existing state of the Russian military, however, it will be some time before Russia will be able to establish such a rapid deployment force. Thus, there is some question about whether Yeltsin's remarks reflected a new policy or an attempt to rationalize and validate events that were already taking place. After the collapse of the Soviet Union, the Russians had tried to create comprehensive civilian control over the military but had failed. Consequently, the Yeltsin government was faced with a far-flung military that was essentially out of control, with local officers taking actions that were neither ordered nor approved by the Yeltsin government. (Lepingwell, 1993a) Sergei Rogov, a military specialist in the Russian Institute for the Study of the USA and Canada, was of the opinion that these local actions had the tacit approval of Yeltsin: "For this I blame Yeltsin, who believes that letting the military do what it wants is safer politically, so the army is uncoupled from the weaker Russian state." (*New York Times,* November 30, 1993, p. A12)

In particular, Rogov had in mind the situation in Moldova. The Russian nationalist uprising on the east bank of the Dniester River had proved intractable, despite the fact that Russians were a relatively small minority within the local population. The Russians who declared this region to be the independent "Dniester Republic" have been strongly supported by the Russian general Alexander Lebed and by the Russian 14th Army. General Lebed and the 14th Army took an active role in fighting the Moldovan troops that were trying to defeat the Russian nationalist forces. (*Washington Post,* June 25, 1992, p. A3) The general cast himself in the role of a "peacekeeper": "My units stopped the war, and I provided for the introduction of peacekeeping forces while the politicians make up their minds, which they're taking an inadmissibly long time to do." (*New York Times,* May 21, 1993, p. 4) The fact that many military officers in the "near abroad" have scant loyalty to the Russian High Command is indicated by General Lebed's comment: "I'm a cat who likes to walk by himself." (*New York Times,* November 30, 1993, p. A12)

In effect, Moscow wields little control over the Russian armed forces. This situation is unlike that which existed in the former Soviet Union. One thing that could be said about the Soviet military was that it had an effective authoritative command structure. The chain of command from top to bottom was intact and fully functioning. The lack of an effective command structure in the Russian military, coupled with the military's heavy electoral support for Russian nationalist and neo-Communist candidates and parties in the December 1993 parliamentary election, creates a dangerous situation.

Moreover, Russia's new peacekeeping posture leaves Russia open to the argument that there is little reason for Russian troops to withdraw from the "near abroad" because they will probably have to return. Is the Russian military the leading edge for an expansionist Russia? According to one commentator: "The military believes there will soon be some sort of reconstituted union. It's not just imperial nostalgia, and it could be very dangerous." (*New York Times,* November 30, 1993, p. A12) Such statements cause considerable concern, not only in many of the independent states (like Latvia and Estonia) but also in the West. Thus, we are brought inevitably to the question, Will peacekeeping (conducted under the auspices of the CIS or not) become Russia's way of restoring its dominance over the former Soviet periphery?

In turn, this question raises the question of the future of Russia. Will it become a stable democratic federation, or will Moscow reinstitute its imperial rule over a periphery made up of the non-Russian subunits to the east and to the south (possibly expanding into the "near abroad")? Alternatively, could Russia's ethnic and political divisions cause Russia to disintegrate like the Soviet Union before it? The relationship between Moscow and the various political subdivisions of the Russian Federation has not been an easy one. Three of the subdivisions refused to participate in the December 1993 parliamentary elections and thus are not represented in the Russian Duma. Is Russia, like the Soviet Union before it, vulnerable to internal ethnic and political forces that are resistant to rule from Moscow? Although the 1993 Constitution gives the ethnically oriented republics considerable sovereignty, it may prove insufficient.

THE FUTURE OF THE RUSSIAN FEDERATION

Russia's constitutional structure is a federal one. Unlike the relatively simple federation of states making up the United States, the Russian Federation has 89 political subdivisions: 21 republics, 1 autonomous region (*oblast'*), 10 autonomous districts (*okruga*), 49 administrative regions, and 6 provinces (*kraia*). (Slater, 1994, p. 24) In addition, Moscow and St. Petersburg are federal cities that have a status equivalent to an oblast. (Teague, 1993) The 1993 Russian Constitution gives less autonomy to the political subdivisions than did previous draft constitutions. It does, however, give them representation in the Russian parliament. The upper house, the Federal Council, is composed of two representatives from each political subdivision.

The republics of the Russian Federation encompass the traditional land of the indigenous groups after whom they are named (see Table 10-1 and Map 10-1). These republics pose the greatest threat to the territorial integrity of Russia. The threat arises from the fact that the indigenous people regard their

TABLE 10-1
Republics of the Russian Federation

Adygea
Bashkortostan
Buryatia
Chechenia
Chuvashia
Dagestan
Gorno-Altai
Ingushetia
Kabardino-Balkaria
Kalmykia
Karachay-Cherkessia
Karelia
Khakassia
Komi
Mari-El
Mordvinia
North Ossetia
Sakha
Tatarstan
Tuva
Udmurtia

Adapted from: Russia and the newly independent nations of the former Soviet Union (map). Washington, DC: National Geographic Society, March 1993.

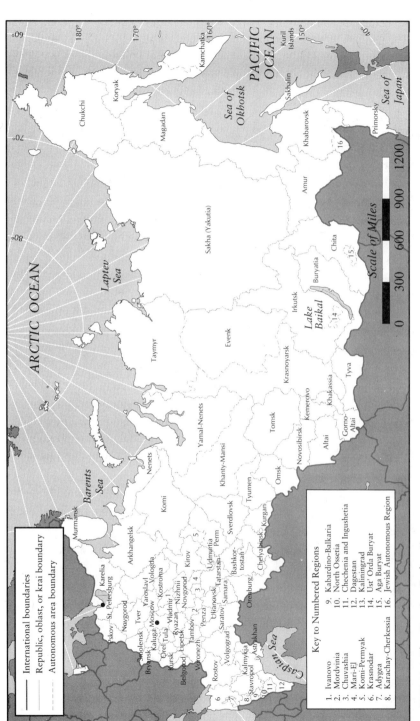

MAP 10-1 The Russian Federation

Source: Aleksandr Sobyanin, Eduard Gelman, and Oleg Kayunov, "The Political Climate in Russia in 1991–1993," *Mirovaya ekonomika i mezhdunarodnye otonosheniya,* no. 9, 1993.

Key to the map:

International boundaries
Republic, oblast, or krai boundary
Autonomous area boundary

Key to Numbered Regions

1. Ivanovo
2. Mordvinia
3. Chuvashia
4. Mari-El
5. Komi-Permyak
6. Krasnodar
7. Adygea
8. Karachay-Cherkessia
9. Kabardino-Balkaria
10. North Ossetia
11. Chechenia and Ingushetia
12. Dagestan
13. Kaliningrad
14. Ust' Orda Buryat
15. Aga Buryat
16. Jewish Autonomous Region

Scale of Miles

0   300   600   900   1200

republics "as the embodiment of their national statehood." In addition, Soviet nationalities policy "promoted the idea that these groups had a right to national statehood and what goes hand in hand with it." (Sheehy, 1993, p. 34) The republics vary greatly in size and population, as well as in economic potential. The largest (Sakha) contains more than 3.1 million square kilometers; the smallest (Adygea), only 7,600 square kilometers. The populations of Bashkortostan and Tatarstan are the largest (about 4 million each). The least populous, Gorno-Altai, has less than two hundred thousand people. The richest are Sakha (especially in gold and diamonds), Tatarstan (petroleum), and Bashkortostan (petroleum).

These facts have significant implications for the future of Russia, because some of the strongest separatist or sovereignty movements have arisen in the largest and richest republics. To date, supporters of these movements have seldom called for complete independence from Russia. Rather, they have wanted more local control over their lives and economic resources (*Washington Post,* May 25, 1992, p. A12) The push for increased local control began during the Soviet period. During 1990, almost all of the autonomous republics and autonomous oblasts in the RSFSR adopted declarations of sovereignty, but only one declaration—Tatarstan's—did not acknowledge connection with the Russian Republic. (Sheehy, 1993, p. 36)

On March 31, 1992, a group of the political subunits of Russia signed a Federal Treaty[15] defining the relationship between the central government in Moscow and the motley group of political subunits that made up the Russian Federation.[16] Tartarstan and Chechnia refused to sign, and Bashkortostan agreed to sign only when President Yeltsin and the chair of the Russian parliament had formally accepted its reservations regarding some of the treaty's provisions. Subsequently, the lack of any general agreement about the distribution of authority between the center and the republics was a major factor delaying the adoption of a post-Soviet Russian constitution.

Like Gorbachev before him, Yeltsin did not give first priority to developing an effective nationalities policy. His attention was focused on affairs in Moscow (particularly his relationship with the Russian parliament and economic reform). The regional political leaders and governments were pretty much left to go their own way. Yeltsin, however, did try to enlist the republics on his side in his protracted confrontation with the Russian parliament. To this end, in October 1992, he created the Council of Heads of the Republics. It was intended to be a consultative body with Yeltsin as chair. This effort was not

---

15. Normally the term *treaty* is reserved for agreements between or among sovereign states. This use of *treaty* is thus unusual. The Federal Treaty, however, is in the tradition of the Union Treaty, which formed the basis of the USSR.

16. There were actually three federal treaties: "one for the republics, one for the krais and oblasts, and one for the autonomous oblast and autonomous okrugs." (Sheehy, 1993, p. 38) All three are usually referred to as the "Federal Treaty."

successful. In only nine of the twenty-one republics did the people vote to support Yeltsin in an April 1993 referendum. In fact, Chechnia did not even take part in the referendum, and Tatarstan's vote was invalidated because of a turnout below the 50 percent required. Even Tatarstan's president Mintimer Shaimiev refused to vote. (Sheehy, 1993)

Why did only one of the republics (Chechnia) pursue independence? Most of the republics had significant Russian populations, ranging from 79.5 percent in Khakassia to 9.2 percent in Dagestan. In fact, according to the 1989 Soviet census, the Russians comprised more than half of the population in nine of the twenty-one republics. (Sheehy, 1993, p. 38) Even in Chechnia there was an acknowlegment that the republic had to have some kind of special relationship with Moscow. Interestingly, in the other republics, demands for some kind of economic sovereignty and more self-rule were often supported by the local Russian population, as well as by the titular ethnic group.

After an outbreak of violence between the North Ossetians and the Ingush during November 1992, the Yeltsin administration finally began to formulate a nationalities policy. The nascent policy had two major principles: (1) The rights of the individual were more important than the rights of ethnic groups. (2) The sovereignty and territorial integrity of the Russian Federation must be preserved. The actual implementation of any nationalities policy, however, was hampered by the effective independence exercised by local officials and governments during the period when Yeltsin was preoccupied with his ongoing dispute with the parliament and with competing economic reform measures. Local governments took advantage of their relative freedom to ignore federal policies and laws they did not like and to set their own rules. Some were even able to wrest significant concessions from Yeltsin in return for their support in his struggle with the Russian parliament. (*Washington Post*, May 25, 1993, p. A12)

Tatarstan is one of the republics that have been particularly important in this struggle with Moscow for power and authority. Unlike Chechnia, which is on the Russian border, Tatarstan is deep within the Russian heartland. Its capital, Kazan, is on the mighty Volga River. Also, Tatarstan is economically and politically more significant than Chechnia. Moreover, unlike Chechnia, its rebellion against Moscow was led by a legitimately elected parliament and president. The strain in the relationship between Kazan and Moscow became baldly apparent in March 1992 when a majority of the population voted in favor of Tatarstan's independence. The question (which was ruled unconstitutional by the Russian Constitutional Court) was: "Do you agree that the republic of Tatarstan is a sovereign state, a subject of international law, building its relations with the Russian Federation and other republics and states on the basis of treaties between equal partners (*na osnove ravnopravnykh dogovorov*)?" The "yes" vote was 61.4 percent, and the "no" vote 37.2 percent—with a turnout of 82 percent. (Sheehy, 1992b, pp. 1, 3)

This event grew out of a long history of resentment. The Tatars were one of the most numerous nationalities in the Soviet Union (see Table 4-1). Because of this fact, they thought they were entitled to be a union republic, not just an autonomous republic within Russia. Stalin, however, decided that a territory had to be located on the border of the USSR in order to become a union republic. Over the years the issue smoldered, but in 1988 it flared up when the Tatar Public Center (TPC), the main political group in Tatarstan, set itself the goal of gaining union republic status for Tatarstan. Later, radical members of the TPC founded the Ittifak Party to push for full independence. Although almost as many Russians (43.3 percent) as Tatars (48.5 percent) were living in Tatarstan, this move was supported by many of the Russians because of the economic wealth of Tatarstan. It was a major center for defense production and for the petrochemical industry, producing 26 percent of the oil of the Russian Republic. From the point of view of many of both the Tatar and Russian inhabitants, the problem was that 98 percent of this productive capacity was under the control of either the USSR or the Russian Republic, not the Tatarstan government. (Sheehy, 1992b, p. 2)

On August 30, 1990, less than three months after the Russian Republic had declared itself sovereign, Tatarstan issued its own declaration of sovereignty. Although Tatar leaders denied that they wanted complete independence from Russia, they demanded that the relations between Russia and Tatarstan be specified in a treaty between equal partners, thus putting Tatarstan on an equal footing with the other union republics. After the failed coup of 1991, Tatarstan sought but failed to gain membership in the CIS. Subsequently, the Tatarstan parliament decided to hold the March referendum. One of the main reasons for this decision was a dispute between Moscow and Kazan over how Tatarstan should be taxed.

During the confrontation between President Yeltsin and the Russian parliament in the fall of 1993, Tatarstan refused to take sides. The Tatarstan prime minister remarked: "Frankly speaking, we have other business to attend to." (Teague, 1993, p. 16) He went on to say that Tatarstan would continue to be ruled by its own constitution, no matter what transpired in Moscow. But after Yeltsin's victory, the Tatarstan government supported his handling of the crisis. In the parliamentary election in December 1993, however, Tatarstan failed to fill its two seats in the Federal Council, as did Chechnia. (Tolz, 1994, p. 2)

In confronting Moscow, Tatarstan is increasingly at a disadvantage. First, the 1993 Constitution greatly strengthens the central government vis-à-vis the republics. Second, Russia plays a powerful economic hand. A political scientist at Kazan University observed that "Russia has powerful means of pressure." (*Washington Post*, November 22, 1993, p. A14) Tatarstan uses Russian rubles, needs Russian orders to keep its factories producing, and requires Russian permission to get its oil to shipping facilities. Although it is likely that the mood in Tatarstan will remain rebellious, the realities that Tatarstan faces are likely to keep it in the Russian Federation for the indefinite future.

It was not surprising, therefore, that Russia was able to exert pressure on Tatarstan to delineate authority and power between the Russian Federation and the Republic of Tatarstan. On February 15, 1994, Boris Yeltsin and

Tatarstan president Shaimiev signed a treaty.[17] It has been both praised and vilified.

In Russia, liberals praised the treaty as a step away from a unitary state and a step toward the creation of a truly federal political entity. Russian nationalists, however, condemned it as "a nail in the coffin of the Russian Federation." (Teague, 1994b, p. 20) Meanwhile, Tatar nationalists denounced the treaty because it did not recognize Tatarstan as a sovereign state and, therefore, violated the Tatarstan Constitution. Nevertheless, the treaty did delineate a wide range of rights for Tatarstan including the right to conduct its own foreign trade, to have its own constitution, to form its own budget, and to levy its own republican taxes. (Teague, 1994b, p. 26)

Moscow wanted the treaty for the reasons specified earlier—to preserve the territorial integrity of the Russian Federation and to ensure the protection of individual rights. The Yeltsin administration also wanted to address demands for greater autonomy before they escalated into full-blown separatist movements in Tatarstan and elsewhere. (Teague, 1994b, p. 20)

A related but somewhat different situation exists in Sakha (formerly Yakutia). Seven time zones east of Moscow, Sakha has a population of 1.1 million people and a territory that comprises one-fifth of Russia. According to the 1989 Soviet census, it has a Russian majority of about 50.3 percent and a Yakut minority of 33.4 percent. Larger than any of the newly independent countries except Russia itself, Sakha is rich in gold, diamonds, coal, and natural gas. Because of its harsh climate, however, Sakha is, if anything, more dependent on Moscow than Tatarstan is. The oil and food that Russia ships up the Lena River enable its people to survive the long and dark winter.

During the Soviet period, Sakha was a classic "resource colony," sending out natural resources to be disposed of by Moscow. The situation was described this way by a sixty-seven-year-old woman: "They took everything from us and gave nothing back." (*Washington Post,* October 8, 1992, p. A41) The people of Sakha feared that this pattern would continue under Russian Federation rule. This prospect caused considerable separatist sentiment. The Sakha government, however, decided to try to force Moscow to give it as much economic control as possible. And in 1992, Sakha leaders were able to persuade Moscow to give Sakha control over a percentage of its diamonds and gold, as well as the right to seek its own economic relationships with overseas investors and trading partners. In return, Sakha promised not to seek independence from the Russian Federation.

This arrangement might seem to benefit the inhabitants of Sakha, but the reality is different. For the most part, members of the old Communist elite have

---

17. The treaty was "The Treaty on the Delineation of Spheres of Authority and the Mutual Delegation of Powers between the Agencies of State Power of the Russian Federation and of the Republic of Tatarstan." Yeltsin claimed that because it was not an international treaty, it did not require ratification by the Duma of the Federal Assembly. However, the situation is complicated by the fact that Tatarstan does consider it an international treaty. (Teague, 1994b, pp. 19–20)

retained power in Sakha and are the main beneficiaries. In addition, infrastructure decay and environmental damage inherited from the Soviet period threaten the economic future of Sakha. Thus, although Sakha has gained a significant measure of local control, the benefits may be largely lost to its people because of inherited problems. Nevertheless, Sakha has kept its part of the bargain, participating fully in the government of the Russian Federation and supporting Yeltsin's dissolution of the Russian parliament. In return for this loyalty, Yeltsin gave Sakha the right to keep all of the federal taxes that it raised. (Teague, 1993, p. 23) This money does not ensure economic prosperity, but it puts Sakha in a position to begin rebuilding its infrastructure and to clean up the worst of its environmental problems—if it chooses to use its revenues for long-term investment rather than for short-term gain.

The issue of Sakha is part of a larger issue: the future of Russia east of the Ural Mountains. There has been a demand for economic sovereignty within some of the subunits of this vast part of Russia (like in Sakha), and a movement for increased economic control extends across the region. The most important organization in this movement has been Siberian Agreement (Sibirskoe Soglashenie), which was founded in November 1990. Siberian Agreement has been at the forefront of a movement aimed at giving the people of eastern Russia "greater control over Siberia's rich resources, the right to engage directly in foreign trade, and an end to what [the peoples of the region] regard as colonial exploitation by Moscow." (Bradshaw, 1992, p. 6) In particular, these various peoples wanted a larger share of the hard currency Russia got from the export of natural resources. Siberian Agreement was important "because it was the only association in which regional heads of administration (governors) and local soviets presented a united front in their dealings with the center." (Hughes, 1993, p. 30) It was also the first association to gain legal recognition from the Yeltsin government.

Like Sakha, most of Russia east of the Urals has been a classic colonial resource frontier region. What industry it has is geared to producing energy and industrial raw materials, which must be sent to European Russia or exported for further processing. Russia east of the Urals, then, is dependent on the rest of Russia and on the CIS for its food, machinery, equipment, and consumer goods. When the Yeltsin reforms freed the prices of these commodities, the prices of raw materials at first remained low. At the same time, because of the decaying infrastructure across the region and the drop in military procurement, production fell. As a result, the people of eastern Russia suffered disproportionately from the declining standard of living associated with the Yeltsin administration's reform efforts. During the Soviet period, people had been willing to brave the hard conditions to work in Siberia because they got higher wages. By 1992, wages across the region were about 20 percent below the Russian average. Wages rallied somewhat by 1993, but were still 15 percent below the Russian average. (Hughes, 1993, p. 30)

Many of the people of eastern Russia wish to create energy-intensive and resource-processing industries and erect an improved socioeconomic infrastructure to take advantage of this vast region's natural resources. Those who want the region to remain a resource-extracting area argue that the poor infrastructure, costly transportation, and harsh environmental conditions would make such an investment prohibitively expensive. The effort to decentralize control over resources in eastern Russia began in the Soviet era and carried over into the post-Soviet period. Although some concessions from Moscow have been obtained (as in the case of Sakha), a high level of economic autonomy is not likely anytime in the immediate future. Russia is simply too dependent on its eastern region as a source of much-needed income, particularly export income. In addition, many of eastern Russia's localities are heavily subsidized by Moscow. They do not have the ability to process the resources they extract, and the industries that they do possess are involved in military production and to a large extent remain government-owned. (Bradshaw, 1992; Tolz, 1993)

We mentioned three scenarios for Russia's future: (1) disintegration, (2) reversion to an imperial form of rule, and (3) establishment of a stable democratic federation. At present, the first seems the least likely. Although there is still considerable separatist sentiment and resentment of Moscow, there is no significant movement to leave the Russian Federation. The richest subunits exhibit far more interest in preventing the perpetuation of the second scenario—imperial rule, colonialism, or the practical equivalent. They want a greater say in their own affairs, particularly regarding the distribution of the wealth generated from their natural resources. They are well aware of their dependence on outside sources. Although they would like to minimize this dependence, they are also aware that they cannot accomplish this goal overnight. Thus, it seems that some sort of federal arrangement is the most desirable. It would permit Moscow to retain control in key areas, such as monetary policy, defense, and foreign relations. It would also permit the regions to have more control over decision-making about their local economies and more opportunity to reap the rewards of their rich natural resources.

Whether such a truly federal arrangement can be reached is, as yet, unclear. Currently, the 1993 Constitution does not give much local control to the republics or to other local governments. But, for political reasons, the Yeltsin government has shown some willingness to grant concessions that will have the practical effect of increasing republic sovereignty in certain key areas. The treaty with Tatarstan is a case in point. Also, the Federal Council may be able to become a reasonably effective representative of republic and local interests in the Russian parliament. Nevertheless, because the institution-building process in Russia is far from complete, how Russian federalism will evolve remains to be seen.

In this chapter, we have considered intraregional relations within the former Soviet Union. Our discussion focused on three aspects of these developing relations: (1) their new international character and prospects for the CIS, (2) the Russian military, its strengths, weaknessses, and future as regional peacekeeper; and (3) the regional problems and possibilities in the Russian Federation. The fall of the Soviet Union, however, has had a major impact on the rest of the world. A new world order seems to be coming into being. In Chapter 11, we consider relations between the newly independent countries and the major actors on the global scene, both international organizations and key nation-states.

REFERENCES

Allman, T. D. (1984). *Unmanifest destiny*. New York: Doubleday.

Angell, R. C. (1969). *Peace on the march: Transitional participation*. New York: Litton.

Art, R. J., & Jervis, R. (Eds.). (1992). *International politics: Enduring concepts and contemporary issues* (3rd ed.). New York: HarperCollins.

Axelrod, R. (1984). *The evolution of cooperation*. New York: Basic Books.

Bradshaw, M. J. (1992). Siberia poses a challenge to Russian federalism. *RFE/RL Research Report, 1*(41), 6–14.

Brown, B. (1994). Three Central Asian states form economic union. *RFE/RL Research Report, 3*(13), 33–35.

Bungs, D. (1993). Progress on withdrawal from the Baltic states. *RFE/RL Research Report, 2*(25), 50–59.

Coplin, W. D. (1971). International organization in the future international bargaining: A theoretical projection. *Journal of International Affairs, 55* (Summer), 287–301.

Crow, S. (1993). Russia asserts its strategic agenda. *RFE/RL Research Report, 2*(50), 1–8.

———. (1994). Russia promotes the CIS as an international organization. *RFE/RL Research Report, 3*(11), 33–38.

Foye, S. (1990). Soviet armed forces face housing crisis. *Report on the USSR, 2*(13), 5–7.

———. (1992). The Ukrainian armed forces: Prospects and problems. *RFE/RL Research Report, 1*(26), 55–60.

———. (1993a). The CIS armed forces. *RFE/RL Research Report, 2*(1), 41–45.

———. (1993b). End of CIS command heralds new Russian defense policy? *RFE/RL Research Report, 2*(27), 45–49.

———. (1993c). Rebuilding the Russian armed forces: Rhetoric and realities. *RFE/RL Research Report, 2*(30), 49–57.

Fuller, E. (1994). The Transcaucasus: War, turmoil, economic collapse. *RFE/RL Research Report, 3*(1), 51–58.

Gregory, P. R., & Stuart, R. C. (1994). *Soviet and post-Soviet economic structure and performance* (5th ed.). New York: HarperCollins.

Hughes, J. (1993). Yeltsin's Siberian opposition. *RFE/RL Research Report, 2*(50), 29–34.

Ikenberry, G. J. (1989). Rethinking the origins of American hegemony. *Political Science Quarterly, 104*, 375–400.

Jacobson, H. K. (1984). *Network of interdependence: International organizations and the global political system*. New York: Knopf.

Kegley, C. W., Jr., & Wittkopf, E. R. (1993). *World politics: Trend and transformation* (4th ed.). New York: St. Martin's Press.

Kionka, R. (1992). Baltic states develop a new *ostpolitik*. *RFE/RL Research Report, 1*(8), 21–25.

Kramer, J. M. (1993). "Energy shock" from Russia jolts Baltic states. *RFE/RL Research Report, 2*(17), 41–49.

Lepingwell, J. W. R. (1993a). Is the military disintegrating from within? *RFE/RL Research Report, 2*(25), 9–16.

———. (1993b). Restructuring the Russian military. *RFE/RL Research Report, 2*(25), 17–24.

Lynch A. (1994). After empire: Russia and its western neighbors. *RFE/RL Research Report, 3*(12), 10–17.

Marnie, S., & Whitlock, E. (1993). Central Asia and economic integration. *RFE/RL Research Report, 2*(14), 34–44.

Martyniuk, J. (1992). Ukrainian independence and territorial integrity. *RFE/RL Research Report, 1*(13), 64–68.

McCormick, J. M. (1989). Intergovernmental organizations and cooperation among nations. In P. F. Diehl (Ed.), *The politics of international organizations: Patterns and insights,* Chicago: Dorsey Press.

Mihalisko, K. (1993). Belarusian leader on first year of statehood: An interview with Stanislau Shushkevich. *RFE/RL Research Report, 2*(3), 8–13.

Olson, M., & Zeckhauser, R. (1966). An economic theory of alliances. *Review of Economics and Statistics, 48,* 266–279.

Riggs, R. E. (1977). One small step for functionalism: UN participation and congressional attitude change. *International Organization, 31*(3), 515–539.

Sheehy, A. (1992a). Commonwealth of Independent States: An uneasy compromise. *RFE/RL Research Report, 1*(2), 1–5.

———. (1992b). Tatarstan asserts its sovereignty. *RFE/RL Research Report 1*(14), 1–4.

———. (1993). Russia's republics: A threat to its territorial integrity? *RFE/RL Research Report, 2*(20), 34–40.

Slater, W. (1994). Russia: The return of authoritarian government? *RFE/RL Research Report, 3*(1), 22–31.

Socor, V. (1994). Moldova: Democracy advances, independence at risk. *RFE/RL Research Report, 3*(1), 47–50.

Stein, A. (1984). The hegemon's dilemma: Great Britain, the United States and the international economic order. *International Organization, 38,* 355–386.

———. (1990). *Why nations cooperate.* Ithaca, NY: Cornell University Press.

Teague, E. (1993). North-south divide: Yeltsin and Russia's provincial leaders. *RFE/RL Research Report, 2*(47), 7–23.

———. (1994a). The CIS: An unpredictable future. *RFE/RL Research Report, 3*(1), 9–12.

———. (1994b). Russia and Tatarstan sign power-sharing treaty. *RFE/RL Research Report, 3*(14), 19–25.

Tolz, V. (1993). Regionalism in Russia: The case of Siberia. *RFE/RL Research Report, 2*(9), 1–9.

———. (1994). Russia's parliamentary elections: What happened and why. *RFE/RL Research Report, 3*(2), 1–8.

Ulam, A. B. (1988). *Expansion and coexistence: Soviet foreign policy, 1917–73* (2nd ed.). New York: Holt, Rinehart and Winston.

Wallace, M., & Singer, J. D. (1970). Intergovernmental organizatons in the global system, 1815–1964: A quantitative description. *International Organization, 24*(2), 239–287.

Whitlock, E. (1993a). The CIS economy. *RFE/RL Research Report, 2*(1), 46–49.

———. (1993b). The return of the ruble. *RFE/RL Research Report, 2*(35), 34–37.

———. (1994). The CIS economies: Divergent and troubled paths. *RFE/RL Research Report, 3*(1), 13–17.

Wolfers, A. (1962). *Discord and collaboration.* Baltimore: Johns Hopkins University Press.

Yearbook of International Organizations, 1991/92. (1991). Vol. 2. Munich: K. G. Sauer.

· 11 ·

THE SOVIET SUCCESSOR COUNTRIES AND THE NEW WORLD ORDER

Plus ça change, plus c'est la même chose.

OLD FRENCH SAYING

Even the sorts of things that haven't changed are different. All sorts of tonalities—emotional, moral, personal—have somehow altered.

CLIFFORD GEERTZ (*New York Times,* May 11, 1988, p. B6)

"The more it changes, the more it is the same thing"—or is it? US president George Bush coined the phrase *New World Order* to describe international relations in the post–Cold War and post-Soviet era. The phrase gained instant popularity because it seemed to capture the changed circumstances of world politics. The concept, however, is easier to use than to define, not because of sloppy analysis but rather because of uncertainty. No one knows how the dust will settle on the international political-economic system. Will *New World Order* simply come to designate a changed distribution of power among new or reconstituted states in a world not essentially different from the power-driven domain historically associated with international relations? If this is the case, then the adage "The more it changes, the more it is the same thing" is apropos. Alternatively, will *New World Order* come to designate something fundamentally different? If this is the case, power as a mechanism of control in the international arena will become less salient as exchange relationships and cooperation through nascent authority structures are increasingly cultivated.

We see the latter trend among the countries of Europe that compose the European Union. They have demonstrated their willingness to surrender significant portions of their economic and political sovereignty in favor of a supranational authority structure. Moreover, as the existing members seek to deepen their political and economic integration, other countries aspire to membership.

These aspirants are willing to surrender their rights to independent action in favor of joint decision-making and explicitly rule-bound behavior.

This trend toward greater integration in Europe and elsewhere notwithstanding, the world remains full of examples of politics as usual. Many states act independently in a relatively rule-less environment. In the traditional domain of international relations, the rules are implicit and informal, typified by sayings like "Might makes right."

In Chapter 10, we discussed the conditions under which states are likely to forgo independent action and pursue cooperation in their international relations. States are likely to seek cooperation when their independent actions do not result in the desired outcome—when their independent actions produce worse outcomes than if they had cooperated. Cooperation, in turn, necessitates joint (rather than independent) decision-making and rule-bound behavior.

As the world approaches the twenty-first century, a number of factors make cooperation the increasingly likely choice for states. Here we need mention only two. First, technology made possible the creation of an international market that has become truly global in scale. Markets necessitate cooperation because participants must agree on the rules of the "market game." Second, over the past century, global issues have emerged that defy resolution through the threat or use of force. The degradation of the global environment is a case in point. Tremendous damage has been done to the environment by those seeking to develop, test, deploy, and use the weapons that efforts to control through power now require. If we are ever to address and resolve the problems of environmental degradation, cooperation—joint decision-making and rule-bound behavior—will be necessary.

As the world becomes more complex and more interdependent, and as the rules that define cooperative relations among international actors become more explicit, an increasingly pressing need for rule-interpretation, rule-adjudication, and rule-enforcement will develop. These circumstances, in turn, are likely to give rise to authority structures capable of meeting these needs. However, this is at best a scenario for the long term. Numerous obstacles must be overcome if international relations are to be transformed along the lines we just described. Cultural biases, ethnic animosities, and mistrust—a natural byproduct of coexistence and interaction in a self-help environment—are but a few of the obstacles. Another obstacle is the resistance to change that is likely to emanate from the actors who can wield the most power and who have the greatest advantage in the existing order.

For the foreseeable future, how we characterize the New World Order (whether as fundamental change or as more of the same) in no small part depends on Russia's and the other successor countries' role in it. The importance of Russia in the New World Order is obvious. It is huge and has an enormous wealth of resources. It has a military-industrial complex second only to that of the United States. Russia's armed forces are large though demoralized and dilapidated, and Russia inherited the nuclear arsenal of the Soviet Union. Moreover, Russian leaders have proclaimed its great-power status, and they are already exercising its considerable power to influence regional politics.

The other successor countries face the challenge of breaking free of the patterns of dominance and subjugation that have historically defined their relationship with Moscow. They must secure their status as independent actors in the international community. To be successful, they must establish new relations with Russia while they actively cultivate cooperative relations with other countries in the region and throughout the world.

In this chapter, we explore a number of issues that will factor prominently in shaping the New World Order. We examine the legacy of the Cold War and its enduring impact on international relations. We consider Russia's efforts to establish new patterns of interaction with the international community. For its leaders, these patterns rest on the assumption that Russia is one of the great powers of the world. In this chapter, therefore, we also explore the great-power concept and its relevance for Russia as an actor in the international system. In addition, we examine Russia's relationship with the United States and with other key actors in the international community. Finally, we look beyond Russia to consider the efforts of the Baltic states, Ukraine, the countries of Central Asia, and Azerbaijan to establish new regional and international ties outside the former Soviet bloc.

THE COLD WAR

From the end of World War II to the Gorbachev era, the Cold War dominated world politics. The Cold War was a hostile standoff between the United States and the Soviet Union. Each claimed to have the political-economic system that should prevail. Each presided over a nuclear arsenal large enough to destroy the world. Each built its policy on the theory that the other was an aggressor and that its duty was to prevent that aggression. In short, the Soviet Union and United States moved from being allies during World War II to being implacable foes in the postwar world. Why did this happen?

There has always been considerable disagreement among both historians and political scientists about the reasons for the Cold War. In geopolitical terms, it can be argued that because the United States and Soviet Union (as well as the Russian Empire) were countries that occupied continent-sized landmasses, they were destined to be competitors. (LaFeber, 1990) Moreover, in a world where there are two dominant powers, such competition is inevitable. Why? As we have said previously, international politics is power driven. Size and military might allow great powers to dominate lesser powers. If there are two great powers, they are bound to have incompatible political and economic interests.

Some would say that this geopolitical argument is incomplete—that the relationship between the United States and the Soviet Union went beyond competition and was characterized by an unusual level of hostility, even paranoia. One reason for this was that the United States and the Soviet Union had very little basis for accurate understanding of each other or for accurate communication with each other. The United States was protected by two great oceans and had relatively weak countries on its borders; it had not been invaded since the War of 1812. In contrast, the Soviet Union was a landlocked power that had suffered numerous invasions by powerful neighbors over the centuries. The most recent invasion, during World War II, had caused enormous human and material devastation. It is virtually impossible for an American to understand, on anything but an intellectual level, what the Soviet people went through during the Nazi invasion and occupation. But for the Russians, those horrific events were yet another reminder of the importance of ensuring their survival by means of military might and defensible borders.

Thus, it is hardly surprising that Soviet political culture was very different from American political culture. Aside from the survival issue, there were many other important differences:

1. Russian political culture was absolutist. American political culture is democratic.
2. The Soviets considered a strong, relatively permanent leader having the power to act arbitrarily to be necessary for their defense against outside threats and internal subversion. Americans, who see unified leadership as dangerous, have a government of checks and balances in which leaders are replaced after set intervals.
3. The Soviet people viewed themselves as subjects. The American people are more likely to consider themselves citizens.
4. In the Soviet Union, conformity and the subordination of the individual to the group were valued. In the United States, great importance is attached to individualism and individual initiative.
5. In the Soviet Union, the formal government institutions were weak, and those who ruled felt little need to inform the populace—let alone take their people's preferences into consideration. In the United States, there are strong (though checked and balanced) government institutions, and the people expect to be as fully informed as possible and to have their wishes heeded by their political leaders.[1]
6. All important policies in the Soviet Union were made by the Party leadership behind closed doors. In the United States, access to political decision-making is thought to be a citizen's right, except in a small number of extreme circumstances dealing with national security.
7. The Soviet economy was a command economy. Americans value their free enterprise system.

In short, the two countries were very different, and their differences, along with the geopolitical context, made enormous tensions and misunderstandings inevitable.

Geopolitical rivalry notwithstanding, at the end of World War II, the United States and the Soviet Union were far from equal in power. Although the United States had suffered some losses, its industrial strength had grown, and it had no

---

1. Ironically, some American presidents (e.g., Richard Nixon and Ronald Reagan), in their efforts to combat the Communist menace, were willing to take clandestine and sometimes illegal action.

domestic war damage to repair. In contrast, the Soviet Union had suffered enormous losses. The Nazis had invaded its most industrialized region, destroying much of the industrial might that Stalin had built. The infrastructure of this region was almost totally destroyed. And the human loss was so great that the effect on the population was still evident twenty years later in the large numbers of single, middle-aged women. Thus, it cannot be said that the United States and the Soviet Union were equal competitors in the years following World War II.

Accordingly, the level of tension that characterized the Cold War had more to do with US actions than with Soviet actions. "The Soviet Union, far from being the aggressor, found itself on the defensive. Although at times the Kremlin reacted belligerently, the burden of responsibility for the Cold War rested on the United States, the more powerful of the two countries . . . and the one with less to fear from the other." (Brands, 1993, pp. vi–vii) True, the Soviet Union had refused to withdraw its troops from eastern Europe, and the United States and its European allies labeled this an aggressive act. From the perspective of Russian and Soviet history, however, it can be argued that the refusal to withdraw troops was a defensive move. A Soviet-dominated eastern Europe constituted a buffer zone between the Soviet Union and its historical enemies.

The other factor that the United States claimed was a sign of the expansionist tendencies of the USSR was Soviet efforts to support attempts to establish Communist systems in other countries. American leaders labeled those efforts "acts of aggression." However, when we take into account the Soviet assertion that their political-economic system represented "the wave of the future," the efforts to spread communism can also be regarded as a sort of political-economic "missionary" campaign.[2] Indeed, this view is reinforced when we remember that after "the Red Army refused to withdraw from where the war's [World War II] end found it . . . the Kremlin captured no more territory by force." (Brands, 1993, p. 223)[3]

The American response to the perceived aggressive tendencies of the Soviet Union was a policy labeled "containment." The containment policy originated in an article written by George Kennan using the pseudonym "X" (1947). From his considerable knowledge of Russian and Soviet history and culture, Kennan concluded that Soviet postwar foreign policy would be premised on two key beliefs in Marxism-Leninism: (1) the innate antagonism between capitalism and socialism and (2) the infallibility of the Communist Party of the Soviet Union. Kennan argued that these beliefs would make the Soviet Union

2. The United States pursued its own "missionary" effort, supporting anti-Communist regimes throughout the world without paying much attention to whether they were democratic or not.
3. The war in Afghanistan, begun in 1979, might be raised to counter this point. One could argue that the campaign, though ultimately unsuccessful, underscored the inherently expansionist tendencies of the USSR. H. W. Brands (1993, p. 223) calls this argument into question by noting, "The Afghanistan fighting was largely defensive . . . intended to ward off the advance of Islamic fundamentalism toward the Soviet Union's Muslim provinces."

difficult to deal with. He did *not* argue, however, that the Soviet Union had "embarked on a do-or-die program to overthrow [Western] society by a given date." (Kennan, 1947, p. 572) Therefore, he recommended (p. 575) that "the main element of any United States policy toward the Soviet Union must be that of a long-term, patient but firm and vigilant containment of Russian expansive tendencies."

Kennan defined containment (p. 576) as "the adroit and vigilant application of counter-force at a series of constantly shifting geographical and political points, corresponding to the shifts and maneuvers of Soviet policy." He believed that the effect of containment, thus applied, would be to nip in the bud any Soviet attempt to expand. He also argued that, given the right circumstances and sufficient time, the Soviet system was vulnerable to collapse. What Kennan did not envision, or recommend, was the kind of globalized containment that the United States put into place. The outcome of the official US version of containment was, in effect, the erection of a wall around the Soviet Union—a wall that was not a response to any particular Soviet act of aggression but left the Soviet Union surrounded by US military might.

According to George Kennan, the militarization of containment had unfortunate consequences:

> The more American political leaders were seen in Moscow as committed to an ultimate military rather than political resolution of Soviet-American tensions, the greater was the tendency in Moscow to tighten the control by party and police, and the greater the breaking effect on all liberalizing tendencies in the regime. Thus the general effect of cold war extremism was to delay rather than hasten the great change that overtook the Soviet Union at the end of the 1980s. (*New York Times*, October 28, 1992, p. A21)

One might extend the argument. Containment not only kept the Soviet Union in but held the Soviet Union together, protecting it from its tendency to fall victim to the flaws in the Soviet political-economic system. Thus, the United States came to embody so fearsome an external enemy that the evils the Soviet people knew seemed preferable to the unknown evils represented by the alien West. The evils they knew, of course, were a political system that was an oppressive empire and an economic system that did not work.

The Soviet educational and propaganda apparatuses continually reinforced fear of the West. Because the flow of information was almost completely controlled, the Soviet people had little information that might have persuaded them that the West was not a destructive monster that they needed to defend against at all costs. The fact remains, however, "that communism [or more specifically, the pathologies of empire and command economies]—not capitalism or democracy—has been the communists' worst enemy. . . . External force usually succeeded only in delaying the discovery [of this fact]." (Brands, 1993, p. 227)

When Mikhail Gorbachev introduced his "new thinking" (*novoe myshlenie*) about Soviet foreign policy toward the West, he did so primarily to divert economic resources away from military production and into consumer production. The core of Gorbachev's new policy was the idea that "military doctrines . . . should be strictly the doctrines of defense." (Gorbachev, 1987, p. 142) His "new thinking" undercut the rationale for containment by effectively ending the Cold War. The removal of the Western threat, in turn, removed the container that had been holding the Soviet system together.

The subsequent rapid collapse of the Soviet Union called into question the wisdom of almost forty years of American foreign policy: "The most obvious question was whether it had been necessary for Americans to get so worked up over an enemy that proved to be a shell. . . . Had the Soviet threat *ever* been very great? How much of the perceived threat had been genuine, and how much a figment of American imaginations?" (Brands, 1993, p. 221)

What is the legacy of the Cold War for Russia and the other successor countries? First, those that inherited significant military production facilities have to deal with the problem of converting much of their defense industry to other uses. The enormity of the problem of defense conversion can hardly be overestimated: "[D]efense production in the Soviet Union absorbed one-third of the country's industrial work force; 60% of the machine building industry; 80% of all research and development personnel; and 20% of Soviet energy output." (Bush, 1992, p. 33) Although selling military-related technologies and producing military equipment for export are options, much of the Soviet military-industrial complex is rapidly becoming obsolete. What's more, Russia and the other heirs to this complex lack adequate financial resources to fund the process of conversion. (Bush, 1993, p. 29; Foye, 1993, p. 58)

Second, for decades the Soviet people were asked to work hard and to sacrifice to defeat the Western imperialist enemy. That enemy has now simply disappeared, but the people are still being asked to sacrifice to remedy the mistakes of the past. This raises the question of how long the people can be asked to accept sacrifice and inferior living conditions. The rebellion against the hardships of reform evinced by many of the Russian voters in the December 1993 parliamentary elections is a sign that time may be running out. (*New York Times,* December 16, 1993, p. A10)

Third, one of the consequences of the Cold War was rampant abuse of the environment. Sooner or later, this will have to be cleaned up and the human consequences dealt with. As we noted in previous chapters, however, technologies that can address some of the problems of the environment may not yet exist. Moreover, even where technologies and environmentally safe alternatives do exist, resource constraints and short-term economic priorities put the issues and consequences of environmental degradation far down on the agendas of regional leaders.

Fourth, the end of the Cold War and collapse of the Soviet Union instantly created nuclear proliferation. Kazakhstan and Belarus agreed to surrender their nuclear weapons and placed them under the control of the Russian military. (*New York Times,* November 29, 1993, p. A10) Ukraine was far less willing to surrender control. Until these weapons are destroyed or moved to Russia, the potential for multiple nuclear powers in this area persists. The initial impulse of

Belarus, Kazakhstan, and Ukraine was to get rid of their nuclear weapons facilities. Ukraine and Belarus had suffered contamination from the Chernobyl accident, and Kazakhstan had suffered contamination from nuclear weapons testing. Since Russian nationalists and Communists have become a significant force in the Russian government, however, these successor countries may decide that they need nuclear weapons as a defense against possible future expansion by a militantly nationalist Russia.

During the Cold War, the US and USSR did not agree on much, but one thing they did agree on was that nuclear proliferation was undesirable. When there were only two major nuclear powers, there existed a perverse stability in the "balance of terror" and the strategy of mutual assured destruction (MAD). The superpowers agreed that the situation would become increasingly unstable with each additional member of the nuclear "club." As the number of nuclear powers increased, the possibility of technical failure, human error, and weapons being acquired by terrorist or radical regimes as well as their being put to other uses was bound to increase. As the heir of the Soviet nuclear arsenal, Russia is still in agreement with the United States on this issue. Russia has agreed to be bound by START I (Strategic Arms Reduction Treaty), negotiated by the US and USSR and signed by presidents Bush and Gorbachev on July 31, 1991. Russia has also negotiated and signed a second START agreement with the United States (START II).

START II would reduce strategic nuclear warheads to 3,000 for Russia and 3,500 for the United States—an approximate 50 percent cut from the levels established by START I. If fully implemented, START II would result in the elimination of all land-based multiple-warhead missiles, which are considered the most destabilizing weapons in both arsenals "because of their greater relative destructive power and their attractiveness as the target of a preemptive first strike." (Crow, 1993a, p. 15) Ratification and implementation of START II, however, are contingent on full implementation of START I, and full implementation will not happen unless and until Belarus, Kazakhstan, and Ukraine ratify START I[4] *and* agree to become non-nuclear powers by signing and ratifying the 1968 Nuclear Nonproliferation Treaty. Only then will the nuclear proliferation problem be settled.

Although concentration of all of the former Soviet Union's nuclear weapons in Russia may be a solution for the problem of nuclear proliferation, many other problems remain. With or without full implementation of START I and II, Russia still will be a formidable military power. This situation raises some troubling concerns about Russia's future. As we discussed in the previous chapter, there is the question of whether Russia will evolve into a true federal democracy. Alternatively, if the Communist and nationalist coalition grows in influence, will Russia try to expand in order to recreate the empire? Or will

---

4. According to the Lisbon Protocol to START I, signed on May 23, 1992, Belarus, Kazakhstan, and Ukraine each became a party to START I, thereby assuming the obligation to ratify and implement it and to guarantee access to inspectors assigned to verify the treaty. (Crow, 1993, p. 14)

Russia disintegrate much as the Soviet Union disintegrated? Either of the last two possibilities presents a serious problem for the rest of the world.

THE FUTURE OF RUSSIA: MISSED OPPORTUNITIES?

When Gorbachev became general secretary of the CPSU in March 1985, he immediately began talking about large-scale reform of the Soviet political-economic system. For the rest of the world this talk of reform was a new and puzzling development. Although previous Soviet leaders had attempted to implement reform agendas, none had a vision for reform that was as sweeping as Gorbachev's.

No aspect of this plan was more confusing to the outside world than his ideas about foreign policy. After decades of regarding the Soviet Union as an expansionist, aggressive state, the non-Communist countries were asked to believe that Soviet foreign policy was being refocused almost exclusively on defense. Quite naturally, they reacted with skepticism. Was it a trick? If so, what did the Soviet Union expect to gain? If not, would the Soviet Union really do what was required to implement the new policy? Finally, how should the rest of the world, particularly the major industrial countries, respond to this new Soviet foreign policy?

American policymakers—and their European and Japanese counterparts—were slow to react to the rapidly changing Soviet foreign policy stance. The United States, as leader of the Western alliance, was particularly cautious. The American president was a conservative republican, Ronald Reagan. He had been a militant anti-Communist for most of his political career and had labeled the Soviet Union an "evil empire." Moreover, he had been so concerned about the Soviet threat that, immediately after winning the presidency, he had embarked on a massive buildup of the military.

After Reagan's reelection in November 1984, his policy stance toward the Soviet Union became considerably more accommodating. What accounts for this change? Reagan as a second-term president began viewing policy, especially foreign policy, with an eye toward the history books. He was concerned about how future historians would assess his record on the matter of peace and global security. The shift to a less confrontational stance was also eased by a change at the State Department. George Shultz replaced Alexander Haig as secretary of state. Shultz was no less hard-line than Haig on military issues, but his statements were far less combative than those of his predecessor. (Brands, 1993, pp. 192–193)

A modified American policy stance vis-à-vis the Soviet Union became perceptible in late 1984. These policy modifications, however, were premised on undiluted Cold War assumptions about the Soviet Union. No one in the Reagan administration was prepared for Gorbachev's "new thinking" and for the ideas and proposals it spawned. Gorbachev proposed that the 1963 nuclear test ban be extended to prohibit underground as well as atmospheric testing. He announced a unilateral Soviet moratorium on testing and suggested the

United States respond in kind. Later, he put forward plans to reduce the strategic nuclear arsenals of the two superpowers by 50 percent if the United States would cease work on its Strategic Defense Initiative (SDI). American policymakers were reluctant to accept Gorbachev's proposals and the new policy premises on which they were based. This reluctance persisted throughout the rest of the Soviet period and into the post-Soviet era, especially with reference to Russia.

The US inclination to proceed with caution is understandable. In retrospect, however, it is possible to see that this slowness to grasp and accept what was happening meant the United States and its allies missed numerous opportunities to shape events in ways that would have been desirable from their point of view. (Evangelista, 1993) One of the major reasons for this series of missed opportunities was the fact that the United States and its allies were hampered by both psychological barriers and material constraints.

US policymakers were used to thinking of the Soviet Union as devious, as well as dangerous. Their first reaction was to regard Gorbachev's foreign policy pronouncements as disinformation, meant to distract them from what he *really* had in mind. This suspicion was compounded by the zero-sum thinking that pervaded the American policy-making community, especially the Pentagon: Anything suggested by the USSR must, by definition, be bad for the United States. Moreover, even if the enemy was not being duplicitous and was merely demonstrating a willingness to compromise, did it not make sense to wait and see if the Soviets might give more? Thus, the persistent perception of the Soviet Union as an intractable foe made it difficult, if not impossible, for Gorbachev's "new thinking" to have its intended effect.

Of critical importance to Gorbachev and his reform efforts was redirecting resources in the Soviet economy away from military applications and toward consumer ones. He was particularly loath to engage in a new arms race over the development and deployment of weapons for strategic defense. He made repeated proposals to try to gain a commitment from the United States to stop work on SDI. At the November 1985 Geneva Summit, Gorbachev tried to convince Reagan of the potentially destabilizing effects of SDI. He argued that SDI did not constitute a purely defensive weapon as Reagan maintained. Gorbachev believed that SDI could easily yield increased offensive capability. He was equally unimpressed by Reagan's offer to share SDI technology with the world. He claimed the United States was pursuing, as it had many times in the past, a one-sided advantage over the Soviet Union. With neither side prepared to budge, the Geneva Summit ended without substantive agreement. (Brands, 1993, p. 197)

The following October, the two men met again in Reykjavik, Iceland. Gorbachev proposed a 50 percent across-the-board cut in the strategic arsenals of both superpowers. The offer was not unanticipated; he had made it before. What was new at Reykjavik was that for the first time Gorbachev promised substantial cuts in the heavy missiles that the United States found so threatening. He also offered to accept the American definition of strategic weapons (a bone of much contention), and he dropped the condition that British and French weapons be considered part of the American arsenal. He even offered to allow the SDI project to continue, with some conditions. Gorbachev and Reagan came close to agreement, but ultimately SDI got in the way. Specifically, would SDI research be confined to the laboratory? That was the Soviets' preference, but this constraint was unacceptable to Reagan. (Brands, 1993, pp. 200–201)

If President Reagan had been willing to make concessions on SDI, Gorbachev could have justified to hard-liners in his own Party his efforts to free up and shift to the civilian sector resources being devoted to the military. That transfer of resources, in turn, might have ameliorated the disastrous decline of the Soviet economy, as well as the precipitous drop in the living standard of the Soviet people. As it turned out, Gorbachev got no concessions, and Soviet hard-liners were left with the impression that in superpower negotiations Gorbachev was willing to give away the store even though the Americans offered little in exchange. In this regard, Marshall Goldman quotes a member of the CPSU Central Committee as saying, "From a hard-liner's point of view, it always seems that when Reagan and Gorbachev meet, Gorbachev comes home without his shirt." (Goldman, 1992, p. 108) Nor was Gorbachev able to stem economic decline. Ultimately, economic decline sapped Gorbachev's ability to implement his reforms, and he lost the support of the Soviet people.

Steps such as taking the military pressure off the Soviet Union by agreeing to limit SDI development can be characterized as passive aid. They would have freed up Soviet resources that could have been shifted to support the reform effort. As the situation in the Soviet Union deteriorated, however, passive aid was clearly too little too late. This posed the question of whether the major industrial nations, acting unilaterally or through international organizations such as the World Bank and the International Monetary Fund, should step into the breach with active aid.

This possibility precipitated a debate between those who saw financial aid as essential and those who saw it as futile because the problems were so great. In addition, some commentators questioned the advisability of aiding the leaders of the "evil empire." Moreover, even supporters of financial aid differed on the nature and amount of aid that might be effective. To take one example, Graham Allison (a Harvard political scientist) and Gregory Yavlinsky (a Soviet economist) put forth a plan called the Grand Bargain. They proposed a set of step-by-step initiatives that international institutions and Western governments could take to aid the Soviet Union, if the Soviet Union held to a relatively fixed schedule of political and economic reforms. The basic underlying premise was that "the accelerating economic collapse [of the Soviet Union] makes the need for reform, as well as support, both urgent and critical." They even referred to what they called "a historic fork in the road: Reform the Soviet system or watch it collapse into chaos." (*Washington Post,* July 7, 1991, p. B3)

On the other side of the debate were those who saw financial aid as nothing more than an attempt to preserve a failing system and a waste of money. They wanted to emphasize other types of assistance. For example, James Hecht (an economist and writer) argued that "a massive program to train Soviet managers, coupled with a program to subsidize joint ventures between U.S. companies and Soviet partners, would be very effective." (*Washington Post,* July 7, 1991, p. B3) This program was based on the premise that a market economy cannot be created in a country where few understand the workings of the free enterprise system. Also, there was the fact that Soviet industry was not capable of competing in the world market and, further, that this situation would not change immediately with privatization, the establishment of property rights, and price reform.

As it turned out, Allison and Yavlinsky's pessimistic view that collapse was imminent was more accurate than they knew. The collapse of the Soviet Union during the autumn of 1991 shifted the topic of the debate from aid to the Soviet Union to aid to the successor countries. The new debate focused mainly on the question of aid to Russia and only secondarily on aid to the other former republics. This shift was accompanied by a significant psychological shift. No longer was the question of aid so closely tied to the issue of how much to help a former (and perhaps future) enemy. Rather, aid became a means of damage control. With the exception of Russia, none of the other successor states had superpower potential. Most policymakers in the West acknowledged that aid was necessary to prevent the resurrection of a reconstituted but nevertheless still hostile enemy. But, again, the type and amount of aid became the issue.

As the 1980s drew to a close, the major industrialized nations slipped into a recession, so the psychological barriers became less important than the material impediments. There was a shortage of resources that could be used to aid Russia and the other successor countries. In addition, the United States confronted a serious budget deficit. During the Reagan presidency, the United States had both lowered taxes and engaged in a massive military buildup. The Bush administration basically continued Reagan's policies. The result was that during the Reagan-Bush years the national debt went from about $1 trillion to about $4 trillion and budget deficits became the focus of a major policy debate. Many Americans questioned using revenue for foreign aid when domestic problems, such as homelessness, were not being addressed adequately for fiscal reasons.

The other major industrialized countries were also experiencing financial problems. The Federal Republic of Germany at first gave more aid to the Soviet Union than did any of the other major industrialized states. But when the wall between East and West Germany came down and a unified Germany became a reality, West Germany's interest shifted to East Germany. Highly prosperous West Germany soon found that East Germany's problems were much more numerous and serious than it had anticipated. And from that point on, almost all German resources were devoted to the effort to bring the East German economy up to the level of the West German economy. Because the West German electorate opposed tax increases to aid the East Germans, the government financed the assistance largely by borrowing. The result was inflationary pressure on the German economy, which stirred memories of the hyperinflation that had brought down Weimar Germany and raised Hitler to leadership. Thus, there was a limit to what the German authorities were willing to do in the way of giving financial aid to any other country.

Of all the major industrialized states, Japan had the deepest pockets, but a long-standing territorial dispute resurfaced to complicate Russian-Japanese relations. After World War II, the Soviet Union gained control over several Japanese islands. Japan still claimed the islands and demanded their return, but the Soviet Union (and subsequently Russia) refused to comply. Not surprisingly, Japan balked at giving aid either to the Soviet Union or to Russia. As the situation in Russia deteriorated, Japan relented a bit but remained unwilling to give direct aid and contributed only through international financial organizations. For various reasons, none of the other major industrialized states felt that they were in a position to devote substantial resources to aiding Russia or the other successor countries.

Even if the resources for aid had been available, there were fundamental questions about how they could best be used. Some suggested that what was needed was a Marshall Plan for the former Soviet Union. Transforming the newly independent countries, however, was a much more complex matter than rebuilding Europe after World War II. In the European case, the challenge had been to rebuild market economies. In the case of the former Soviet Union, the challenge was far greater: to transform a command economy into market economies. One thing the CPSU had done really well was to destroy or make illegal almost every vestige of market activity that had existed prior to Stalin's revolution from above.

The task in the former Soviet Union was not just to restore the economic infrastructure. It was to dismantle the old and build the new—in both material and human terms. Many of those who grappled with questions about the type and amount of aid that would be needed did not fully understand the problem. Essentially, there were three tasks:

1. The old economic infrastructure had to be eliminated. This meant eliminating not only outmoded factories and other economic institutions but also jobs, goods, and services.
2. The people who made the economy of the former Soviet Union work had to change their entire conceptual framework and view their relationship to their jobs and to the economy in general in a new way.
3. A new economic infrastructure had to be erected and people found who could make it work.

In comparison, the Marshall Plan was child's play: The only task was to rebuild the economic infrastructure; the people who could make it work were already there.

Therefore, by default, the situation in the former Soviet Union was approached in a disorganized and tentative way. More aid was promised than was delivered. Aid that was delivered was often not delivered in a timely manner and seldom had its intended effect. Not infrequently, aid fell into the hands of the mafia (*mafiia*). Large amounts were syphoned off from those really in need to enrich the Western bank accounts of the newly rich, many of them former Party bosses or black-marketeers.

In 1992, when the attempt at shock therapy did not produce rapid economic improvement, people still hoped that stabilization and gradual improvement would replace economic deterioration. In Russia and many of the other newly independent countries, reform efforts tended to bog down because of political infighting, which fragmented the reformers, led to government deadlock, and gave credibility to nationalists and those advocating a return to some form of state-run economic system. This problem was particularly acute in countries that were attempting a genuine, simultaneous transition to democracy. The electorate began to put pressure on elected officials to stop the deterioration in the standard of living—at any cost.

In the midst of the grave economic and political problems that beset the newly independent countries during the years that immediately followed the fall of the Soviet Union, the Soviet successor countries were eager to become full-fledged members of the international community. Most of them made active and persistent attempts to join various international organizations. Because Russia was heir to the Soviet seat on the United Nations Security Council, it was able to lay claim to the Soviet Union's great-power status, and it made a concerted effort to gain membership in other key international organizations.

RUSSIA AND THE INTERNATIONAL COMMUNITY

From 1945 to 1991, the United Nations had functioned mostly as a forum for the discussion of international problems. Because of the Cold War, it had not functioned as the collective security organization envisioned by its founders.[5] Each of the five permanent members of the Security Council (the United States, the USSR, the United Kingdom, France, and China) was given veto power over any decision taken by the council. Thus, any proposal to take military action was inevitably opposed by the United States or by the Soviet Union.[6] Either of them could stop collective security actions by threatening to use its veto power.

This situation changed dramatically because of Gorbachev's new foreign policy. In August 1990, when Iraq invaded Kuwait, the Soviet Union cooperated in the United Nations effort to liberate Kuwait. The USSR did not use its veto to stop the creation of the international military force that drove Iraq out of Kuwait, and it put diplomatic pressure on Iraq to cease its aggression. The immediate effect of the Soviet response to the Iraqi invasion was the restoration to the Security Council of its original role. Since then, the Security Council has been a resource that the member nations can call on to do what its 1945 charter said it should do: "maintain or restore international peace and security."

---

5. The major exception to this was the so-called police action in Korea. The vote to send troops into Korea was taken when the Soviet Union was boycotting the Security Council and thus was not in a position to veto the proposed action.

6. Until 1971, the China seat was occupied by the nationalist Chinese, who had fled to the island of Taiwan. In that year, the United Nations General Assembly voted to seat Communist China in the world body.

All fifteen former Soviet republics are now members of the United Nations General Assembly. For the most part, Russia has maintained the cooperative stance the Soviet Union showed at the time of the Gulf War. The situation, however, became more complicated as the focus of United Nations activity shifted from the Middle East to eastern Europe. Specifically, at the time of the United Nations intervention in the conflict between the Serbs (a Slavic and Christian people) and the Bosnian Muslims, Russian nationalists put pressure on the Russian government to lend support to the Serbs. (Lynch & Lukic, 1993; *New York Times*, December 2, 1993, p. 5) Thus, it seems that Russia will be more inclined than the pre-Gorbachev Soviet Union was to support the international security activities of the Security Council.

The Warsaw Pact was officially disbanded on July 1, 1991. With the end of the Cold War, many began to question the future role and purpose of NATO. The former satellite countries, however, and even some of the former Soviet republics (e.g., Lithuania) have been eager to join NATO, fearing a Russian threat to their future security. Russia opposed this. The NATO members were sensitive not only to the security concerns of some of the former Soviet satellites and republics but also to Russia's position that it was not a threat. In 1993, when this issue was being discussed, the foreign minister of Russia made the following point: "[W]e do not understand the discussions to the effect that NATO must give security guarantees to the countries of Central Europe and in the long term accept them as members. . . . How are these states threatened and by whom?" (Crow, 1993b, p. 22)

As an intermediate position, the United States proposed the Partnership for Peace. From an American perspective, the proposal allowed the United States and its NATO allies to reconcile three somewhat contradictory policy concerns. First, it addressed the security interests of the states that fear a rekindling of Russian expansionism. The program would permit the affiliated "partners" to participate in NATO exercises and meetings, but it would postpone the question of whether they should or would become NATO members. Second, it allayed the anxieties of the former Soviet satellites and of some of the newly independent countries without piquing Russia's fear of being isolated and without arousing Russian nationalists and hard-liners. Third, supporters of the Partnership for Peace believed it would help to define a new post–Cold War mission for NATO—a mission not requiring the identification of a new enemy but nevertheless set to tackle the major threats to European security in the New World Order. Those threats include (1) the possibility of a resurgent Russia, (2) the potential for outbreaks of ethnic conflict, and (3) the increase in political and economic instability associated with the political-economic transformation in east and central Europe. (Mihalka, 1994, p. 1)

A number of leaders from east-central Europe voiced disappointment with the Partnership for Peace proposal, arguing the necessity for NATO security guarantees. But despite their dissatisfaction, they quickly became signatories. By June 1994 twenty states had joined the Partnership for Peace. For the most part, the leaders of these states recognize the advantages and potential benefits offered by the partnership program, but they nevertheless prefer to view the program as a first step toward NATO membership. (Reisch, 1994, p. 18)

On June 22, 1994, Russia became the twenty-first state to join the Partnership for Peace. Russian leaders obviously calculated that participation was the best way to avoid isolation and to forestall as long as possible the issue of expanding NATO membership (unless, of course, such an expansion were to include Russia itself). The issue for Russia is not so much whether a particular eastern European state joins NATO but rather "that Russia neither be nor appear to be excluded from emerging security frameworks." (Lynch, 1994, p. 16) From this standpoint, the Partnership for Peace program could promote "negotiated transitions to security arrangements that complement or supplement existing ones." (Lynch, 1994, p. 16)

In April 1992, Russia became a member of the International Monetary Fund (IMF) and the World Bank.[7] Membership made Russia eligible for the types of economic aid that these international economic organizations offer to members. Both organizations were created at the Bretton Woods Conference in 1944. Designed to be part of the post–World War II economic order, they were created to help the world avoid the financial instability of the interwar period and the Great Depression. The Soviet Union attended the conference but declined to join. Thus, Russia could not inherit membership as it had inherited membership in the Security Council of the United Nations.

Charged with stabilizing the international financial system, the IMF is a short-term lender. It makes loans to countries that have problems meeting their international financial obligations. The money for the loans comes from the contributions of the IMF's more than 160 members. The loans are conditional: They depend on the borrowing country's willingness to adopt economic policies that the IMF considers sound. The IMF also assesses the economic performance of its members and provides them with advice when warranted. (Spero, 1990) With the fall of the Soviet Union, the IMF took on a major new task: helping to guide the former Soviet republics and satellite states in their transition from command to market economies.

The World Bank, the IMF's sister institution, was created to help rebuild Europe after World War II. Over the last forty years, its primary focus has shifted to making long-term loans to less developed countries to support economic development. It funds the creation and improvement of infrastructure, like roads, dams, electrification projects, and bridges. The World Bank also gives loans to fund other kinds of economic projects. For example, it has given aid to Russia to help refurbish petroleum-producing facilities.

Two other economic organizations have been important in the international effort to help Russia and the other successor countries in their efforts to transform their economies. These are the Group of Seven (G-7) and the Paris Club. The G-7 is made up of the seven leading industrial democracies: Britain, Can-

7. Currently, all of the former Soviet republics are members of these two organizations.

ada, France, Germany, Italy, Japan, and the United States. They initially came together in 1974 to develop cooperative strategies to deal with the global oil crisis that arose when a group of the major oil-producing countries drastically increased the price of crude oil. After 1977, they met annually to assess world economic conditions. They are the major contributors to the IMF and the World Bank, and they have determined the size and makeup of the economic aid packages offered to Russia since the breakup of the Soviet Union. Russia aspires to membership in the G-7. (*New York Times,* July 8, 1994, p. A8)

Originally formed in 1962 by ten members of the International Monetary Fund, the Paris Club aims to unify loan terms and conditions for debtor countries. It meets only when a developing country is experiencing significant difficulty in meeting its international financial obligations. Western creditor states evaluate the terms of loans or other types of assistance being extended to the troubled country. The Paris Club can negotiate to ease these terms. The club does not make direct loans to developing countries.

Gorbachev went to the 1991 meeting of the G-7 to ask for aid. He was turned down. Looking back, the members saw this refusal as a lost opportunity—it may have contributed to the coup attempt that brought down not only Gorbachev but the Soviet Union. Thus, even before the 1992 meeting the G-7 members had agreed on a $24 billion economic assistance package for Russia. The package included the authorization for up to $4 billion in borrowing power from the IMF, a $6 billion IMF stabilization fund to help in making the ruble fully convertible, and $14 billion in aid from individual countries. (*Washington Post,* June 25, 1992, p. B10) From the outset, implementation of this program proved difficult.

Because the IMF loans were contingent on an agreed-upon economic reform program for Russia, the failure of the Yeltsin government to develop and implement a comprehensive economic reform package meant that Russia and the IMF were never able to reach an agreement that lasted for very long. From the beginning, the IMF was forced to accommodate Russia in ways and to an extent that it had never done for any other country. Early in the summer of 1992, the IMF (with US agreement) prepared to advance Russia $1 billion in IMF loans, although a complete agreement had not yet been reached. The goal was to encourage Russian reform efforts both psychologically and financially. Because most of the $24 billion could not be disbursed without an agreement, by the end of 1992 approximately half had not reached Russia. Most of the half that Russia did get came from individual countries. (*New York Times,* September 28, 1991, p. A7) The stabilization fund remained unused. Its goal was to stabilize the Russian ruble when it became a fully convertible currency, but this had not happened. In addition, for a number of reasons, Russia never qualified for the remaining $3 billion in IMF loans.

Russia was considered a poor risk not only because of its failure to negotiate an acceptable agreement with the IMF but because of the trouble it was having making payments on its existing debts. If creditor countries were to be willing to advance Russia new loans, Russia had to renegotiate its schedule for paying back its existing loans. One reason why Russia had this problem was that it had assumed virtually the entire Soviet debt of $86 billion. The biggest creditor nation was Germany (approximately $38 billion in loans); US loans to the Soviet Union had been relatively modest (approximately $4 billion). (*New York Times*, December 16, 1992, p. A14) In December 1992, the Paris Club agreed to postpone for five to ten years more than $15 billion in debt payments. Russia was required to make only $2.75 billion in payments by 1994—a fraction of the $17 to $18 billion that would otherwise have been due in principal and interest payments. This concession was unusual, because the Paris Club normally does not reschedule government-to-government debt payments in the absence of an agreement between the debtor nation and the IMF. The agreement was made with the understanding that Russia would continue rapid economic reform.

In April 1993, the foreign and finance ministers of the G-7 met in an extraordinary session and put together a new aid package of $28.4 billion. (*Washington Post*, April 16, 1993, pp. A1, A18) The problems that had plagued the previous $24 billion package continued, however; and by the end of 1993, the amount of aid delivered to Russia ($8 billion) again fell far short of the amount promised. (*New York Times*, February 1, 1994, p. A6) The conservative vote in the December 1993 parliamentary elections had essentially been a protest vote by the Russian people against the hardships of rapid reform. Subsequently, Yeltsin and his prime minister put together a new cabinet that was more moderate in its approach to reform. As a result, it would be yet more difficult for Russia and the IMF to hammer out an acceptable agreement.

In short, what the IMF wants and what Russia may find hard to deliver in the long run are (1) that inflation be kept at a relatively low level to encourage investment and stabilize the economy; (2) that the government stop subsidizing unprofitable economic activity; and (3) that other reforms, such as the privatization of industry and the establishment of market prices, continue. (*Washington Post*, February 2, 1994, p. F1) The G-7 countries must consider what they can do to help Russia and mediate the relationship between the IMF and the Russian government.

Early in 1994, the Clinton administration proposed that economic policy toward Russia be governed by three factors: (1) getting some aid to the Russian people in order to lessen their pain and make them more receptive to additional reform; (2) continuing with the $4.1 billion in aid that the United States had pledged to support local programs that promoted capitalism and democracy; but nevertheless (3) refusing to weaken the IMF demands for reform before large-scale G-7 aid is sent to Russia. (*New York Times*, February 1, 1994, p. A6) Despite predictions to the contrary, in March 1994 Prime Minister Viktor Chernomyrdin appeared willing to accede to IMF demands. In exchange for his pledge to keep to an anti-inflation, tight-credit policy, the IMF agreed to release a $1.5 billion loan that had been held up since mid-1993 over doubts about Russia's commitment to economic reform. The loan had been eagerly sought by the Russian government, not only for the money but also for the certification of fiscal soundness it represents—a kind of IMF "seal of approval," necessary for attracting investors and soothing creditors. (*Washington Post*, March 23, 1994, p. A24)

For the major international economic organizations—the G-7, the IMF, and
the World Bank—Russia represents an unprecedented challenge. These organizations have had considerable success helping other formerly Communist
states make the transition from command to market economies. (*Washington
Post*, February 2, 1994, p. F2) The problem presented by Russia, however, is
on an entirely different scale.

First, there are the geographical realities. Russia constitutes approximately
one-sixth of the earth's landmass. Much of this land is not arable or only
marginally so. When Russia lost Ukraine, it lost its breadbasket. Russia has
abundant natural resources, but they are in inaccessible places, and the equipment Russia possesses for their extraction is obsolete and crumbling.

Second, Russia's command economy was more complete than the command
economies of any other formerly Communist country. Thus, both the people
and the mechanisms that might form the basis for a market economy are
scarce. Given the fact that people get set in their ways with increasing age, this
problem may be remedied only with generational turnover.

Third, the formerly Communist countries that have been making the most
successful transitions are relatively homogeneous. Russia is almost as heterogeneous as the Soviet Union was. In this regard, the most comparable country
outside Soviet territory is the strife-torn former Yugoslavia.

Russia has the potential to play a major role in the world, but what that role
might be is a problem. That is why international organizations like the G-7 and
the IMF cannot leave Russia to its own fate. For this reason also, Russia is—
even in its current state of poverty and confusion—a force to be reckoned with.

RUSSIA AS A "GREAT POWER"

The term *great power* is usually associated with the so-called modern era. It
dates from the post-Renaissance period, which witnessed the emergence of
nation-states and of a transoceanic global system of states. (Kennedy, 1987) A
country becomes a great power if it has significant military might and is willing
and able to use it to gain influence in the international arena. Great-power
status depends on several other factors as well.

A great power has historically been a relatively large country wih an effective state apparatus. Great powers have well-developed economies relative to
their competitors in the international system. Great powers are relatively efficient at generating wealth, which, in turn, allows them to extract the resources
and produce the material on which military power is based. There is, however,
a paradox associated with being a great power: A country requires a strong
economic base in order to become a great power. But the emphasis on production for military purposes ultimately tends to sap a country's long-term economic vitality. (Kennedy, 1987)

With the advent of the Cold War, the multipolar world of great powers was
eclipsed by a bipolar world of superpowers. The United States and the Soviet
Union had huge nuclear arsenals as well as formidable conventional forces.

Their armed might, plus their enormous size, put them in a category that was qualitatively different from the other great powers. With the fall of the Soviet Union, the United States became the sole superpower, but this position does not mean that it is able to perform the role of global policeman in the New World Order.

In his speech to the Russian Federal Council when it met for the first time after the election of December 12, 1993, President Yeltsin repeatedly called Russia a "great power." (*Washington Post,* January 12, 1994, p. A13) His assertion that Russia is a great power, however, does not make it one. Certainly, Russia has the landmass necessary to make such a claim. In addition, it inherited considerable military might from the Soviet Union. Herein, however, lies the problem. To create this formidable military machine, the Soviet leadership poured a disproportionate amount of resources into the military sector of the economy, effectively "starving" the other sectors. The collapse of the Soviet Union was largely due to the failure of its economy, not the failure of its military. And just before and after the fall of the Soviet Union, the sorry state of the economy began to have major effects on the military.

One effect was the growing inadequacy of the arsenal. Fewer resources have been available to support and update Russia's military. The military budget has barely been sufficient to support the troops; almost nothing has been left for necessities such as fuel, maintenance, and research and development. (*New York Times,* November 28, 1993, p. A1) In fact, between 1989 and 1993, spending on weapons and other military equipment fell 78 percent in real terms. Thus, the production of weapons fell precipitously. For example, there was a 92.9 percent drop in the production of attack helicopters and a 76.3 percent drop in artillery and nuclear-tipped missiles. (*New York Times,* December 3, 1993, pp. A1, A18)

Moreover, among both officers and soldiers there has been a serious morale problem. It too has an economic basis. As we noted in Chapter 10, the military faced a severe housing shortage. When Soviet troops began to return after the liberation of the satellite states of eastern Europe, they found that they had no place to go. Even more worrisome, by 1993, 70 percent of the officer corps "did not believe that their units were capable of carrying out their missions." Capability aside, a great power has to have a loyal military, but by 1993, even loyalty was in question. The problem can be seen in the comment of a senior officer: "You can forgive Yeltsin our pauper's pay, the destroyed health of our wives and children, our eviction from warm houses [in eastern Europe and the Baltics] virtually into open fields, but we cannot forgive that lands conquered by our fathers and grandfathers and our people living on them, have been given away." (*New York Times,* November 28, 1993, pp. 18–19) It is not surprising that a significant portion of the military voted for nationalists and conservatives in the December 1993 election. (Lepingwell, 1993c)

Russia clearly has the potential to be a great power. It has the land, the natural resources, and the military. Currently, however, it lacks the economic ability to utilize its resources effectively, and its army is underfunded and demoralized. Also, greatness is a relative concept. At the moment, Russia

THE POLITICS OF CHANGE

does not look like a great power when it is compared to the United States and its NATO allies. Unlike Russia, the NATO countries have strong economic bases, and viable militaries. NATO, "after four decades of grandiose spending and anxiety about the Soviet military buildup, no longer rates Moscow's non-nuclear forces even as a threat." (*New York Times,* November 28, 1993, p. 18) The former Warsaw Pact countries and the former Soviet republics, however, still fear possible future Russian expansionism. Thus, relative to the larger NATO countries, Russia does not look like a great power. Compared to the formerly Communist European states and the "near abroad," however, it does.

Not surprisingly, therefore, Russia has reasserted its role as a great power in international efforts to bring peace to the troubled Balkan peninsula (the former Yugoslavia). Russia's interest in the Balkans dates back at least a hundred years. It was as defender of the Slavic people of the Balkan peninsula that imperial Russia was drawn to support their cause against the Austro-Hungarian Empire after the assassination of the Austrian archduke in 1914. This same interest—support for the Slavic Serbs—has compelled Russia's involvement in what have been called "the Wars of the Yugoslav Succession." (Lynch, 1994, p. 10)

Beginning in 1992, Russia adopted and consistently followed a diplomatic approach with regard to the former Yugoslavia. The objective was a settlement to the war in Bosnia and Herzegovina that would not require the use of military force by the West. Throughout 1992 and 1993, Russia's diplomatic efforts worked to reinforce, not counteract, similar efforts of the Western powers. Indeed, in mid-1993, "the United Kingdom and France found that cooperation with Russia in effect shielded them as members of the UN Security Council from the need to veto US efforts to lift the arms embargo against the Bosnian government." (Lynch, 1994, p. 10)

Russian efforts to influence events in the Balkans intensified in late 1993. In September, Russian Foreign Minister Andrei Kozyrev cautioned Croatia that human and minority rights must be guaranteed in Krajina—Serbian-held territory in western Croatia. In November, Russia engaged in shuttle diplomacy, sending its deputy foreign minister to the capital cities of Serbia (Belgrade), Bosnia and Herzegovina (Sarajevo), and Croatia (Zagreb), and to "the seat of the Bosnian-Serb Parliament" (Pale), to try to reach agreement about the lifting of economic sanctions against Serbia. Subsequently, Russia reversed its resistance to a US-backed plan for a six-month extension of the mandate for United Nations peacekeeping forces in Croatia, Bosnia, Herzegovina, and Macedonia. Nevertheless, Russian leaders continued to oppose the use of air strikes against the Serbs in Bosnia. (Lynch, 1994, pp. 10–11)

Thus, the Russian Federation's intervention on behalf of the Bosnian Serbs in February 1994 demonstrated more a continuation of existing policy than a major new policy departure. What was new in February was Russia's dramatic attempt to move from a supportive to a leading role in the international efforts to bring peace to the region. Nevertheless, the limits of its great-power influence became apparent in April 1994 with NATO's initial limited air strikes against Serbian nationalist forces that were attacking the United Nations "safe area" of Gorazde. (*New York Times,* April 12, 1994, p. A1) Boris Yeltsin vigorously protested because he was not consulted before the air strikes were launched, but the Russian reaction was clearly a measured one. In the face of dwindling political support at home and enormous economic problems, Yeltsin could not afford to antagonize the United States and the other members of the G-7. For a "great power," Russia found its options severely constrained by its dependence on other states for political and economic support.[8]

Ironically, this dependence extended to the Serbs. Russia has needed to support the Serbs in the Balkan conflicts primarily because of domestic political pressures. The need to placate Russian nationalist sentiment leads to the potential for Russia's manipulation by the Serbs. This was dramatically acknowledged in April 1994 by Deputy Foreign Minister Vitalii Churkin, who for months served as Russia's point man in Bosnia. Churkin denounced the Serbs, noting that they demonstrated no genuine willingness to negotiate and were using Russia only to play for time. Upon his return to Moscow after a particularly frustrating round of negotiations, Churkin announced, "The time for talking is over. The Bosnian Serbs must understand that by dealing with Russia, they are dealing with a great power and not a banana republic." He added, "Moscow must decide if it can allow a group of extremists to use the politics of great Russia for achieving its own goals." For Churkin, the answer was an unequivocal "never." (*New York Times,* April 19, 1994, p. A10) Given the fact that his remarks received little coverage by the Russian press, however, it is unclear how widely shared his views are.

It is important not to lose sight of the fact that greatness is a relative notion. The major industrialized countries are much too strong to be intimidated by Russia, and the Serbs are able to manipulate domestic political pressures in Russia to their advantage. The comparative weakness of Russia's neighbors in the "near abroad" and in east-central Europe is very real. Considered against this weakness, Russia is indeed a "great power." This perception has contributed to a Russian foreign policy that treats the rest of the world differently from the way it treats its neighbors. Russian analyst Dimitrii Furman has suggested that Russia is pursuing a dual foreign policy. Toward the industrialized world, it has a "dinner jacket" policy conducted by the rules of the current diplomatic game. Toward its neighbors (particularly the "near abroad"), it has a "flak jacket" policy, conducting business on the basis of brute force "just as it did during the days of Soviet power." The "main actors are the Ministry of Defense and the directors of the military-industrial complex." (Teague, 1994, p. 11) Thus, although Russia cannot yet be regarded as a global great power (except with reference to its huge nuclear arsenal), it is pursuing a regional policy that is reminiscent of the way the great powers played old-style great-power politics.

---

8. The situation in the former Yugoslavia has also plagued other great powers, leading Edward Luttwak to question the continued viability of the "great power" concept in contemporary international relations. (Luttwak, 1994)

RUSSIA AND THE UNITED STATES

Throughout the history of Soviet-American relations, US policymakers became used to developing policies based on the idea that the Soviet Union was a state run primarily by one individual, the general secretary of the CPSU. Thus, Americans tended to think of the Soviet Union in highly personalized terms. This notion was, of course, appropriate when enormous power did lie in the hands of whoever held the top leadership post. With Gorbachev, however, the Soviet Union entered a period in which it was attempting to increase the importance of stable institutions. Gorbachev attempted to effect a transition from a state ruled by men to a state ruled by law. When the Soviet Union collapsed, Yeltsin pledged himself to continue this effort.

Not trusting this institution-building effort, American policymakers continued to focus on the top leader—first Gorbachev and then Yeltsin. This focus had two important effects. First, American policy was tacitly or explicitly based on the notion that the person holding the top post was critical. Thus, a tendency to support (or refuse to support) individual leaders or potential leaders caused American policymakers to ignore the process of institution-building in their foreign policy thinking. In other words, instead of supporting institutions, they supported individuals. Second, having spent most or all of their lives in a bipolar world where the United States and the Soviet Union were mortal enemies, American policymakers had difficulty shaking off their suspicions of Soviet leaders. They were constantly on the lookout for deception and were hypersensitive to any evidence that a leader was taking or demanding too much power.

The result of these two tendencies was a discrepancy between what was really happening in the Soviet Union (and, later, Russia) and what American policymakers thought was happening. It took the American government a long time to realize that Gorbachev was "for real"—that he was sincere in his effort to bring about major reform in the Soviet system. Then, once America had decided that he was "for real," it embraced him with a fervor that ignored his waning popularity in the Soviet Union as well as the failure of much of his reform effort.

Gorbachev's popularity with US policymakers and with the American people led the Reagan and Bush administrations to put too much faith in his leadership and to discount other potential leaders, such as Yeltsin. It also caused them to discount the importance of institutional legitimacy. An important example of the discounting of institutionalized legitimacy was the American downplaying of the fact that Gorbachev did not become USSR president by popular election and Yeltsin did become Russian Republic president in a popular, contested election. Once the Soviet Union had disintegrated, instead of shifting its main support to the institution-building process in Russia, the United States fixed its attention and support on Yeltsin, treating him in much the same way as it had treated Gorbachev.

Throughout the Gorbachev era and in the years immediately after the demise of the Soviet Union, the United States was constantly being "surprised" by developments and had to scramble to adjust American policies in a reactive rather than a proactive way. For example, because Americans had a tendency to pay disproportionate attention to the reformers, particularly the ones around Yeltsin, the United States failed to appreciate the rise of Russian nationalism in the period before the parliamentary election of December 1993. When the nationalists and their conservative allies gained a plurality in the Duma, the Clinton administration maintained its strong loyalty to Yeltsin and argued that this election result would not hamper the reform effort. Soon, however, the reformers who were most respected by Americans began to leave their government posts, and economic experts from abroad began to pack up and go home. Then, gradually and almost reluctantly, American foreign policymakers conceded that perhaps the election results were going to slow the pace of reform—if not reverse it. But they still voiced their support for Yeltsin. One American official remarked, "The ultimate reformer is Yeltsin and he is still there." (*Washington Post*, January 29, 1994, p. A1) At the same time, other observers saw Yeltsin in a different light. For example, Michael Dobbs, former Moscow bureau chief of the *Washington Post*, observed that although Yeltsin had "rejected communist ideology," he had "retained an authoritarian way of thinking." (*Washington Post*, December 12, 1993, p. C2)

Earlier, we discussed the duality in Russian foreign policy—the difference between the "dinner jacket" and "flak jacket" approaches. American foreign policy has historically also had its own duality. On the one hand, Americans (e.g., Woodrow Wilson) have rejected old-style power politics in favor of collective security arrangements through international organizations. They have maintained that it is in a state's interests to be cooperative rather than conflictual. This kind of thinking is associated with traditional idealism or liberalism. On the other hand, US policymakers in the postwar period have frequently followed a foreign policy based on realist assumptions that are radically different from assumptions held by the idealists. Realists assume that nation-states are the only relevant actors in international relations and that states define their interests in terms of power. In other words, force is the most important instrument of foreign policy, and conflict (rather than cooperation) is the natural condition of international relations. Neither set of assumptions is wholly correct or incorrect. Rather, both are correct to some degree, depending on the situation.

This duality has complicated the conduct of American foreign policy, especially when it confronts the duality present in Russian foreign policy. President Bill Clinton, in his speech at the 1994 NATO Summit, outlined his vision for the future of Europe: "I say to all those in Europe and the United States who would simply have us draw a new line in Europe further east that we should not foreclose the possibility of the best possible future for Europe, which is a democracy everywhere, a market economy everywhere, people cooperating everywhere for mutual security." (*New York Times*, January 10, 1994, p. A6)

These themes echo idealist assumptions about international relations. Thus, the Clinton administration strongly influenced NATO in its decision not to accept the membership of the eastern European states.

Realist critics, like former secretary of state Henry Kissinger, questioned the wisdom of this policy posture. Kissinger argued that it might be more prudent to extend NATO security guarantees to eastern Europe to discourage any expansionist ideas that Russia may entertain in the future: "It is in fact ambiguity about dividing lines, not their existence, and ambivalence about Western reactions, not their certainty, that tempt militarists and nationalists." (*Washington Post,* January 25, 1994, p. A19) It is important to add, however, that Kissinger did not discount the importance of continued economic aid and the need to encourage Russian inclusion in international cooperative arrangements. In contrast to the early policy stance of the Clinton administration, Kissinger advocated a two-pronged approach. Interestingly and importantly, in 1994 the two-pronged approach gained increasing salience within the Clinton administration.

This difference in perspectives highlights the dilemma for American policymakers. On the one hand, they want to encourage the cooperative stances of the "dinner jacket" Russian foreign policymakers. On the other hand, they do not want to make any moves that would encourage the "flak jacket" Russian policymakers. In particular, they do not want an extension of NATO membership to the former satellites of eastern Europe to awaken the ancient survival fears of the Russians. If NATO seems to be moving in on Russia from the west, Russian nationalists and militarists who argue that the best defense is a strong offense and that their age-old enemies in the West are still to be feared might gain credibility.

From the Russian point of view, Russia needs to be integrated into the world economy. It needs Western aid and investment to rehabilitate its national economy. Despite the difficulty of acquiring assistance from the West, Russia's interests continue to be served by pursuing cooperative economic relations. Similarly, its interests are served by the mutual reduction of strategic nuclear arsenals. Toward this end, START I and II have been negotiated, signed, and may someday be implemented. Where Russia has demonstrated far less willingness to adopt a cooperative posture in its international dealings is in areas where historical Russian security concerns are an issue. When dealing with its immediate neighbors, Russia is much less likely to settle for less than its optimal policy preferences. This attitude extends not only to the countries of the "near abroad" but also to the countries that bordered on the Soviet Union.

The points of contention in US-Russian relations are likely to be areas in which Russia has taken a "flak jacket" approach. But cooperation in other areas could be severely compromised if a working understanding about these sensitive areas cannot be reached. In response to Russia's claims of a "special status" vis-à-vis the countries in its immediate vicinity, the United States has had to deal with the security concerns of countries like the Baltics and Ukraine—not to mention the former satellites. In this regard, President Clinton conceded that the United States was willing to acknowledge Russia's special interest in the "near abroad" but stressed that that concession did not mean that Russia could interfere in the internal affairs of those governments without their express consent. In his 1994 State of the Union address, Clinton said: "We will seek to cooperate with Russia to solve regional problems while insisting that if Russian troops operate in neighboring states, they do so only when those states agree to their presence and in strict accordance with international standards." (*Washington Post*, February 5, 1994, p. A12)

RUSSIA'S BILATERAL RELATIONSHIPS WITH EUROPE, JAPAN, AND CHINA

The relationship between Russia and the United States is not Russia's only important relationship. As former president Richard Nixon noted, Russia holds the key to global stability. (*New York Times*, March 5, 1993, p. A29) So the relationship between Russia and other major international actors could prove to be just as important as the US-Russia relationship. Paramount among these other actors are Europe, Japan, and China.

In the era of the European great powers, Russia was counted as a European state. During the Cold War, the Soviet Union's relationship with Europe changed. The Soviet Union had an imperial relationship with eastern Europe and an adversarial relationship with western Europe. The questions for the future are whether the patterns of dominance and subjugation can be broken and whether cooperative relations can be cultivated with an increasingly integrated Europe.

The nationalist conflicts that had troubled Europe from the late nineteenth century through World War II were largely quiescent during the Cold War. There were three reasons: (1) the forging of economic integration through the European Economic Community; (2) the strong rule of Marshal Tito in Yugoslavia; and (3) the Soviet Union's ability to suppress ethnic rivalries in its satellite states. With the withdrawal of the Soviet Union from eastern Europe and the subsequent fall of the Soviet Union, interethnic hostilities and violence have again become a pressing issue in Europe. The Conference on Security and Cooperation in Europe (CSCE) has attempted to address this issue.

During the Cold War, the CSCE played a major role in furthering talks between the East and the West on human rights, military security, and other volatile matters. Beginning in 1989, the CSCE attempted to redefine and restructure itself in order to play a role in stemming the spread of interethnic conflict in eastern Europe. In this connection, it tried to play the role of peacemaker in areas ranging from Nagorno-Karabakh to Bosnia, offering the services of fact-finders and mediators. Most recently, it began to play a greater role in identifying and containing possible future conflicts in order to avoid the outbreak of violence. (Huber, 1993)

The issues of security and safeguarding territorial and political integrity have not disappeared from Europe in the aftermath of the Cold War. This is evident in the desire of some eastern European states to join NATO and in

NATO's rejection of their membership in favor of the Partnership for Peace. It is also evident in Europe's concerns about the disposition of conventional military forces.

In 1989 and 1990, NATO and the Warsaw Pact tackled this difficult issue and negotiated the Treaty of Conventional Armed Forces in Europe—the CFE Treaty. The CFE Treaty was signed in November 1990 by the members of NATO and the members of the Warsaw Pact. By setting limits on five categories of offensive conventional weapons (tanks, armored combat vehicles, artillery, combat aircraft, and attack helicopters), the CFE Treaty aimed to reduce the likelihood of conventional wars in Europe. When the treaty came into force on July 17, 1992, however, neither the Warsaw Pact nor the USSR still existed.

The new political configuration in Europe challenged the forty-year-old assumptions about military strategy in the event of a conventional war. These assumptions rested on the idea that such a war would erupt somewhere along Europe's East-West divide. The end of the Cold War and the fall of the Soviet Empire rendered these assumptions moot, but no country except Russia wanted to adjust the CFE Treaty to reflect new realities. Most arms control experts and diplomats have been more interested in preserving as much of this agreement as possible. They have opted simply to divide among the successor countries the weapons allocated to the former Soviet Union in the treaty, but without reconsidering the assumptions about the military strategy that give rise to the allocations in the first place.

Russian military leaders were unhappy with the limits the CFE Treaty placed on the number of offensive weapons they could retain in the St. Petersburg and North Caucasus districts. According to the treaty, these districts had a "rear-echelon" role. In the new geopolitical reality, however, these districts represent Russia's "first line of defense." (Clarke, 1993) The North Caucasus district has grown in prominence because of the civil wars in Georgia and the Armenian-Azerbaijani conflict. In 1992 and 1993, Russia made informal suggestions to the other CFE Treaty signatories that treaty-specified limits on offensive weapons in those districts be adjusted. Although Russia's suggestions were virtually ignored, the issue is unlikely to go away. Its resolution is crucial, not only to the future of the CFE Treaty but also to Russia's future relations with its European neighbors: "The resolution of this issue is likely to be the Russian military's litmus test in judging just how sincere its new Western security colleagues are about promoting the equal security of all the treaty's signatories" (Clarke, 1993, p. 38)

Although Russia has been historically treated as a European country, the fact of the matter is that it stretches to the Pacific Ocean. It shares borders with both Japan and China, and in both cases these borders are a matter of dispute. At this point in time, relations between Russia and China are less problematical than relations between Russia and Japan, although that state of affairs may change.

Russian-Japanese relations have been considerably strained over four disputed Kuril Islands.[9] These islands are at the bottom of a chain of small islands that stretch between the Japanese island of Hokkaido and the Russian peninsula of Kamchatka. The Soviet Union seized them from Japan at the end of World War II. Now that the Cold War is over, Japan wants them back. Having experienced the disintegration of its inner and outer empires, however, Moscow has balked at surrendering them.

Even though there is a distinction to be made between the Soviet Union and Russia, there is considerable feeling among the Russians that the Soviet Union represented a "greater Russia." This notion is strengthened by the fact that in many ways Russia has been the heir of the Soviet Union in the international arena. Thus, what was the Soviet Russian Republic's territory should now properly be Russia's.

To the Russians, who have lost most of what constituted the periphery of both the Russian and Soviet empires, the four tiny islands are a symbolic rather than a substantive issue. As Otto Latsis, a journalist for the Russian newspaper *Izvestiia*, commented, "By all criteria, this loss would be almost unnoticeable." But it is precisely because of what these islands symbolize about Russia that the Yeltsin administration has decided to draw the line against further losses. Latsis, thus, continued: "Things so happened that our capacity to assess the situation soundly and to resolve problems confidently ran dry precisely at this stage." (*New York Times*, September 11, 1992, p. A12)

Thus, sentiment in Russia has run against returning the Kuril Islands to Japan. It is felt that the Soviet Union won them "fair and square," that they were part of the Russian Republic, and that they should remain part of the Russian Federation. Moreover, the Russians were insulted by Japan's heavy-handed efforts to use its economic power to force Russia to give back the islands.

For the Japanese, also, this is a symbolic issue. In 1992–93, President Yeltsin abruptly canceled two state visits to Japan. Although the cancellations were officially attributed to other factors, the failure to make progress on resolving the territorial dispute was widely recognized as the real reason for them. A senior Japanese diplomat observed, "The second trip fell apart for essentially the same reason as the first did. They were not prepared to talk about the islands at all, and we could not completely shelve the issue. We said that there had to be some hint of progress." (*New York Times*, May 7, 1993, p. A11)

During the same period, however, the United States and other members of the G-7 pressured Japan to relax its position on economic aid to Russia—Japan had tied any significant assistance from Japan to the return of the islands. Japanese officials relented and in the 1993 G-7 aid package for Russia pledged $1.8 billion in economic aid and trade insurance. Thus, Japan lost considerable leverage over Russia with regard to the disputed islands, and its policy toward Russia was left

---

9. The Kuril Islands originally belonged to the Russian Empire. In 1875, however, Russia gave them to Japan in return for the southern half of Sakhalin Island. (Riasanovsky, 1984, p. 390)

in disarray. Its only remaining economic card is the promise of future "massive aid" if Russia surrenders the islands. In the wake of the nationalists' success in the December 1993 elections, however, it appears unlikely that Russia will be willing to give up the islands anytime soon. Thus, they are likely to remain an obstacle to good relations between Japan and Russia.

Historically, there have been many problems in the relationship between Russia and China. This is not surprising, because they share a border of approximately 2,500 miles. The border has been the subject of considerable dispute since the Russian Empire extended its reach into the Siberian Far East during the nineteenth century. At the point when Russia was expanding, China was particularly weak, "at war with Great Britain and France and torn by a rebellion." The Russian Empire took advantage of this weakness to force two "extremely advantageous treaties" on China. (Riasanovsky, 1984, p. 390) Most important, the Treaty of Aigun forced China to give Russia the north bank of the Amur River. Thus, the Amur became the major boundary between the two countries and a chronic source of border disputes.

In 1949 the Communists came to power in China, and there was a brief period of friendly relations between the two countries in the 1950s. By the end of the decade, however, the relationship was deteriorating because of border disputes and ideological differences. In May 1989, Mikhail Gorbachev visited China. This trip marked the end of the long-standing ideological differences between the two countries, but the border dispute was not resolved. It remains a latent but potentially explosive issue.

Currently, both Russia and China are interested in redefining their relationship on a pragmatic instead of an ideological basis. During President Yeltsin's 1992 visit to China, the two countries concluded numerous agreements aimed at achieving cooperation. These included accords on trade, business, education, science, arms sales, and nuclear power. (*Washington Post,* December 19, 1992, p. A16) For the moment, therefore, it is to the advantage of both countries to have good relations.

From the Chinese point of view, it is desirable to encourage a stable, rather than an unstable, Russia. From the Russian point of view, China is a large and potentially lucrative market, especially for Russian arms. Also, the Russians want Chinese help in converting a large part of their military-industrial complex to civilian production—an area in which the Chinese have considerable experience. (*Washington Post,* December 17, 1992, p. A40) The Russians are also determined to prevent "inadvertent or dangerous military confrontation between their forces" in the event of future internal instability in either of their two countries. (*New York Times,* December 5, 1993, p. A8)

IN RUSSIA'S SHADOW: THE BALTICS, UKRAINE, AND THE CENTRAL ASIAN COUNTRIES

In three other areas relations between former Soviet republics and the outside world are likely to play a role in shaping the international relations of Eurasia.

To the northwest are the Baltic states of Lithuania, Latvia, and Estonia. They are the only remaining former Soviet republics completely unaffiliated with the CIS. Their foreign policy is directed at becoming part of Europe and avoiding problems with their huge Russian neighbor. To the southwest is Ukraine, the only one of the three nuclear powers of the "near abroad" to resist surrendering its nuclear weapons. Ukraine's foreign policy has been aimed at achieving security guarantees and pledges of economic aid. Toward these ends, former president Leonid Kravchuk attempted to use nuclear weapons to gain leverage with both Russia and the United States. To the south are the Muslim countries of Central Asia and Azerbaijan. Their foreign policy is directed at establishing relations with other Muslim countries, as well as with Western industrialized states. In this connection, they are faced with two models of political development: (1) the secular model presented by Turkey and (2) the Islamic fundamentalist model presented by Iran.

The Baltic states want to integrate more fully into Europe to further their security and economic interests. Of the three, Lithuania was the first to secure the full withdrawal of Russian troops. Getting Russian troops out of Latvia and Estonia proved to be more of a problem, for two major reasons. First, there was the lack of housing in Russia. Housing was so scarce that there was little or no space left for returning troops. Second, there had been significant tensions between the ethnic Balts and the Russian minorities. In Lithuania tensions were minimized; but in Estonia and Latvia tensions continued, and Russian nationalists were concerned about what they perceived to be a hostile climate toward Russians in those countries. Thus, Russia was reluctant to pull out all of its troops. To the Latvians and Estonians, these were not reasons but mere excuses. The Estonian position was supported by the CSCE, which found no basis for Russian charges of human rights violations against Russians living in Estonia. (Kand, 1994, p. 92)

On April 30, 1994, Latvian and Russian leaders signed a treaty and other related accords on the withdrawal of Russian troops from Latvia. In Latvia, popular reaction to the treaty was mixed. Some praised the treaty as a necessary first step toward freeing the country of Russia's military presence. Others believed the treaty did not go far enough. For example, Russia was permitted to operate the Skrunda radar station for another four years. Critics also noted provisions for social security guarantees for Russian military pensioners. They feared Russia could someday use these provisions to justify a renewed military intervention in Latvia. (Bungs, 1994, p. 1)

In the years since they achieved independence, the Baltic states have increased their efforts to move toward a united defense posture, establishing a hot line linking their defense ministries. In addition, they began using military equipment that met NATO standards. (*Washington Post,* December 18, 1993, p. A20) They have also joined NATO's Partnership for Peace.

Along with Russia, the Baltic states joined Denmark, Finland, Germany, Norway, Poland, and Sweden in creating the Council of the Baltic Sea States. This organization was designed "to promote democratic and economic development in the region, foster cooperation among the member states, and strengthen ties between the members and nonmembers of the [European Union] in the region." (*RFE/RL Research Report,* March 20, 1992, p. 64) Lithuania also expressed an interest in pursuing membership in the European Union. (Girnius, 1994, p. 101)

On May 23, 1992, Ukraine along with Russia, Belarus, Kazakhstan, and the United States signed the Lisbon Protocol to START I. Although vague on particulars about the ownership and control of the nuclear weapons at issue, the protocol achieved its major objective: to find a way to ensure that all the concerned states ratified and participated in START I. The protocol also called for Ukraine, Belarus, and Kazakhstan to join the Nuclear Nonproliferation Treaty "in the shortest possible time." (Lepingwell, 1993b, p. 11) The protocol, however, did not directly and explicitly link together participation in the nonproliferation treaty and ratification of START I. Moreover, each signatory sent a letter to President George Bush specifying the interpretation and conditions that each attached to the protocol. (Lepingwell, 1993b, p. 11)

From a US perspective, the Lisbon Protocol, despite all its limitations, represented a significant accomplishment. It was a step toward the realization of two important policy goals vis-à-vis the former Soviet Union: (1) the ratification and implementation of START I, and (2) the securing of non-nuclear weapons status for three of the four states that had inherited nuclear weapons from the USSR. Basically, the United States was interested in arms reduction and nonproliferation, and the same could also be said of Russia. Russia, however, weighted these goals differently.

First and foremost in the Russian view was nonproliferation—securing the non-nuclear weapons status of Ukraine, Kazakhstan, and Belarus. Arms reduction, though very important, ranked second. It is hardly surprising, therefore, that Russia tried to impose a deadline for accession to the nonproliferation treaty (the Lisbon Protocol itself did *not* specify that accession must be achieved before ratification of START I). (Lepingwell, 1993a, p. 1; Lepingwell, 1993b, p. 11)

The Ukrainian perspective on nuclear weapons evolved to be quite different from the perspective of the Americans and the Russians. Rather quickly Ukrainian sentiment moved from supporting nonproliferation and endorsing non-nuclear weapons status for Ukraine to recognizing the deterrent value of nuclear weapons and coming to view them as essential for Ukraine's national security. Why this shift occurred is not difficult to understand. Security concerns were bound to emerge in a state that had just achieved sovereignty after centuries of imperial domination and in the face of such menacing developments as the rising tide of nationalism in Russia. Over the course of 1992 and 1993, it became clear that in order to eliminate nuclear weapons from Ukrainian territory a combination of strong incentives and reassurances about Ukraine's territorial integrity would be required. (Lepingwell, 1993a, p. 2)

The 1994 trilateral agreement signed by the Ukrainian, Russian, and American presidents represents the culmination of a months-long effort to combine both carrots and sticks with modest security guarantees to get Ukraine to commit anew to START I and to non-nuclear weapons status. In retrospect, it

appears that the event that was the catalyst for the trilateral talks that produced the agreement was the November 18, 1993, vote by Ukraine's parliament to ratify START I, but only conditionally. After the vote, Ukraine confronted an international backlash. It became very clear to President Kravchuk
that Ukraine was risking international isolation because of its stance on nuclear
weapons. The United States and other Western countries threatened to block
economic assistance and its membership in NATO's Partnership for Peace
program if Ukraine did not change its stance on nuclear weapons. More ominously, Russia increased its diplomatic pressure on Ukraine, hinting that it
might apply economic leverage. Under these circumstances, the Ukrainian president renewed his commitment to nuclear disarmament and thereby gave new
impetus to negotiations. Significant progress toward an agreement was made
when trilateral talks began in December 1993. For the first time, the United
States participated in the negotiations, acting as mediator between Ukraine and
Russia. (Lepingwell, 1994, p. 12)

The text of the agreeement signed in 1994 emphasizes the importance of
equal partnership among the three states, as well as "respect for the independence, sovereignty, and territorial integrity of each nation."[10] The insertion of
that phrase was particularly important to Kravchuk, who wanted to establish
for Ukraine a status on a par with that of Russia and the United States. The
agreement also reasserts the "commitment that Ukraine would accede to the
Nuclear Non-Proliferation Treaty in the shortest possible time." (Lepingwell,
1994, p. 13) It is significant that the language on this point is virtually identical
to that of the Lisbon Protocol, because it was precisely this point (Article 5 of
the protocol) that the Ukrainian parliament had rejected in November 1993.
The agreement also calls for "simultaneous actions on the transfer of nuclear
warheads from Ukraine and delivery of compensation to Ukraine in the form
of fuel assemblies for nuclear power stations." In addition to compensation,
Russia and the United States committed to limited security guarantees for
Ukraine (once START I enters into force and Ukraine becomes a non-nuclear
weapons state). These guarantees include their commitment to (1) refrain from
the use of economic coercion "to secure advantages of any kind" and (2) seek
immediate action of the United Nations Security Council "if Ukraine should
become a victim of an act of aggression or an object of a threat of aggression in
which nuclear weapons are used." (Lepingwell, 1994, p. 14)

For Ukraine, the road to nuclear disarmament remains fraught with uncertainty. The trilateral agreement is an important step, but it is just a step. The
Ukrainian parliament must ratify it; and even if it does so without amendment
(which is unlikely), many more agreements specifying the details of nuclear
weapons transfer must be ratified. Moreover, a similar process must occur in
Russia. Thus, "the trilateral agreement . . . may be the best possible agreement
on the elimination of nuclear weapons in Ukraine. Yet, even the best agreement

---

10. The text of the trilateral agreement was distributed by the US Information Agency wire
service. It is reprinted in Lepingwell (1994, pp. 14–15).

may not be good enough." (Lepingwell, 1994, p. 20) Competing interests both within and between Ukraine and Russia will make it very difficult for the same agreements to be ratified and implemented by their respective parliaments. Failure of the trilateral agreement, however, could sour relations among the three states and seriously delay the process of nuclear arms reduction specified in START I and START II.

As of mid-1994, Ukraine continued to send mixed signals about its policy on nuclear arms. During the first half of the year, Ukraine dismantled and shipped missiles to Russia, as specified in the terms of the trilateral agreement, despite the fact that the Ukrainian parliament had yet to ratify it. Shortly after his election as Ukraine's president, however, Leonid Kuchma equivocated on whether Ukraine would become a signatory of the Nuclear Nonproliferation Treaty. (*Washington Post,* July 14, 1994, p. A16) Ukrainian failure to sign the treaty could jeopardize Russian ratification and implementation of START I.

When the Central Asian countries achieved independence, they were almost immediately invited to join the CSCE. Some in Europe queried the wisdom of inviting the newly independent Central Asian countries to join, because they were not European countries. But the issue was resolved in favor of admission on the grounds that it was wise to bring these countries into the orbit of the secular West, lest they come under the influence of the fundamentalist Islamic movement. In fact, a major concern in much of Western policy-making with regard to the Central Asian countries was whether any particular policy decision would push them toward becoming secular or religious states.

Turkey was the most salient model for a secular Central Asia. The people of Central Asia are essentially a Turkic people with ancient ties to Turkey. Except in Tajikistan, they speak a mutually intelligible language closely related to Turkish. Thus, a tie with Turkey would have many advantages. Tajikistan, unlike the other Central Asian countries, has close historical ties with Iran, and the Tajiks speak a language close to the Farsi spoken by Iranians.

After the demise of the Soviet Union, Turkey lost little time in establishing embassies and signing economic protocols with the newly independent Central Asian countries. Turkish leaders believe their country can serve as a bridge between the Central Asian countries and Western investment and economic cooperation. Turkey is uniquely situated to play this role. Besides its ethnic and linguistic ties to Central Asia, it is the geographic gateway between Europe and Asia. In addition, over the past forty years Turkey has cultivated close security and economic ties with Europe. It is a member of NATO and has long sought membership in the European Union. The advanced industrial states of the West have encouraged Turkish efforts in this regard because they prefer the secular Turkish model of a Muslim state over the Iranian fundamentalist model. (Marnie & Whitlock, 1993, p. 41; *Washington Post,* March 22, 1992, p. A1)

Since early 1992, Turkey has offered loans and credit guarantees to the countries of Central Asia. In 1992 alone, Turkey granted a total of $1 billion in aid and trade credits. It established a scholarship program for students from Central Asia to attend Turkish universities and high schools and a training program for Central Asian bankers and diplomats. In addition, by means of the Intelsat VI, which orbits above the Indian Ocean, Turkey began beaming television programs to the area. It also initiated a major project that will link Turkey's telephone system with that of Central Asia. The plan is to have Turkey's state-owned telecommunications manufacturer supply "small-capacity public exchanges to each country." (Marnie & Whitlock, 1993, p. 41) This exchange network will be linked by the Turk-Sat telecommunications satellite to the Turkish exchange and by extension to the rest of the world. This arrangement is of considerable importance because the telephone system left in place in the Central Asian countries after the collapse of the Soviet Union routed nearly all international calls through Moscow. (Marnie & Whitlock, 1993, p. 41; *Washington Post,* March 22, 1992, p. A1)

The leaders of the four Turkic states of Central Asia have encouraged Turkey's involvement in their countries. Thus, in addition to developing regional projects, Turkey has signed a number of bilateral agreements. To cite just two examples: In July 1992, Uzbekistan signed its first credit agreement with Turkey; and in August 1992, President Nursultan Nazarbayev of Kazakhstan announced a pipeline project to deliver crude oil from his country to Turkey. Totaling $595 million, the agreement between Uzbekistan and Turkey enabled the Uzbeks to purchase Turkish grain, sugar, medicine, and consumer goods. The announced pipeline project was just one of several energy-related projects jointly undertaken by Kazakhstan and Turkey. (Marnie & Whitlock, 1993, p. 41; Olcott, 1992, p. 266)

Iran has also been active in the region. Iran borders on Turkmenistan and Azerbaijan and has long-standing cultural and religious interests in Tajikistan. In recent years, Iran has funded the construction of mosques and religious schools and has distributed religious literature in Tajikistan and throughout Central Asia. (Olcott, 1992, p. 266) In the years immediately after attaining independence, Turkmenistan was particularly active in pursuing close relations with Iran. Cultivating this relationship, Iran promised extensive assistance with economic development projects, particularly ones relating to the Turkmen oil and gas industries. (Marnie & Whitlock, 1993, p. 41)

Thus, since the breakup of the Soviet Union, both Turkey and Iran have stepped up their respective roles in Central Asia. Separately, each has pursued its own agenda through regional and bilateral economic aid projects. They have also worked cooperatively through the Economic Cooperation Organization (ECO) on various development projects. ECO members are especially interested in forging transportation and communication links as well as in creating a network of power grids and pipelines. Needless to say, these infrastructure projects are long-term as are the broader economic policy goals of the ECO. Thus, though important to the Central Asian countries, the ECO cannot meet the short-term economic needs of its newest members. (Marnie & Whitlock, 1993, p. 41)

This raises an important point. The question of whether these countries will develop along secular or religious lines is interesting and important, but for the leaders of the newly independent Central Asian countries it is superseded by the challenge of meeting their short-term political and economic needs. These needs, of course, are intertwined. Securing the financial assistance and invest-ment necessary to promote economic development will aid and abet their efforts to guarantee their political independence in the long run. They also recognize that achieving and maintaining political stability is a necessary pre-requisite to the accomplishment of their economic goals. Thus, to achieve the intertwined goals of political security and economic development, the leaders of Central Asia[11] have become pragmatists in the conduct of regional and international relations.

They both need and fear Russia. They look to Russia as a source of financial or technical aid and regional stability. At the same time, however, they recognize that, given the historic record of imperial relations in the region as well as Russia's enduring regional interests both political (e.g., stability along its borders) and economic (e.g., its interests in petroleum and gas reserves), Russia remains a formidable neighbor. Under these circum-stances, the leaders of Central Asia have been "determined to draw the Rus-sians back in only far enough to preserve their own independence." (*Washing-ton Post,* February 10, 1994, p. A27)

The desire to strike a balance in their relations with Russia was evident in a number of statements made by Central Asian leaders. At the 1994 World Economic Forum Uzbek president Islam Karimov refused to dismiss as insignifi-cant threats to the region from Islamic fundamentalism and the war in Afghani-stan and in this regard acknowledged that "Russia is the guarantor of security in Central Asia." (*Washington Post,* February 10, 1994, p. A27) At the same conference he and the president of Turkmenistan also insisted that they would resist Russian efforts to reassert economic dominance in their countries. On this point, Karimov pointedly remarked, "We give priority to Russia and to Turkey," purposely placing the Turks and the Russians on the same economic footing. (*Washington Post,* February 10, 1994, p. A27)

As part of their pragmatic approach to regional politics, Central Asian leaders also appealed to the West, particularly the United States. This part of their regional strategy appeared to have two components. First, the Central Asian leaders wanted to convince the West to make future aid to Russia contin-gent on Russia's progress toward democratization. President Nazarbayev of Kazakhstan suggested in an interview that the West should "emphasize that aid will be given only if Russia follows a democratic path—and you should stick to this in practice." (*Washington Post,* February 8, 1994, p. A11) Nazarbayev clearly believes, as do many other observers of Russian politics, that a demo-cratic Russia is far less likely than an authoritarian or an autocratic Russia to pursue restoration of the empire.

Second, the Central Asian leaders aimed to convince the West that Russia has received a disproportionate share of the aid distributed to the former Soviet Union and that increasing the share of aid directed to the other newly indepen-

---

11. We except Tajikistan from this discussion because it has largely surrendered its political and economic sovereignty to Russia in its effort to quell civil war.

dent countries would be in the mutual interest of the West and the countries of Central Asia. On this point Nazarbayev remarked, "We [in the other countries] all see that aid is provided only to Russia, and so Russia thinks it can do anything it wants with us." He also stated that Kazakhstan, in particular, offered the West a golden opportunity to promote democracy and economic development in Central Asia and thereby discourage any future Russian expansion: "Here you could make a proving ground for democracy and a market economy." (*Washington Post*, February 8, 1994, p. A11)

THE FUTURE OF RUSSIA AND THE NEW WORLD ORDER

The contours and dynamics of the New World Order will, in no small part, be determined by Russia's role in it. Will Russia redefine its relationship with the United States and the other advanced industrial democracies along cooperative rather than conflictual lines? Will it establish new, nonimperial patterns of regional relations with the countries of the "near abroad"? Answers to these questions will depend on internal developments in Russia—developments that can be influenced only at the margins by policies advanced by the other major actors in international relations. Nevertheless, it would be a mistake to dismiss such policies as wholly insignificant for shaping Russia's future. At a minimum, the policies of the United States and of the other major states must be crafted to avoid the outcome that everyone in the international community wants to avoid: the restoration of an autocratic regime in Russia, one with an expansionist, anti-Western foreign policy.

Western policy cannot be premised on either idealist or realist assumptions about Russia and the so-called New World Order. Western leaders must not assume that political and economic reforms will inevitably produce in Russia a stable democracy and a market economy and that Russia will be an active participant in a new order of mutual cooperation. However, neither must Western leaders assume that reform in Russia will ultimately derail and that a return to old patterns of power politics in international relations is inevitable. No one knows how events in Russia will unfold, so a pragmatic policy that aspires to the former and is prepared for the latter (without provoking it) is the one that should be pursued.

This is a difficult policy balance to strike. Analysts and commentators have suggested possible components of such a foreign policy vis-à-vis Russia and the other countries of the former Soviet bloc. The components include (1) shifting the focus from building democracy in Russia to building it in eastern Europe, where democracy has a greater chance of success, at least in the short run; (2) redirecting Western aid to send a greater portion of it to the countries of the "near abroad"; and (3) maintaining support, both economic and political, for Russia's reform efforts without passing judgment about how reform is going or should go. Of these components, the third offers the greatest challenge. It would require a flexible and nuanced policy—one committed to reform on Russian, not American or other, terms.

Such a policy would be difficult to accomplish because the United States, in particular, is accustomed to viewing the Soviet Union (and now Russia) in stark contrasts of black and white, friend or foe. This bipolar thinking contributed to the intensity of the Cold War and could sabotage American-Russian relations in the future. Americans need to appreciate the complexity and enormity of the processes of transformation under way in Russia. They need to recognize that there is tremendous potential for both conflict and cooperation between the United States and Russia, and they need to figure out how best to defuse the potential for conflict and enhance the potential for cooperation.

REFERENCES

Brands, H. W. (1993). *The devil we knew: Americans and the Cold War*. New York: Oxford University Press.

Bungs, D. (1994). Russia agrees to withdraw troops from Latvia. *RFE/RL Research Report, 3*(22), 1–9.

Bush, K. (1992). Russia's latest program for military conversion. *RFE/RL Research Report, 1*(35), 32–35.

———. (1993). Conversion and unemployment in Russia. *RFE/RL Research Report, 2*(2), 29–32.

Clarke, D. L. (1993). The Russian military and the CFE Treaty. *RFE/RL Research Report, 2*(42), 38–43.

Crow, S. (1993a). START II: Prospects for implementation. *RFE/RL Research Report, 2*(3), 14–18.

———. (1993b). Russian views on an eastward expansion of NATO. *RFE/RL Research Report, 2*(41), 21–24.

Evangelista, M. (1993). Internal and external constraints on grand strategy. In R. Rosecrance & A. A. Stein (Eds.), *The domestic bases of grand strategy* (pp. 154–178). Ithaca, NY: Cornell University Press.

Foye, S. (1993). Russian arms exports after the Cold War. *RFE/RL Research Report, 2*(13), 58–66.

Girnius, S. (1994). Lithuania: Former Communists fail to solve problems. *RFE/RL Research Report, 3*(1), 99–102.

Goldman, M. (1992). *What went wrong with perestroika*. New York: Norton.

Gorbachev, M. (1987). *Perestroika: New thinking for our country and the world*. New York: Harper & Row.

Huber, K. J. (1993). The CSCE and ethnic conflict in the east. *RFE/RL Research Report, 2*(31), 30–36.

Kand, V. (1994). Estonia: A year of challenges. *RFE/RL Research Report, 3*(1), 92–95.

Kennan, G. F. ("X"). (1947). The sources of Soviet conduct. *Foreign Affairs, 25*, 566–582.

Kennedy, P. (1987). *The rise and fall of the great powers: Economic change and military conflict from 1500 to 2000*. New York: Random House.

LaFeber, W. (1990). *America, Russia, and the Cold War* (6th ed.). New York: McGraw-Hill.

Lepingwell, J. W. R. (1993a). Introduction: The problem of former Soviet nuclear weapons. *RFE/RL Research Report, 2*(8), 1–3.

———. (1993b). Ukraine, Russia, and the control of nuclear weapons. *RFE/RL Research Report, 2*(8), 4–20.

———. (1993c). Is the military disintegrating from within? *RFE/RL Research Report, 2*(35), 9–16.

————. (1994). The trilateral agreement on nuclear weapons. *RFE/RL Research Report,* 3(4), 12–30.

Luttwak, E. (1994). Where are the great powers? *Foreign Affairs,* 73(4), 23–28.

Lynch, A. (1994). After empire: Russia and its western neighbors. *RFE/RL Research Report,* 3(12), 10–17.

Lynch, A., & Lukic, R. (1993). Russian foreign policy and the wars in the former Yugoslavia. *RFE/RL Research Report,* 2(41), 25–32.

Marnie, S., & Whitlock, E. (1993). Central Asia and economic integration. *RFE/RL Research Report,* 2(14), 34–44.

Mihalka, M. (1994). Squaring the circle: NATO's offer to the east. *RFE/RL Research Report,* 3(12), 1–9.

Olcott, M. B. (1992). Central Asia's post-empire politics. *Orbis, 36* (Spring 1992), 253–268.

Spero, J. E. (1990). *The politics of international economic relations* (4th ed.). New York: St. Martin's Press.

Reisch, A. (1994). Central Europe's disappointment and hopes. *RFE/RL Research Report,* 3(12), 18–37.

Riasanovsky, N. V. (1984). *A history of Russia* (4th ed.). New York: Oxford University Press.

Teague, E. (1994). The CIS: An unpredictable future. *RFE/RL Research Report,* 3(1), 9–12.

· 12 ·

REBUILDING

Soviet power ... bears within it the seeds of its own decay, and ... the sprouting of these seeds is well advanced.
GEORGE KENNAN (1947, p. 580)

No other country in living memory has been so gripped by simultaneous economic, political, and ethnic crises as the former Soviet Union.
EMIL PAYIN (Morris, 1993, p. 1)

Soviet power did, indeed, bear within it the seeds of its own decay. The Soviet Union had a political system—empire—that was vulnerable to stagnation and disintegration. It had a command economic system that was unworkable. In addition, it sat on the powder keg of a myriad of different and often mutually hostile ethnic groups that it had failed to blend into a single Soviet people. One reason why the Soviet Union lasted as long as it did was the willingness of the Soviet leadership to base its rule on the use of coercion. Another reason was the unity that stems from having a common enemy. The primary social glue holding Soviet society together was power. As Soviet leaders after Stalin became more and more reluctant to use brute force and as the economic system became more and more dysfunctional, the Soviet Union fell into an unstable state of stagnation, which led to political and economic disintegration.

Faced with deteriorating economic conditions, as well as an unwieldy and corrupt political system, the new generation of leaders who replaced the elderly Brezhnev, Andropov, and Chernenko saw that something needed to be done to arrest the political and economic decay. In 1985, under Mikhail Gorbachev, they launched a brave and sweeping set of political and economic reforms. They never intended to do away with the system completely; they never saw themselves as initiating a process of revolutionary change. For the most part, they were dedicated members of the CPSU. They fully intended to keep the basic structure of the Soviet system. They believed that it had gotten off track and their job was to get it back on track. The differences that emerged within the CPSU leadership under Gorbachev were not over whether reform was necessary. There was widespread consensus that something needed to be done. The disagreements were over the nature and timing of reform.

What the leaders did not realize was that they were trying to reform the unreformable. Most of the problems that had gotten the Soviet Union into the condition it was in by 1985 did not stem from the failure of previous leaders to run the system properly. Rather, they were largely due to flaws inherent in the system itself. Mere reform would not set things right. Revolutionary change was necessary.

In fact, efforts to reform the existing system only aggravated its problems. As the reform effort progressed, it became clear that ethnic and economic problems overshadowed all the rest. Glasnost (and later democratization) unleashed powerful ethnic loyalties and interethnic hostilities that had long lain dormant under a Soviet nationalities policy that repressed all but the most superficial manifestations of ethnic identity. Perestroika revealed that the problems in the Soviet economic system could not be alleviated by mere adjustments. As more and more economic reforms were put into place, things got worse instead of better. It became increasingly clear that the cure was to abandon the command system completely and to try to put a market system in its place.

Gorbachev and his advisers had trouble even acknowledging that these problems called for drastic measures. In a sense, they were captives of their own pasts. Most of them had gotten into positions of influence within the old system. They were very much products of that system. It had worked for them in the sense that it had allowed them to attain leadership positions. Although they were ready to make changes, they were not ready to throw everything out and start over. They were unquestionably brave and innovative, and their achievements should not be minimized. Nevertheless, they had their limits. At the time, it seemed as if they were acting in a truly revolutionary way. The early period of reform was a time of heady optimism, both inside and outside the Soviet Union. Then everything began to unravel. The reformers had set into motion forces they did not adequately understand and could not effectively control. By the end of 1987, they were scrambling to keep up with events. They had lost the capacity to lead in anything but a reactive way. They were overwhelmed by one crisis after another until the final crisis, the failed coup of August 1991.

In all fairness, it should be noted that Emil Payin, whom we quote at the opening of this chapter, is right. The problems they faced were unprecedented. Everything was falling apart at the same time. Every action they took to alleviate one problem had ripple effects on a multitude of other problems. They could not reform everything at once. If, however, they did not, the context in which they instituted their reforms made those reforms ineffective at best and harmful at worst. What they were unable to see and accept was the fact that reform could not save the Soviet political-economic system. The system itself needed to be replaced by one that could work. This was easier said than done. After all, an entire physical superstructure was in place and could not easily be transformed. Both the leadership and the people had grown up under the old system. It was what they were used to—an evil, perhaps, but a known evil. And in times of crisis, people tend to fall back on what they know, the familiar ways of doing things.

Leaders both in the former Soviet Union and in most of the successor countries have faced and are still grappling with enormous political and economic problems. For the most part, they are poorly equipped to deal with these problems. They have little practical knowledge of or experience with democracy or market economies, and they lack the financial resources that could ease the transformation.

The one thing that the leaders of all of the successor countries have in common is that economic policy is their primary concern. Some of them have been making a genuine effort to build democratic institutions and market economies at the same time. Others have continued to govern much as they did under the old Soviet system and, within this political context, are trying to move toward market economic systems. In successor countries that have chosen to move toward both democracy and market economies, the leaders have had to contend with the fact that there is a limit to the amount of hardship they can impose on their people—if they want to remain in office. This constraint has been a powerful conservative force. The standard of living for most people has dropped precipitously. In effect, would-be democratic leaders are caught between the proverbial rock and hard place: If they choose to impose some form of rapid change, or shock therapy, they are likely to be thrown out of office by a suffering and angry electorate. But if they do not, the result is likely to be much the same. There are no panaceas, no easy ways out.

Successor countries where the leadership has continued to play politics by the old rules have tended to be more politically stable and thus more attractive to foreign investors. Some, like Turkmenistan, look as though they could make a smooth transition to a market economy. The smoothness of the transition, however, depends on factors such as the stability of the government and the extent to which the stability stems from authority rather than from power. The countries also need sufficient capital (including foreign investment) to develop industries related to their natural resources, as well as to create a diversified domestic economy.

THE CREATION OF NATION-STATES

We have referred to the former Soviet republics as "successor countries." This label evades the question of whether all can be said to have achieved statehood. State-building has two aspects. To be regarded as a state, a country must have external sovereignty. The international community must recognize it as an independent state with clearly defined borders. For the most part, this recognition has been formally extended to all of the former Soviet republics. To be regarded as a state, a country must also have internal sovereignty. The former Soviet republics differ greatly in the extent to which they have met this criterion for statehood.

With reference to external sovereignty, the major issue is the future role and influence of Russia. Powerful political forces in Russia support a range of policies with regard to the other former Soviet republics. On the one hand, there is much support for the assertion that Russia should have a "special relationship" with them or play a "special role" in the territory that was once the Soviet Union. On the other hand, many extremist politicians advocate a return to the empire. In between is a range of types and intensities of policy preference that could prove threatening to the external sovereignty of the other newly independent countries. If Russia remains intact, it will—at the very least—be the regional hegemon by virtue of sheer size and relative power.

The central issue is: To what extent will Russia act in ways that compromise the external sovereignty of the other former Soviet republics? If Russia is effectively controlling the government of one of the other post-Soviet countries, to what extent will that control compromise the sovereignty of that country in the eyes of the international community? For example, during the entire period of Soviet rule, the United States maintained symbolic diplomatic recognition of the Baltic republics. It was not, however, recognition of their external sovereignty. Everyone knew that Lithuania, Estonia, and Latvia had little external or internal sovereignty. Such symbolic recognition does not make a country a state. For the establishment of statehood, the recognition of the external sovereignty of any of the successor countries has to be real, not symbolic.

With reference to internal sovereignty, there is a great deal of variation in the extent to which the newly independent countries have been able to establish a viable administrative and coercive apparatus. On one end of the spectrum are countries like Georgia and Tajikistan, which, torn by internal strife, have barely begun to try to establish viable internal institutions of administration and coercion. On the other end are countries like Estonia and Kyrgyzstan, which are well along in the institution-building process.

Thus, while the creation of external sovereignty is contingent on recognition by other states, the creation of internal sovereignty is largely an exercise in institution-building. An institution is a social structure (e.g., a parliament) that performs vital social functions. For internal sovereignty, the institutions needed are those of coercion and administration. Establishing a state, then, is a matter of creating effective coercive and administrative institutions. A state's institutions for administration and coercion may be more or less well developed. In order for internal sovereignty to exist this apparatus must only be adequate to the current needs of the state. What is adequate varies with several other factors.

First, is the basis for rule power or authority? If the basis for rule is mainly power, the administrative and coercive apparatus must be much more highly developed than it would need to be if authority were the basis for rule. Under rule by means of power, the psychological basis of behavior is simple compliance. To ensure compliance, a high level of supervision and the potential for coercion are necessary. Empires, for example, need a more developed administrative and coercive apparatus than democracies need. Why? Democratic rule is based mainly on authority. If the basis for rule is mainly authority, there is less need for supervision because the inhabitants of the state have internalized its key rules of behavior, especially the rules for managing or settling conflict. The need for close administrative supervision and coercion is limited to situations in which the participants have failed to internalize the relevant rules.

Another important factor is homogeneity in the population. The bases for homogeneity include culture, language, ethnic identity, and common goals. Frequently, these overlap in real-world situations. The need for supervision and coercive control is lessened when the inhabitants of a country perceive themselves as part of a unified whole—when they think in terms of "we," rather than in terms of "us versus them." A common identity tends to be associated with a fairly high degree of shared values. Shared values are essential for the building of community based on trust. When rulers are viewed as "us" and are trusted, there is much less need for an explicit rule system and a highly developed administrative and coercive structure to impose it. People naturally act in ways that are appropriate, because of their internalized values. And there is room for individual variation, because trust leads to more tolerance of diversity.

The notion of tolerance of diversity leads from the topic of state-building to the topic of nation-building. Nation-building is a much more subtle process than state-building. It happens primarily in people's minds. Nation-building is the process of creating identical or—more realistically—reasonably similar sets of ideas and values in the minds of a population. People are loyal to a nation-state because they perceive it in terms of "us." Other states, rather than groups within the state, are seen as "them." Here again it is a matter of degree. The intensity of nationalist loyalty felt by the inhabitants of a state may vary as may the proportion of the population that shares these nationalistic feelings.

The key question is: Are the intensity and pervasiveness of national identity adequate to the country's current needs? A highly homogeneous country like Lithuania can afford to be relaxed in welcoming and extending citizenship to non-Lithuanians. Estonia, with a large and relatively unassimilated Russian minority, has been much more threatened by the Russians. Its response has been to erect major barriers to the assumption of Estonian citizenship by Russians and to offer Russians incentives to return to Russia. Thus, Lithuania is much better situated to build a viable nation than is Estonia. Countries like Estonia, Kazakhstan, and Moldova, with large or restive Russian minority blocs, find it difficult to assimilate their Russians, because of Russian nationalism and questions about the relationship between their Russian inhabitants and Russia. These concerns make it difficult for a country to create a viable nation.

The feelings of connection and trust that arise from a successful nation-building effort, however, are a strong basis for the legitimacy that undergirds authority. Forging institutions of democracy can bolster this psychological stance. True nation-states are less likely to need rulers whose actions are primarily based on force. Nationhood creates an environment in which there is less need for a powerful coercive and administrative apparatus. If people know, understand, and have internalized the rules—be they norms, traditions, statutes, or constitutions—there is less need for supervision and enforcement.

(Barkun, 1968) Thus, nation-states are more likely than empires to be ruled mainly by authority. It follows, then, that nation-states tend to be more stable political entities than empires. Nation-states that are not democracies are, correspondingly, in a better position to move toward democracy than are countries that have not yet become nation-states.

THE POLITICAL OUTLOOK

Aside from economic problems, the greatest threats to the building of viable nation-states by the newly independent countries are threefold: (1) domestic violence, (2) ethnic animosities, and (3) the heritage of all-or-nothing politics. The first two are related in countries like Armenia, Azerbaijan, Moldova, and Georgia. Tajikistan's violence has been more political and religious than ethnic. Other countries, like Kazakhstan, Latvia, and Russia, have major ethnic problems, but have not experienced serious related violence as of this writing. Finally, none of the newly independent countries has a cadre of political activists or governmental leaders with long experience in the give-and-take of democratic politics. In fact, for many, willingness to compromise is taken as a sign of weakness or incompetence.

It has been said that war is the mother of all states. This is true to the extent that war requires that a country build a coercive apparatus sufficient to defend its borders, as well as maintain domestic peace. In addition, war can unite a nation to rally against a common enemy. Ongoing violence, however, can also have a destructive impact on both state-building and nation-building. In at least five of the former Soviet republics violence has been a major problem from the start.

In Armenia and Azerbaijan, the war has been international and has had a different impact on the institution-building efforts of each country. Although both have had to attempt to create and maintain effective coercive institutions, the creation of effective administrative institutions has suffered especially in Azerbaijan, where the vicissitudes of war have led to numerous changes of regime. The political leadership of Armenia has been more stable, but institution-building in areas removed from the war effort has been difficult. For example, the war has delayed indefinitely efforts to rebuild and recover from the devastating Armenian earthquake of 1988. Both of these countries are relatively homogeneous (with the exception of Nagorno-Karabakh in Azerbaijan), and both have international recognition and significant coercive apparatuses. If the problem of Nagorno-Karabakh could be settled satisfactorily, both have the potential to become viable nation-states. The violence, however, must stop permanently.

Unlike international war, civil war is the destroyer of states. Civil war has been a major problem for Moldova, Georgia, and Tajikistan. In Moldova, many of the issues causing civil unrest were at least temporarily settled by a consensus-building process. But the problems with the Russian nationalist "Dniester Republic" have proved less amenable to compromise. Russian control of a significant portion of Moldova calls into question the validity of Moldova's established borders. It also calls into question Moldova's internal sovereignty, for the coercive and administrative apparatus that has been established in the rest of Moldova does not function in the so-called Dniester Republic. For example, the government of Moldova supported Yeltsin during his parliamentary crisis in the fall of 1993, but the "Dniester Republic" not only supported the parliamentary opposition but also had representatives fighting on that side in Moscow. (Socor, 1993) Until the Moldovan government can establish control throughout *all* of its territory, its hold on both internal and external sovereignty will be precarious.

Georgia also remains so fragmented that its leadership cannot really make a claim to fixed borders or internal sovereignty. The ability of the Abkhazian rebels to take control of a large part of western Georgia in 1993 calls into question the validity of the borders that Georgia claims. Unless these situations can be remedied, the international recognition that Georgia achieved after the disintegration of the Soviet Union will become more symbolic than real—at least with regard to the extent of the territory regarded as Georgian. Correspondingly, the fact that the Georgian coercive and administrative apparatus has been unable to control large portions of its territory calls into question Georgia's internal sovereignty. Until these problems have been solved and the territory is at peace, nation-building will not even be an issue. Thus, the prospect that Georgia will establish a viable nation-state anytime in the foreseeable future is dim.

The civil war in Tajikistan is similarly a barrier on the road to building a viable nation-state. In one respect, Tajikistan is in better shape than Moldova and Georgia. Its borders are not being challenged, although there is considerable movement of contending forces back and forth across the Afghan border, as well as involvement by Afghan fighters. The basic problem, therefore, is one of establishing internal sovereignty. There is simply no Tajik coercive apparatus that can subdue the rebels. The administrative apparatus is a shambles. By the end of 1993, the Tajiks had given Russia significant control over their economy, and Russian troops were actively supporting the Tajik government in the civil war. (*Washington Post,* Janurary 8, 1994, p. A20) Thus, there is a question as to whether the administrative and coercive apparatus is controlled by Tajiks or Russians. Under these conditions, it cannot be said that the Tajiks clearly possess internal sovereignty. Lack of internal sovereignty, in turn, undermines Tajikistan's claim to statehood, in spite of the fact that it is recognized as a state by the international community. Needless to say, under these conditions, nation-building is not yet even an issue.

The rest of the countries that succeeded the Soviet Union have been able to sustain a reasonable measure of domestic peace and thus are better situated to claim actual, as opposed to symbolic, statehood based on both external and internal sovereignty. For them the problems of building viable nation-states revolve around two major issues: (1) To varying degrees, they must solve the problem of nation-building, and (2) to varying degrees, they must make key decisions in their institution-building process. Although most of them have viable claims to external sovereignty, their claims to internal sovereignty will depend on the quality of the government and economic institutions they are establishing. Given continued domestic and international peace, however, their chances of building workable and stable nation-states offer, to varying degrees, a real basis for optimism.

For some, like Russia, the prospects for ethnic or political violence are good. The 1993 insurgency in Moscow is an indicator of the potential for serious conflict, as are the makeup and leadership of the parliament emerging from the December 1993 elections. By pardoning the leaders of the insurgency, as well as the leaders of the 1991 coup attempt, the new Russian parliament set a dangerous precedent. In other countries, like Estonia and Latvia, there is the hope that violence can be avoided and ethnic differences resolved to a sufficient degree that an effective nation-building effort can be pursued. The great unknown is the future of Russian nationalism, both in Russia and in the "near abroad." To the extent that Russia is willing and able to interfere in the affairs of its neighbors, it will interfere with their efforts to build viable nation-states.

Finally, many of the newly independent countries have found it difficult to build viable democratic institutions for two related reasons. First, no one in a position to assume leadership has had much experience with democratic processes. On the contrary, all of them grew up under the rule of Moscow. Even on the local level, the Party bosses did not permit much in the way of popular participation—claims to the contrary notwithstanding. Thus, the trust, bargaining, and compromise so crucial to the effectiveness of the democratic process have not come naturally. And, democratic participatory skills have not been easy for the post-Soviet political leaders to learn, much less to internalize.

Moreover, in many of these fledgling democracies, there is a political culture that regards compromise as a dirty word. Political figures are expected to take a stand on issues and to maintain that position in the face of all opposition regardless of the consequences. This is the heritage of the political culture of absolutism and strong leaders. Inflexibility is confused with having solid, well-thought-out convictions. In the former case, compromise is impossible; in the latter, it is difficult—but possible if the opposition presents a convincing argument for change. As long as the political leader who bargains and compromises is seen as lacking character or as a weakling, viable democracy will be difficult to establish and maintain.

THE ECONOMIC OUTLOOK

The task facing all of the newly independent countries is to restructure their economies while maintaining internal political and economic stability. Under any circumstances, to do both at the same time is difficult. Given the current situation in most of the former republics, the task of restructuring while maintaining stability is particularly difficult.

Decision-making, information, and incentives are radically different in command and market economies. In command economies, decision-making is centralized, information is generated bureaucratically, and most incentives are coercive. In market economies, decision-making is decentralized, information is generated through relative prices, and most incentives are related to individuals' perceptions of material self-interest. To move successfully from one system to the other, a country needs a consistent plan. This has been lacking in most of the newly independent countries. One consistent policy that might be followed is shock therapy, a rapid movement from one system to the other. Another is a slow, deliberate, but consistent movement from one system toward the other. Although there has been talk about shock therapy, it has not been seriously attempted in the former Soviet Union. In Russia and in many of the other newly independent countries, economic transformation has been attempted in a series of starts and stops—innovations and retreats.

The absence of a clear and consistent plan for economic transformation complicates and confuses the process of change. Lack of clarity and consistency creates confusion about the locus of, and responsibility for, decision-making. In Russia, for example, efforts to privatize the economy (and thus to decentralize decision-making) have been proceeding. Heavy industry, however, has remained strongly tethered to the Central Bank, and the Central Bank's willingness to issue credits to keep obsolete and unproductive factories from failing has compromised decentralized decision-making. The Central Bank thus has freed managers from the responsibility of making and being held accountable for hard choices that will affect their firm's financial solvency and its work force. As a result, there have been almost no bankruptcies in Russia. Waiting for government subsidies, however, has had serious negative consequences. Production lines have been slowing down or stopping altogether. Instead of being fired, employees have been put on unpaid vacations or on leave without pay. According to one commentator, "a peculiarly Russian version of economic depression is being manifested, in which most people work only in theory and get paid that way too." (*Washington Post*, February 18, 1994, p. A30) Technically, therefore, there has been very little unemployment. An ongoing stream of credit to unproductive and uncompetitive factories is the perfect recipe for inflation and ultimate industrial collapse.

Inconsistency has also riddled efforts at price decontrol. The tendency has been to remove price controls and then, in the face of soaring inflation, to put them back into place. Although this practice may benefit people who are hard-pressed to make ends meet, it negates the value of relative prices as a source of information for economic decision-making. Too many prices have had too little relationship to conditions of demand and supply. This problem has been particularly acute in countries trying to move toward both democracy and a market economy. There has been an enormous amount of political pressure from hard-pressed constituents when rising prices cut too far into their buying power. And, of course, these constituents have spent their entire lives in a country, the Soviet Union, where prices seldom changed.

With some exceptions, primarily in the small-business sector, incentives based on material self-interest have been slow to take hold in Russia's transforming economy. Managers and workers in the industrial sector have preferred to wait for the central government to take care of them, and the central government's policies have frequently done little to encourage them to do otherwise. Most of the population tends to fear risk-taking and is accustomed to a parental relationship with political leaders.

The bottom-line necessity for the transition from a command economy to a market economy is consistency. Because restructuring rapidly without creating serious political and economic instabilities would be difficult, the best course of action seems to be slow but steady movement. Unfortunately, the position taken by the advanced industrialized states pushed the successor countries in the direction of shock therapy. Even if they were politically stable, homogeneous countries, that approach would be difficult, though it would be feasible. But the newly independent countries have been neither stable nor homogeneous. Thus, their political leaders have been caught in a bind: The requirements of economic reform have pushed them in one direction while political forces have pulled them in the opposite direction.

A massive infusion of foreign capital has been desperately needed. Foreigners, however, are looking for good investments, and they are reluctant to invest in countries that are unstable. They also need to be able to "do business" with some degree of ease. They need a clear, unchanging, and reasonably accommodating atmosphere in which to operate. Instead, in the successor countries they have found laws that are confusing or obsolete. To cite but one example, a popular American joint venture hotel, the Radisson Slavianskaia, found itself with its bank accounts frozen and faced with a multi-million-dollar lawsuit over the claims of two maids to permanent employment—claims based on Soviet labor law. The potential for this kind of legal action based on obsolete laws enforced by Soviet-style courts makes Western business interests slow to invest in Russia. According to the hotel's director, Vladimir Draitser, "The legal infrastructure isn't in place, along with a lot of other stuctures. The legal foundations for the overall changes, outside the beautiful declarations of the Constitution, just aren't there. And until they're in place, the main reform, that of the minds of the people, won't happen." (*New York Times,* February 14, 1994, p. A9)

Would-be investors also confront the remnants of one of the most immovable bureaucracies of the twentieth century. Despite a disastrous lack of adequate medications, for example, foreign drug-makers faced a bureaucratic nightmare when they tried to obtain permission to market their medicines in Russia. Thus, while they tried to clear the scientific and bureaucratic hurdles that were placed in their way, there were epidemics of treatable and preventable diseases. Ultimately, the Russian government made a pact in which it promised to automatically approve American medicine and vaccines that had been found to be safe and effective by the US Food and Drug Administration. (*New York Times,* February 17, 1994, p. A16) Though somewhat unusual, this pact opens the way for American pharmaceutical companies to invest in production and marketing in Russia. Before Russia and the other newly independent countries can become economically viable, they must take many more such steps to invite and encourage foreign investment.

RUSSIA IN EURASIA AND THE WORLD

The Soviet Union left the former union republics ill equipped to become self-governing, independent political-economic systems. Their integration into the Soviet command economy has made it difficult for them to pursue diversified economic development, and most have little or no military capacity to defend themselves against Russia or anyone else. These two points are intertwined. For the foreseeable future, Russia must remain a necessary, though potentially dangerous, ally.

What will protect the newly independent countries from Russia? NATO's Partnership for Peace has moved into this vacuum in east-central Europe. How the Central Asian and Transcaucasian countries will handle their security is still not clear. The one thing that is certain is that they must deal with the possibility of Russian expansionism and the volatility of the larger Muslim region.

Economically, all of the successor countries are still tightly tied to Russia. Trade with Russia as a proportion of their international trade seems to be declining, but Russia remains their most important trading partner. Some are highly dependent on Russia for energy supplies. Even those that are rich in energy-related natural resources have a limited capacity to process and transport these resources. Moreover, much of their infrastructure, such as oil pipelines and electrical power grids, passes through and thus can be controlled by Russia. The best strategy for the "near abroad" to offset Russian economic influence is to cultivate economic relationships with countries other than Russia. To this end, the Baltic countries are courting western Europe, and the Muslim countries are looking toward Turkey and Iran.

For its part, Russia is accustomed to regarding the other former Soviet republics as military buffer states and resource colonies. Under what conditions is Russia likely to intervene in these countries? The answer to this question depends on several factors. First, the likelihood of intervention will increase if there is significant political and social unrest. The situations in Georgia and Tajikistan have already illustrated this possibility. Second, if internal instability in Russia leads to the rise of rabid Russian nationalism, the likelihood of intervention will increase because of the significant Russian minorities in most of the successor countries bordering on Russia. Moreover, to make matters worse, many of the boundaries in these areas are disputed.

These two factors, however, are mitigated by a third. Russia is financially strapped, and its economy is in bad shape. Policies of expansionism would be difficult to finance and in the face of domestic economic hardship difficult to justify. Given these circumstances, therefore, it is not surprising that when a Russian-speaking nationalist was elected president of the Crimea—a Ukrainian peninsula with a Russian-speaking majority—there was no rush of sentiment within the Russian parliament supporting the reintegration of the Crimea into Russia. Likewise, the newly elected Duma almost unanimously opposed a Russian-Georgian friendship treaty, despite the fact that it would have given Russia generous access to Georgian territory for the purpose of establishing military bases. In both cases, Russia was not motivated by sensitivity to its neighbors' concerns about possible Russian expansionism. Rather, Russia was unwilling to assume other countries' burdens while struggling with its own economic problems. (*Washington Post,* March 1, 1994, p. A1)

Moreover, Russia needs as much economic aid as it can get. The major potential sources of this aid in the industrialized world have indicated that aid from them depends on how Russia conducts its affairs—both internally and externally. Any blatant or overt acts of expansionism would probably result in a sharp deterioration of relations between Russia and its prime sources of aid. Thus, expansion, if it occurs, will likely be "by invitation"—countries of the "near abroad" seeking Russian military assistance in the context of social unrest or civil war. The "invitation" to expansionism, however, could conceivably come not from the governments of the countries of the "near abroad" but ostensibly from the Russians who call these countries their home. Serious clashes between the Russians and Kazakhs in Kazakhstan, for example, might give Russia an excuse for "peacekeeping" or intervention to protect the Russians. This could naturally lead to a situation in which the relationship between Kazakhstan and Russia might evolve into one reminiscent of that between the Soviet Union and its satellites in eastern Europe. Or, even worse, Russia could try to annex large portions of northern Kazakhstan.

The promise of economic aid can work to moderate Russian policy toward the "near abroad" only as long as Russia continues to look toward the West for assistance. Throughout much of Russian history, however, there has been tension between those who argue that Russia should turn outward (Westernizers) and those who argue that it should turn inward (Slavophiles). The Westernizers have insisted that Russia should be integrated into the family of nations and should follow Western models in its political and economic development. The Slavophiles have favored policies that would emphasize Russia's uniqueness and would in effect keep Russia as self-sufficient as is humanly possible. There are parallels to this age-old debate in the current policy dialogue between the "radical reformers" and the nationalist conservatives. If the latter were to prevail, Russia might stop being so concerned about world opinion. In that case, the second scenario might become far more likely.

Since the fall of the Soviet Union, the industrialized countries have strongly emphasized aid to Russia and paid much less attention to the needs of the fourteen other newly independent countries. The two major Russian aid packages of 1992 and 1993 were not delivered in their entirety because Russia failed to meet the conditions on which the aid was contingent. This failure raises important questions. Is the kind of aid being offered appropriate to Russia's needs? Also, there is a growing recognition that Russia's political and economic problems are far more serious than anyone realized when the 1992 and 1993 aid packages and their requirements were negotiated. Thus, policy-makers in the donor states are becoming more concerned with the distribution of aid among the newly independent countries. To what extent should aid be more widely distributed throughout the former Soviet Union? If Russia's expansionist tendencies are to some extent related to the level of stability in the other successor countries, aid that strengthens the "near abroad" might make Russian expansionism less likely.

SOME CONCLUDING THOUGHTS

The Soviet Union has disappeared and is now a historical memory. Yet its shadow lingers, affecting the lives and fortunes of all the peoples that once lived under its rule. Since the Soviet Union existed for little more than seventy years, its legacy is closely tied to the legacy of the Russian empire that preceded it. At the core of both of these political-economic systems was acceptance of strong leaders who acted and were expected to act in essentially rule-less ways. Authority figures, such as the tsar and the Communist general secretaries, wielded power in ways that were only minimally rule-bound. The myth of the strong leader assumed to be acting for the general good—virtually a parent figure—provided a rationale for this rule-less behavior. Even when the leader's actions were clearly not beneficial to the people, his ability to use rule-less power discouraged the voices of opposition.

The fact that rule-less behavior was viewed as normal political behavior that happened with regularity gave the rule-less exercise of power a kind of tacit legitimacy. Trust based on blind acceptance of whatever the rulers did was basic to the subject mentality of the people. For the most part, Russians are not noted for their political activism; they are noted for their capacity to endure. In both empires, this also had to be the stance of the non-Russians. Trust based on blind acceptance, however, cannot be the basis for a democratic polity. Nor can it be the basis for a market economy.

Exchange is crucial in democratic political systems and market economies. In both, trust is a key component. This trust cannot be based on blind acceptance. Rather, it must be based on the confidence that all participants will permit themselves to be bound by certain rules. This creates a political-economic environment in which the participants can form reasonably accurate expectations about the future. These expectations enable them to make personal choices with the confidence that their predictions about the behavior of salient others are basically accurate.

There are two implications. First, every party to a political or economic transaction must be bound by the same rules and those who violate the rules will experience sanctions. Second, people in different roles are bound by different rules. They cannot, however, define the rules for themselves, but are bound by the prevailing authoritative definition of their roles and the associated rules. The bottom line is that rules are understood, internalized, and obeyed.

Why is this important for democracy? Trust is essential to majority rule, minority rights, and the ability to reach compromise. If the majority is to rule, the minority must trust that its rights will not be violated and that it can oppose the majority safely. Also, minorities must have some assurance that their needs will not be ignored, that the majority will be willing to compromise—giving them some of what they want. In both cases, an exchange is the key. Minority loyalty is exchanged for majority willingness to be sensitive to the wants and needs of the minority and majority willingness to allow the minority to periodically challenge the majority in a free election. Moreover, when compromises are reached, the parties must trust each other to live up to their part of the bargain. In other words, the trust necessary for a successful democratic system flows from the rule-bound behavior of the participants in the democratic process.

With regard to the countries of the former Soviet Union, there is a chicken-and-egg problem. A regularized system of democratic procedures is needed as the basis for trust. However, a certain fundamental trust is necessary in order to create and institutionalize the democratic process. The leaders and people of the newly independent countries are caught in this paradox. With a heritage of rule that was based on the virtually rule-less exercise of power, it is difficult for the people to trust their leaders. The leaders, on the other hand, are continually tempted to break the rules in order to do what they think is necessary to meet the crises that threaten to overwhelm their rule. If they do, they may be able to meet the crises more effectively in the short term, but they sacrifice the trust of the electorate that they need for long-term democratic rule. Leaders who act in a rule-less way also sacrifice their long-term effectiveness with regard to the rest of the political elite.

Why are trust and rule-bound behavior important for market economies? In an economic system based on decentralized decision-making, respect for property rights is crucial. People need to trust that their choices with regard to the control and disposition of their property will be honored by relevant others. This respect must also exist with regard to contracts. People must trust that deals struck at one point in time will be honored in the future. Furthermore, if property rights are not respected and contracts not honored there must be some recourse for the injured parties. Governments have historically played this role. Executives and legislatures must establish authoritative rules governing property rights and contracts; the judiciary must interpret them, and the executive enforce them. It is also necessary for government officials to have as much respect for these rules as everyone else.

The idea that the government must be bound by its own rules is especially important for the countries of the former Soviet Union. Why? The old order required most of the people to accept the premise that they were bound by rules but their leaders were not. If they did not accept this idea voluntarily, they were forced to do so. In return for their acceptance, the Soviet people were guaranteed some degree of personal security and an economic safety net. At times (e.g., during the purges of the 1930s) the political leadership violated this "social contract," but for the most part, if the people were careful enough about what they said and did, they could expect to be left alone and to have a low, but tolerable, standard of living.

This "social contract" reinforced the inherent passivity and proclivity to minimize risk-taking that were characteristic of the subject peoples of the Soviet Empire. This mentality is inappropriate to market economies. The taking of risks is essential to market activity. People, at minimum, have to trust that they will not be punished by the authorities for their risk-taking. More importantly, they must believe that risk-taking will pay off in the long run, even if they experience short-run failures. In other words, there must be a fundamental trust that the economic "rules of the game" will prevail and that people can plan their entrepreneurial activities accordingly.

Thus, the core problem for all of the heirs of the Soviet Empire is the challenge of establishing the rule-boundedness and basic trust without which democratic systems and market economies cannot be created and persist. Each of the successor countries is struggling with the challenge in its own way. This process of change is unprecedented and offers a valuable laboratory for those interested in studying institution-building, nation-building, and state-building. The Soviet successor countries are being presented with an opportunity to recast the social order within their boundaries. Their efforts to do so can be studied in a systematic way, yielding a new understanding of the process of political change.

REFERENCES

Barkun, M. (1968). *Law without sanctions*. New Haven, CT: Yale University Press.

Kennan, G. F. ("X"). (1947). The sources of Soviet conduct. *Foreign Affairs, 25,* 566–582.

Morris, J. M. (1993). Settling ethnic conflicts in post-Soviet society. *Woodrow Wilson Center Report, 5*(3), 1–3.

Socor, F. (1993). Dniester involvement in the Moscow rebellion. *RFE/RL Research Report, 2*(46), 25–32.

GLOSSARY

Absolutist system: A system in which the powers exercised by the government are formally unrestrained.

Administrative power: Control that is exercised through the manipulation of people's activities and the quality of their lives.

Anarchy: The absence of any authority to enforce laws.

Apparatchik: Middle- or low-level bureaucrat in the administrative hierarchy of the Soviet Union.

Autarky: Complete economic independence.

Authority: The ability to elicit a particular type of behavior because of the legitimacy of either the person or the institution issuing the command.

Autocracy: Rule by one person.

Azeris: The majority ethnic group in Azerbaijan; also called Azerbaijanis.

Black market: An illegal exchange system for goods and services produced outside the state-sanctioned economic system.

Bolshevik Revolution: The October 1917 revolution.

Boyar clans: Russian nobility from the tenth through the seventeenth century. A council of boyars advised the princes of Muscovy.

Brezhnev, Leonid: CPSU general secretary from 1964 to 1982.

Capitalism: An economic system in which the means of production are privately owned.

Central Asia: The region of the former Soviet Union that comprises the five predominantly Muslim countries of Kazakhstan, Kyrgyzstan, Tajikistan, Turkmenistan, and Uzbekistan.

CFE Treaty. See **Treaty of Conventional Armed Forces in Europe.**

CIS: Commonwealth of Independent States. The political-economic organization that succeeded the Soviet Union. Its original purpose was to provide a forum in which issues left unresolved by the collapse of the USSR could be dealt with in an orderly way.

Cold War: The period from 1947 to 1989 during which there was high tension between the Soviet Union and the United States but no actual war.

Collective farms: Farms that in theory are voluntary associations in which the

357

means of production are the collective property of the cooperative and the members elect their leaders.

Collective goods: Goods, such as national defense, bridges, ports, and public parks, that are seldom, if ever, produced through exchange and markets and are provided for public consumption by the government.

Collectivization: Stalin's policy of forcibly relocating Russia's peasants onto collective farms in the 1930s in order to establish cooperative agriculture.

COMECON: Council for Mutual Economic Assistance. An international governmental organization established in 1949 as a means for the Soviet Union to further integrate its economy with the economies of the satellite states of eastern Europe. COMECON was developed to counter the Marshall Plan, the massive economic aid plan launched by the United States after World War II to rebuild Europe.

Command economy: An economy in which the means of production and distribution are controlled by the state.

Conference on Security and Cooperation in Europe: An organization formed in 1975 as part of the Helsinki Agreement to reduce the confrontations between NATO and the Warsaw Pact.

Containment: An American policy based on a proposal by George Kennan in 1947. It was designed to prevent further Soviet expansion.

Convertible currency: The currency of one country that can be traded for the currency of another country. A given number of French francs, for example, is worth a given number of US dollars. The Soviet ruble was not a convertible currency.

Cooperative: A property form in which, theoretically, the means of production are jointly owned and any residual income is evenly divided among the members of the cooperative.

Council of Europe: An international governmental organization established in 1949 "to achieve a greater unity among its Members for the purpose of safeguarding and realizing the ideals and principles which are their common heritage and facilitating their economic and social progress." (Article 1 of the Statute of the Council of Europe)

CPSU: The Communist Party of the Soviet Union.

CSCE. See **Conference on Security and Cooperation in Europe.**

De-Stalinization: The repudiation of Stalin as hero and savior of his country and the systematic removal of most of the overt symbols of Stalin. Nikita Khrushchev began the program of de-Stalinization in 1956.

Destiny myth: A myth that tells the story of a country's ultimate role in history.

Duma: The lower house of the Federal Assembly.

ECO: Economic Cooperation Organization. An organization founded by Iran, Pakistan, and Turkey in 1985 to eliminate tariff and other barriers among members. In 1992, the former Central Asian republics, as well as Azerbaijan and Afghanistan, joined.

EEC: European Economic Community. Established in 1957 by the Treaty of Rome, the EEC was originally a customs union. It is now the European

Union and has sixteen members. It aims to integrate the economies of its members to create a single market.

Efficiency: The pragmatic allocation of resources in order to eliminate as much waste as possible and thereby maximize society's well-being.

Empire: A relationship of dominance and subjugation between an imperial center and its periphery, where center and periphery constitute separate societies. In an empire, the periphery is forced to surrender effective control of its society to the imperial center.

Ethnocentrism: The belief that one's own ethnic group is superior to other ethnic groups.

European Union. See EEC.

Exchange: A mechanism of social control on which markets are built and political compromise is based. It involves voluntary agreement between two or more people to freely trade some item or service for some other item or service, and it is motivated by calculations of self-interest.

External sovereignty: The international community of established states' acceptance of the right of an existing government to make decisions for the people who live within its boundaries.

Federal Assembly: The Russian parliament formed under the 1993 Constitution. The lower house is called the Duma. The upper house is called the Federal Council.

Federal Council: The upper house of the Federal Assembly.

Federation: A system of government that divides sovereignty between a central government and the governments of its major subdivisions.

Five-year plan: The official production goals set by the Soviet planning authorities for a given five-year period.

Foundation myth: A myth that tells the story of a country's origin.

GATT: The General Agreement on Tariffs and Trade. An international trade organization whose purpose is to reduce and eliminate trade barriers among member states.

GDP: Gross domestic product. The account of all goods and services produced domestically by a country.

General Secretary: The head of the Communist Party of the Soviet Union. The general secretary was the true leader of the Soviet Union even when he held no government post.

Gerontocracy: A ruling elite composed of the elderly.

Glasnost: Openness. Gorbachev's policy of open discussion of social problems and shortcomings.

GNP: Gross national product. The account of all goods and services produced by a country, including goods and services produced by companies abroad.

Gorbachev, Mikhail S.: The last general secretary of the Communist Party of the Soviet Union (1985–91).

Gorkom: A city committee of the CPSU.

Gosagroprom: The first Soviet superministry, created in November 1985 to increase economic efficiency in agriculture.

Gosbank: The Soviet State Bank.

Goskomtrud: The Soviet State Committee for Labor and Social Questions.

Goskomtsen: The Soviet State Committee for Prices.

Gosplan: The Soviet State Planning Committee.

Gospriemka: The Soviet State Quality Acceptance Committee.

Gossnab: The Soviet State Committee for Material and Technical Supply.

G-7: Group of Seven. An association of the world's seven most advanced industrial democracies: Canada, France, Germany, Great Britain, Italy, Japan, and the United States.

Hard currency. See **Convertible currency.**

Hegemony: The predominant influence of one country over other countries. The subordinate countries are unable to modify the status quo even though the hegemonic state does not try to absorb them.

Hierarchy: A pyramidal authority structure in which orders flow down from above and are carried out by people at lower levels who specialize in implementing such orders.

Hyperinflation: Inflation so severe—in excess of 1,000 percent per year—that people try to get rid of their currency before prices rise still higher and render their money worthless.

Ideology: An integrated intellectual belief system that sets forth a particular world-view and proclaims a vision for the future.

IGO: International Governmental Organization. An institutional body formed by agreement among two or more sovereign states.

IMF: International Monetary Fund. It makes short-term loans to countries that have problems meeting their international financial obligations.

Imperial center: The locus of control in an empire. It constitutes a separate and distinct society from the subjugated periphery.

Import substitution: A development strategy whereby a developing country seeks to escape reliance on imports by manufacturing goods at home.

Industrialization: The process of moving from an economy based on agriculture to one that relies predominantly on manufacturing.

Inflation: A persistent increase in prices and costs and decrease in the purchasing power of money.

Internal sovereignty: The ability of a political entity to exercise control over the territory and the people under its jurisdiction. In an empire, internal sovereignty is largely secured by the coercive and administrative apparatus.

International Bank of Reconstruction and Development: The World Bank. It was initially formed to help rebuild Europe after World War II. Over the last forty years, its focus has shifted to making long-term loans to less developed countries in order to advance their economic development.

International regime: The norms, principles, procedures, or other implicit or explicit rules that inform the actions of states in a given issue area. An international regime is the product of joint decision-making and works to increase the rule-bound behavior of states. An international regime thus enhances cooperation among the states that choose to respect its rules.

KGB: Committee for State Security. It functioned as a secret police force in the Soviet Union.

Khrushchev, Nikita S.: The Communist Party first secretary (general secretary) from 1953 to 1965.

Kolkhoz: A collective farm.

Kolkhoztsentr: The bureaucratic agency that forced collectivization.

Kulak: A relatively successful farmer. Kulaks were singled out for destruction during the period of forced collectivization.

LDLP: Lithuanian Democratic Labor Party (formerly the Lithuanian Communist Party).

Legitimacy: The belief that something is right and proper and is in conformity with significant values.

Lenin, V. I.: The leader of the 1917 Bolshevik Revolution and the founding father of the Soviet Union.

MAD: Mutual assured destruction. A posture adopted by both sides during the Cold War; it virtually guaranteed a second retaliatory nuclear strike.

Market economy: An economy in which decision-making is decentralized and relative prices inform the choices of decision-makers. The incentive system that operates in such an economy is based on material self-interest and competition.

Master myths: A society's broad, all-encompassing myths.

Money: A universally recognized medium of exchange and store of value.

MVD: Ministry of Internal Affairs. The internal police force of the Soviet Union.

Myth: A belief that is held in common by a large group of people and that gives events and actions a particular meaning. The meaning is typically socially cued rather than empirically based.

Nation: A relatively modern concept of group identification typically associated with people who share a common cultural heritage. Central to this concept is the notion of a political community that bonds its members to one another and helps legitimate the exercise of authority by nationally sanctioned elites.

Nationalism: Loyalty and devotion to the culture and interests of a nation. Nationalism is usually symbolized by flags, national anthems, and beliefs emphasizing commonality among the members of a nation.

Nation-building: The process whereby the inhabitants of a state's territory come to identify themselves as a political community.

NATO: North Atlantic Treaty Organization. An alliance among the United States, Canada, and many western European states that was formed after World War II under the leadership of the United States. The NATO treaty is a collective security pact that considers an attack on one member to be an attack on all the members.

Near abroad: Russia's term for the other fourteen successor countries.

NEP: New Economic Policy. A plan that Lenin instituted after the period of War Communism. NEP allowed a limited market to operate in the Soviet

Union to aid in the recovery of the economy from the 1917 revolutions and the civil war.

Nomenklatura: A list of high-level positions filled by CPSU committees throughout the USSR.

OAS: Organization of American States. An international governmental organization created in 1949. Its members are countries of the Western Hemisphere.

October Revolution: The revolution that brought the Bolsheviks to power in Russia.

Oligarchy: Rule by a limited group of individuals.

Outer empire: The Soviet satellites of eastern Europe. These states, which functioned as the western protective border of the USSR, included Bulgaria, Czechoslovakia, East Germany, Hungary, Poland, and Yugoslavia.

Paris Club: An organization formed to aid developing countries that are experiencing difficulty in meeting their international financial obligations. The Paris Club helps to renegotiate the terms of loans, but it does not make direct loans to developing countries.

Partnership for Peace: A program that offers affiliation with, but not membership in, NATO for the former Warsaw Pact countries and the newly independent countries of the former Soviet Union.

Perestroika: Gorbachev's program for restructuring the Soviet economy.

Persuasion: The transmission of information intended to elicit a targeted and voluntary behavioral response. Persuasion is a mechanism of social control.

Politburo: The major policy-making body of the Communist Party of the Soviet Union.

Political culture: The assumptions that members of a society make about the political world.

Political ideology: Ideas that explain and justify a preferred political order, either existing or proposed.

Power: The ability to compel someone to do something he or she otherwise would not have done or to refrain from doing something he or she otherwise would have done. The practical basis of power is the ability to coerce. Those using power control through fear.

Pre-Petrine period: The period before the reign of Peter the Great, who ruled from 1682 to 1725.

Product cycle: A cycle in which a new technology, developed by an advanced industrial economy, matures and becomes a standard technology that developing countries can use to become low-cost producers and thereby generate revenues to expand their own economies. Through innovation, the cycle repeats itself.

Productivity: A measure of output per worker.

Property: Any object or resource (including knowledge and personal skills) that can be owned.

Proto-party: A political party in its infant stages before it officially becomes a viable organization.

Public goods. See **Collective goods.**

Purges: The imprisonment or execution of thousands of people in the 1930s. They were designed to create absolute loyalty to Stalin.

Reform: Changes in the rules of political conflict that leave intact most of the overall rule structure, as well as the political cultural assumptions on which it rests.

Relative prices: The mechanism used to compare the demand for and supply of goods and services.

Residual income: Any income that remains after all financial obligations associated with maintaining and operating a property have been met; profit.

Revolution: A deliberate attempt to make basic changes in the rule structure of a political-economic system, not just to get rid of the regime currently in power.

Ritual: A ceremonial activity that expresses and defines social relations by means of symbols.

RSFSR: Russian Soviet Federated Socialist Republic.

Russification: The imposition of the Russian language and Russian culture on non-Russian groups.

SDI: Strategic Defense Initiative, or Star Wars. A US antimissile weapons program initiated during the Reagan administration.

Secretariat: The major administrative or bureaucratic arm of the Communist Party of the Soviet Union.

Shock therapy: An economic reform plan calling for all major changes to be implemented at the same time.

Social rule structure: A patterned set of role relationships that serve as the building blocks of the social order.

Sovereignty: The right and ability to exercise supreme control within a given territory.

Sovkhoz: A Soviet state farm.

Speculation: The buying up and resale of commodities or other articles with the goal of profit.

SSR: Soviet Socialist Republic.

Stagnation: A period of little or no growth in an economy.

Stalin, Joseph V.: A Communist leader who took control after Lenin's death and decisively changed the direction in which the Soviet political-economic system was moving. He was leader of the USSR from 1927 to 1953.

State: A political entity that occupies a specific territory, has an organized government, and possesses internal and external sovereignty.

Store of value: An asset that people are willing to accumulate because they expect that at some point in the future they will be able to use it to acquire other things of value.

Subject: A person dominated by power who has little control over his or her own destiny.

Sustaining myth: An ideal that justifies the existing social order.

Symbol: A visible object that evokes something that cannot be seen.

Symbolic incentive: An incentive that is designed primarily to make the person receiving it feel good about his or her contribution to society.

Transcaucasia: The landmass that lies between the Caspian and Black seas. This region includes the countries of Armenia, Azerbaijan, and Georgia.

Treaty of Conventional Armed Forces in Europe: A treaty signed by NATO and Warsaw Pact members in 1990 calling for massive reductions in numbers of tanks, armored combat vehicles, artillery, combat aircraft, and attack helicopters in Europe.

Union Treaty: The treaty that brought the USSR into being in 1922. It was signed by representatives of the four original republics: Byelorussia, the Russian Soviet Federated Socialist Republic, the Transcaucasian Republic, and Ukraine.

Unitary system: A system of government in which the central government is supreme over both regional and local governments.

United Nations: An organization founded in 1945 to provide collective security for member states. It acts as a forum for the discussion of international problems and sponsors peacekeeping operations.

USSR: Union of Soviet Socialist Republics.

War Communism: The period of civil war following the Bolshevik revolution, 1918–21.

Warsaw Pact: An alliance formed under the leadership of the Soviet Union to counter NATO. This organization also functioned as a means for the Soviet Union to exercise imperial control over the states of eastern Europe.

World Bank. See **International Bank of Reconstruction and Development.**

Yeltsin, Boris N.: The first popularly elected president of Russia.

Xenophobia: An extreme form of nationalism in which everything having to do with something foreign or alien is considered threatening.

INDEX

ABOUT THE AUTHORS

CAROL BARNER-BARRY (Ph.D., Syracuse University) is an associate professor of political science at the University of Maryland, Baltimore County. Her books include *Contemporary Soviet Politics,* fourth edition (Prentice Hall, 1991, with Donald D. Barry), and *Psychological Perspectives on Politics* (Prentice Hall, 1985; reprinted by Waveland, 1991; with Robert Rosenwein). She has also published works on the former Soviet Union and in political psychology for a number of journals, most recently "Soviet Marxism-Leninism as Mythology" for *Political Psychology* (forthcoming, with Cynthia Hody).

CYNTHIA A. HODY (Ph.D., University of California, Los Angeles) is an assistant professor of political science at the University of Maryland, Baltimore County. Her areas of specialization include international and comparative political economy, international relations, and comparative foreign economic policy. She is currently working on a book on U.S. foreign economic policy.